Praise for THE MUSIC OF THE REPUBLIC

"This book is a windfall twice over for lovers of Plato—and indeed, for lovers of thinking overall. First, it makes widely accessible a revised and expanded edition of Eva Brann's 'Music of the *Republic*,' a legendary work whose influence has already made it something of an underground classic among Plato scholars. It also brings together a wonderful array of additional pieces on Platonic texts and Platonic themes, some of them essays that would otherwise be difficult to procure and some appearing in print for the first time. Those new to Brann's writings will find the essays in this book to be engaging, insightful, and wise, a pleasure to read and to anticipate re-reading. Now collected together, they will establish her as one of the great readers and interpreters of the Platonic dialogues in modern times."
—*Bruce Foltz, Eckerd College*

"This collection of Eva Brann's is one of the most valuable aids a lover of Plato could have. By luminous, graceful prose and dialectical reflectiveness, the reader is drawn into Socratic conversations. How very welcome that Brann's long-treasured, substantial essay 'The Music of the *Republic*,' which gives this collection its center and title, is here made readily available for all who share her enthusiasm for Plato's writings." —*Walter Nicgorski, University of Notre Dame*

"In these wonderfully insightful essays, Eva Brann helps us hear the music of Plato's dialogues and join the conversation. With learning, wit, and an affectionate appreciation for her texts, Brann guides the reader of Plato into that circle of talk where, as Socrates himself suggests on more than one occasion, philosophy itself resides. If these sympathetic and inviting essays are a good introduction to Plato, they are also a fine introduction to the philosophical life, to the unbroken conversation that centuries of Plato's readers have joined. Reading Brann's essays, I found myself filled with envy for her students and happy, with this book, to now be included among them."
—*Anthony T. Kronman, Yale University*

"Eva Brann's superb papers on Plato are models of clarity and intelligence. They combine the charm of a fresh approach with rigor and precision. She offers us an illuminating exploration of what Plato means by his 'ideas,' subtle discussions of the importance of the *Sophist*, charming accounts of the opportunities and perils of translation, and deep analysis of the *Republic*. The reader will not find a better collection of essays." —*Mark Blitz, Claremont McKenna College*

THE MUSIC OF THE REPUBLIC

ALSO BY EVA BRANN

*Homeric Moments: Clues to Delight in Reading
the* Odyssey *and the* Iliad

The Past-Present

Paradoxes of Education in a Republic

*Late Geometric and Protoattic Pottery, Mid 8th to
Late 7th century B.C.*

Trilogy of the Human Center

The World of the Imagination: Sum and Substance

What, Then, Is Time?

The Ways of Naysaying: No, Not, Nothing, and Nonbeing

TRANSLATED BY EVA BRANN

Greek Mathematical Thought and the Origin of Algebra,
by Jacob Klein (from the German)

Plato's Sophist
(from the Greek, with Peter Kalkavage and Eric Salem)

Plato's Phaedo
(from the Greek, with Peter Kalkavage and Eric Salem)

THE MUSIC OF

ESSAYS ON SOCRATES' CONVERSATION

EVA BRANN

WITH PETER KALKAVAGE AND ERIC SALEM

 PAUL DRY BOOKS   PHILADELPHIA, 2004

THE REPUBLIC

AND PLATO'S WRITINGS

First Paul Dry Books Edition, 2004

Paul Dry Books, Inc.
Philadelphia, Pennsylvania
www.pauldrybooks.com

Text type: Sabon
Display type: Lithos and Optima
Composed by P. M. Gordon Associates
Designed by Adrianne Onderdonk Dudden

1 3 5 7 9 8 6 4 2
Printed in the United States of America

Library of Congress Cataloging-in-Publication Data
Brann, Eva T. H.
    The music of the Republic : essays on Socrates' conversations and
Plato's writings / by Eva Brann with Peter Kalkavage and Eric Salem. —
1st Paul Dry Books ed.
        p.   cm.
    ISBN 1-58988-008-0 (hardcover : alk. paper)
    1. Plato. Dialogues. I. Kalkavage, Peter. II. Salem, Eric. III. Title.
    B395.B749 2004
    184—dc22
                                                        2003025707

ISBN 1-58988-008-0

"Then where, Socrates, are we to get hold of a good singer of incantations—since *you* are abandoning us?"

"There's a lot of Greece, Cebes; I suppose there are good people in it—and there are many races of barbarians too. . . . You must search for him in company with one another too, for perhaps you wouldn't find anyone more able to do this than *yourselves.*"

Phaedo 78 a

IN MEMORY OF JASHA KLEIN (1899–1978),
WHO TAUGHT US MOSTLY
WHAT WE'D ALWAYS KNOWN.

CONTENTS

PREFACE

Who has spent a lifetime reading Plato's writings and does not regard the *Republic* as his central work? It reaches higher and wider and displays a more lucid design and more artful devices than any other dialogue. It is, moreover, Socrates' longest conversation. It is inexhaustible.

Consequently the middle of this collection consists of four pieces on the *Republic*. The earliest and longest one, "The Music of the *Republic*," dealing mostly with the philosophical center of the dialogue, was first published in 1967 and reprinted occasionally by students; I have thoroughly revised it. The latest piece, about the last book of the dialogue, was delivered as a lecture in 2003. The *Republic* has surely been the dialogue closest to my soul.

Yet the dialogue that has given me most to think about is the *Sophist*. It contains what seems to me the third most portentous ancient discovery for philosophy (after Parmenides' revelation of Being and Socrates' hypothesis of the forms): the reinterpretation of Nonbeing as Otherness, which turns out to be indispensable for an understanding of that most fascinating of human abilities—imaging. So this book contains three pieces on that dialogue, the first of which is an introduction written in collaboration with my colleagues Peter Kalkavage and Eric Salem for our translation of the *Sophist*.

Translating the *Sophist* (and then the *Phaedo*) together was an exhilarating experience of learning compounded with friendship, such as Socrates would have smiled upon. In the course of our collaboration we established some principles and practices for turning Socrates' conversations into English, which are reported herein.

Drawing students into these conversations is a part of our mission at my college. The pieces on other dialogues and themes are the fruits of this effort. The last little essay summarizes my notion of what might work for a teacher and what couldn't possibly.

I want to say, finally, that although this book is full of pretty confident interpretive conclusions concerning the Platonic text, in retrospect they all look more like preludes to new, perhaps deeper, questions.

Eva Brann
St. John's College, Annapolis
2004

THE MUSIC OF THE REPUBLIC

EVA BRANN, PETER KALKAVAGE, ERIC SALEM

1

INTRODUCTION TO THE **PHAEDO**

In the first book of his *Inquiries,* Herodotus tells the story of Solon and Croesus. The Athenian wise man gives the Lydian tyrant a piece of advice. "Look to the end," he says, if you want to know whether a human life has really been blessed or happy. As he makes abundantly clear to Croesus, Solon means by "end" no more and no less than how a man has died.

If there is any truth to Solon's words, we would do well to pay close attention to the *Phaedo* in our pursuit of the question "Who is Socrates, and was he blessed or happy?" In the *Phaedo* the philosopher Socrates "meets his end." He does so in the double sense of the phrase: He reaches the termination of his death-bound life, and he reflects, in the company of his friends, on the deathless intellectual vision to which his life had been devoted. To pay serious attention to the *Phaedo,* then, is to do more than investigate what Socrates talked about and did on the day he died. It is to pursue the question that underlies and pervades all the dialogues of Plato: Who is the true philosopher, and is he really the most blessed and happiest of men?

Like all the other Platonic dialogues, the *Phaedo* has its own setting, circumstances and limits. Socrates is a perpetual mystery, the perennial questionable questioner, and Plato is careful to present him, never "as such" or "in himself," but always in a continually shifting, and therefore lifelike, context with an ever-varying set of interlocutors. The *Phaedo*, though revelatory as befits the story of an end, speaks from its own perspective and within its own confines. Like all the other dialogues, it has its share of concealment, unresolved perplexity, omissions, exaggerations, and deliberately contrived "bad arguments"—all meant to make us think in ways we are left to discover for ourselves. The reader must steel himself to the fact that the story of Socrates' end will not easily or unproblematically open itself up to his gaze.

The *Phaedo* is the most poignant and personal of all the dialogues. The conversation is literally a matter of life and death as the soon-to-die Socrates, in the company of adoring and anxious friends, takes up the question of what happens to us at the moment of our death. But there is another poignancy to the *Phaedo*: Socrates here attempts to transform our worry about death into a reflection on what it means to be fully and truly *alive,* into a discursive hymn in praise of the philosophic life. This hymn is deeply perplexing. On the one hand, Socrates encourages both himself and his friends with the hope for a more-than-mortal life after the soul leaves the body. On the other hand, the means to this encouragement consist in giving arguments that are full of patent logical flaws. As noted above, we find such deliberate illogic in all the dialogues. But here the illogic has an especially perplexing and troubling character since what is at issue is nothing less than our individual selves. How are we to reconcile the strength of Socrates' encouragement with the weakness of the actual arguments? Granting that the *Phaedo* is most centrally about the praise of philosophy in its care for deathless being, what does Socrates actually think about the fate of the individual soul, *his soul,* at the moment of death? Where does the last conversation of Socrates leave us at the end?

The dialogue's opening word, "self" (*autós*), brings us to the very core of the mystery before us. Echecrates asks whether Phaedo *himself* was present at Socrates' death. The intensive pronoun is an excellent example of how the deepest philosophical problems for Plato tend to lie right at the surface of ordinary language. Echecrates' question makes us wonder what words like "himself" and "itself" ultimately mean, wonder what it means to *intensify identity*. Here in the *Phaedo* and in other dialogues, those ultimate thinkables—the forms—are often referred to as "the things themselves all by themselves." Echecrates' opening question thus calls to mind not only the human self, of which "Phaedo himself" is an example, but also the forms. The *Phaedo*'s opening word "self" leads us directly to questions that are at the very heart of the dialogue: What is the soul? What is the relation between soul and form? And does our selfhood, our identity, make any sense without the body to which our soul is mysteriously attached?

The *Phaedo* belongs to the class of narrated or, to use Socrates' word, recollected Platonic dialogues. To the class of nonnarrated or directly presented conversations belong dialogues like the *Meno* and *Gorgias*. Of the narrated sort, some are virtual soliloquies with an unidentified listener, like the *Republic* and *Parmenides*. Others are narrations embedded within a directly presented conversation. Dialogues that belong to this class include the postmortem recollections of Socrates: the *Symposium, Theaetetus,* and *Phaedo*. Their very form compels us to ask: Why is it important to keep the memory of Socrates alive?

The *Phaedo*'s recollection of Socrates is a perplexing blend of *lógos* and *mythos*, argument and story. As we hear early on, Socrates' death had been delayed—by "a bit of chance," as Phaedo says. Every year, the Athenians, in accordance with their vow to Apollo, send an embassy to Delos. Before this embassy returns to Athens, the city must keep itself pure and not put anyone to death. The embassy commemorates Theseus's rescue of the fourteen young Athenians (the Twice Seven, as Phaedo calls them, in keeping with the fact that the group was composed of both youths and maidens) from the Minotaur or Bull-man of Crete. The *Phaedo* is a playful recasting of this well-known myth. Socrates is the new, philosophic Theseus. He is the heroic savior of the friends who gather around him as he is about to make his final journey—fourteen of whom are named; and their discussion of the soul and her fate, particularly in the final and most problematic stage of the argument, indeed resembles a logical labyrinth. Phaedo himself plays an important role as the fifteenth named member of the group around Socrates: he is the Ariadne[1] whose narrative thread leads us into and through Plato's labyrinth of arguments.

But who or what plays the role of the Minotaur? From what, in other words, must Socrates' companions be saved? Is it their fear of death? Or is it the great evil known as misology or "hatred of arguments," the evil which, near the center of the dialogue, threatens to drown the conversation in disillusionment and despair? Or perhaps these are meant to be taken together— as the two "horns" of a dual-natured monster. This much is clear: the dialogue becomes ever richer as we think through the many points of contact between it and the myth it mimics. By the time we reach the very end of Phaedo's thread, we wonder: Is the Minotaur—whether as the fear of death or the hatred of argument—ever slain once and for all? Or, as its bullheadedness suggests, is it slain only to keep coming back to life again and again after each defeat?

Phaedo tells his story to Echecrates in Phlia, a city in the Peloponnese connected with the followers of Pythagoras. Indeed the spirit of Pythagoras, known to his disciples as *Autós,* pervades the *Phaedo.* The teaching that the body is the soul's prison is Pythagorean in origin, as is the transmigration of souls; and the notion of soul as a *harmonía* or tuning recalls the Pythagorean connection between ratios of whole numbers and musical intervals. But the Pythagorean theme closest to the heart of the dialogue is that of purification. Socrates returns to this theme often in the course of the discussion. The philosopher is depicted as the man who is, above all, pure and therefore free. The true philosopher, in Socrates' depiction, seeks to purify himself of all bodily entanglement in order to dwell with being or the forms. The *autós* language that pervades the dialogue is intimately bound up with this philosophic quest for purity.

But Socrates' relation to Pythagoreanism is problematic, to say the least. On the one hand, Socrates seems eager to form an alliance with the Pythagorean devotion to purity, mathematics, musicality, and health. On the other, Pythagoreanism, at least in its teaching that soul is a tuning, plays right into the hands of the Minotaur-as-the-fear-of-death by implying that the soul is deathbound rather than deathless. The attack on soul-as-tuning is only one of several clues that the Pythagorean guise of the philosopher in the *Phaedo,* the ascetic depiction of philosophy as the practice of death and hatred of the body, is perhaps more caricature than characterization. If philosophy is hatred of the body, how do we account for the fact that Socrates at the age of seventy has a baby son (60 a)? Or that, as Alcibiades tells us in the *Symposium,* Socrates, when pressed, always out-drinks everybody else, never gets drunk, and seems to enjoy himself more than other people (220 a)? Or that, as we discover in the *Phaedo,* Socrates enjoys playing with Phaedo's beautiful hair?

The *Phaedo* consists mostly of a conversation between Socrates and the two close friends, Simmias and Cebes, whose Pythagorean loyalties are elicited and called into question throughout the dialogue. Their friendly two-ness is played on in various ways as they wrestle with Socrates, with one another, and with their fears and distrust. Simmias, although he occasionally expresses distrust, seems on the whole closer to trust, edification, musicality, and right opinion. He agrees unquestioningly with Socrates' harsh depiction of the philosopher as a hater of the body and a practitioner of death. And it is Simmias who, late in the dialogue, is the prime recipient of the myth about the true earth. Cebes, by contrast, is the more logical and rigorously skeptical of the two. It is he who follows Socrates through the labyrinthine last argument. The differences between Simmias and Cebes cause us to reflect on the different and complex ways in which the human soul appears, and on how philosophic discussion, no less complex than the human soul, draws its sustenance and life from contrary but complementary sources.

The philosophic core of the *Phaedo* is usually thought to reside not in its drama but in the so-called "proofs for the immortality of the soul." Four such arguments are put forth in the dialogue: the argument from *contraries,* the argument from *recollection,* the argument from *invisibility,* and the argument from *cause.*

These arguments present the reader with a variety of difficulties. The meanings of crucial terms shift from argument to argument. For instance, in some places the all-important term "soul" refers to the principle or cause of life, including plant life; in other places it clearly means intellect. Again, all the arguments are affected to some extent by Socrates' openly taken decision to "tell stories" or "sing incantations" on this his final day. The effects of this decision are particularly apparent at those points where "there" and "then," place and time, are readily attributed to souls and forms—where, for instance, it is quickly concluded that forms constitute a region, albeit invisible, from which souls "came" or to which they will "go."

But perhaps the greatest difficulties stem from those "much-babbled-about" things, the forms. Three of the four arguments rest on them, and they are readily accepted by both Simmias and Cebes. Can we afford to be so blithe? Even if we manage to persuade ourselves that not all talk about forms is mere babble, and if we go along with them—Socrates' ruling hypothesis—difficulties remain, for the forms turn up in different guises in different arguments. Sometimes they appear as very distant objects of thought, unreachable in this body-ridden life. At other times, they turn up as features of our everyday experience, as, for instance, what we must be seeing whenever we note that equal sticks are not altogether equal. Or again, they show up right in front of us, engaged in mortal combat with their contraries whenever snow melts or numbers are added. Can these different "looks" be put together? No wonder Socrates admits at one point that the argument is "still open to suspicions and counterattacks" and yet encourages Simmias and Cebes to "look into" and "sort out" their "first hypotheses" with greater care. In spite of the difficulties they present, indeed precisely because of those difficulties, Socrates' arguments—taken up in the right spirit, without the blindness of mere faith or the emptiness of mere skepticism—become a rich soil for questions and reflections of the most fundamental type.

The drama of the *Phaedo,* the drama in which the arguments just discussed have their philosophic life, may be playfully divided into fourteen parts, in imitation of the Twice Seven in the myth of Theseus. A brief synopsis of each part will give us both an overview of the whole and a thread of sorts through Plato's labyrinth.

I PHAEDO HIMSELF [57 A – 59 B]

Echecrates discovers that Phaedo himself was present on Socrates' last day and asks him to recount everything that was said and done. After telling Echecrates why Socrates' death was delayed (the embassy to Delos), Phaedo begins by speaking of the wondrous mix of pleasure and pain he experienced that day in prison. It is with this mix of emotions that contrariety, so central to the entire dialogue, first comes on the scene.

II SEPARATENESS AND THE CARE OF DEATH [59 B – 69 E]

Phaedo begins the account proper by telling Echecrates the fourteen names of those he remembers to have been present. Plato, so Phaedo thinks, was ill and consequently absent. As the group of friends enters Socrates' cell, they come upon Socrates just released from his bonds. The pleasure he feels inspires him to reflect that Aesop would have done well to make up a story about pleasure and pain, about how the gods settled their constant quarreling by tying their heads together.

Socrates' last conversation, as fabricated by Plato, does not begin as a conversation about the deathlessness of the soul. Indeed it looks at first as if Socrates himself might be inviting the group to discuss, not life and death, but the wondrous and Aesop-worthy relation between the two contraries, pleasure and pain. Phaedo had already expressed wonder at the mix of emotions in himself and in the group, and now Plato presents Socrates as echoing a similar experience. How, then, does the deathlessness of the soul come to be the central topic of Socrates' last conversation?

The mention of Aesop impels Cebes to ask about Socrates' own compositions, his musical settings of Aesop's fables and a hymn to Apollo. Evenus the poet-sophist wants to know, says Cebes, why Socrates has suddenly taken up composition. Socrates tells Cebes about his recurring dream and the divine exhortation to "make music." He ends by telling Cebes to tell Evenus that he, Evenus—"if he's soundminded"—should follow Socrates in death as soon as possible. This in turn leads to a discussion of why the philosopher, although a follower of death, will never take his own life. Even at this point, although the discussion turns in the direction of death, the question "Is the soul deathless?" is not yet explicitly raised. Instead the issue becomes: Is Socrates just in his willingness to abandon his friends and the gods? Simmias and Cebes bring charges against Socrates. They require Socrates to give an *apología* or defense of why anyone who is truly wise would be as willing, as Socrates seems to be, to get free of a good and divine master—of why Socrates is so willing to die. The analogy with Socrates' trial and the charges brought against him by Athens for impiety and corruption of the youth informs the entire conversation as it is related by Phaedo. Socrates is not only compelled to give an account in the theoretical sense; he must also give an account of *himself* before the court of Simmias and Cebes. He must seek to persuade them that the philosopher's calm acceptance of death is not a case of injustice against those who love him.

Here begins the emphatic denigration of the body that will continue throughout the dialogue. This denigration has an important rhetorical function in regard to the charges of Simmias and Cebes. By denigrating the body and everything attached to body (including what we call "personality"), Socrates is attempting to wean his two friends from the attachment to the man Socrates, whom they refuse to let die.

And so Socrates begins his defense. The true philosopher, he says, is "dead" to the body and its allurements, and philosophy is the practice of dying and being dead. The only good philosopher, it seems, is a "dead" philosopher. The body, we hear, is a kind of prison, from which the true philosopher seeks release. The philosopher strives for a precise and unerring vision of what *is*, and the body, with all its senses and emotions, is nothing but a continual nuisance and obstacle. As the effort to give oneself up to inquiry and therefore to free oneself from the body, philosophy is nothing less than "the care of death," a phrase Socrates will use at a later point. Since death is the release and therefore separation of the soul from the body, and since the philosopher, in all his inquiries, has always done nothing other than strive for such separateness and purity, it is only reasonable, argues Socrates, that the true philosopher will not make a fuss about death.

With this defense, Socrates proceeds to discuss wisdom or thoughtfulness as the highest and truest virtue and defines such virtue as a form of purification. He concludes his defense in a mythical mode by expressing the belief that There, in the Hades that awaits us all, he will dwell with gods and with "good comrades."

III THE ARGUMENT FROM CONTRARIES
[69 E – 72 E]

The entire preceding defense of the true philosopher (which Socrates has conducted in a mysterious Orphic-Pythagorean mode and has attributed to "those who rightly philosophize") has been addressed to Simmias. Socrates' lofty tone and his concluding analogy between his defense before Simmias and Cebes and his defense before the Athenian judges, make it appear that Socrates is ready to "close his case." But Cebes speaks up and compels Socrates to talk some more. As Cebes points out, to argue that the philosopher should be cheerful in the face of death because There, in Hades, he will achieve the separation of soul from body that has been his practice and care throughout life, is to presuppose that the soul will still *be* once this separation has occurred. At this point, there begin the arguments for the deathlessness of the soul.

In turning the conversation to the proof of deathlessness, Cebes brings up two interrelated themes that will haunt the rest of the dialogue: fear of death and distrust. Cebes speaks for all human beings. He moves the conversation from the depiction and praise of the highest life of philosophy (Socrates' preceding Orphic defense) to life and death in general. It is Cebes who compels the conversation to take up the soul and her fate in relation to coming-to-be and passing-away—in a word, to process. It is because of Cebes, in other words, that the *Phaedo* combines a concern for the human soul with physics as the study of "becoming" as such.

Socrates rises to Cebes' challenge, or rather his probing anxiety, by appealing to the behavior of contraries. Echoing his earlier observation that pleasure and pain seem to evoke each other, Socrates puts forth the view that all contraries come into being from one another: the bigger from the littler, the worse from the better, the just from the unjust. He extends this view to include contrary processes like separating and combining, and cooling and heating. If indeed contrary processes or "becomings" always come in pairs, then the process of dying cannot fail to evoke its correlative process—returning to life. If the dead are generated out of the living, then the living must in turn be generated out of the dead. Becoming is a circle. And because of this circle, the soul—whose presence or absence marks a being as either alive or dead—must *be* before arriving in a body.

IV THE ARGUMENT FROM RECOLLECTION
[72 E – 77 A]

Cebes, recalling his earlier reminder about human distrust, tells Socrates that "we're not deceived in agreeing to these very things." He provocatively connects what Socrates has just put forth—Socrates' psychophysics—with the teaching that all learning is in fact recollection.

At this point, Simmias takes over the argument. He asks to be "reminded" of the demonstration of this teaching. Socrates obliges and goes through several examples, showing first that recollection can take place by means of associations other than similarity: The lover sees the beloved's lyre or cloak and recalls the beloved himself. Socrates then switches to recollection based on similarity. Plato leads us to wonder why the kind of recollection that's based on non-similarity, which Socrates provocatively connects with erotic experience, was brought up in the first place.

Earlier, in the high-flown defense addressed to Simmias, Socrates first made reference to the forms, designating them as "each of the beings that's unadulterated and itself all by itself." In the argument from contraries, Socrates in effect turned away from the forms to natural processes. With similarity-based recollection, the forms, again referred to as the "things themselves all by themselves," re-enter the conversation, this time as an integral part of a proof for the soul's deathlessness. Whereas recollection based on non-similarity was connected with erotic love, recollection based on similarity is connected with the sobriety of mathematics. Socrates uses the perplexing example of a "relational" form—the Equal. If equal sticks and stones indeed "remind" us of the Equal Itself by *falling short* of that Equal, and if we therefore have to have "seen" the Equal "beforehand" (that is, before we were embodied), then "our soul *is,* even before we were born." Simmias seems entirely convinced. He speaks of an "overwhelming necessity" to Socrates' argument, adding that "the account is taking refuge in a beautiful conclusion." But we are left with perplexities: Why does Socrates use as his example of a form a mathematical relation rather than a mathematical property of an individual thing (for example, an object's circularity)? And why *this* relation?

Many things are noteworthy about Socrates' treatment of recollection here. For instance, Socrates does not directly connect the recollection that "proves" the deathlessness of the soul with philosophic inquiry, as he does in the *Meno,* though the arguments in both dialogues begin with mathematical discovery. That Socrates does not here argue for deathlessness based on recollection as inquiry is perhaps due to the fears of Simmias and Cebes. Anxiety over the future, the fear about what happens to the soul *afterward,* has usurped the place of philosophic *eros,* which tends, not onward and down, but *backward* and *up* to the truly deathless beings. This direction of inquiry is figured in the very word for recollection, *anamnesis,* the *ana* part of which means both "back" and "up." The fears of Simmias and Cebes, we might say, compel the argument to go "down" rather than "up." Socrates, who is unwilling to abandon them to their fears and who no doubt realizes that fear is an impediment to philosophic love, "descends" with them.

V SONGS FOR CHILDREN [77 A – 78 B]

But has Cebes, the down-to-business fellow, been persuaded? Simmias comments on his friend's capacity for skepticism, calling Cebes "the mightiest of humans when it comes to distrusting arguments." He also suggests that he too is subject to "the fear of the many." What if the soul, he worries, were somehow put together at birth and then taken apart at death? Couldn't the circle of becoming then go on without the soul's continued existence? Cebes praises Simmias's perspicacity and remarks that only "half" the necessary argument has been given. Socrates reminds the two friends that the allegedly missing half of the argument has already been taken care of. Nevertheless he is willing to humor what he calls their "childish" fear of death. This lighthearted reprimand conveys a most important teaching: that one should not take the fear of death *too* seriously—if one's highest concern is with the pursuit of deathless Being. Cebes, laughing, tells Socrates to go ahead: "Try to persuade us as if we were afraid." The little interlude ends with Socrates telling the two friends that now, since he is about to go away, they must search everywhere, even among "barbarians," for the "good singer" who knows how to charm away the bogeyman named Fear of Death.

VI THE ARGUMENT FROM INVISIBILITY
   ### [78 B – 84 B]

Socrates now gets down to business with Cebes. Together they explore the attributes of soul. If soul is found to be composite, the old fear returns, for a composite soul could, and no doubt would, suffer decomposition into the parts or elements out of which she was made. A non-composite soul would not suffer this. Socrates bases the inquiry on the distinction brought up earlier between the "beings themselves" and their sensuous participants. The former belong to the class of the unvarying and unseen, the latter to the class of the changing and visible. Soul is quickly found to be akin to Being itself by virtue of her invisibility and natural hegemony over the body. She is "most similar to" the divine and deathless, while body is "most similar to" the human and the deathbound.

Socrates then reverts to his earlier mythical mode of speech. With a play on the word "Hades"—which closely resembles the Greek word for "unseen"—Socrates tells Cebes that the soul that has spent her days in philosophic purity, communing with Being itself, goes off at the moment of death to a place like herself—"noble and pure and unseen." The play on "Hades" suggests that the philosopher, while alive in a mortal body, nevertheless "goes to" a deathless "place" whenever he engages in philosophy. It suggests the here-unexplored possibility that the true Hades is not really an afterlife at all, that it is not "where you go next" but where you have the power to go *now*. To his happy portrayal of the philosopher, Socrates appends an ominous "likely story" about the fate of the impure, body-loving soul. He belabors his attack on body, telling Cebes that every pleasure and pain alike "nails the soul to the body." Socrates' rhetoric here seems intended to counter the fear of death with a fear of the basest enslavement. Socrates ends this section of the conversation by emphasizing to Simmias and Cebes that death, for the pure or philosophical soul, is the escape from this enslavement and that the philosopher, if anyone, has no reason to fear death.

VII THE LYRE AND THE WEAVER [84 B – 88 C]

Socrates' encouraging speech about not fearing death has, however, an unsettling coda. He gives an all-too-familiar, all-too-vivid depiction of just what we, in our childishness, fear: that our soul will be "scattered" and "blown away" at the moment of death, that she will "vanish and no longer *be* anywhere at all!"

The long silence that descends with Socrates' words envelops all present. Simmias and Cebes have a private exchange, but Socrates brings them out of hiding. He exhorts them strongly to voice their distrust. Then Socrates laughs and compares his "swan song"—his musical *lógos*—to the song of real swans, who, he says, sing for joy on the day of their death. Simmias picks up the thread of the argument and speaks of the need for courage and resourcefulness. If a human being can't determine what's true, then, sailing upon human accounts as upon a raft, he must find among these accounts the one that's "best and least refutable." Simmias's speech foreshadows the "second sailing" we hear about later. It also summons as a model for philosophic virtue the figure of Odysseus, that man of many ways. Odysseus is invoked at crucial moments in the *Phaedo*. He, Theseus, and also Heracles form a sort of heroic triumvirate in the dialogue. They provide a paradigm for Socrates' and his friends' efforts to slay the monstrous enemies of discourse.

Simmias voices his distrust through the image of a tuned lyre. If soul is to body as the tuning is to the lyre, then just as the tuning is destroyed along with the lyre, so too the soul is destroyed along with the body; for soul would be nothing more than this: "a blend of the elements of the body."

We then hear Cebes' distrust. He too uses an image. His objection is a more radical version of the one Simmias had put forth. Even if soul were "stronger and more long-lasting than body," even if she could outlive her body in the course of a great many deaths, what is to prevent the soul from eventually "wearing out?" It's like an old weaver-man, says Cebes, who wove and wore out many cloaks but wasn't "durable enough" to wear out all such cloaks for all time. Who knows? The soul's current "cloak"—Cebes here, or Simmias, or Socrates—may well be her last!

VIII THE HATRED OF ARGUMENT [88 C – 91 B]

At this perilous moment, we approach the very center of the *Phaedo,* the heart of Plato's labyrinth. Echecrates irrupts into the conversation. He breaks in because Simmias and Cebes have just, each of them, made serious objections that threaten to undo Socrates' arguments. He wonders how he can trust any argument from now on. Back in Athens, Socrates has foreseen just this defeatism, and as if to speak to Echecrates from the grave, he turns to Phaedo, who will be telling Echecrates what happened next.

What follows is surely one of the most remarkable moments in the Platonic dialogues. Socrates plays with Phaedo's hair (something he did habitually, we are told) and guesses that tomorrow, when Socrates is no more, Phaedo will cut off those beautiful locks of his, adding that they both will have reason to cut their hair even today, "if the argument meets its end." This affectionate gesture is alone sufficient to dispel any notion that Socrates is simply a hater of bodily things.

Socrates calls on Phaedo to be his Heracles, as he will be Phaedo's Iolaus, in this exploit of saving the life of the account—incidentally illustrating what Phaedo has just told Echecrates: that he never admired Socrates more than on this occasion, because he was so kind and admiring in dealing with the young men's criticisms. For Heracles is the great hero and Iolaus his young companion, and Socrates is modestly proposing to reverse the proper roles. Now he warns of a danger, a certain experience they must guard against. To name it, he coins a word in analogy to "misanthropy," the hatred of human beings. It is "misology," the hatred of argument. Just as someone comes to distrust and hate all human beings because he has been repeatedly "burned" by an ill-placed trust, so a naive and artless way of trusting in arguments makes someone finally distrust and hate them all because no thing and no argument ever stays put, ever gratifies his demand for an argument that is deception-free. Then, instead of blaming his own ineptitude, he foreswears the activity of giving accounts and making arguments.

This remarkable drama between Socrates and Phaedo, so carefully placed at the center of the dialogue, suggests that the hatred of argument is more terrible than the fear of death, that this hatred is the true and deepest Minotaur in the soul. It also helps us understand the musical, incantatory function of Socrates' discourse—here, as elsewhere in the dialogue, no doubt connected with Orpheus's power of song. We hear on several occasions about the singer who can charm away the fear of death. That charm is perhaps no different from what we see actually going on in the drama before us, not just in the non-argumentative moments of the dialogue but also in the arguments themselves. The Cebes-like "business" in which philosophy ordinarily engages is possessed of a Simmias-like "music." The music of philosophic discourse calms the human anxiety about death, not by constructing irrefutable "proofs for the immortality of the soul," but by engaging the soul in the philosopher's everyday business of tending arguments.

IX TUNING UNDONE [91 B – 95 A]

Socrates now turns back to Simmias and Cebes. He helps them demolish the argument most familiar to them as disciples of Pythagoras, the argument that soul is a tuning, a mere relation of parts. Here begins the close-in fighting for the survival of reasonable speech and argument. Socrates briefly summarizes their respective forms of distrust and with that takes up the objection of Simmias. In his first "attack on Harmonia," he points out to Simmias and Cebes that the tuning-thesis doesn't "sing in accord" with the teaching that learning is recollection: If you trust the one, you've got to reject the other.

In his second assault, Socrates, now addressing himself to Simmias, argues that if the soul were a condition of tuning, and if being tuned always meant being made orderly and good, then all souls would be orderly and good: Vice would be impossible. Not only that, but since one tuning can't be any more tuned or orderly than another, all souls would be equally virtuous.

The third and final attack appeals to the behavior of contraries. The crucial assumption here is that a tuning must always follow the disposition of its parts and never run contrary to them. If soul were indeed some sort of tuning, then since her parts would be the bodily elements in tension with each other, the soul could never run contrary to her body: The body would always lead. But this conclusion runs contrary to what had been agreed to earlier—that soul, by nature, rules. Socrates supports this view of soul's natural hegemony over the body by appealing to the countless occasions on which we restrain or check our bodily desires.

The attack on soul-as-tuning ends with an appeal to poetic authority. As the "Divine Poet" shows us, Odysseus (whom Simmias had indirectly invoked earlier in his image of the raft) speaks to his heart and controls himself. But the reference points to a difficulty that Socrates does not mention. In the passage from Homer, Odysseus is controlling his anger and spiritedness rather than his bodily desires. He is in fact restraining himself from killing the maidservants for their having sacrificed all honor and loyalty to the pleasures of the body. If the soul is non-composite, and if the only opposition to be considered is that between soul and body, how do we account for what seems to be a tension *within* the soul of Odysseus in Socrates' craftily chosen example?

X THE THREAT OF BLINDNESS AND THE SECOND SAILING [95 A – 102 A]

Socrates now turns to the objection of Cebes. Here he adopts a whole new strategy in order to make the argument, as he says, "more gentle." He pauses for a long time to consider something within himself—the very image of recollection. This pause is a signal that something very mysterious is coming; what they are searching for is "no trivial business," as Socrates says in the understated manner he habitually uses at crucial junctures, and it is indeed related to recollection. He shows them that what is at stake here is understanding "the cause of generation and destruction as a whole."[2]

Socrates begins by giving Simmias and Cebes an insight into his intellectual development, in the course of which he is twice nearly brought to the very despair in reason that he has just so fervently denounced. When he was young, he was "wondrously desirous of that wisdom they call 'the inquiry into nature.'" At first, he would give the most ordinary answer to explain generation and growth: A human being grows by eating and drinking and adding flesh. But that was entirely unsatisfactory. Then he read a book by Anaxagoras, who said that Mind orders the world. He was delighted, until he saw that this "wise man" didn't actually use Mind in his causal explanations. For instance, Anaxagoras would have said that Socrates was sitting in prison not because of any mindfulness but because his bones in their sockets were bent in a certain way. He would have neglected to show that it was Socrates' mind that judged it best for Socrates to endure the penalty imposed on him by the Athenians rather than to run off. Although Anaxagoras had asserted that Mind was the cause of all things, in the end he was just one more materialist. He could not explain why it was best for things to be as they are. Socrates here is like Odysseus, who is on the verge of his homecoming when an opened wind-bag blows him off course.

Socrates then tells Cebes that he had simply "had it" with looking into beings themselves and had begun to fear that he might become "soul-blinded." He sought refuge, as he puts it, in *lógoi* or verbal accounts. Thus begins Socrates' famous "second sailing" in search of cause.

The passage about blindness and the refuge in *lógoi* is one of the most difficult in the *Phaedo*. What exactly is the blindness Socrates fears? And what does *lógos* refer to here? Socrates appears to be describing a conversion from the direct, intellectual perception of "things themselves" (presumably the head-on vision he sought in the physics of Anaxagoras), to the indirect but no less Being-oriented activity of philosophic accounts based on the forms. The turn is not the conversion from "beings themselves" to images or likenesses of beings, as Socrates goes out of his way to make clear. Nor is the refuge in *lógoi* the turn to the investigation of "language." Nor is *lógos* here a "theory" or "concept," which would in effect displace philosophy's directedness to Being with the directedness to the mere thinking of Being and the invention of artificial structures. It appears to be the turn to a philosophic way of speaking that indeed "catches" the Being of things, indirectly and therefore "safely," by attending to what speeches and things have in common—the genuine intelligibility of form, *eídos,* as opposed to the beguiling but sham intelligibility of process physics.

Socrates outlines a "method" of hypotheses, a way of inquiry that seems like an elaboration of the Odyssean raft Simmias had earlier described. These hypotheses, literally "puttings-under," are not hypotheses in the modern sense of the term—rational, often mathematical conjectures intended to be verified by experiment—but rather suppositions that support thinking and make speech possible. Speech here means all speech, our ordinary everyday speech as well as account-giving and the arguments in which Socrates has taken refuge. The first hypothesis is that there are forms—the Beautiful itself by itself and many others—each of which is itself a hypothesis. "Itself by itself" is a kind of formula Socrates has devised for these ultimate thinkables; it betokens the intensity of their being and their independence from the variety of the things of sense that we call by their name. Communion with these beings of thought is the intelligible cause of both the coming to be and the abiding of the things of sense. Above all, the forms are responsible for our ability not only to name things but also to engage in reasoned speech. Socrates makes it clear that he regards this hypothesis as a return, on a clarified plane, to his early innocence, before he became discombobulated by the "wise," that is, sophisticated, causes given by those who inquire into nature. He calls his own way simple, artless, and naive, and he recommends it to Simmias and Cebes as the way for all lovers of wisdom.

The rest of the dialogue up to the myth is devoted to showing how one can think by means of hypotheses. This next part of the dialogue thus serves, beyond its proper matter, as a demonstration for Simmias and Cebes, but even more for us, of reasoning on the supposition of the forms.

XI THE ENTHUSIASM OF ECHECRATES [102 A]

Once again, Echecrates cannot contain himself. He breaks in a second and last time, signaling that this central episode is over. It has consisted of two complementary parts: a passionate defense of account-giving and a particular way of doing it. Echecrates now voices his enthusiastic approval of Simmias and Cebes for agreeing with Socrates on the right use of hypotheses. The slight interruption serves to remind us that the drama is not strictly confined to Socrates' cell. By mediating between the actual events and his listeners, Phaedo in his own way "brings the *lógos* back to life." He perpetuates it for Echecrates and his friends, just as Plato brings Socrates back to life for us. Eche-crates says outright what Plato surely intends us to infer: that Socrates' way of hypotheses travels well and can be taken up fruitfully in far off places and distant times.

XII THE ARGUMENT FROM CAUSE
[102 A – 107 B]

Phaedo picks up the thread of his narrative. At first Socrates talks with Simmias, but soon Cebes enters and continues with Socrates to the very end of this last section of the argument.

Here we reach the densest, most labyrinthine section of the dialogue. The basis for the entire discussion is the mutual exclusiveness of contraries, an exclusiveness that Socrates mythically (and somewhat comically) portrays in the language of combat and retreat. Socrates takes up the example of the Big and the Small. He argues that "the Bigness in us never abides the Small, nor is it willing to be exceeded." The Big and the Small are presented as at war with one another, like pleasure and pain in Socrates' much earlier reference to Aesop. The forms are possessed of inviolable identities, and this virginity makes a form inimical to its contrary. At the approach of its contrary, a form must either "flee" or "perish." An unnamed listener at this point speaks up and shows that he has been paying close attention to the conversation all along. (Perhaps he is not one of the named fourteen because he doesn't need to be saved from inappropriate emotions and is simply "following the *lógos*" with great interest.) He reminds Socrates that earlier it had been agreed that contraries, far from excluding one another, come to be out of one another. Socrates counters the objection by saying that the earlier assertion had not been about forms but about things. He then returns Cebes to the apparently indisputable claim that "a contrary will never be contrary to itself."

Socrates pursues the point by shifting to a new example, the Hot and the Cold and their influence over the behavior of fire and snow: The forms Hot and Cold behave as contraries usually do, according to what has been said so far. When one of them approaches, the other "either flees or perishes." But fire and snow, says Socrates, also behave in this way. When the Hot approaches snow, the snow that was once cold does not turn into snow that is now hot: It can either "move away" or else stay and perish *as snow.* Nor does fire "get cold" with the approach of snow. It too must either "get out of the way or perish."

Socrates then extends the argument to include the behavior of Odd and Even in relation to numbers. Why, we wonder, has Socrates chosen these examples in particular and this sequence? Do the examples, when taken separately and explored, point to the same or different conclusions? And do they tend to further the argument or undermine it? In any case, Socrates seems eager to draw a general conclusion: Contraries, as it turns out, aren't the only things not to admit one another—those things that *contain* contraries act the same way.

At this point something unexpected happens. Socrates takes Cebes back to the very beginning of the argument and revises the earlier agreement about cause. He says he will now go beyond that first answer—the safe and unlearned one about the presence of a form. If somebody asks him, "What made this body hot?" Socrates will now say not "Hotness" but "fire." It is with this "fancier" or more sophisticated answer (an answer, we must note, that nevertheless continues to rely on the forms) that the argument—questionably, to be sure—reaches its end. Socrates returns at last to the soul, now regarded as "that by which the body will be living." The reasoning embodied in the previous examples (Hot and Cold, Even and Odd) is now unquestioningly applied to soul in relation to body. Life and Death are contraries. Things that "contain contraries" behave the way contraries themselves do—they mutually exclude, and are inimical to, one another. That which doesn't admit Death must, however, be the deathless, and soul, since she brings Life to what she possesses, must "contain" the contrary of Death. Therefore, "soul is a deathless thing." Has this conclusion finally been sufficiently demonstrated? The usually skeptical Cebes seems to think so. He responds with an enthusiastic "Very adequately demonstrated indeed, Socrates." Socrates adds one more questionable condition to the argument—that the soul be shown to be imperishable or immune to decay as well as deathless. Cebes readily agrees that indeed the deathless must also be immune to decay. Socrates concludes: "So when Death comes at a man, his deathbound part, as is likely, dies, but his deathless part takes off and goes away safe and undecayed, getting out of Death's way." Socrates then returns to his earlier point, one of the constant refrains in his philosophic song: If the soul "takes off," then there must be some *place to which* she takes off. That place is Hades—the Unseen.

Cebes now says that he no longer has any distrust in the earlier arguments. He encourages Simmias "or anyone else" to speak up—while there's still time. Simmias too says he's no longer distrustful, "given what's been argued," but he qualifies his agreement with Cebes. He confesses to a lingering distrust based on the sheer magnitude of what they have been talking about and, by contrast, the weakness of human nature. Socrates responds by reinforcing this distrust while at the same time transforming it into a lifelong task. He sobers up Simmias's vague anxieties about infirmity by in effect telling Simmias to get down to work. Even our "first hypotheses," Socrates says, "must nevertheless be looked into more clearly." This presumably means, in particular, the hypotheses of the forms.

Earlier in the dialogue, Socrates invoked the figure of Penelope. There the true philosopher was *not* like Penelope, whose web was done only to be undone. He did not, once free of bodily entanglement, let his soul then fall shamelessly back into a liaison with body. But here, at the very end of the arguments in the *Phaedo*, Socrates both indirectly recalls and rehabilitates the figure of Penelope. The true philosopher is indeed like the wife of Odysseus. At the end of an argument, when a conclusion has been "woven," he must then go back to the beginning, separate the strands of which the argument is composed, and undo the web of *lógos*. The *lógos*, whose return to life the new Heracles has tried to bring about, is perpetuated precisely in this oscillation between weaving and unweaving. Argument goes on and is, in a sense, deathless—not just because valiant souls keep it up but because philosophic *lógos* is itself inherently incomplete and never "meets its end."

XIII   THE TRUE EARTH [107 B – 115 A]

Socrates now turns away from argument, and from our trust and distrust in argument, to his myth about the true earth. Like the myths Socrates presents in other dialogues, this one has as its central point the extreme importance of taking care of our souls now in our mortal lives. The myth presents a genuine "cosmos," a beautifully ordered whole. In this it may be said to accomplish, however mythically, what the Mind of Anaxagoras could not. In place of the many earlier references to Hades, Socrates now presents an elaborate description of the shape and workings of the Whole. He combines the language of body-in-process, the language of physics, with an account of how various souls fare within this Whole.

According to Socrates' myth, the earth itself comes in three layers: the true earth, the hollows within it where we dwell (thinking we dwell on the surface), and the earth beneath us. The Earth Itself, round and pure and resplendent, remains at rest as a whole in the middle of the heavens. No pushes or pulls, no Atlas or air, no external force, in other words, is needed to keep it in place. The "self-similarity," that is, the equipoise of the heavens and the earth's own equilibrium suffice to keep it at rest. Life on the surface of the true earth mirrors this cosmic state of affairs. None of the tugs and pulls, none of the turmoil and violence that mark our life in the hollows, is to be found there. True freedom, in other words, is the escape both from all process and from its attendant seriousness. The inhabitants of the surface of the true earth float free, dwelling in unconcealment, reveling in the sight of the things that *are*, like sightseeing tourists on an eternal vacation. There are no faction-ridden cities, indeed no cities at all, on the surface of the true earth.

In the nether world, the world that lies below what we call earth, things are very different. Here force and constraint, turmoil and violence, characterize both the "look" of that world and the "lives" of those forced to stay there. Indeed the surgings and rushings of liquids under great pressure, the absence of light except in the presence of great heat, seem to mirror the inner turmoil of the most desperate of that world's inhabitants, who are in turn swept along, always at the mercy of something or someone other than themselves.

Yet for all its apparent chaos, the nether world turns out to have a structure: Not order and disorder but different principles of order make for the difference between above and below. The order of the lower world is the order of oscillation, of movement constrained or governed by and about a point—in this case the center of the earth. The center of the earth is also the center of a great tube that passes through the earth, the channel of Tartarus. This tube and its center together determine all fluid flow within the lower world. The *position* of Tartarus defines, in general, the path of flow, the meaning of "to" and "fro." The lower world is riddled by channels filled with everything from water to liquid fire, but every channel, however circuitous its path, must exit and sooner or later re-enter Tartarus. The center of Tartarus, in turn, defines the possible *extent* of flow: Just as a pendulum bob can never, over the course of its motion, end up at a point higher than its point of release, so too, liquid flowing out of Tartarus at one point can never re-enter it further from the center than the initial point of outflow.

Within this structure of ordered surgings, four rivers stand out along with Tartarus: Ocean ("Swift-flowing"), Acheron ("Distressing"), Pyriphlegethon ("Fire-blazing"), and Cocytus ("Shrieking"). Here, too, a certain order is present—an order of contraries, as it were. Ocean and Acheron are paired with one another, as are Pyriphlegethon and Cocytus. They circulate in contrary directions and have their points of discharge "directly opposite" from one another, that is, at diametrically opposed positions on either side of the center. Moreover, Pyriphlegethon and Cocytus come nearest to one another when they pass by the Acherousian Lake. Those who have committed great but curable misdeeds spend most of their time in violent motion within Tartarus and are swept past the Acherousian Lake on the rivers only in order to ask forgiveness of those they harmed. In other words, this constellation of rivers seems to function as the moral center of the lower earth.

Where are *we* in this picture of the earth? The most beautiful things around us are mere fragments, yet fragments of things above. Though our vision is clouded, we see the same heavens the surface-dwellers see. And some of the dappled beauty of their world comes from the mist and air around us, the "sediment" of the aether. Yet we seem to be equally connected to the earth below; indeed it is sometimes difficult to tell, in Socrates' account, where the hollows leave off and the underworld begins. That our Ocean's waters mix with and are governed by the same laws as their waters, that their Pyriphlegethon occasionally bursts forth in our world, are sufficient signs of the connection. Our own middling lives are suspended between these two extremes, and how we live now has everything to do with what region we will—or perhaps do—inhabit.

The myth, we must note, is addressed to Simmias, who, as has been said, seems to be the more lyrical and less dialectical. Socrates concludes his speech to Simmias with an exhortation. He speaks of the "noble risk" involved in taking the myth to heart, that is, not in believing all the mythical details but in doing everything in life "so as to partake of virtue and thoughtfulness." Socrates again returns to that "good singer" who knows how to charm away the bogeyman, Fear of Death—but now the singer is *us*. We must take heart for our souls in the belief that the cosmos and the divine that lives within it are responsive to our quest for purification, especially the purification that is philosophy. Much of the *Phaedo* is about not what is absolutely and demonstrably true but about what the philosopher should tell himself—in a word, what he should trust. Here Socrates reminds us that such trust in the goodness and order of the Whole is induced by philosophy as a form of music.

XIV THE END OF SOCRATES [115 A – 118]

Socrates now says that he must "turn to the bath" and save the women the trouble of bathing a corpse—a gesture that combines care for his own purity with care for the sensibilities of others. At this point in the drama, Plato focuses our attention on the all-too-human Crito. Crito wants to cling to the man Socrates and to every precious minute and mortal concern that remains. Gently but firmly, Socrates attempts to guide Crito back to an understanding of the extreme importance of what Socrates has always told them: They must care for their souls by "walking in the footsteps" of that which their conversation has shown them. Crito, however, quickly reverts to his care for Socrates' body: "But in what way shall we bury you?" At this point, Socrates asks the others to "make a pledge" before Crito, to swear that Socrates will not remain behind at his death but will be "off and gone."

We now reach the concluding narration, in which Phaedo tells us how Socrates died. How does Plato's depiction of Socrates' final moments affect all that has been said up to this point? What exactly do we witness, and what can we conclude, as we watch the actual approach of Death?

It appears that the accounts and arguments which Socrates has spent the day giving to and eliciting from his friends are more persuasive as examples and enactments of the way of life in which Socrates believes than as proofs of the survival of the soul after bodily death. Therefore Socrates' demeanor in the hour and the moment of his death might matter even more than if he faced death utterly convinced by his own proofs that there is a life beyond. If he is really blithe even in his last moments on earth, we might suppose that he is a man who finds eternity in *this* life day by day, who does not need to wait for physical death to die the philosopher's death and turn away from the pleasures of the body to the delights of thinking. He might be a man who needs no special deliverance to live in the region of Being; that is what his warmly human friend Crito does not quite understand.

But does that mean that Socrates is deceiving Simmias and Cebes—or even himself—when he sings them charms to banish the fear of death and when he casts himself as Theseus, their savior from the bull-headed monster, the Minotaur? Not necessarily. Socrates recognizes that his young friends are frightened and that he has things to say to them that he himself may not need to hear. He is willing to enact a drama of conquered fear for their sake. If it is deception at all, it is also candor and kindness that makes him lead them through the labyrinth by the clue of his conversation to face—what?

After Socrates bathes, he sees his three sons and gives instructions to the women of his household. The servant of the Eleven arrives and bids a fond farewell to Socrates, calling him "the noblest and gentlest and best man among those who've ever arrived here." Socrates praises him for his noble tears and calls for the potion. Crito, with touching desperation, urges Socrates not to hurry—after all, there's still some sun on the mountains, still time to enjoy even the pleasures of sex before dying! Socrates then tells Crito that by acting as others do, he'd only be a laughingstock in his own eyes. He urges Crito: "Obey and don't act in any other way!"

When the potion-bearer arrives, Socrates treats him with all the respect due to one who has knowledge. He seeks advice on how to cooperate with the natural powers of the drug. Socrates at this point graciously takes the cup. Throughout the dialogue Socrates' glance has been emphasized. He looks at each speaker, keenly and attentively. Now near the end, when the man brings the potion that is both a poison and a cure, Socrates looks up at him from under his brows "with that bull's look that was so usual with him." A strange description, and it almost seems as if just at the stroke of death Socrates the Minotaur-slayer had himself turned into the Minotaur, whose death the young men have to watch so that they themselves may become monster-slayers. Socrates shows them the drama of the slaying of Death so that they may see how harmless the monster is when approached in a safe and sure way.

We already know that Socrates has been judged by the potion-bearer not to be in an excited mood. Early on, he had warned Socrates not to engage in so much conversation as to become heated because then a double dose of the poison would be needed to kill him. Now, when Socrates offers, in an enigmatic way, to use part of the potion to pour a libation to "somebody," it is clear that the man has judged that Socrates is calm and has brought only the minimum amount. So Socrates says that he must at least pray to the gods for an auspicious "emigration from here to There." And with that, he drinks.

All self-control breaks down at this point as the assembled friends seem to be devoured by yet another Minotaur—Grief. The whole company, including Phaedo, joins in the threnody of Apollodorus, who, throughout the entire conversation, has been weeping rather than following the argument. The music of discourse, it seems, has been utterly lost on him. Socrates rebukes them for their impious anti-music and exhorts them to propitious silence. Their shame restrains their tears. These tears, we must note, are not the noble tears of the servant of the Eleven, whom Socrates praised. What, we wonder, is the difference between them? Why are the former ignoble and the latter noble? Perhaps it has something to do with the form as well as the extent of the grief. Perhaps it is one thing to grieve but accept the death of Socrates and another to grieve but not accept. This distinction fits with the servant's parting words to Socrates: "Farewell and try to bear these necessities as easily as possible." The servant may be noble because, although he weeps, he does not do so uncontrollably; he is willing to say farewell!

And now the approach of Death. In obedience to the potion-bearer, Socrates walks around until his legs feel heavy and then lies down, covering himself. Slowly Death comes upon him in the form of the Cold and the Stiff. It starts from below and works its way up: first the feet, then the legs, then the thighs. The potion-bearer calmly demonstrates the natural process by which Death operates. He tells the company that when the effect of the potion reaches the heart, Socrates will be gone. Even as he says this, the parts of Socrates' lower belly grow cold.

Socrates now uncovers himself to make the last request Crito has been so eager to receive. "Crito," he says, "we owe a cock to Asclepius. So pay the debt and don't be careless." Some readers think that, since Asclepius is the god of medicine, Socrates is ordering a thank-offering (perhaps the one he was not allowed to pour himself) for being released from the disease of life. That explanation certainly fits with the fact that cocks were also sacrificed to the Egyptian god Anubis, identified with the Greek god Hermes, who guides souls to the underworld and by whom Socrates is fond of swearing. But why do "we" owe the thank-offering?

How we interpret the last words of Socrates, so redolent of the Theseus-theme of salvation, depends on how we answer the questions: What has Socrates been attempting to save his friends from? Who do we think the real Minotaur of the *Phaedo* is? The fear of death is a prime candidate, and no doubt Socrates in his closing words expresses his gratitude to higher powers for his having been successful, at least on this occasion, in preventing his friends from being consumed by that fear. But as we have seen, at the center of Plato's labyrinth lurks not the fear of death but the hatred of argument. Perhaps this is the deeper reason behind Socrates' thank-offering: On the day he dies, surrounded by intensely anxious friends, he does indeed somehow manage to ward off the fear of death. But he does so not, as we have seen, by constructing irrefutable "proofs for the immortality of the soul," but by redirecting his friends' care to the renewed life of philosophic inquiry and discourse. Socrates thus dies bequeathing a task, not just to Simmias, but to all who know of Phaedo's account, when he says: "What you say is good, but also our very first hypotheses must nevertheless be looked into for greater surety."

Perhaps there is a second and harsher reason why Socrates himself, just before he drinks the potion, takes on the guise of the Minotaur. Perhaps there is something deadly about even Socrates—especially about *him*—something from which, along with the fear of death and hatred of argument, his friends need to be saved. Socrates in the *Phaedo* is surrounded by loving admirers who cannot bear to lose Socrates the man. The conversation began, we recall, with Socrates' apparently blithe acceptance of death. This blitheness, stressed throughout the dialogue by Socrates' jokes and smiles, is taken hard by Simmias and Cebes, at least at first. In their indignation born of grief, they accuse Socrates of injustice to his friends. In effect, they cast him as a Theseus who saves his friends and fellow journeyers from all sorts of dangers only to abandon them in the end, as Theseus abandoned Ariadne on the isle of Naxos. It seems appropriate, therefore, that just before he dies, Socrates try to deliver his friends from the final Minotaur—their engrossing love of Socrates the man, a love that threatens to fill their souls with grief and indignation. He shows them a new view of the face that had the power to rivet attention on the man rather than on the speech and vision for which the man lived. The understandable fixation with Socrates the man is touchingly enacted in Crito's stubborn attentiveness to Socrates' body. This may explain why Plato presents himself as absent on that momentous day. Unlike Apollodorus, Crito, Simmias, Cebes and all the others, Plato is not threatened by the most potentially seductive of all Minotaurs: He knows Socrates well enough to be willing to let the man Socrates die. Ironically, he is also the one who, in his dialogues, keeps Socrates perpetually alive for us—alive, enchanting, and perhaps also *dangerous*.

Socrates then falls silent. After a little while, he makes a motion of some sort and is uncovered once more. He has composed his expression, and his mouth and eyes are open. Crito closes them.[3]

The course of Death has been knowingly plotted for us by the potion-bearer. We have watched its approach. As for the moment itself, the arrival and very deed of Death—that remains cloaked in mystery, as does Socrates' final encounter. The final look of Socrates, however, while it may not tell us what Death is or even what Socrates experienced before he "composed his countenance," does offer a fitting, perhaps even comic, picture of what Socrates lived for. In the open eyes and mouth, we have the very image of a man who devoted himself to vision and speech. If we put together the open eyes and mouth, we also have the gesture of wonder. The gesture seems to say, "So this is Death!" without, however, revealing what Death Itself *is*.

Phaedo's narration ends, appropriately, with the praise of Socrates. If it is indeed the case that Socrates dies blithely and with welcoming wonder, a puzzling fact about Phaedo's last words in praise of Socrates begins to make sense: During his life, Socrates thought and talked about four particular virtues—wisdom, courage, moderation, and justice. When Phaedo sums up Socrates' virtues, calling him the best, the most thoughtful, and the most just of all men whom he and his friends have known, he leaves courage conspicuously unmentioned. Perhaps Plato is saying, through Phaedo, that a human being impassioned by the love of wisdom and absorbed in the search for being does not need courage in the face of death.

Was Socrates also the happiest of human beings? Phaedo does not say. And yet, we may infer from Socrates' lightheartedness, displayed throughout the dialogue, that Socrates dies as he lived—neither indignant at misfortune and death, nor a passionless Stoic, nor when all is said and done, a hater of the body who is glad to be relieved of the disease of life. He dies in full keeping with the conditions for happiness set out by Solon in Herodotus. He has served his city as soldier and gadfly and now dies in the fullness of old age (and with several sons), surrounded by a group of devoted friends. The condemnation by Athens even tends to ennoble him as a great man wrongly accused—a man who, on the day of his death, seems to give ample proof of his belief in "good gods" and his scrupulous care for the souls of the young.

The heart and soul of Socrates' happiness, however, extends far beyond the temporal boundaries for happiness we find in Solon and Herodotus. This "higher" happiness lies in Socrates' pursuit of the divine and his devotion to speech and vision—a divine which, as the exact opposite of the divine in Herodotus, is not envious but rather opens itself up ungrudgingly, if perplexingly, to the exertions of inquiry. Throughout the *Phaedo,* Socrates appeals to those deathless beings that the philosopher longs to "see" and "be with"; and throughout the *Phaedo,* the singer Socrates evinces a light and even comic mode in an effort to deliver his friends from their tragic Muse. These two facts are connected. To give oneself to the love that is philosophy is to be liberated, above all, from tragedy and its deathbound Muse.

There is a story to the effect that Plato, after he met Socrates, went home and burned his tragic compositions. It was on that day that Plato slew at least one Minotaur and thus prepared to write a philosophic comedy entitled *Phaedo.* If Plato's readers are themselves delivered from their tragic-minded anxiety and are turned to the pleasant labors of philosophy, Plato himself might well have reason to say: "We owe a cock to Asclepius, reader. So pay the debt and don't be careless!"

2

SOCRATES' LEGACY: PLATO'S **PHAEDO**

This is a view, very sketchily stated, of Plato's *Phaedo* which might help a serious student in reading the dialogue. By "serious" I mean "interested in the application of the text to live questions."

I have never met anyone who is in the least persuaded by the four arguments for the immortality of the soul that Socrates mounts on his last day among the living. In fact he himself seems unpersuaded: Why would he try so many ways if one were conclusive?

Here is a notion that came to me while I, together with two colleagues with whom I was translating the dialogue, was wondering about its purpose. It made sense that Socrates might want to comfort these young men who feel that he is abandoning them, but not that he would do it with implausible contrivances. It seemed equally unlikely that he himself was so afraid of death that he might wish to soothe or trick himself with sophisms about an afterlife, for that World Beyond which he cares about is not the one which might come at the end of a lifetime, but the earthly death he achieves *within* life whenever he is lost in thought.

Here is what I think Socrates is up to: Open the dialogue just about at its literal middle and you will come upon its center. It is Socrates' real worry that the life of the *lógos* might end, that philosophical inquiry might die from "misology," hatred of rational speech (89 d). Socrates intends in this last conversation to bequeath philosophy to his young friends. He does it, however, not only by open exhortation but also by engaging in actual, though implicit, teaching. Embedded in the arguments about the soul he presents a list of his concerns, his unfinished legacy. Socrates may indeed be interested above all in human excellence, but for him such goodness flows from knowledge of supra-human matters, the knowledge that will come to be called "ontological," because it gives "an account of Being." Therefore, on his last day the dialogic emphasis is on such inquiries, and the purity of soul that he advocates is meant to further the cause of the *lógos*.

Here then is my list of the unfinished inquiries, the *aporíai*, the impasses and perplexities, Plato's Socrates insinuates into the purported demonstrations of the soul's immortality. In fact he makes these proofs depend, not altogether convincingly, on tentative answers to these questions. Since he is talking to young friends who are quite familiar with his way of inquiry, the human bond among these participants is particularly strong in this valedictory conversation; I should warn that I'm stripping away, at least for a moment, just that human drama which gives their talk its vitality.

Even before the conversation turns to the ostensible search for proofs of the soul's immortality, Socrates raises, in a more personal mode than that of the central inquiry, certain preparatory, term-setting topics:

a Speaking from present experiences he asks: What is the nature of pleasure and pain, such that they are attached as a pair of *contraries* (60 b)?

b Philosophizing being a voluntary death, i.e., *freedom from the bodily senses* (though real suicide is impermissible), how can Socrates defend himself from the charge of deficient human attachment (63 a)?

c If thoughtfulness requires freedom from interference by the senses so that the soul on its own can reach true Being, how can a philosopher, how can he, *fear death* (67 e)?

d If the excellences Socrates cares about—courage, moderation, justice, and "virtue as a whole"—are conditioned on thoughtfulness, what is the fate of *those who lack it* (69 b)?

These are the unfinished teachings, the legacy of *aporíai*, that Socrates, as it seems to me, bequeaths to his youngsters and to us:

1 What is becoming (*génesis*)? Does anything come into being from nothing or rather from its own contrary, as "just" from "unjust," i.e., is Becoming a passage from Not-being to Being? Are there two opposed becomings: coming into being and going out of it (70 e)?

2 How do we learn non-sensory truth? Is it by "recollection," a recovery of pre-natal knowledge, or by a kind of intellectual connection, whose sensory analogue is being reminded by association, as a friend's possessions put us in mind of the friend (73)?

3 If by comparing sensory equals, which always fall short of true equality, we are led to the thought of an Equal itself, when in human life is that knowledge acquired (75)?

4 *Are* there intelligible beings, such as the Equal, the Beautiful, etc., and what is their relation to the soul (76 e)?

5 What is the nature of such beings? Are they self-same or changing, composite or simple, seen or unseen (78 d–79 a)?

6 Is the soul more closely related to the realm of the Invisible, and the body to the Visible (80 b–81 d)?

7 Is there a penalty attached to immersion in physical pleasures and a contrary reward for the life of thought (81 c–84 b)?

8 How are we to account for the generation and destruction of things? Are natural qualities or powers, like Heat and Cold, responsible or natural substances, like blood or the brain? Are differences to be accounted for in strictly physical terms, for example, one person is bigger than another "by a head" (96 d)?

9 How is multiplicity generated? In adding units, do two ones together turn into a two, or is it the second unit that makes them a duality (96 e)?

10 How can natural causes explain the excellence or necessity of the world, its being the best possible? How can a mechanistic explanation account for a moral choice, i.e., how can a physical configuration account for Socrates sitting in prison? Since it is unsatisfying, should we give up the inquiry into natural causes in favor of ideal, i.e., rational accounts (98 d)?

11 If accounts seem to require hypotheses, "suppositions"— the Forms—shouldn't we assert as the cause of something being or coming to be big, beautiful, or good, its participation in the Big, the Beautiful, the Good itself? What makes such beings, reached by the *lógos,* intellectually satisfying? Mustn't we continue the account of each such being in terms of a higher hypothesis, i.e., shouldn't there be an effort to establish a *lógos* of an ideal hierarchy among the causes of natural things (100 c–101 d)?

12 Then if someone is big, for example, isn't he big not by reason of what he himself or anyone else is—for his being does not change in accordance with his comparative size—but by Bigness? Hence, if he is small in relation to someone else only by taking part in Smallness, it cannot be because either of these beings have turned into the other, can it (103 c–e)?

13 Doesn't that mean that when we said before that contraries come from contraries we were talking not of the hypothesized beings, the Contraries themselves, but of things in this world (103 a–b)?

14 But aren't there also natural things that are in fact destroyed when invaded by an opposing form, such as snow by the Hot?

And aren't there yet other things that, although they do not go by the name of the form itself, yet invariably take part in that form, as three does in the Odd (103 d–105 b)?

15 Doesn't that suggest a more sophisticated (if less safe) answer? Couldn't we say that the hot body got hot by fire or fever, which in turn bear the form Hot preeminently, so that there is an intermediate physical causal agent? Then wouldn't the soul be one such intermediary bringing the form life to a body? Similarly for an even number, wouldn't it become odd not immediately by Oddness but by reason of the remaining indivisible unit (105 c)?

16 Why does the dialectical *lógos,* the thoughtful argument, need a completion in a mythical image, a depiction of the cosmic setting in which the philosophizing soul is at home (107 c–115 a)?

17 Is the way a human being lives and acts incidental or essential to the trustworthiness of his philosophy (115 to end)?

This list, extracted from Socrates' final conversation, seems to me to be a compendium, the most extensive to be gotten from any of the dialogues, of Socrates' unfinished business. But it is also a list of living concerns for people to whom philosophy is the inquiry by means of *lógos* into the nature of those things that have large human consequences. To give a summary of a summary of these: What is the nature of that in us which makes us thoughtful? Is it an emergent condition of the body or a separable and indestructible soul? What roles do feelings and sensory impressions play in inducing reflection? Are the impasses reached by explanatory speech to be regarded as the primary incitements to thought? What is it that human speech reaches when it names objects? Is the answer to hypothesize stable ideal beings behind the shifting appearances? If so, how would the sensory world connect with them? How do numbers arise, and are they models for our accounts of nature? What are the causes of generation and decay and of temporally ordered change? In what terms are the effects of nature best accounted for: by elements of the same order as these effects (as when matter moves matter), or by natural powers of a different level (as when force moves matter), or by meta-physical causes (as when intellect moves matter)? Is a comprehensive rational account of our world possible, or does it always have to be completed by an encircling story? And above all is philosophy a morally neutral profession or necessarily implicated with virtue?

We might be tempted to call these items "problems" since even today they are the recognizable issues of philosophy, though perhaps in highly evolved terms. For us a problem is a question formulated in fairly fixed technical vocabulary awaiting a satisfactory solution. I think we get that meaning from Aristotle, who, as the first historian of philosophy, establishes a list of received problems in his *Metaphysics* (III). He, however, still uses Socrates' term *aporia* for these, though in a tighter sense.

Socrates, on the other hand, even were he philosophizing at a time when all questions had a well-worked history, would—I imagine—still be at the beginning. He would not care so much about devising well-formulated breakthroughs for received issues as for staying with the inquiry at its origin in wonder. He is not inviting these young men, who trust him, to solve problems that will then enter the graveyard of superseded history; he is rather asking them to keep his perplexities alive. For that is what philosophizing means to him.

3

THE OFFENSE OF SOCRATES: **APOLOGY**

I

A first reading of Socrates' defense before the court of the Athenian people as reported by Plato induces an exalted feeling in favor of Socrates.[1] That is my experience and, I think, the experience of most students: We hear a philosopher nobly coping with a persecuting populace.

It is a perennial perception. To cite only two of the very numerous testimonials,[2] one from the nineteenth century and the other from the twentieth: John Stuart Mill, referring to the *Apology* in his essay *On Liberty*, says that the tribunal "condemned the man who probably of all then born had deserved least of mankind to be put to death as a criminal," while Alfred North Whitehead asserts that Socrates died "for freedom of contemplation, and for freedom of the communication of contemplative experiences." By and large the defenders of Socrates are to be found among those who might reasonably be called liberal, whether in the thoughtful or the lightheaded vein.

A rereading of the speech, however, can check this first feeling and raise suspicions that subsequent readings confirm. I am taken aback by the intransigence with which Socrates is shown to go on the offensive and to convert his defense before the court of the Heliaea into an accusation against the "men of Athens." A small formality sets the tone: He never once accords the court the customary address of "Judges"; he reserves it for those who vote for his acquittal (40 a).

What is more, the speech intensifies in provocation toward its end. In the section, delivered after conviction, where Socrates avails himself of the opportunity granted by Athenian law for proposing a penalty to counter that demanded by the prosecution, he first suggests maintenance at the public table for himself, so that he might have more leisure for exhorting the Athenians; next he suggests a derisory fine about equivalent to a prisoner's ransom; and only finally, urged by Plato, Crito, and other friends, reluctantly offers a reasonable sum thirty times as great. As a foreseeable consequence, eighty juror-judges, evidently convinced that this Socrates, once convicted, must be executed, now vote for the death penalty (Diogenes Laertius, II 42). Still later, after judgment, when Socrates is allowed to speak once more, he issues dark threats against the city through its children (39 d).

This perspective on the event, resistant to Socrates' cause as it is, also has a lineage of testimony. Its sources vary, for the most part, from respectably conservative through illiberal, even to reactionary—from Jacob Burckhardt, who calls Socrates "the gravedigger of the Attic city," through Nietzsche and Sorel, to the Nazi writer Alfred Rosenberg, who regards his defense as an intimation of the degeneration of Greece. This rough division of views will have a certain bearing on what I have to say.

The variety and bulk of comment concerning the *Apology* is itself significant. Yet the one discovery that might really startle us—what Socrates did in fact say—is totally beyond our reach, as it was even beyond that of a contemporary like Xenophon. In his own *Apology,* which both counters and complements the Platonic version, he calls every current account of Socrates' speech deficient and says that the only aspect on which all agree is its "grandeur of utterance" (¶ 1). So we are thrown back on the consideration and reconsideration of the major version, Plato's—which is surely what Plato wanted.

II

I can see two lesser and one prime reason for offering still another reading of the *Apology*. The first of the weaker reasons lies in the special position that the *Apology* occupies in Plato's Socratic works. It is the only speech among them; the auditors participate only by shouting, and its single interlocutor, the reluctant witness Meletos, is impressed into a dialogue. It is the only work in which the author, who is explicitly absent even at Socrates' death (*Phaedo* 59 b), reports himself present, a fact Xenophon omits. I understand these circumstances to indicate that what Socrates said and did here is to be seen as casting its shadow over the other works, including those preceding the trial in dramatic date. I mean not only the dialogues explicitly associated with the *Apology*, namely its prologue, Socrates' conversation about *piety* with Euthyphro; its complement, about *patriotism*, with Crito; and its consummation, on *death*, with Phaedo and others. Nor am I particularly referring to the works that contain clear allusions to the trial, such as Anytos's threats in the *Meno* (94 e) or the prediction of the philosopher's death in the *Republic* (517 a). Rather *all* Platonic conversations, even those at which Socrates is absent, are colored by his defense—in just what way is the question to be discussed.

III

A second reason for attending to the *Apology* is that it belongs to a group of works whose subject forms a topic in moral education, though I would hesitate to call them a literary genre, because of the solemnity of their occasion. They are accounts of the trials of men who have offended authorities by thought or speech *but not by actual deeds*. For example, two days before his conviction for high treason and less than two weeks before his execution, Helmut von Moltke wrote a letter to his wife reporting on his trial before the National Socialist People's Court. In the letter, which was smuggled out of prison, he said: "We are cleared of every practical action; we are to be hanged because we thought together."[3] He goes on to praise the otherwise despicable judge for his clarity of perception in this respect.

Anyone who dies for his deeds also finally dies for his thought. But what distinguishes these deaths for thinking and speaking alone, attended by no provable intention to incite particular action, is the acute form they give to the question concerning the work of thought in the world.

IV

First among these comparable accounts stand those of the trial of Jesus. There is, in fact, a very long tradition setting Socrates' and Jesus' ordeals side by side; it is done in the writings of Origen, Calvin, Rousseau, Hegel, and Gandhi, to name a small selection.[4] The apparent similarities begin with the very fact that there are varying accounts of what was said and done.

Both defendants are the objects of popular passion channeled by a group of implacable opponents, led respectively by Anytos for the reestablished democracy and Caiaphas for the Sanhedrin. Both are attended by a band of adherents, friends or disciples, to whom they are suspected of imparting secret teachings, and both deny the charge. Both are intransigent in their refusal to defend themselves effectively. Both show a shocking unwillingness to evade death, and for both, their deaths only confirm their influence. A most striking parallel, furthermore, is the chief explicit charge, irreverence in the case of Socrates and blasphemy in the case of Jesus.

It is, however, at this point also, when charges have been brought, that the incommensurability of the two cases begins to appear. Socrates speaks before the Heliaea, while Jesus "holds his peace" before the Sanhedrin and answers Pilate with "never a word" (Matt. 26:63, 27:14; a divergent account lets him answer with counterquestions and evasions). His silence arises from his situation. He is suspected of claiming the power and being of the Messiah. That claim is undeniably blasphemy if it is false. But the Jewish court has already prejudged its falsity, and since Jesus has certainly asserted the claim in secret (16:15–20), his only course is to obscure its assertion publicly. Again, when the Jewish authorities represent him to the Roman governor as seditious because he has assumed for himself a new sovereignty, Jesus follows a similar course; he admits and at the same time denies this assumption by putting it in the mouth of the governor—"Thou sayest it" (27:11)—and by denying that his rule is political—"My kingdom is not of this world" (John 18:36).

So far he and Socrates are nevertheless still comparable, for both withhold themselves from the court; both present themselves as less than they are. But there is this all-important difference: The writers of the Gospels believed, after all, that Jesus' claim was true; that the defendant at this trial was, acknowledged or not, God.

So while both cases are the consequence of an irruption into the community of powerful claims incompatible with its authority, they are quite incomparable in a way very revealing for the *Apology*. For Jesus, as the long-awaited Christ, is represented as fulfilling in his life and death a prophecy and a mission, while Socrates, who specifically denies having even superhuman *wisdom* (20 e), is a man, and a man unheralded and unordained. Therefore, while the Passion is an inevitable consummation, Socrates' end is no part of a prefigured unique drama but a deliberate, human deed. It is consonant with this difference that Socrates *speaks* where Jesus is silent, and speaks boldly, if selectively, to his city, in *this* world. The *Apology* is part of a thoroughly political event.

V

There is a prosecution with which the trial of Socrates allows even more obvious comparison. Sir Thomas More, "our noble, new Christian Socrates," as his biographer Harpsfield calls him, was brought before the King's Bench, indicted under a statute that made it treason to deny—or in the court's interpretation, to refuse to affirm—the King as Supreme Head of the Church of England.

Socrates' and More's conduct are similar in these points: Both have an opportunity for evading their trials as well as their sentences—Socrates by voluntary silence or exile, More by agreeing to "revoke and reform" his "willful obstinate opinion." Both defend themselves before the court and both speak again, more bluntly and intransigently, after having been pronounced guilty, revealing that they consider the real cause for prosecution to be other than the stated indictment, but also that they are in spirit, at least, guilty as charged. Finally, both explain their conduct by reference to otherworldly considerations—More to "the hazarding of my soul to perpetual damnation," Socrates to his welcome among the heroes in Hades.

More makes a wily, subtle defense by standing on the letter of the law in claiming his right to silence and revealing only after the verdict his implacable opposition to the king's heterodoxy. He says:

> Ye must understand that, in things touching conscience, every true and good subject is more bound to have respect to his said conscience and to his soul than to any other thing in all the world besides, namely, when his conscience is in such a sort as mine is, that is to say, when the person giveth no occasion of slander, of tumult and sedition against his prince, as it is with me; for I assure you that I have not hitherto to this hour disclosed and opened my conscience and mind to any person living in all the world.[5]

More, then, as a statesman and a lawyer defends himself with all legal care, while as a man and a Christian he preserves inviolate his inmost thoughts, as did Jesus. But Socrates, a private man who has scarcely held office and claims no experience of courts (17 d), handles his defense very cavalierly, while as a citizen and a philosopher he, unlike his Christian counterpart, has no notion of privacies of conscience. The comparison therefore throws into relief his freedom in the *Apology*. His resolve derives not from hidden recesses of conviction, but from a ground that by its very nature is common and in need of communication.

VI

The most vivid reason, finally, for restudying the *Apology* is the desire to come to some answer to this question: Was Socrates rightly convicted and rightly condemned to death? It is a question of several aspects.

First, why did the Heliastic court convict Socrates and in addition accept the prosecution's view that this was a capital case? It is essential here to recall not only that Socrates himself considers irreverence and corruption of the young definable offenses and agrees with the authorities that such charges could lie, but that, as the *Crito* shows, he is in deepest accord with the Solonic fundamental law from which they arise.[6]

Because we have no report of the case for the prosecution, this first question can only be resolved by examining Socrates' defense, which I will do later. That task is complicated by the fact that Socrates turns his defense into an *offense,* into an accusation against his accusers and his fellow citizens that is at once an insult and an assault. For it would be ludicrous to attempt to examine the substance of his attack, which would require trying to determine whether the Athenians are more sluggish in self-examination than are, say, Thebans, Spartans, or Americans. Indeed, it might be argued that such charges, which are universally true of all humankind, are pernicious when pointedly leveled at one particular community. Hence his very attack might become evidence to the jury of Socrates' bad faith.

A second aspect of the question concerning Socrates' conviction is this: Shortly after Socrates' execution a backlash seems to have occurred. Meletos may have been condemned to death and Anytos to exile.[7] Socrates the persecuted philosopher was vindicated in the repentant city. How then ought a Heliastic juror have voted, had he been able to foresee subsequent events, particularly the most immediate result, that a convicted Socrates would cooperate with his accusers by moving to force the court to inflict the death penalty?

But the most important aspect is the one framed in contemporary terms: How should I be disposed in analogous present-day situations? For despite the fact that such cases can no longer arise, at least in this country, with the judicial directness possible in the ancient city, the Socratic issue is always present when persons of more mobile intellect, more extensive education and more leisure than the people at large come into collision with the religious beliefs and moral traditions of those whom they are intent on serving.[8]

VII

To begin with, then, I examine the sufficiency of Socrates' defense.

Xenophon takes Socrates' "grandness of utterance," a feature present in all previous accounts of the speech, as his point of departure. This tone must, he says, appear as "rather mindless" unless it can be shown that Socrates was in fact deliberately inviting death as an escape from the decay of old age (6). Here is the classic statement in the tradition of propounding self-euthanasia as an explanation of Socrates' strange conduct in court. For it is evident that Socrates' defense is a deliberate failure.

Plato, however, attempts to forestall that explanation of this striking fact in the dialogue of Socrates' last day, the *Phaedo*. There Socrates himself argues that suicide is impermissible, no matter how desirable death might seem (62 a). To regard Socrates as manipulating the Athenians into killing him and to confuse his welcoming acceptance of death with suicide is to trivialize the events of that day in court. Only the fact that Socrates invited conviction stands.

VIII

Let me then present a critical rehearsal of Socrates' speech, stated in the least well-disposed terms.

Socrates begins by accusing his accusers of lying when they warn the court that he is a skilled and formidable speaker. Unaccustomed as he is to public speaking, he is not formidable, "unless they call him formidable who speaks the truth" (17 b). This truth he will present, and indeed in the subsequent speech, "alien to the diction" of a crowd though he may be, he is complete master of the situation. He even contrives for a stretch to introduce his own dialectical mode into the proceeding, as he interrogates Meletos, a co-accuser, who is by law obliged to submit to examination. Anytos, his senior opponent, he wisely omits to call.

He attacks this inadequate young man, who goes running to accuse him "to the city as to his mother," as Socrates puts it (*Euthyphro* 2 c), with an ad hominem argument: Meletos himself does not care about the substance of the accusation. But what weight in law can that have, supposing it were so? In any case, Socrates does not allow Meletos to answer his question—Who, then, does make the young better?—in the only way Meletos and those behind him can answer it, namely, by asserting that the laws, but most of all the citizens, improve the young (24–25). For in the *Meno* (92 e) he had already disallowed Anytos's answer that it is the respectable citizens of the city, its gentlemen, who transmit excellence from generation to generation. Now Socrates wants Meletos to tell the court which particular professional, such as a horse trainer, exercises the young of Athens into excellence. But, of course, this is precisely what Meletos's backers resist—the notion that their children's moral formation should be in the hands of such experts.

As a part of Socrates' wider attack on the good faith of his accusers he substitutes for the formal indictment a charge of his own devising. In bringing his charge, Socrates claims, Meletos trusted to an "old slander" (19 a, 28 b), a long-standing hatred in the city against him, which Socrates associates with Aristophanes' comedy *The Clouds*. But there are difficulties. Not only does he himself later refer to the high esteem in which he is held in the city, where "the opinion prevails that Socrates is something more than most men" (35 a), but the relation of Aristophanes to Socrates in the *Symposium* and Plato's veneration for the playwright make it hard to maintain that Socrates' friends ordinarily saw that old comedy as working over nearly a quarter of a century toward his undoing.

IX

Socrates, then, makes up a suppositious indictment based on *The Clouds* (112, 117) that runs: "Socrates does wrong and meddles, searching into the things below the earth and into celestial things and making the worse reasoning the stronger and teaching others these very things" (19 b).

By means of this reformulation he pretends that the real charge of irreverence—which he himself recognizes in the *Euthyphro* (5 c)—is directed at his supposed researches into the nature of heavenly bodies and similar matters. These he gave up long ago, when still in his youth, for reasons set out in the *Phaedo* (96 b). Of such matters, he somewhat plausibly argues, he no longer knows anything, nor do they any longer concern him. And yet in that very dialogue, he gives a vivid topology of the things above and below the earth (198 e ff.), as he does in the *Republic* and in other conversations. Can he really argue in good faith that he no longer has *any* interest in cosmology and eschatology, when he makes up novel stories and private myths about the upper and lower realms—the very enterprise that disturbs the Athenians?

His chief defense, however, against the "old slander"—which is at bottom nothing but the imputation of sophistry—rests on a tale he tells (20 e). Chaerephon, his crony in *The Clouds,* had perpetrated a coup in Delphi: he had gotten Apollo's oracle to declare that no man was wiser than Socrates. Whereupon Socrates modestly undertook to prove the god mistaken, but, to his own regret, failed! He calls this undertaking "giving the god's business the highest priority" (21 e), and regards its mention as a sufficient defense against the charge (24 b).

X

The correct indictment, as Socrates cites it, is: "that Socrates does wrong, corrupting the young and not respecting the gods whom the city respects, but other, new half-divinities" (24 b).

Here is how Socrates meets the actual charge of irreverence, when he finally reaches it. The wording of its first point, if the meaning of the verb *nomizein* is translated very carefully, is that Socrates "does not regard the gods in the customary way." Against this point Socrates has no defense. He himself admits its truth to Euthyphro. For he tells him that he, Socrates, cannot accept the traditional stories of the gods, that is, the common myths of the Greeks; this, he adds, is the reason for his prosecution (*Euthyphro* 6 a). In cross-examining Meletos, however, he traps him into thoughtlessly agreeing with an altered formulation, namely that Socrates "does not regard the gods as existing" (*nomizein einai,* 26 c, d). Now he can defend himself, and he produces an argument as logical as it is ludicrous. Using the indictment itself, he argues that he who is accused of introducing new half-divinities cannot be charged with not believing in the full gods who must be their parents, any more than someone who acknowledges the existence of mules can be supposed not to believe in their parents, namely horses and asses (27 c). So much for irreverence.

There remains the charge concerning the introduction of new divinities. Socrates makes it clear in the *Euthyphro* (3 b) and again in the *Apology* (31 d) that he understands the accusers to be thinking of his notorious *daimónion,* the "half-divine thing" within him, and that they regard him as a "maker of gods" on account of it. Nonetheless Socrates not only makes no effort to allay their apprehensions, but even dwells on his "divine sign" more aggressively here in court than anywhere else.

XI

How next does Socrates defend himself against the corruption charge? His version of it in terms of the "old slander" is that Socrates is a "clever one," the unique indigenous sophist and excogitator who dispenses dangerous wisdom to a clique from within a cogitatorium. Of course, as everyone in and out of the dialogues knows, Socrates actually has no establishment of his own, so the comic claim needs no refutation. Its serious counterpart in the real accusation, on the other hand, is that he offers esoteric teachings. Socrates calls this charge a lie and asserts that no one has ever heard anything from him in private that all were not welcome to hear (33 b). Had I been in that courtroom I would simply have refused to believe him. Nothing is clearer than that Socrates does not say everything to everyone.

Furthermore, Socrates knows perfectly well that his accusers are not very precise in their knowledge of sophists, that intrusive traveling tribe of professionals. In the *Meno,* Anytos wanders into the conversation expressing a horror of these people, but readily confesses that he has never met one. Socrates is in no position to ridicule him for that lack of experience, for in the *Republic* he himself argues that it might be useful for a physician to have experienced disease in his own body, but that it is in no way good for someone who is to govern the soul by means of the soul to be experienced in corruption (409 a). A magistrate like Anytos might well claim that it is a staunch caution which keeps him from seeking acquaintance with those whom his sound sense makes him despise.

Since, therefore, the description of the sophists' competence is left to Socrates, he chooses to present them as people who "might be wise with a greater than human wisdom" (20 e). That is, *they* are the ones who are expert in the things above and below, while Socrates has the reputation only of "a certain wisdom," which is "perhaps human wisdom." At this point the Athenians make a disturbance, for they know that this Socratic wisdom, this "unwilling wisdom" (*Euthyphro* 11 e), has but one content: the knowledge of Socrates' own ignorance and the determined exposition of the ignorance of everyone else in the city (21 d).

Part of the charge of sophistry is the charge of "teaching." The actual indictment does not specify teaching, but Socrates imports it and tricks Meletos into amending the wording to include it (26 b). Why? Because he intends, in making the point that his activity is not teaching, to bring out these three circumstances: that he takes no money, that he conveys no subject-matter, and that he accepts no responsibility (33 b).

But if he takes no money, that only means that he is uncontrollable—he cannot be engaged or dismissed, as a parent might hire or fire a professional. And if he takes no responsibility for the careers of his young associates—why, that is usually called irresponsibility. And if he conveys no positive matter to these young men, that is the very worst of all, in the light of what he shows them instead. For with disingenuous innocence he himself gives a vivid description of what is conveyed to them in his company: He goes about engaging public men, poets, and craftsmen in conversations that are really examinations, in the course of which it emerges that they do not, in truth, know what they are doing, although they think they know it well enough—while the young men stand by and watch and smile; for, as he says charmingly: "it is not unpleasant" (33 c). Afterwards, he reports, they range through the city imitating him, presumably like those skeptical puppies who have inopportunely gotten hold of dialectic, whom he himself describes in the *Republic* (529 b). This is what Socrates calls "not being anyone's teacher," and this is how he makes himself palatable to his fellow-citizens!

He completes his defense against the corruption charge by pointing out that no one who either considers himself to have been corrupted or is a parent of a corrupted child has in fact come forward to complain (34 b). But then, of course, aside from the unlikelihood that a parent would proclaim his child's corruption in public, the whole town knew that the chief accuser, Anytos, considered himself to be just such a parent. Xenophon records this circumstance (*Apology* 29).

XII

This then is Socrates' defense as Plato permits us to construe it in the mind of a Heliastic juror. There is undoubtedly something deliberately self-incriminating about it.

Socrates does not even scruple to use phrases to the court which intimate in his own terms the equivocal nature of his own activity. I am referring to the phrases that in the *Republic* give the working definition of right or justice, namely "to do one's own business," and of wrongdoing, namely "to be busy at many things" (433 a), to meddle, "to do everything," the latter being Socrates' favorite description of the sophists' activity (596 c). Yet for Socrates in Athens the two apparently coincide—he claims that in his private interrogations he is both "doing his own business" (33 a), which happens to be going about meddling in theirs (31 c), and that in doing theirs he is also doing the god's (33 c).

So he intimates something possibly pernicious, while he never takes cognizance of the real fears of his judges. Those fears concern the substance of the city, which is compounded of traditions—particularly the deep old myths about its gods and the established respect for the wisdom of its citizens—of whose collapse Socrates' scrutiny makes a spectacle for the young. So also, because he never acknowledges that he teaches, he avoids rendering a candid and comforting account of the essential loyalty of his intentions, such as even a very unconforming citizen-teacher would feel obligated to give to apprehensive parents; he never says that he and they in the end care for the *same* city.

It is necessary here to recall that Socrates' indictment was judicially correct. Under these circumstances it seems to me that even a decent juror, realizing in the course of the speech that both charges, irreverence and corruption, have the same root, which the defense had in no way reached, might feel compelled to convict, while he might pray that execution would be avoided.

XIII

Indeed a case can be made for the convicting Athenians. Hegel, who takes a very comprehensive view of the affair, is their brisk defender, and some of the points that follow are, in fact, made in the *History of Philosophy* (Vol. II, "The Fate of Socrates"). But what is of more interest is that they all come from the dialogues themselves.

First, the common view that this was a political trial, the attack of the rabid, returned democracy against a man with aristocratic views and associates, will not hold up. Socrates himself recounts at his trial how he has been in difficulties under various regimes, certainly—to his credit—under the oligarchical Thirty, who included his own interlocutors Critias and Charmides (*Apology* 32 e; ch. 4). Furthermore, the chief accuser, Anytos, was a *moderate* democrat, an "orderly and well-conducted man" of respectable reputation by Socrates' own account in the *Meno* (90 b).

The very description of Socrates as an antidemocrat is not very convincing. Read without prejudice, the vignette of the democratic regime in the *Republic,* a dialogue itself set in the democratic stronghold of Athens's harbor, shows, for all its outrageousness, one vital, redeeming feature: This regime is, Socrates says, a perfect supermarket of constitutions, and anyone who wishes to erect a city, "*as we are now doing,*" should go there (557 d; cf. *Statesman* 303 a). Socrates' activity is at home in a democracy, not to speak of the fact that the Athenians regard Socrates as instigating that very forwardness in the young which he describes as endemic to democracies (*Republic* 563 a).

As Socrates himself observes in the *Crito* (52 e), the Athenians have borne with him for seventy years, in spite of the supposed "great hatred" against him (28 a). Even his two incursions into politics, for which, as he tells the court, he might "perhaps" have died (32 d), passed off safely. So the man who tells the Athenians that they will kill anyone who publicly opposes them (31 e), has actually been allowed to live a long life of semipublic resistance.

Even this late conclusion need never have come. Had they managed better, Crito sadly observes, the case need never have come to court (45 e). Nor need Socrates have died, for voluntary exile was possible, as the laws remind him when he makes them speak (52 c). Even in that court and in spite of Socrates' intransigence, 220—nearly half—of the 500 (or 501) jurors either think the accusation insufficiently proved or are moved by a strong sense of Socrates' excellence or agree with him that the city could profit by his existence or consider that the city would be better served by forbearance. These 220 refuse to find him guilty. Their number surprises Socrates, who has evidently not done justice to the well-disposed condition of some Athenians (36 a).

Once the verdict is in, Socrates is again allowed to speak freely, as is the civilized Athenian custom, and to reaffirm his partnership in the city by participating in the formulation of his sentence. Socrates abuses this occasion by reiterating his view of the incompetence of the Heliastic court. Moreover, once he is sentenced and in prison, the city of Athens allows him daily conversation with his friends and accords him a bloodless death among them. Not so in Jerusalem, London, or Berlin!

Indeed, his freedom to speak before the large public of the courtroom or to the intimate circle of friends in prison is complete. The formal issue of a mere right to free speech, contrary to Whitehead, is of no concern to Socrates or to the Athenians; both care only about the substantial question of whether Socrates' speech does damage.

In this light even Anytos's harsh recommendation that the case must either not come before the court at all or come as a capital case (29 c) can at least be taken to evince a state of mind the opposite of trivial, a state of mind Plato must respect. For in the *Statesman,* a dialogue dramatically contemporary with the trial (*Theaetetus* 210 d), the stranger to whom Socrates has turned over the conversation says that, in the absence of true statesmanship, the laws and the ancestral customs must rule. Since no one is to be wiser than they, if anyone is seen to be searching into the useful crafts that have been legally established, and waxing wise about them, he can be indicted on a charge of corrupting the young and made to suffer "the most extreme penalties" (299 b).

In sum, the very seriousness with which they take Socrates' nonpolitical activity gives the Athenians a claim to our respect, for the modus vivendi of many of us is to regard philosophers lightheartedly. To be sure, it is not good to interrupt a speaker, but their clamor is brief and controllable—and it comes correctly, at crucial points. Here, in effect, the attention of a whole city has been gained by one man, a philosopher. Of what other people can that be said?

XIV

Clearly this Socrates, who confronts and affronts such a city in this way, is Socrates in a very oblique aspect. The aspect is just that described by Kierkegaard in a passage from *The Concept of Irony.*

> Thus we see clearly how the position of Socrates with respect to the state is thoroughly negative, how he wholly fails to fit into it, but we see it even more clearly at the moment when, indicted for his way of life, he surely must have been conscious of his disproportion to the state. Yet undismayed he carried through his position, with his sword above his head. His speech is not the powerful pathos of enthusiasm . . . but instead we have an irony carried through to its last limit.[9]

By "irony" Kierkegaard means not what Socrates means when
he uses the term with respect to himself—namely his dissimula-
tion, his pretense of knowing less than he does—but a kind of
self-levitation by which one is raised above all positive knowledge. Such a zestful abstention from content does, in a way, characterize the Socrates of the *Apology*. At any rate, Socrates with
his sword above his head is a man of *negation*.

XV

And these are his features: First and foremost there is that uncanny naysayer within him, which he calls his *daimónion* and
which plays a larger role in this than in any other dialogue generally accepted as genuine. He describes it as a sort of inner voice
that has been with him from childhood (31 d); that is to say, it
is innate but not in need of "recollection," of being searched out
by thought. This "half-divine" and even "divine something"
never aids thought and never urges action. It speaks only to warn
him *not* to do a deed.

To what realm of being this notorious *daimónion* belongs is
unfathomable, but the role it plays in Socrates' life is not beyond conception. Enthusiasm means literally the state of having
a divinity within (*éntheos*): the *daimónion* is Socrates' *negative*
enthusiasm, a permanently implanted restraining power. Socrates is no enthusiast, because the exaltations of thought are not
due to a special agency, though he does need a special negative
faculty. For it is his chief teaching that excellence is knowledge
(e.g., *Protagoras* 360 e ff.), and that deeds of excellence are the
direct consequence of knowledge. By the (logically independent) inverse proposition, all wrong deeds stem from ignorance
and are always in some deep sense inadvertent; no one does bad
things in full consciousness. Consequently, since they are by their
very nature beyond the context of reason, they require, once
fancied, an uncanny power for their prevention. The *daimónion*
is Socrates' ability to avoid wrong, his *negative* excellence.

In particular the *daimónion* makes Socrates refrain from engaging in politics (31 d) because that would have been tanta-

mount, he says, to a futile, premature sort of self-destruction. Nonetheless he describes himself in the *Gorgias* (521 d) as being the only man in Athens who does truly engage in politics. That is to say, he has devised for himself a mode of being privately public (or the reverse); by his description it is a way of "conferring in private the greatest benefit on each citizen" (36 c). This mission that he has assigned to himself he will not give up even if he "is to die many times over" (33 c). That is Socrates' *negative* politics: to deny that the public realm is the truly political realm and to assert his inner *lógos* intransigently in the service of the city. In this respect Socrates most differs from Thomas More. More unwillingly but dutifully accepts high public office, and yet asserts to his death the right to open his mind to no one but his God. It is, in capsule, the distinction in matters political between a philosopher, who cares for Being in its commonness, and a Christian, who worships a Person in intimacy.

XVI

Last and most important, when Socrates formulates what is to be within this speech "the greatest good for man," it is in altogether negative terms: "The *un*examined life is *not* livable for a man" (38 a); what people at present care for is nothing much (30 a); positively stated, the truly worthwhile work is that of examining, testing, refuting, exposing impartially both oneself and others. In this one respect at least he finds himself wise: He knows he knows *nothing* (21 d); his fellow citizens, on the other hand, *fail* totally under examination—and it is precisely Socrates' offense that he publishes these failures. He claims, however, without irony, that to fall silent would be disobedience to "the god" (37 e).

To put it another way: The *first* culmination of Socrates' nondidactic teaching is usually his notorious *aporía*, literally "waylessness," a profitable perplexity or embarrassment, induced in the learner for his own sake (e.g., *Meno* 84). Insofar as Socrates represents his activity as a public service, however, his interlocutor is embarrassed not for his own sake but as an object lesson, nor does the conversation continue to positive learning; in this setting Socrates is indeed a *negative* teacher.

Here, then, the philosophic activity is presented as an entirely negative effort, without an end or a substance—significantly the substantive *philosophía* is never used, but only the verb *philosopheín*, "to carry on the effort for wisdom." But most particularly, at the literal center of the speech (29 b), and again at its end, Socrates asserts his ultimate negative wisdom—his knowledge of his ignorance concerning Hades, the realm of death.

XVII

To offset clearly the negative Socrates in the dock, whose defense he appears to record, Plato writes a second defense for Socrates in prison. The conversations of the *Crito* and the *Phaedo* are the deliberately positive complements to the oratory of the *Apology*.

In the beginning of the *Crito*, Socrates awakes from a deep, blank sleep, just like that so longingly described at the end of the *Apology*, to a conversation in which he accepts his condemnation as he never would before the court, namely as duly proceeding from the laws he has very willingly lived under all his life (53 a). In a tone the very opposite of that in the *Apology*, he has the laws upbraid him: "Do you think the right thing is the same for you and for us, so that whatever we undertake to do to you, you think it is right to do the same back to us?" (50 e).

This other, positive Socrates is even more strongly delineated in the *Phaedo*, the dialogue on death which explicitly contains his second and, he hopes, more successful defense (69 e). On this his last day he is not a harsh and offensive rhetorician but a charming and attentive listener, as the narrator makes a point of noting (89 a). Here he speaks not as a relentless interrogator, but as one who is prepared, if his interlocutor wishes it, to "talk it through in tales" (*diamythologeín*, 70 b). Here he does not present himself as proudly ignorant, but is presented as the one and only knower (76 b); nor does he pretend to be without a teaching, but he appears, instead, as one who—the recipient of Phaedo's account interrupts to remark—makes philosophical matters astonishingly clear (102 a). Here all the great Socratic notions are recapitulated: his supposition of the *eidé,* the invisible "looks" or forms; the myth of recollection; the true good beyond the merely human good of refutation (ch. 2). In this conversation Socrates frequently refers to *philosophía* and presents it as the inquiry into the realm of death, the "invisible Hades" (*Aídes aeidés*), which is also the place of the invisible *eíde* (80 d), the place of Being (76 d). Here he is not ignorant of death but well-studied in it, and the death the city confers on him is not an absconding into sleeplike nothingness but an "immigration" to the realm of Being (40 c, 117 c), a felicitous alternative to exile.

So there can be no doubt that before the court Socrates deliberately curtails his explanations and withholds himself.

XVIII

The question then becomes: Why? Why does Socrates deliberately offend the court, why does he go on the offensive against the Athenians, why does he use his defense to document his offense against the city?

Since Socrates actually lived and actually had to defend himself before the Heliaea, there must be some aspects of Plato's *Apology* (the title means "Defense") that derive from the actual circumstances. Once a defendant, Socrates became a *resister,* the defender of philosophy from the city's attack. He must have thought that this public occasion was a moment to display spirit, to confirm the lifelong business of words in deed, to be what Achilles, to whom he compares himself, was in war—a hero, a hero in philosophy (28 c).

In part his conduct must have been an accommodation to the conditions of the occasion, namely, the short time he has to speak and the great crowd to whom he must address himself. Twice he mentions the lack of time for quiet persuasion (19 a, 37 b). This lack of leisure and of intimacy is not a peripheral matter—nothing Socrates thinks can be expeditiously conveyed by public deliverance; it must always be slowly engendered in leisurely direct conversation with its accompanying inner dialogue (*Theaetetus* 172 d). Socrates' positive wisdom stated concisely in public would appear simply bizarre.

The negative and positive Socrates are each other's obverse. Refutation, the breaking up of an accepted opinion, goes over into the search for a truth. But in public, whether Socrates has been summoned to court or has been accosted by a man who is not a friend, the transformation will not take place—the conversation is curtailed. The *Apology* leaves aside the widest and deepest questions concerning the right relation between the political community and the care of souls, but it implies this much: When philosophy comes upon the city it comes as a negation and a *threat*.

XIX

It is possible to surmise *why* Plato put on record for times to come so detailed and emphatic a statement of Socrates, the resister. A startling moment in the *Apology* throws light on this matter. For the first and last time Plato himself irrupts into his own work (38 a). Socrates hears him raise his voice to suggest a sober and sensible money penalty—to subvert, as it were, Socrates' own proud and derisory proposals. The suggestion is very much like a rebuke, and Socrates accepts it. It is as if in this work, in which Plato does not speak through Socrates but represents himself as spoken to by him, Plato is recording something he has heard in court which must cast its shadow over the other dialogues, and so over the philosophical tradition. He has heard that *Socrates' activity is publicly indefensible*.

XX

Let me conjecture. The life, if not the letter, of the Socratic conversations would by and large pass into oblivion, as the positive content of Socrates' wisdom, its deep suppositions and encompassing myths would shrivel into conformity with his successors' more strenuous, technical systems. One such successor, Aristotle, would soon appear in Athens.

On the other hand, Socrates' speech, his defense delivered before the largest public of his life, would continue to be at work across the millennia. Its heroic intransigence, which had once driven the court to extremes against him, would serve thereafter to reestablish him. Hence it would be the Socrates of refutations who would prevail. In a softened popular coloring this is the Socrates of Cicero's well-known description:

> Socrates was the first who called philosophy down from the heavens, settled her in the cities and even introduced her into private houses and compelled her to ask questions about life and moral matters and things good and bad (*Tusculan Disputations* V iv 10).

But the so-called Socratic method would also make harsher reappearances, as "radical doubt," as "enlightenment," as "critique," as the "re-examination of all values," or as the general encouragement of a questioning disposition. In each of these modes, philosophy would yet again penetrate the pretenses to credit proffered by another communal way.

Without supposing that Plato could have foreseen all these developments, it is yet possible to imagine that he had intimations, that he was as apprehensive about the facile vindication of Socrates' way as he was about the learned ossification of his thought. To prevent the latter—or rather to provide a permanent possibility of revival—he wrote numerous Socratic conversations. To forestall the former—or rather to put perennial obstacles in its way—he wrote one Socratic speech. This oration, proud and noble in accordance with the event, was so written as to reveal on re-examination that Socrates had appeared to Plato to have committed an undeniable offense against the city and that he had seen his teacher, once at least, as *truly* dangerous. The speech would serve as a warning to future friends—and as an enticement.

To append a modern application: In our American polity, Socrates' offense is not a capital crime, nor are his modern successors of his stature. Furthermore in a court of law an American citizen juror would be guided and restrained by the Constitution and its interpretations and laws. The judicial issue is therefore much less excruciating—what is more urgent is to form some general opinions about such situations. And here the *Apology* makes a clear comment, which, stated most cautiously, says: The side resisting enlightenment also has something vital to defend and should be heard.

There is yet one more thought. Socrates himself would, I am persuaded, live out his life among us doing no harm and receiving none. The great question then to be considered is: Ought such immunity be a source of high satisfaction or should it too be a cause of deep misgiving?

4

THE TYRANT'S TEMPERANCE: **CHARMIDES**

I'll begin by telling you when and how I came on this little drama, the *Charmides,* which is not among Plato's most-read dialogues. It was during a cold Greek winter in the late 1950s, and I was working by myself in the storage rooms of the American excavations at Corinth, the great commercial center of ancient Greece. At night I would come back to the guest house where an invisible staff had made a fire and prepared a meal. There were no colleagues there either, but the common room had a complete set of Loeb volumes, the olive and gold edition of all of Greek literature with Greek on the left pages and English on the right. There I conceived and carried out two deeds of intemperance: First, I got hungry late one night and sneaked into the kitchen and ate a bowl of the far-famed Corinthian yogurt, real goat's-milk yogurt, creamy, with a thick skin, which I topped with mounds of brown sugar. Alas, I had incontinently eaten the starter yogurt, the seed pearl of yogurts, and this famous strain disappeared from the archaeological world forever, to my disgrace. Second, I, in my hybris, decided to read my way straight through all of Plato's thirty-six dialogues that winter in Corinth and Athens. As is usually the case with such study plans of overweening ambition, I remembered nothing and everything. I certainly remembered the *Charmides* for its intensely charming frame and its forbiddingly dry dialectic. That was the first time I had come on the close juxtaposition of the inflammation of love and the intensity of reason that appears in a number of Socrates' conversations. I might have said "the concreteness of passion and the *abstraction* of thought," but I avoid the term "abstract" like the plague when speaking of Socrates' or Plato's thinking. "Abstraction" has to do, literally, with drawing away from the particularities of life and producing mere rational residues. For Socrates, however, what is reached by our thinking has more genuine life, more vibrant being than the particulars of experience which jump-start Socratic conversations. I say this now because in the *Charmides* someone does engage in abstraction (*apháiresis*) in that attenuating, rarifying sense— though the word itself wasn't used in that way until Aristotle introduced it into philosophy.

The next time I thought seriously about the dialogue was forty-five years later, when I met with a small group of friends in Annapolis for a day to have our own conversation about Socrates' conversation. (As happens several times in the Platonic dialogues, there were two brothers in our group.) As also happens in Socratic conversations, from the participant who was probably the least used to reading these works came the tone-setting observation: a sense of unease with the dialogue, a feeling of opaqueness and hidden agendas. We began to look for those hidden agendas, and this piece is something of a record of what came to us in our animated talk.

Let me here bring in the subtitle of the *Charmides*. We don't know who supplied it, but it is quite accurate: "Concerning Temperance: Tentative." The dialogue is certainly tentative; it makes an unsuccessful try at discovering the meaning of a term and seems to have purely negative results. But just remember how useful negative results are in all sorts of investigations: they tighten the confines of the positive possibilities.

There is, furthermore, no question that the dialogue has a single theme: temperance. The Greek word is *sophrosýne,* which means literally "safe-" or "sound-mindedness," just as *Socrates* means "sound power"—but that is pure serendipity, and though I'd like to say later on that Socrates' meaningful name resounds in the dialogue I scarcely dare claim it; Socrates himself will, to be sure, play on his younger partner's parental name.

Sophrosýne is rendered variously as "temperance" (and I've used that in my title, "The Tyrant's Temperance" for the small joy of alliteration), as "modesty," as "moderation," as "self-control," and as "self-possession." All of these are interpretative versions, and it is good to keep them in mind when the effort is to get to the center of this ring of meanings. From now on I'll stick mostly with the literal translation: sound-mindedness.

Still meandering about the outskirts of the dialogue, I now have to raise a problem of the sort called "hermeneutic" by scholars, as follows:

Suppose yourself in conversation with a forceful, clever young man of about twenty-eight, called Slobodan Milošević. You know by a time warp that he will do such atrocious deeds that he will come before an international war crimes tribunal. Will that fact work retroactively, will a curious kind of pre-emptive indictment taint the present conversation and your perspective of the young man's arguments? I think it would be practically unavoidable.

Well, that's the case for Charmides and Critias, who are Socrates' partners in the conversation—not that I seriously think even the worst Greek tyrant can quite match in *style* the gross but cunning boorishness of a modern Balkan dictator.

We may suppose that the dialogue is an invention of Plato, though the participants are contributions from the real world. Logicians of fiction call such persons, people who wander from the world of fact into the texts of fiction, "immigrant characters."

I hope we all agree that the real people in their factual world probably never said anything as significant and revealing of truth as they say in their fictionally revised moments. But if the truth is in the invented conversation, why allow these immigrants into the dialogue at all and so often? After all, Charmides and Critias aren't the only immigrants whose future casts a shadow on their dialogic present. Flagrant Alcibiades (incidentally a close friend of Critias) and iniquitous Meno are two others. It must be, I think, because their lives, known to contemporaries and to us from reports (sometimes from other dialogues), are supposed to be silent yet shrill descants above the plainsong of the conversation, and we are intended to hear both strains. Now that possibility poses something of a problem for me. At St. John's College, we pride ourselves on going at the text directly and getting out what's in it, and not diverting and distracting ourselves with extraneous knowledge. And here I am about to breach this hermeneutic, that is, this interpretational principle, to draw attention to the later lives of the participants in the *Charmides*. My excuse is that I think the dialogue itself calls for such knowledge to be brought to bear on it. Or to put it somewhat paradoxically: Even someone who knew nothing further of Charmides and Critias could tell that there was something further to be known, something lurking behind the conversation. What was it?

Critias as master spirit and Charmides as a follower belonged to the regime of the Thirty Tyrants. They put down the democracy of Athens and ruled the city from fall of 404 to spring of 403 B.C.: eight months of carnage, plunder, and sacrilege. Their rage to purge all opposition makes one historian compare their regime to the Reign of Terror that degraded the French Revolution. Here in Athens there seems to have occurred an early, perhaps the earliest, example of ideological purification; all persons even suspected of democratic inclinations were eliminated by judicial murder. More fellow-Athenians were killed by these Athenians in eight months than had died in ten years of the Peloponnesian War. The democratic exiles eventually mounted a battle in which Critias and Charmides died. Finally the Spartans were called in to superintend the end of the Athenian civil war. All this happened twenty-nine years and more after the dialogue we are examining. These are unforgettable facts. I might add that it is reported (Aeschines, I 173) that "Socrates the Sophist" was executed—this was in 399 B.C.—"because he educated Critias." We shall see whether Plato thinks that Socrates taught Critias anything or was his mentor. It adds to the poignancy of the setting that all these people are blood kin: Charmides was Plato's maternal uncle, while Critias was Charmides' and Plato's mother's cousin (as well as guardian), and so Plato was Critias's first cousin once removed. It will become problematic whether this dialogue does what some people think: sets an honorable monument to these two monstrous embarrassments to the family, who died when Plato was about twenty-six, not far from Critias's age in the dialogue, and when he was just a few years from giving up the composing of tragedies in favor of writing dialogues celebrating Socrates.

Critias turns up in other dialogues, most significantly in the one named after him. Let me give a most abbreviated version of its contents: Critias describes the old, prehistoric enemy of an Athens that existed long before the historical Athens. This antediluvian Athens (which Socrates' friends pretend was an incarnation of something like that "beautiful city" described in the *Republic*) had to face a terrifying invader, Atlantis. Critias describes this island realm with such relish that to this day people think of it as a lost idyll, submerged in the great flood that also eroded Old Athens. In fact Atlantis is the prototype of a totalitarian state, whose imagined architecture prefigures in its gigantism the Nazi building programs under Hitler's architect and minister of armaments, Albert Speer: Its land has been regimented by a geometric abstraction, a great grid; its city is an impregnable nest of concentric circles of deep moats and enormous walls, in whose center bloody sacrifices are performed. By an uncanny coincidence the colored stones used in this building program are the Nazi colors of white, black, and red (*Critias* 116 a). Poseidon, the most resentfully persecutional of all the gods, fathers the Atlantic kings by a rape. Of all this Critias is the admiring verbal architect. Surely Plato is shuddering at his work.

To my mind it took courage on Plato's part to make this whole brilliantly awful crew turn up in the dialogues devoted to his teacher—but perhaps he thought that one Plato who turned out to be a credit to Socrates could outweigh them all and that he could show by intimations that Socrates never had any illusions about those of his companions who went to the bad. If our reading group's hunch about this dialogue worked out, it would show that Plato was never the captive of his clan and class convictions and, more generally, that any argument which begins "He belonged to an aristocratic family and therefore he . . ." is apt to be a *non sequitur.* Where there is thinking there are no inadvertent loyalties.

That is enough bumbling about in the outer precincts of the dialogue. Let me plunge into the work itself by setting out a preview of its main contents. Many Platonic dialogues display this feature: Just as you think you've grasped the subject, you are asked to follow Socrates into something apparently different. The *Phaedrus* begins with love and ends with rhetoric; the *Republic* begins with politics and centers in on liberal education; and the *Charmides* declares itself to be about soundmindedness and slithers off into theory of knowledge, knowing about knowing. We are to apprehend the connections between these apparently disparate matters.

Just as real people take part in this dialogue so it has an exact date: 431 B.C., at the beginning of the Peloponnesian War when Potidea, a city that had abrogated its alliance with Athens, surrendered after more than a year's siege. Socrates, who had been away for quite a while on this campaign, has returned the night before. Though he is thirty-nine, he probably has no family yet. At any rate, he turns up the very next morning at a wrestling school. There he has a conversation which he relates at some unknown later time to an unknown person; perhaps we're supposed to think it is Plato. We don't know when Plato wrote the dialogue down, nor does it matter—though it's generally thought to be an early work.

There are other dialogues, like this one, that Socrates tells in the first person. One is the *Protagoras.* There the cousins, Charmides and Critias, then a few years older, appear with Pericles' sons, as well as the wild and beautiful Alcibiades, in the company of Protagoras and several other sophists (315 a). The other famous first-person dialogue is the *Republic,* in which Socrates discusses that very narrational form of writing with respect to its truthfulness (393 f., p. 151). There are three forms of narration, he says: An author can candidly stand behind his work, so that we can readily infer his presence. He does that by speaking of his characters in the third person and in indirect discourse. For example: "Socrates came to the wrestling school as soon as he was back from Potidea, and there he met Critias, and Critias said '. . .'" Or the author can, like a tragic poet, disappear from our consciousness and make himself an imitator of each of the characters who are saying their lines in their own personas, hiding himself behind their dramatic masks, in this fashion— Socrates: "Good morning, how has philosophy been faring since I went on campaign? Any interesting boys?" Critias: "Wait till you see my cousin Charmides." Or an author might mix the candid and the imitational modes.

Both the *Republic* and the *Charmides* are written in a yet different narrational mode. First, Socrates speaks in his own person, impersonating no one but himself—an honest proceeding. But then, he mimics the dialogue of the others—not so honest. And third, Plato is hiding beyond our ken and consciousness in bringing on the stage a Socrates who speaks for himself out of his first-person mask—very shifty. These first-person dialogues—

in which Plato imitates Socrates directly, contrary to his own canons of candor—betoken tricky business, to my mind. I'll try to show what that tricky business is.

When Socrates arrives at the gymnasium he is greeted first by a kind of philosophical nut, a histrionic person named Chaerephon, who has attached himself to Socrates. His presence shows that Socrates has slipped back into his old life, and that not all his followers are very self-controlled; Chaerephon is a kind of immoderate innocent, harmlessly unsound of mind. He brings Socrates to sit down with Critias, who will not be so harmless. They all want to know the news from the field. Socrates reports, evidently modestly saying nothing about his own part in the campaign, which we hear of from Alcibiades in the dialogue *Symposium* (219 e f.). According to him, Socrates was famous in the camp for his terrific hardiness, his self-control under conditions of wintry cold and hunger, his daylong sieges of standing motionless in the summer sun rapt in thought, and his heroic rescue of Alcibiades in battle. Clearly Plato is presenting *sophrosýne* incarnate—Socrates is a model of modesty, hardy self-control, and, we'll soon see, of moderation.

Now he asks for the news he cares about: How is philosophy doing, have any of the boys become prominent for wisdom or beauty (in that order) or, what he would evidently welcome most, both together?

At this moment a noisy crowd of fans comes in, announcing the celebrity himself, Charmides, who is probably about fourteen and just grown into adolescence; he is called a stripling— a long narrow shape of a boy. You have to read the dialogue to feel the intensity of its charm: the erotically charged atmosphere of the gym, the Dionysiac entrance of the beautiful and well-born boy with his rout of followers, the ludicrous eagerness of the men pushing each other off the benches so he'll sit by them. Since he's Critias's cousin and ward, Critias calls him over on the pretext that Socrates can cure some morning headaches he's been suffering. Chaerephon lets loose a *bon mot* and is heard from no more: If the boy stripped, he says, you would think he had no face—his beauty of form (*eídos*) is so perfect. Socrates says soberingly: The man—not "boy"—would be impossible to beat in battle if he had one tiny additional thing, a well-grown soul; that soul is what we should undress. Now Charmides looks at Socrates, and his mantle falls open (or he lets it fall open). Socrates confides to the person to whom he is telling this event something that is rare. We know from other dialogues that he can be passionate for his beliefs, deeply contemptuous of incurable ignorance, and angry with conceited cleverness. But now, just once, he's on fire, burning—so he says, and no longer "in himself"—that is, he is ecstatic and beyond self-control.

Here I must say something about that notorious Socratic irony. The Greek word means "pretending, dissembling"—in Socrates' case, pretending for pedagogical purposes to know a good deal less than he does. The Romantic concept of irony, set out by Kierkegaard in his doctoral dissertation on Socratic irony, makes irony a kind of noncommittal hovering above the issue, a deliberate withholding of commitment. I have a feeling that here, in this one dialogue, Socrates comes close to the modern notion: He may well be aroused by a charming boy who is what we vulgarly call "coming on" to him. At the same time he's looking at himself smilingly, ironically, from a safe place beyond.

At any rate he collects himself quickly and admits to the boy (who's been advertised to him as philosophical and also "wholly poetical") that he does have a headache drug, but the guru from the northern provinces who gave it to him also told him that it is ineffective unless accompanied by an incantation. Socrates has taken an oath never to administer the drug without it. At first Charmides wants to take this charm down in writing so as to use it at will; laughingly he agrees to do it only with Socrates' consent. Socrates asks him: "Do you know my name accurately?"—I pointed out before that Socrates means something like "sound power." All this byplay is amusing—and also ominous, as we will see. There's a game and a battle here, in this direct Platonic mime of Socrates.

Now Socrates expounds a theory of treatment that we would call holistic medicine: You can't treat the eyes without the head, the head without the body—and the body without the soul. The implication is plain to us if not to the boy: his headache betokens that his soul isn't well. You don't have to know the boy's future to conceive a suspicion of this young celebrity.

The incantation consists of beautiful words—dialectic conversation—that will engender soundmindedness (and here the governing word of the dialogue appears). Critias bursts in to say that his nephew outdoes all the other boys in this virtue—never mind that temperance and modesty aren't very good candidates for inviting the kind of competitive possessiveness Charmides attracts.

Socrates asks Charmides directly if he's so very soundminded, and like a well-bred boy he weasels; he can't, after all, prove his guardian a liar, and he won't praise himself.

Here begins the dialectic part of the dialogue. In reading it we must work our way through the arguments, but we don't need to like them. They are often, as here, intended to be refutational, to show people (1) that they hardly know what they're talking about and (2) that they can't even defend the skeletal thoughts they do have from picky and tricky attacks. I think this refutational testing is intended to evoke the intelligent outrage of the alert reader and to drag into the conversation the concatenation of terms needed to carry on the inquiry. You might say that refutational logic is the spinach of the dialectical diet: It's good for you.

Socrates starts with the two necessary conditions for such talk: experience of the thing (we are to think that Charmides has some perception of soundmindedness) and a common language in which to articulate the experience (Charmides speaks Greek). Then Charmides is to say what he thinks soundmind-

edness is. His first notion is that it is a sort of quietness, a subdued decorousness—a funny perception for a boy who has been
led into the gym by a noisy bunch of squabbling kids. Socrates
quickly shows that this notion is nowhere near the central meaning of what ought to be, whatever else it is, a good thing, since
nervy quickness is often a better mode than elegant languor.
Charmides tries again: Soundmindedness is modesty, bashful-
ness. This is indeed how upper-class European children used to
be brought up: to be shy, seen but not heard, on the hypothesis
that an inhibited youth makes for a self-possessed maturity. Socrates points out that shyness is not always a virtue—by an appeal to the *Odyssey,* where Homer has someone say that bash-
fulness is no good for a needy man.

Charmides has been dialectically driven to the end of his own
experience, not because what he says is wrong—in fact, in its ordinary use *sophrosýne* encompasses the features he picks out—
but because it comes to him too easily. Now he tries something
secondhand. Socrates knows right away that this formula comes
from Critias, but both cousins deny it. It's a playful white lie but
also something darker: an intrusion of caginess where it is least
wanted, in a philosophical inquiry. The formula Charmides remembers is that soundmindedness is "doing one's own thing."
Readers of the *Republic* will recall that this is its operative notion of the virtue of justice. In its application to the soul it means
knowing oneself, that is, knowing how one's soul is constituted
and then letting each capacity do its work, in particular letting
the desires reach out for possession, the spirit tense and tone the
psychic fabric, and the reason issue restraining commands to
the whole. In the *Republic* soundmindedness is the harmonious
adjustment of these three parts, so in that dialogue justice and
soundmindedness are not so easily distinguishable: Justice seems
to belong to each capacity in itself; soundmindedness seems to
belong to the three in their relation to one another. But outside
of this psychological context the formula "doing one's own thing"
is unintelligible, and Charmides is soon reduced to perplexity.

It can't mean, as Socrates suggests, that a scribe is supposed to write only his own name or that you're supposed to make your own shoes. Again Critias explodes. Charmides is garbling what has suddenly become *his* definition and is ruining his reputation.

Socrates switches partners, and from now on he talks to the sophistical and savvy older cousin, Critias, who appeals to the poet Hesiod for some tricky word-mongering of the sort he has evidently learned in the school of Prodicus the Sophist. The upshot is that "doing your own thing" is now turned into "doing good things." It doesn't mean making your own shoes or scribbling only your own name but doing useful and noble things. But, Socrates pushes him, don't the craftsmen and professionals often get useful, helpful results without quite knowing what they're doing? Yet things done helpfully are done soundmindedly. (Socrates introduces here a term important for later use: *ophélimos*, "helpfully" or "serviceably.") If that's so, couldn't someone be acting soundmindedly without knowing what he was doing? Critias is scandalized: that's impossible.

Critias here demonstrates, as he will again later, that ready flexibility in argument can be a token of being fundamentally disengaged. He withdraws his previous claims, and this time appealing to the famous inscriptions on the temple of Apollo at Delphi, comes up with a new formula: What the god means by "Know thyself" is "Be soundminded!" By means of some silly sophistry he argues away the other famous inscription on the temple: "Nothing too much."

Two points are to be remarked. Once again Critias feeds back to Socrates formulas which are Socrates' own, but without the Socratic context that gives them meaning. Socrates makes no mystery of what he means by the injunction to self-knowledge. He doesn't mean rummaging around in your own "subjectivity" but getting clear knowledge of your soul's constitution, so that you'll know whether you are a complex monster or a quieter, simpler creature (*Phaedrus* 230 a). Nor does he mean something terrifically abstract, some purely logical self-reflection—as Critias will later on. The second point is that for the moment Socrates lets Critias get away with setting aside the most normal understanding of moderation, the "Nothing too much," the Golden Mean that is for Aristotle (who always takes his departure from normality) the master schema according to which all the virtues are means between extremes. Socrates himself regards such balanced, steady self-control as the master virtue in the *Gorgias* (507 b f.), and he makes its absence a specific vice of tyrants in the *Republic* (571 ff.). This straightforward moral virtue is the one Critias pushes aside. The translators of my favorite version of the *Charmides,* Thomas and Grace West, note this crucial fact.

Critias wants Socrates to agree to all this derivative cleverness, but Socrates balks. He's trying to mount an inquiry and doesn't know the answer without taking a moment to consider. Socrates is introducing in his own conduct the possibility of knowledgeable ignorance. So here begins the serious dialectic, a difficult but trick-free investigation. It will bring into the world at least two incipient notions with huge futures.

In the Middle Ages one of these will acquire the still current name of *intentionality*. Intentionality means the capacity for "aboutness," and it can be claimed that all thinking possesses it preeminently. I don't know if it can be proved, but I believe that *only* thinking has it, which would mean that wherever there is aboutness there is thought, for instance that feelings which are about something are necessarily thought-imbued. Here is what I mean by aboutness. Thinking always has an intention, an object at which it is directed. Even if you think of nothing, then Nothing becomes your object. When we ask "What was all that about?" we are implying that someone had something in mind. The non-conscious world isn't about anything, except by our attribution; for example, we may impute an intention or feeling to nature (which imputation is called the Pathetic Fallacy). In short, to think is to think *about something,* and to know is to know *something,* and this aboutness is the exclusive mark of thinking.

That's exactly Socrates' next thought. If soundmindedness is knowledge at all, it is knowledge of something. Yes, of self, says Critias. Well, objects Socrates, why do all the other kinds of knowledge have objects *other* than themselves, as medicine has health?

Critias tells Socrates he is inquiring incorrectly. Geometry for instance has no independent product. But, says Socrates, it does have a separable subject; now really, what's temperance a knowledge *of,* what is to be known that's different from temperance itself?

Critias blows up again and accuses Socrates, who is now certainly in the inquiring mode, of being in the merely refutational mode. Soundmindedness, he claims, is simply different from all the other kinds of knowledge. It is—not his own term—reflexive, its own object. But Critias slips in an addition to gain not one but many objects for his soundmindedness as well: It is the knowledge of itself *and* of other sciences. Socrates pacifies the beleaguered Critias, who concedes that what Socrates says "observes the *mean*"; he unwittingly uses a term reintroducing the sense of moderation that he had excluded from consideration.

If soundmindedness is a knowledge of itself and of other knowledges, it must also be a knowledge of ignorance (insofar as it will judge the scope and competence of these knowledges). This little addition is a characteristic Socratic ploy; it makes apparently innocuous little shifts that turn out to have large consequences.

So I must stop again to point out that the question of the knowledge of ignorance is really a serious preoccupation for Socrates, for on it depends the possibility of inquiry. The dialogue *Meno* is concerned with this very question: How is discovery of the unknown possible, how do we recognize a new truth, how do we know what it is we do not know? So also Socrates' notorious claim to know that he knows nothing is not a discountable bit of Socratic irony but the formula for a lifelong question: *What* do we know if we know our ignorance? To Socrates soundmindedness is not a set of abstracted impersonal notions. When he summarizes the inquiry so far, he humanizes all the talk of knowledge and self-knowledge and products and subjects: The soundminded human being will know himself and will discern what he knows and doesn't know, and will have some judgment about what others know and don't know.

But again, in the presence of these cousins all the issues are being stripped of their Socratic pathos and put in the service of a perilously hollow agenda.

For what Critias is formulating is a perfectly self-aware master-knowledge which will give him total control with minimum effort and will, on top of everything, bear the grand name given it by that mythical "law-giver," the originator of names: *sophrosýne.* Whoever possessed *this* virtue, this *power,* could certainly tyrannize the world. Cloaked in the good name of a moderating virtue, he could direct for his own ends and from afar all the work of the world, judging it by a knowledge abstracted from all concrete objects and totally imbued with the sense of its own knowing—a self-certifying knowledge, isolated and impregnable to the influence of human circumstances.

The good old-fashioned tyrants, from those ruling the early Greek city-states to certain Roman emperors, were, it seems, given to sensuality and sadism: Socrates describes the type of the tyrant in the *Republic* as self-tyrannized rather than self-controlled—tyrannized, that is, by his own ravenous appetites. But Critias, as Socrates gets him to reveal himself to us, seems to have in him a hint of a more austere modern type first fully seen, apparently, during the French Terror, a fierce purifier of all opposition and exterminator of all opponents, an ideologue with a master knowledge, a knowledge of knowledge which enables his regime to regulate all knowledges without knowing any of their objects, to judge and censor ignorance or falsehood without knowing how ignorance is possible—an unreasonable rationalist. More concretely, it is a characteristic of the most destructive modern tyrannies that they are ideological, in the sense that in them one knowledge, one schematic idea—it could be any—certifies itself and all other knowledge as within or without its pale, while human good and bad are mere derivatives of these mental figments. In a word, this knowledge, objectless because indifferent to its object's truth, has one true intention: power. Critias, to my mind, prefigures the modern totalitarian ruler, a creature who rules by abstractions, an austere ideologue albeit with excessive and inhuman appetites. What I'm saying is a hunch, a speculation, but it is based on an eerie sense of watching an inchoate evil, one that will emerge more clearly at the end of the dialogue.

Socrates begins the third and last part of his inquiry with Critias. The first part dealt with Critias's claim that soundmindedness was doing one's own thing. The second was the transformation of this borrowed formula into knowledge of self and of other knowledges and of ignorance. Now Socrates asks whether such a knowledge, a knowledge of nothing other than itself and of other knowledges and non-knowledges, is even possible.

Socrates thinks it is impossible. He cites all kinds of disparate examples of aboutness. He shapes this inquiry as a question concerning the genitive relation, really the preposition "of." "Vision of," "opinion of," "desire of"—none of these can be completed reflexively: vision of vision, opinion of opinion, desire of desire—none of these capacities seem to apply to themselves. But Socrates doesn't trust himself to be up to analyzing this question further. Like an infectious yawn, this perplexity seizes Critias as well.

Here is the second future-fraught issue of the dialogue. We moderns might not agree that these second-level capacities are so unthinkable: "Desire of desire" is a well-known Romantic notion, that of self-excitation. "Opinion of opinion" pretty exactly describes opinion research, a respectable second-level subject in political science. But "knowledge of knowledge," above all, is more than a mere possibility for us, for the chief task philosophers of the seventeenth and eighteenth century set themselves was to establish a knowledge of knowledge, even a science of science, and its name was epistemology. Its great aim was not only to certify the discoveries of science and thus to be truly a master-knowledge, but also to set the limits of human knowing, to be a knowledge of ignorance. I name Descartes and Kant to remind you of what I'm speaking about; this epistemological project is checked by Hegel's grand critique of it in his introduction to the *Phenomenology of Spirit*. (I omit the "thought of thought" [*nóesis noéseos*] that is the activity of divinity at the apex of Aristotle's world, for it is not reflexive but self-penetrating: It does not turn on itself as an instrument for working on an object, but rather its activity has become identical with its object—the thought of being and the being of thought are at one.) Socrates does not so much deny this reflexivity (which is the turn toward the future) as he finds himself not up to affirming it. No thoughtful person could call the Greek philosophers simple-minded, but they do seem to have had a certain sound-minded simplicity. I think it appears in the Socratic rejection of reflexive self-intention, the mind's focusing on its own functioning. I'm far from having thought that out, although it does appear that some things seem hardly possible to Socrates that are a staple of our common opinion. He cannot believe, for example, (1) that anyone should willingly and knowingly choose evil; or (2) that any human thinking can be free of "value"; or (3) that aboutness in its abstraction should gain independence from and mastery over its original objects. For Socrates, recall, the master knowledge, the knowledge of his philosophizing kings, is not the knowledge of knowledge but the knowledge of the Good (*Republic* 540 a).

Because clever Critias has no great interest in the good that his epistemic soundmindedness might bring, Socrates now calls him by his father's curious name: son of "Callaeschrus," which he takes to mean "Beautiful-Shameful."

But to help Critias over his shame at appearing inadequate Socrates concedes for the moment that a knowledge of knowledge might be possible (although he finds it in principle unintelligible that knowing, empty of an object, should turn on itself). Yet how does such a knowledge help a human being to know *what* one knows or doesn't know? Surely, Critias says, a man who possesses such a reflexive science will be similar to what he has, and thus he will also know himself. Socrates concedes this too, though he can scarcely believe it. It is, as we would say, too abstract.—This reflexive knowledge is not Socratic self-knowledge; just to know knowledge and to know oneself as knowing is not to know one's human self. Although he makes the concession, Socrates, who is, as he says, "always the same," meaning that he has a stable inner being, still doesn't understand how such knowledge can help him know anything substantial about himself or other subjects. By Critias's knowledge he can only know *that* he knows, not *what* he knows.

Socrates clearly thinks that this is a fairly empty thing to know, but again he is both broaching and rejecting a future doctrine. When Kant establishes the limits of reason in his *Critique of Pure Reason,* he argues repeatedly *that* there are things beyond our experience—he calls them "things in themselves"—but that we are, *ipso facto,* unable to know *what* they are. It is the Socratic formula with a positive sign. For what Socrates considers unintelligible, that we might claim that we know something without a clue as to what it is, that the question of existence might be answered without any reference to essence—this very possibility is positively asserted by Kant so that he might be able to refer to the farther side of the limits of human reason.

If there were a knowledge—call it soundmindedness—that knew the "what" of all the other knowledges, it would truly be a science for rulers, be they the rulers of homes or city-states; soundmindedness would rule so that all that was done was done for the best, because no one would try to do what he was not competent to do, and everyone would instead let those who knew how to do it better, do it.

This is probably attributing too great a power to sound-mindedness, Socrates says, and so our inquiry has found nothing useful. Critias thinks Socrates is saying something very strange. Socrates agrees, using his very own oath: "By the Dog." The Dog is apparently Anubis, the Egyptian god of the underworld, whence come dreams. So Socrates tells his dream; it may be from the underworld gate of false dreams or of true dreams, he doesn't know. Suppose soundmindedness regulated everything, and there was no pretense in the professions. We would indeed be healthier and safer and have better utensils. But in always acting knowledgeably, would we necessarily do well and be happy? That's what we haven't yet been able to learn, my dear Critias, he says.

Critias can't really argue that shoemakers and brassworkers and other specialists are particularly happy. Supposing there *were* someone who knew everything. Which of all the things he knows *would* make him happy?—Not prophecy or playing the dice or even health science, they agree.

Critias finally coughs up what Socrates has been after: The knowledge of good and bad. Socrates bursts out in pretended indignation—or perhaps in a pretense of pretended indignation, for he knows Critias's soul and is at bottom disgusted. "You scoundrel!" You've dragged me around in circles, hiding the fact that living knowledgeably does not make us happy, and that *your* soundmindedness is not helpful (*ophélimos*). Socrates blames himself: If I had been useful to a noble inquiry, then what is agreed by all to be the noblest thing would not have come out seeming unhelpful to us. We've made unwarranted concession after concession: that there was a knowledge of knowledge, that it would know what other knowledges know, and most unreasonably of all, that a man can know what he doesn't know. (Recall here that Socrates in fact has a memorable way of making us believe that we can know what we don't know, set out as the Myth of Recollection in the *Meno*.)

Socrates concludes: Although the inquiry found us so simple-minded and flexible (a euphemistic description of Critias's sophistic slipperiness), it hasn't been able to find the truth, but helped by our agreements and constructions, it has "hybristically," tyrannically, shown us the unhelpfulness of what we posited that soundmindedness was; Critias's soundmindedness has no necessary relation to the human good.

With this mention of the tyrant's flaw of *hybris*, "impertinent pride," in conjunction with "unhelpfulness," Socrates ends his passionate summary. The whole conversation has been one of illuminating false starts. Using terminology that is at once anachronistic and appropriate to this future-fraught conversation, we ourselves might summarize it this way: A value-free consideration of human virtue is going to get us nowhere. Such is Socrates' conviction—not a conclusion but rather a point of departure for his more conclusive inquiries about the Good as the source of all knowledge (*Republic* 507 f). Since virtue is knowledge (a proposition argued in some form in many dialogues), it is, of course and even primarily, under the aegis of the Good. Furthermore, "all knowledge divorced . . . from virtue is villainy"—Socrates' word here is *panourgía*, "all-doing" (*Menexenus* 246 e). It is the necessary goodness of all genuine knowledge, and so of the virtue here discussed, that is occulted in this conversation with clever Critias, the prospective "all-doing" tyrant: As he has an empty, if all-encompassing, view of knowledge, so his understanding of temperance is divorced from goodness; it is intended as mere potency, capable of anything.

Here is my last chance to state what is so significantly unusual about Socrates' dialectic in this dialogue. Almost always in other conversations he insists that the discovery of *what* something is, particularly a virtue, what its name signifies, must precede all other inquiries: how it's acquired, what it's good for (but see p. 131). Here in the *Charmides*, he would have reversed the order

had Critias allowed it. Why? Because, it seems to me, his conversational partners are usually decent-minded if unthinking
folks, who, although somewhat clueless about the meaning of
the terms they live by, hold them in proper reverence. They know
that soundmindedness, self-control, temperance, moderation are
good, are what we call "values," whatever they may be. But in
Critias Socrates is facing an opponent who seems to have no notion that any understanding of a virtue must include some sense
of its making life good. Hence he has to wish to reverse his usual
order of inquiry, though without success.

So Socrates turns back to Charmides: In your behalf, Charmides, he says, I am very anxious. That for you who are so remarkable in physical form and so very soundminded in soul—
that for you this soundmindedness should be of no help in your
life!—if indeed you have this virtue, which I think is a great
good. Socrates manages to concede and deny the virtue to the
boy in the same speech. And Charmides picks up this hesitation.
I don't know, he says, whether I have it or not. But I do need
your incantation. Critias chimes in and unilaterally commits his
ward to Socrates' companionship; Charmides will obey his
guardian. Evidently they are whispering at this point. Socrates
wants to know what they are plotting. The language becomes
increasingly political. So you'll take me by force, Socrates says,
without even a proper arraignment? I'll use force, Charmides
says, since Critias has given the order. And he asks Socrates:
What's *your* plan? Here is how Socrates reports the parting
words of this ominous conversation.

> *Socrates:* There's no plan left to me. For once *you* set out to
> achieve anything by force, not a man can oppose you.
> *Charmides:* Then don't *you* oppose me.
> *Socrates:* Then I won't oppose you.

Some three decades later Charmides was a middle-aged associate of that public conspiracy called the Thirty Tyrants. They

ordered Socrates, along with four other men, to arrest a certain Leon of Salamis whom they wanted to kill. The others obeyed, but Socrates, risking his life, *did in fact oppose the tyranny* by refusing to execute the order. Instead he just went home (*Apology* 32). And no one dared touch him—at the time. That event, which appalled Plato (as he tells in his *Seventh Letter* 325 a), is, I think, the ominous subtext of this strange little dialogue with its unwontedly personal setting and its oddly abstract dialectic.

5

INTRODUCTION TO READING THE **REPUBLIC**

The *Republic* is a dialogue, that is to say, a conversation. Since it is a conversation recorded between the covers of a book we cannot help but begin by *reading* it, but I think the author wants us as soon as possible to *join* it, to be converted from passive perusal to active participation, to be drawn in among the other silent "interlocutors." As it happens, in a number of Platonic dialogues there are people present who say nothing or next to nothing out loud; in the *Republic* we are told of four (328 b). In fact one of these, Clitophon, who makes only a brief intrusion into the conversation here, is to be thought of as having a few things to say on his own about the topic at hand, which is justice. For there exists a brief but brisk dialogue between him and Socrates, a companion piece to the *Republic* which, if it is not by Plato, is at least by someone versed in the spirit of Platonic dialogues. The reader is, I think, invited to be present just as these people are, and with them to smile or snicker at witticisms and inside jokes, to groan in outrage at trick arguments, to nod approval at satisfying formulations, to recall contradictory passages of conversation, to appreciate the return of a

theme, and in sum, to check and fill out the recorded conversation with an unwritten inner accompaniment—to be always just
on the brink of breaking in. Indeed the vocal characters themselves make it clear that they are by no means Socrates' unwitting stooges, but wary and critical participants. For example, at
one point Adeimantus somewhat pugnaciously breaks in:

> "Socrates, no one could dispute what you say—your listeners are
> in the same position as always. . . . They think that because of
> their inexperience at question and answer the argument leads
> them astray a little bit at a time until finally, when all the bits
> are collected, they find themselves lost in apparent contradic-
> tion to what they said at the start" (487 b).

—a rebuke to which Socrates yields quite gracefully.

Perhaps nothing about the Platonic dialogues in general is
more worth dwelling on than their dialogic form, especially in
the *Republic,* which itself contains a discussion of its own literary type. In Book II (392 d ff.) Socrates divides all myth telling
and poetry into two styles. One is the *narrative* style, in which
a poet candidly and on his own account retells an event. The
other is the *imitative* style in which he speaks as a dramatist
with the voice of another and conceals his own authorship. The
former style is honest, the latter deceptive. It is to this latter style
that the *Republic* itself appears to belong, since Plato is entirely
hidden behind this imitation of a conversation between Socrates and others.

This distinction between narration and drama may not appear so very interesting until one becomes concerned with the
truth-telling and thought-provoking powers of the written word,
the word which has been abandoned by its speaker. For then it
appears that narrative, from myth to treatise, is indeed an undisguised attempt by an author to talk *at* a reader, an attempt which
leaves that reader the defense of well-directed resistance or bored
disengagement, while drama and dialogue draw him helplessly
into a fictive world of vivid but spuriously attributed speech.

Now Plato will not talk *at* us, that is, write clear and convincing treatises, because he considers that knowledge cannot be simply conveyed into the soul by words (518 c), nor will he involve us in one of those exciting tragic dramas which provide nothing but an artificially heightened appearance. One ingenious solution is the dialogue written, like the *Republic,* in the *first person*. For that form does retain some of the immediacy of drama, and yet at least one of the authors of the dialogue, namely Socrates, is very much present and responsible as the teller of the tale. Such a dialogue form overcomes the dangers of poetry while preserving its power to move the soul. Given a chance, that is what the reading of a Socratic dialogue will do.

A long introduction risks standing in the way of giving readers that chance to come to grips with the dialogue immediately, for example, when their author's supposed social or cultural circumstances are injected between him and his work. Is it not possible for a writer to be so deep, so original in the strong sense, that he can be defined neither from, nor even against, his social setting? It is a question to be especially asked about a writer who gives this description of the way in which a philosopher might be received by his society upon his return from the realms of thought:

> ". . . They'd say he came back from above with ruined eyes. . . . And if they could get their hands on the man who was trying to release them and lead them upward, wouldn't they kill him?" (517 a).

—the very fate, of course, of Plato's older friend Socrates. Hence an introduction to a work in terms of the author's background is apt to amount to an implicit denial of its radical originality.

Nor does the historical or political setting necessarily make a text more accessible. For example, the "dramatic date" of the dialogue *Republic,* that is, the time at which it is taking place, is an interlude of peace during the Peloponnesian War (whose main parties were Athens and Sparta) in the latter part of the fifth century B.C. Athens is at this time still a democracy. The scene of the dialogue is the port of Athens, the Piraeus, a proletarian stronghold of democratic feeling, at the house of a rich merchant whose family will later be destroyed by the antidemocratic party. A trenchantly mordant description of democratic modes and morals is put by the aristocrat Plato into the mouth of the craftsman Socrates (562 c ff.), who has already foretold his own execution by a later democratic regime. Hence students are usually introduced to the *Republic* as a deeply antidemocratic book. But let me cite a bit of text. Socrates has just been satirizing democracy:

> "And, you know, it's just the place to go shopping for a regime."
> "How come?"
> "Because it's permissive and has every kind, so that anyone who wants to construct a city, *as we just did,* ought to shop in a democracy as in a regime bazaar. . . ." (557 d).

I have italicized the telling phrase. It seems to me to indicate that the book is far from being uncompromisingly antidemocratic, for within it attention is being drawn to the fact that a dialogue concerning ideal cities is best carried on, and is in fact being carried on, in a democracy. In this point introductions sometimes prejudice our reading of a text whose judgment on our favored political form is justly complex by making too coarse an application of historical circumstance. So also with economic conditions: The fact that the privileged Plato, a slaveowner to boot, conceives through Socrates a communitarian society so radical as to leave modern communisms, scientific or utopian, looking quite pale should warn the reader to use the author's local situation most cautiously in interpreting his work. For where real thinking is going on, external facts determine at most the point of departure of the inquiry. Mere circumstance is what thought penetrates and goes beyond.

Biographical facts may sometimes have to be sparingly supplied. Those that have significance, like Socrates' trial and con-

demnation for corrupting the youth of Athens, are often written into the dialogues. One circumstance, which lends the *Republic* a certain pathos, is indeed not mentioned in that dialogue,
namely the fact that Socrates' young conversational partners,
Glaucon and Adeimantus, are Plato's brothers. Neither of them
appears to have achieved any distinction in later life, and that
too turns out to have a certain significance, as we shall see. So
also Plato's trip to Sicily, the middle one of three, made subsequent to the composition of the *Republic,* throws a certain backward light on the book's intention. He had gone rather reluctantly, yielding to the demand that he should have the courage
to try in practice his alternative plan for the realization of the
best regime: that "kings and regents become genuine philosophers." All this he tells himself in his *Seventh Letter.* Long before the composition of the *Republic,* its first and preferred plan,
namely that philosophers might themselves be accepted as kings,
had been demonstratively dashed by the execution of Socrates.
Now the philosophical education of the Sicilian tyrant Dionysius had proved to be a failure as well. We may cautiously conclude that before, during, and after the writing of the *Republic*
(which he kept revising until his death), Plato knew that its central proposal was indefensible.

Finally, it might be helpful to mention the dialogue we know
to be Plato's last work, the *Laws,* and to contrast it with the *Republic*. The Greek title of the *Republic* is *Politeía,* which literally means "Political Regime" or "Constitution" and signifies a
conception of thought, while the *Laws* naturally contains a multitude of practically applicable laws. The latter dialogue explicitly refers to itself in comparison with the *Republic* as a "second
sailing," that is to say, a second best or even least worst way.
Both the speaker Socrates and the very word philosophy are
missing from the *Laws,* which takes place during a long day's
walk under the Cretan sun, just as the *Republic* goes on well
through the night at a house in the port of Athens. The differences between the two dialogues is, crudely, that between theory and practice.

From introductory backgrounds let me turn to introductory interpretations. I have some misgivings about anticipating the reader's own understanding of the text with preemptive explanations. Nonetheless in the hope of helping rather than hindering access, I will offer some hints for reading the *Republic*. For beyond appearing as a lively and open-ended conversation for the reader to join, the dialogue is also a discussion carefully guided by Socrates and a work artfully composed by Plato. That suggests that the conversation may be contained within a revealing structure and marked by significant turns and pregnant omissions, all designed as invitations to speculative interpretation. To mention the omissions first, Socrates deliberately withholds the very teachings for which the dialogue is to be a preparation: the full-scale inquiry into the parts of the soul and the direct discussion of the Good (504 b, 506 e). The latter in fact belongs among the so-called "unwritten doctrines" of Plato's school, unwritten because, in the words of his *Seventh Letter* (341 c), "it is not sayable as are other kinds of learning." Now to the more or less explicit teachings of the dialogue.

THE CENTRAL DIALOGUE: THE PHILOSOPHER'S CITY

The observation of structures and patterns can yield a clue to the author's intention. The *Republic* has indeed a rather large and obvious architecture, a symmetry which suggests too much to be a mere pattern. Let me set it out roughly by books:

I and **X**: The rewards of justice;
II–V and **VIII–IX**: The construction and corruption of the best city;
II and **X**: The critique of poetry;
VI and **VII**: The philosopher's function and education.

This arrangement may be imagined as a set of concentric circles with the themes lying on a diameter through them (p. 117). The major themes are repeated going into the center and coming out, of course under a different light. For example, the critique of poetry in political communities in the second book is confined to its content, its misrepresentation of excellence and of the gods. However, in the tenth book, in the light of the preceding philosophical discussion, the critique becomes a radical condemnation of poetry as a kind of perverse absorption in images and a deliberate distancing from Being. (See ch. 7.)

But the concentric construction primarily effects the clear definition of a dialogic center, namely Books VI and VII, in which are contained the heights and the depths of the dialogue. What is presented there is "a way to be pursued"—this is the literal meaning of the Greek word *méthodos* which as yet has no connotation of a systematic procedure. It is an education which has scarcely any of the usual modern aims: It is intended neither to broaden or sharpen the mind, nor to inform or indoctrinate it, and least of all to train people to "be creative" or to "develop their whole personality." Instead it is meant to employ the appropriate parts of the soul to lead the young learner in accordance with the nature of things to a view of the Whole. That is to say, it is an education intimately related to philosophy, even to *a* philosophy, one that founds communities.

In the center of the Western tradition's first book on political theory, then, politics is replaced by philosophy. This is an observation backed by an acute although not disinterested reader, Rousseau. He says in his fictive pedagogical case history, *Émile,* a book intended to be the individualistic modern replacement of Plato's work:

> To get a good idea of communal education read Plato's *Republic.* It is not a political treatise, as those who merely judge books by their titles think. It is the finest treatise on education ever written.

Perhaps then it is better to say that Socrates transforms a political question into an educational one. To mark this transformation, the dominating desire of the dialogue, namely that justice should be proved to be compatible with and even conducive to happiness, is for the moment thrust aside: To those who guide and those who undergo such an education the doing of justice is, on the whole, not a source of happiness but a simple sacrifice. For justice demands that they should descend from the realm of Being to act in the world of appearance (516 c ff.), and this is for them a mere harsh duty, a moral obligation without assured reward; indeed, they must rather expect loss of bliss, submission to distraction, risk of contumely, and even danger of death. That is the judgment of Socrates who himself "went down," among the populace. (The *Republic* begins with the word *katében*, "I went down.")

This transformation of politics into pedagogy is necessitated by what might be termed the "founding paradox" of the ideal city. For suppose such a city has been constructed in argument, how is it to be realized? It is under the pressure of this question from Glaucon that Socrates gives the absurd, or at least not very commonsensical, answer already cited: Such a city can come about only if either philosophers become kings or kings philosophers. But for kings to become philosophers there must take place one of those wrenching conversions described in the Cave Image (515 c ff.; p. 208), which has to be effected with the aid of someone who has, in turn, already somehow, perhaps by a miracle of birth, become a philosopher—yet, as was mentioned, nothing within the dialogues or in Socrates' and Plato's lives supports the expectation that if such a philosopher were to appear, he could bring about such a conversion. If, on the other hand, philosophers are to be kings, the ordinary circle of conditions must somehow be replaced: The likely candidates would have to grow up in a city that can give them a truly philosophical education such as will keep them from becoming like those smart injurious intellectuals rightly rejected by the people. It would, further, have to be a city already so constituted as to be willing to accept the rule of philosophers, or there would scarcely be much incentive for educating them to it. In sum, the future philosophers must already be born into Socrates' ideal city. But that city can come about only if some true philosophers happened to be born into some existing city, happened to come to power there, and happened thus to be in a position to send all the adults into the wilds and to seize command of their children's education (540 d ff.)—the comic counsel of despair with which Socrates closes the discussion of the philosophical curriculum.

The resolution to this paradox of circularity is given in the passage which seems to reveal most directly the inner intention of the *Republic*. When the argument, now past the center, reverts to the original task of proving justice advantageous, Glaucon and Socrates have their last exchange concerning the philosopher city:

> ". . .You mean the city we've been founding in words; I don't think it exists on earth."
>
> "But perhaps it is laid up as a model in heaven for anyone to look at who wishes *to found himself*. It makes no difference whether it exists or ever will exist here. He'll practice the politics only of it and of no other" (592 b).

I have italicized Socrates' oddly abrupt phrase "to found himself." It reveals in direct words that the point of the *Republic* is not a political but a personal founding, a self-constituting, which is accomplished both in and by the dialogue. Socrates resolves, or rather, bypasses, the founder's paradox by founding, through conversation, *right here and now* an educational community whose members are all the present and future participants in the dialogue. The very development of this community "in speech," that is, the course of the argument itself, educates his interlocutors "in deed." ("In speech and in deed" is a common Greek opposition which Socrates himself employs in this context, 473 a.) The establishment of this dialogic community and the conversion and reformation of *its* philosopher-citizens is itself *the* So-

cratic accomplishment—not the preparation of future philosopher kings, as the choice of the prospectively obscure Glaucon
as chief interlocutor signifies.

The course of education which Socrates sets out for the
sake of our education has what we no longer expect of such a
curriculum—an end, a culmination. It is intended to effect not
so much an advance into a subject matter as an ascent to this
end, which is called with stupefying grandeur, "the idea of the
Good," or simply, "the Good" (508 e). It is not some one good
thing, nor a moral imperative or rule of right conduct, nor an
excellence or a substance, nor, indeed, a being at all. Rather it
is "beyond Being," beyond all beings. It is their governing
source. We know that in other contexts its name was "the One."
Here it is referred to as "the source of the Whole" (511 b), which
might be rendered as "the source which is the Whole," or as
"the ruling principle of everything." (The Greek word for
source, rule, principle, even government, is *arché*.) As I have
mentioned, Socrates refuses to explicate the Good directly because it is not to be attained and conveyed in speech, certainly
not in summary speech, but he does provide a likeness, the Sun
Simile (506 e). The Good is like the sun in two ways: It gives
Being and substance to the realm of invisible beings, the forms,
as the sun gives growth and sustenance to the whole visible
world, and it gives intelligibility and articulation to the different beings within Being, as the sun gives illumination and dis-
tinctness to the appearances within the world. The Good is "beyond Being" because it is not yet one more being in addition to
the forms, but rather the wholeness and oneness itself of all Being (194 ff.).

THE DIVIDED LINE   Under the presidency of the Good,
then, there arises a cosmos of substance and shadows, of being
and appearance, which Socrates sets out by means of a geometric diagram, the Divided Line (509 d ff.). The proportioned segments of this line represent the realms which arise as Being is suc-

cessively reflected: First it casts its rational shadows, the objects of mathematics; these are in turn imaged in the bodies of the natural world, and these, again, throw off surface reflections. (See p. 220 for the diagram.)

Corresponding and appended to these four realms are four appropriate powers of the soul. Now if there is any mode of thinking which might be called characteristic of the dialogue it is this mode of correspondences or correlations: To the parts of the soul correspond the chief passions and their controlling excellences (435 c ff.); to different human types correspond different political regimes (544 e); and to different powers of the knowing part of the soul correspond different objects of knowledge (477 b). In most cases Socrates begins the correlation with what is closest to us, with ourselves and our powers:

> "Then we clearly agree that opinion is different from knowledge . . . and *being different powers each naturally pertains to a different thing:* knowledge pertains to what *is,* to know how it is, whereas opinion, we say, conjectures [about becoming]" (478 a).

This central section, however, is an exception, for there he is giving a preview, albeit an abbreviated and inadequate one, of the ascending realms of Being, and therefore he presents the objects as prior to the powers by which they are known.

Reversing Socrates' order in the following interpretative setting-out of these powers and their objects, I begin with those represented by the highest and presumably largest segment of the line. There intellection or thought (*nóesis*) moves, rising and falling among the things of thought, the beings or forms, by and through which it approaches and departs from the Good. This motion is called "dialectic," which here does not have the usual meaning of dialogic discussion, argument or refutation, but is the specific activity of the intellect among the forms, the highest kind of thought. In the *Republic* Socrates is reluctant to say much about it or its objects. We are, however, to understand that a form (*eídos*) is that intelligible being, that "thing itself," which stands behind and above the mere appearances, giving them whatever determinate looks they may have. (See ch. 12.)

The next segment below stands for thinking or understanding (*diánoia*). It is a more restless, technical, and incomplete activity which works through pure non-sensory images, such as mathematical shapes. Its business is the making of assumptions or hypotheses, such as are the axioms and objects of mathematics. In fact the words with which we name the forms of Being without quite knowing them, words like "justice," for instance, are also hypotheses of the understanding—these are the very assumptions dialectic turns into knowledge. The movement of mathematical understanding is characteristically deductive, downward, as in Euclid's geometric proofs. It descends to conclusions but it does not ascend beyond its own suppositions. These two upper parts together represent the realm of knowledge (*epistéme*).

Opinion (*dóxa*) is represented by the two lower lengths, which are cut in the same ratio as the upper two, both subsections reflecting the overall ratio, that between knowledge and opinion.

The third segment down stands for trust (*pístis*). It is the way we have of dealing with all the apparently solid things in the world around us. By and large we take them for granted, believe in them and trust them to behave predictably: The sun will rise, the ground will support us. It can be proved that as this line is divided, the two middle segments are of equal length (see p. 357), which shows that the realm of mathematics and its phenomenal reflection, the realm of nature, are coextensive, that is to say, fitted to each other in the scale of being. (In another dialogue, the *Timaeus,* which is a sequel to some occasion when Socrates retold his conversation on city building, some friends, to reciprocate, invite him to a feast of cosmos construction; among other things, they show him in a most modern vein an idea prefigured by the ancient Pythagoreans, that the physical world is literally constructed *out of* mathematicals, which is to say that the two realms are more than coextensive—they are identical.)

Finally, at the bottom, is the shortest segment standing for the most peculiarly Socratic power, the most dubious and the most necessary, the lowest and the first. It is the power whose name *eikasía* is often, not very plausibly, translated as "conjecture." Actually, Socrates has appropriated a rare word and used it in its literal sense, which is "imagizing." It can be rendered as "imagination" or as "imaging." It is the wonderful power of dealing with an image (*eikón*) *as* an image, the power of recognizing likenesses. To recognize a likeness *as* a likeness is the first of philosophical feats, for it involves seeing that something (an image) has the look of something else (the original) which it is *not*—thus it is the first step in distinguishing Appearance from Being. Socrates signals the pervasive nature of this power when he performs the mathematical operation of "alternation" by which he transforms the proportion:

Intellection is to understanding as trust is to imaging

into:

Intellection is to trust as understanding is to imaging,

which means that understanding, the power of doing mathematics, is immediately related to image-recognition (534 a). This relation will be very plausible to anyone who has ever drawn a misshapen ovoid on a blackboard and said "Let this be circle C," meaning, "Recognize this as an image of a true, physically unachievable circle." That "imaging" should be *the* pervasive power is not surprising where the ascent of learning depends on recognizing the objects of each lower realm as shadow images cast by a higher.

In fact an overwhelming interest in the nature of images and their seeming, in what makes it possible that a shape should at once *be* and *not be* that which it is, runs through a number of dialogues (chs. 6, 8, 10). Understandably so, for the image which is not what it seems to be is a kind of prime exemplar of that realm between Being and Nonbeing (477 ff.), that shifting shadow world of mutability, variousness, and seeming that is our world of appearances and which Plato sometimes calls "Becoming." Within the *Republic,* this interest shows itself in a way that must always have scandalized readers, namely in the thorough censoring of the products of the imagination. They are called "music," that is to say, the poetry, song, painting, and other works of the Muses, which together with physical training, form the prephilosophical upbringing of children in the ideal city. His fierce attacks on the poets as irresponsible image-mongers stem from the fact that, unlike many of us, Socrates is dead serious about the potency of poetry. For he sees it as a seductively charming corruption of the primary power of philosophical ascent, which is precisely the power of image-recognition.

THE CAVE IMAGE   In Book VII Socrates turns to the human costs and effort of this ascent. He begins, cleverly, with an invitation to use this very power of image-recognition: We are to recognize our world as a cave (see p. 206). He describes the wrenching, disorienting conversion undergone by the unchained prisoners when they are first forced to turn around to look at the opinion-making and image-manipulating that goes on behind their backs. The first turnabout enables them to recognize as mere images of images the shadow plays performed for them on the screen at the bottom of the cave before which they have been sitting enchained all their early lives. (The contemporary application to television viewing is comically obvious.) Then they are dragged and hauled, still unwilling, up into the blinding light of the sun, the very sun of the Sun Simile. Just when they have begun to rejoice in this bright upper world, they must force themselves to descend again and to undertake the dangerous task of enlightening their fellow citizens in turn.

THE PHILOSOPHER'S EDUCATION Then follows a detailed account of a curriculum which is the realization of that upward haul, the "winch to lift the soul from Becoming to Being" (521 d). It picks up where the training in gymnastics and music (which corresponds to the lower two parts of the Divided Line—those representing nature and images) had left off, leaving habituation and training behind in favor of thinking and true education. It is the first detailed systematic exposition of the traditional liberal arts, particularly of those four skills of mathematics and physics called the "quadrivium" in medieval times. The mathematical "method" here is not a technical but a philosophical preparation, a road leading not to application but to reflection—that is what makes it liberal.

The first and fundamental subject is nondimensional *mathematics,* that is, arithmetic. It is the study of collections of units, and its importance lies not in training students to reckon but in its being a logical preparation for the approach to *the* One, that is, the Good. Thereafter the studies advance dimensionally through plane and solid geometry up to harmony, the study of sounding solids in rational motion—pure *physics,* as we would say.

The crowning study, not to be undertaken until maturity, is *dialectic,* the thoughtful motion of the intellect among the forms (532 ff.), aided by internal and external dialogue, that is, by reflection and conversation, and culminating in a view of the Whole, the idea of the Good.

Now what is most remarkable in this curriculum, ostensibly meant for philosopher-statesmen, is that it excludes completely all political theory and all science of government. I have already argued that this education is in fact meant more for philosophers than for statesmen. But it turns out that from the point of view of the curriculum that hardly matters. For were these philosophers destined actually to govern, they would do so not through the study of law and the science of government—the constitutional and administrative features of the philosopher's city are minimal—but in the light of the Whole, by a contingently applied wisdom. That is the reason why the One is in this dialogue named the Good (see p. 204)—because from its contemplation flows the possibility of action which is not rule-ridden but truly adjusted to each case. Only because it is not a mere neutral oneness which encompasses and unifies the world, but the *Good,* can the world be the scene of unifying, fitting, effective, human, personal action (517 c), in short, of *justice.*

THE OUTER DIALOGUE: THE DEGENERATE CITIES   The outer rings of the dialogue are concerned with the building up and the breakdown of the just city, but "in speech," as Socrates repeatedly says—that is, for the sake of argument. In fact on the way into the center of the dialogue, a whole series of "cities" (the Greek word is *pólis,* which is best rendered as "political community") is described, each embodying justice with more complexity than the preceding one. Past the center their degeneration, as the citizens lose their moral tone, is pursued through symmetrically similar stages: First the philosophers' knowledge fails, then the soldiers lose their spirit, then the traders become intemperate, and finally the craftsmen throw off their justice. Each of these stages is a commonly recognized real regime. A chart may be useful:

Ideal City	Real Regime
Philosopher City	————————
Guardian City	Aristocracy (rule of the best)
Warrior City	Timocracy (rule of the honorable)
Trader City	Oligarchy (rule of the wealthy few)
Craftsman City	Democracy (rule of the people)
————————	Tyranny

I think that the four left-hand patterns leading up to the philosopher city are at once stages in the genesis of the ideal city and seperably imaginable *political* entities. But I have already argued that the highest and happiest city is actually a *dialogic* community including Socrates, Glaucon, and the reader, a league of learning which, though surely not a full-fledged political foundation, is yet not a merely private affair. The lowest and worst and the most miserable of real regimes, tyranny, is, however, truly private, for the tyrant is defined by the fact that he exploits the whole city as his private means for servicing his boundless desires. So both of these cities, the ideal best and the real worst, are really not true political communities.

It is the Guardian City which has, as an apparently realizable political ideal, given most scandal and even brought on Plato the charge of totalitarianism. This is the city in which the older warriors of the Warrior City are separated off to become the guardians (414 b) of a new, radically communistic city, in which there is no private property, wives and children are held in common so that the family is abolished, men and women are equally trained for war, and a rigid caste system resting on the testing of human types is enforced.

Let me at least suggest certain mitigating factors. First, the city is not totalitarian but unitarian, for it is not so much under total control as completely unified—that, at least, is Aristotle's criticism, who thinks that such unity is contrary to nature. Second, the ruling group itself lives under the harshest communal discipline (in contrast to totalitarian regimes, where the rulers live in luxury), while the members of the lower class are, as far as one can tell, allowed to form families, accumulate property, and engage in all the ordinary pleasures and private latitudes.

JUSTICE IN SOCRATES' CITY   But the argument which supersedes all others is the circumstance, so often repeated by Socrates, that this is a city only built for the sake of argument. It is quite literally a utopia (a Greek word coined by Thomas More, meaning "no-place"). It is, after all, only a device Socrates has introduced for the sake of answering the main question: What is justice? That device is a projection of justice on the largest possible screen, the political community, so that its nature might be easier to discern (368 d ff.). It should be noted that this projection becomes possible only by reason of another such principle of correspondence as was mentioned above: Each excellence is located analogously in the city and in the soul.

In their preliminary arguments about justice in Book I, the participants had assumed, rather as a matter of course, that justice is a matter of relations among people, a matter of external conduct. But even then Socrates had already pointed out that insofar as it is indeed an excellence, and if excellences are powers and functions of the soul, justice might rather have to be primarily a matter of internal soundness (353 d ff.; see ch. 7).

It is, of course, impossible to construct a constitution which will display justice unless a hypothesis about its nature is built in from the beginning. This supposition about justice will, not surprisingly, be rediscovered at the end of the exercise as the sought-for feature of the construction. Socrates' presupposition is precisely that justice is not a condition or procedure like the fair distribution of goods or equal treatment under the law, but an excellence, an excellence concerned with self-relation. The definition of this justice, as it emerges in Socrates' city, seems at first disappointingly drab and uninspiring. It is quite literally, "to do one's own thing" (433 b), not of course in the current sense of expressing and pleasing oneself, but in the sense of having a competence and not overstepping its limits. (It is a definition made more immediately plausible by the fact that the Greek word for a vicious type is a *panóurgos*, which means a "do-all.")

In its political application this definition means that a just city is, first, an aristocracy, that is to say a "government of the best," of those best fitted and most competent to govern, and second, a thoroughly articulated community in which no one is allowed or, indeed, even wishes, to step out of his properly assigned place. In such a city justice belongs to the whole community, but it is the peculiar excellence of that majority whose part it is to do their own specialized work, work which is vital in its place, but limited in scope. Socrates' justice belongs specifically to "the people."

In respect to the individual, this definition of justice means that that soul is just each of whose parts performs its function well and submits to the direction of the part which is best and most fit for rule, the reasonable part. Hence a just soul is a potent yet controlled soul, happy in the vigor of its parts and the clarity of their relations, a well-adjusted soul, whose just external relations are a mere reflection of its inner order.

What gives aptness and force to justice as "doing one's own business" is that so understood it becomes the excellence of excellences in a world under the rule of the Good. For that the Good rules must mean that in its light each being is both good in itself and good as a part of the whole. That is precisely what justice accomplishes in the working world, which is a reflection of the realm of Being: To be just according to Socrates is to be both good on one's own and good for others.

THE FINAL MYTH   In the middle books of the *Republic* Socrates uses projections, similes, diagrams, and images to lift the discussion, as it were, above itself. In the introductory first book, however, only the notorious Socratic dialectic appears, dialectic, that is, in the usual understanding—a winding argument, full of quibbles, quandaries, and refutations. By contrast, the last book concludes with a very grand myth. In every major Socratic dialogue the logical argument is complemented by a mythical tableau. A Socratic myth is always a cosmic image which encompasses the world of heaven and the world of hell, the realm where the soul sees true being and the realm where it meets retribution—the world above and the world below, between which lies our earthly place. It provides that vision of the Whole which no argument can convey.

In the Myth of Er with which the *Republic* ends we are shown a cosmos that is a setting for the judgment of former and the

choice of future lives. The strange and suggestive visual ambi-
guities of this word-image of the invisible form of the Whole are
interpreted in ch. 8, p. 260. As a narrative, however, the myth
is meant to foster the conviction that the process of living has
behind it a controlling form, the pattern of our life taken as a
whole, which we ourselves have already chosen, expressing in
that choice the disposition of our soul. But the moment for another choice, the myth implies, cannot fail to come, is indeed
now at hand, and the best preparation for doing well then is to
engage seriously in the inquiry concerning justice now.

6

THE MUSIC OF THE **REPUBLIC**

SURVEY OF ARGUMENTS

I MÝTHOS

A The *Republic* is composed of concentric rings encompassing a center. *[116]*

B The outer ring represents Socrates' descent into the house of Pluto-Cephalus (Books I and IX–X). *[116]*

   1 The oath "By the Dog" is an appeal to Hermes the Conductor of Souls. *[118]*

   2 Socrates assumes the role of Heracles, founder of cities. *[119]*

   3 His longest labor is the bringing up of the triple monster Cerberus—the soul. *[121]*

   4 His greatest labor is the release of a new Theseus. *[121]*

II LÓGOS

A The second ring represents the founding and degeneration of cities "in speech" (Books II–IV and VIII–IX). *[122]*

B These cities are "in speech" only, since they can be neither generated nor regenerated. *[124]*

1   The Phoenician tale implies that men can be mined as a public treasure. *[124]*

2   The just city founders on the unnaturalness of human nature and on the "founding paradox." *[126]*

3   The degenerate cities themselves are actual, but the argument about them is detached from their vices. *[129]*

C   In Polemarchus's house justice, defined as "doing one's own business," is the craftsmen's specific virtue. *[130]*

1   The "demiurge" is opposed to the "panurge" in all his forms. *[130]*

2   The inner justice of the philosopher converts the definition of justice into "knowing one's own soul." *[133]*

3   For the philosopher the argument that justice is profitable fails. *[134]*

III   ÉRGON

A   In the center of the *Republic* Socrates founds the philosopher city "in deed" (Books V–VII). *[135]*

1   A public vote forces Socrates to propose his communal design. *[135]*

2   Other works corroborate the assertion that the philosopher city is not identical with the guardian city. *[137]*

3   Socrates' city in the *Timaeus* differs from that of the *Republic*. *[138]*

B   The paradoxical condition for bringing about the city is that its founder must already live within it. *[139]*

1   Socrates lives so as to fulfill this condition. *[139]*

2   Glaucon has some qualifications of a young ruler. *[141]*

3   The bodily community of the guardian city is replaced by a dialogic community. *[142]*

C Democracy, the exact inverse of the just constitution, perversely proves to be the soil for the just city. *[143]*

D The just city can be brought to life by providing a fitting macrocosm, as in the *Timaeus*. *[146]*

    1 Temperance replaces justice in this city. *[146]*

    2 Antiquity in the *Timaeus* represents spurious actuality. *[147]*

    3 The city of the *Laws* is non-Socratic. *[148]*

IV MUSIC

A Glaucon's education in Books V–VII is Socratic music. *[150]*

    1 The guardians' training is accomplished by purged traditional music (Books II and X). *[150]*

        a Socrates corrects the myths of gods and Hades but postpones the correction of the myths of man. *[150]*

        b The *Republic* itself exactly obeys the stylistic requirements of "purged music." *[151]*

        c This poetic music is explicitly excluded from the plan of the philosophers' education. *[153]*

    2 Socrates' new music is "philosophical music." *[153]*

        a Socrates has spent his life making music. *[153]*

        b Socratic *mímeses* of truth are *images* rather than *myths*. *[153]*

        c Such images are sketched in the soul by long reflection. *[154]*

        d Socratic images *induce* a *lógos,* while myths are *preceded* by one. *[154]*

        e Socrates fulfills his own requirement that all poets make an "image of the Good." *[155]*

        f Socrates corrects the Promethean Myth of Man in the "Cave Image." *[155]*

g These two images respectively represent the *One* and the *Indefinite Dyad* of Plato's "Unwritten Teachings." *[156]*

3 Socrates' plan for the philosophical education is presented musically as the "prelude" of mathematics and the "hymn" of dialectic. *[157]*

4 The central dialogue is a symmetric texture of images and their explications and correlations. *[158]*

B The discovery of opinion (*dóxa*) is Glaucon's introduction to philosophy. *[159]*

1 The outer dialogue requires the "helmet of Hades," which obviates reputation or "good opinion" (Books II and X), but the central conversation is governed by "true opinion." *[159]*

2 Summary of 474–480 (Book V). As becoming is between being and non-being, so opinion is between ignorance and knowing. *[160]*

3 "Opinion" corresponds to "spirit," the mean between reasoning (*logistikón*) and desire (*epithymía*) in the tripartite soul. *[162]*

4 The *logistikón,* properly called the "calculating power," is a lesser faculty than "knowledge." *[163]*

5 After the new division of the soul as an "instrument of learning" the terms for the lower tripartite soul designate desires. *[164]*

6 The finer division of the soul by the device of finding the middle is the dialogue's main pre-dialectical exercise. *[166]*

C The orator Socrates is elected to defend philosophy before the democracy (487–505, Book VI). *[166]*

1 Adeimantus is the expert on corruption. *[166]*

2 Socrates, by his images, persuades the Many to accept philosophers as kings. *[166]*

3 He refuses Adeimantus access to the "highest study," the Good. *[169]*

D Socrates tells Glaucon of the Good in a true image, the Sun Image. *[170]*

1 Summary and tables of 506–511 (Book VI). The Sun Image is explicated by the Divided Line. *[170]*

2 This representation requires Glaucon to exercise the two lower, "doxastic," powers of the soul. *[173]*

a The lower of these, likeness-making and likeness-recognizing (*eikasía*), known to Glaucon as a game, is Socrates' chief instrument in this context. The Divided Line itself forces Glaucon to recognize the visible world as a *mere* image or likeness. *[173]*

b His trust (*pístis*) in the visible world is shaken and a belief in the rule of the Good is substituted. *[175]*

c Socrates' non-dialectical or "doxastic" presentation of the Good serves both to avoid misunderstanding and to instill a kind of artificial recollection in Glaucon. *[176]*

3 The Divided Line, a figure for knowledge, provides training for Glaucon's power of thinking (*diánoia*). *[177]*

a *Diánoia,* "thinking things through," involves a higher *eikasía* in two ways: Natural objects are here regarded as images, and thoughtful analogies are made by recognizing likenesses. *[177]*

b The mathematical faculty characteristic of Glaucon, *diánoia,* is discovered by him as a "mean." *[180]*

c Socrates particularly invites Glaucon to a dialogue on number; this passage is the only approach to dialectic in the *Republic. [180]*

d *Dialégesthai* has three meanings: *conversation* among the many, *dialogue* between a knower and a learner, and *dialectic,* the movement of the soul within itself and through the forms (*eíde,* sing. *eídos*). *[181]*

4 The mathematical model of proportion (*analogía*) is fully exploited. *[184]*

a The Good is not a "study" in the usual sense. *[184]*

b The absence of the dialectical accounts (*lógoi*) of being is expressed by the absence of definite ratios (*lógoi*) between the line segments. *[185]*

c The "embodied soul" has solidity; the "knowing soul" is "non-dimensional." *[185]*

d Socrates forms four proportions from the Divided Line, showing Glaucon even before he knows the parts themselves how sameness of relation runs through the Whole. *[188]*

e This induces Glaucon to trust the bond of similarity (*homoiótes*) required for dianoetic ascent, which is through likenesses. *[191]*

f The Good, by exercising a downward *eikasía* and likening things to itself, makes the ascent possible. *[192]*

g The mimetic arts are condemned for usurping the power of the Good (Book X). *[193]*

5 The image of the Good *implicitly* introduces Glaucon to the fundamental problems of dialectic. *[194]*

a The Good has three capacities: as *progenitor* it fathers the sun; it is the *responsible cause (aitía)* of knowing; and it is the *ruling source (arché)* of being. These are presented in reverse order of importance to a *pólis*. *[194]*

b A diagram shows how Being is articulated doubly by the Good, and particularly why Becoming is doubly apprehended, namely in *sense perception* and *opinion*. *[195]*

c The Good is not a differentiating but a unitary binding source, complemented, the image implies, by a secondary "dyadic" or doubling source. *[197]*

d Likeness, which fails to account for the participation of natural objects in the *eíde* within the realm of Being, takes the place of the Other beyond Being. It is that bond by which the Whole becomes one, the bond which the three-term proportion of the Divided Line expresses. *[200]*

e   In the dialectic progress from "what each is" to "what the Good is," the latter is revealed as the order (*táxis*) of the Whole, and thus as the pattern of all political community. *[203]*

f   The One is treated explicitly in no Platonic dialogue, not even in the *Parmenides*. *[205]*

g   The Myth of Er contains the mythical counterpart of the Sun Image—a model of the world within the world. *[206]*

E   Socrates tells Glaucon of evil in a second "true image," the Cave Image. *[207]*

1   Summary and table of 514–517 (Book VII). The cave is to the upper world as the place of visibility is to the place of thought. *[207]*

2   While the Sun Image shows the places prepared by the Good for the soul, the Cave Image shows the actual dwelling of men; thus the Cave Image explicitly includes ignorance and even deceit. Ignorance, however, corresponds to Nonbeing. *[209]*

3   Therefore a different correlation of the images is implicit: *[211]*

	Sun Image	Cave Image
Being	: intelligible realm	
Becoming	: ←——— sensible realm ———→	
Nonbeing	:	underground realm

4   Nonbeing is the mother corresponding to the Good as father. *[211]*

a   Politics as the dissembling art of managing human stupidity has a special place in the Cave Image. *[211]*

b The cave as a womb is a figure for Nonbeing, to which is opposed the realm of Being under the sun; between them lies the road along which "coming into being" takes place. *[212]*

c Socrates identifies the cave as the *mortal Hades,* the "sightless place." The backward position of the prisoners signifies human perversion, which is corrected by the Socratic conversion (*periagogé*). *[213]*

d Socrates alludes to Pythagoras's descent into Hades; in fact the dialogue itself has the form of a Pythagorean recollection exercise. *[215]*

F Socrates recites the "hymn of dialectic" for Glaucon. *[216]*

1 The ascent from the cave represents the road of learning, which has three parts: *[216]*

a *Conversion* is not within the formal plan because it is, in effect, now being accomplished. *[216]*

b The *haul upwards* is effected by Socratic mathematics, pursued not for its own sake or as giving the order of Being, but as *inverse* dialectic. It consists of the analytical solution of such problems as the construction of a hypothetical cosmos according to a purified Pythagorean mathematical order. Its analytic approach permits a constant return to its own hypotheses, which reflect the requirements of the *lógos. [217]*

c *Dialectic* itself is withheld from Glaucon as accessible only by the long path of study; instead its praises are sung in a "hymn." *[237]*

d Having heard the plan, Glaucon, as an initiate of the mysteries of learning, becomes a fellow law-giver. *[237]*

2 The ages for study and practice are set out as in a formal curriculum. *[238]*

a   The education of the rulers always leads out of the city, which contains nothing "fair" for them; in it *geometry* is substituted for *eros*. *[238]*

b   Because of the hypothetical character of all "patterns," the rulers in the *Constitution* do not study constitutions, but learn to rule "in the light of the Whole." *[241]*

c   Socrates introduces the dead philosophers as new divinities. *[243]*

d   Socrates has brought up his Theseus from Hades. *[243]*

I MÝTHOS
A

". . . Socrates begins most of his investigations not at the center but at the periphery. . . ."

At the center of Plato's second longest dialogue, the *Constitution* (*Politeía*), usually called the *Republic,* there is an *érgon*, a deed or accomplishment. In order to fix this center it is necessary to establish the periphery. The *Republic* is composed on the plan of concentric rings; the themes on the diameter reappear in reverse order as if they were reflected through a central axis. (See the diagram on the next page.) The outermost periphery is a setting of *myth*. A broad inner ring consists of the construction and destruction of the successive forms of a pattern city in "speech," *lógos*. The themes of this ring, for instance the attack on the poets, are also symmetrical with respect to the center. This center itself, clearly defined as such by the plan of the dialogue, presents the actual founding of a city "in deed" (*érgoi*). The *Republic,* as will be shown, exemplifies the insight quoted above, which Søren Kierkegaard expressed in his dissertation *The Concept of Irony, With Constant Reference to Socrates* ("Plato").

B

Anyone who has used an annotated edition of the *Republic*[1] will have read the curious anecdote told by Diogenes Laertius and

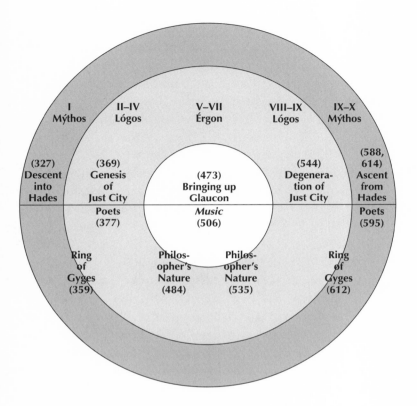

Dionysius of Halicarnassus about the beginning of the work. Dionysius reports that there were many current stories about the care Plato took to "comb and curl" his dialogues, especially one about a tablet found at his death, which contained "that beginning of the *Republic* which goes 'I went down yesterday to *Peiraeus* with Glaucon the son of Ariston,' transposed with subtle variety." We may infer that some special meaning was to be conveyed by the beginning. Indeed, there is something curious about its style: ancient as well as modern Athenians, when they visit their harbor, usually go not "to *Peiraeus*" but to *the Peiraeus* (e.g., Thucydides, VIII 92 9);[2] this is Cephalus's own usage (328 c 6), and since he lives there he ought to know. The phrase is to be heard in a special way. It happens that the Athenians did hear a certain meaning in this name—it meant the "beyond-land," *he Peraíe,* the land beyond the river that was once thought to have separated the Peiraic peninsula from Attica.³ Therefore let us try reading: "I descended yesterday to the land beyond the river, together with Glaucon, the son of Ariston . . ."; "in order to offer my devotions," he goes on, "to the goddess. . . ." The goddess, we learn at the end of the first book (354 a 11), is Bendis, a Thracian stranger identified with Hecate,⁴ the guardian deity of the underworld. Socrates is on his way back up to town when Polemarchus with his companions detains him and presses him to come to his house, where they find Cephalus, Polemarchus's rich old father, sitting in state. He is on that "threshold [to Hades] which is old age" (328 e 6).⁵ As he himself explains, he scarcely has a body anymore; he is, as his name signifies, a mere "head"—as Socrates slyly points out, he sits on a head-rest, a *proskephálaion* (328 c 1). His wealth, his *ploútos* (331 b 7), Socrates suspects, is his great comfort. A strange light is thrown on him and his house by an ancient source that reports that he was over thirty years dead at the dramatic date of the dialogue, which is between 411 and 405 B.C.; his son himself has only a few more years to live before his death at the hands of the Thirty Tyrants.⁶ *We are in the city of shades,* in the house of Pluto.

1   What is Socrates' business down there? To detect the myth that provides the venerable setting for Socrates' descent it is necessary to go somewhat far afield for a moment.

On certain occasions Socrates uses an oath that was evidently considered in antiquity to be his very own: "By the Dog!"—and in the *Gorgias* (482 b 5) more explicitly: "By the Dog, the Egyptian god!"⁷ Socrates utters the oath twice in the *Republic* and, as elsewhere, in passages concerned with the philosopher's part both in true speech and in politics (399 e 5, 592 a 7; cf. *Cratylus* 411 b 3). Who is the Egyptian dog-god on whom Socrates calls? Plutarch (*On Isis and Osiris* 368 e–f) describes him in this way: He is born of an underworld mother but nursed by a heavenly goddess and thus belongs to both these realms; he can see his way both by light and by dark and therefore has the office of mediating between the upper and the lower worlds. His Egyptian name is Anubis, but to the Greeks he is Hermes, the Interpreter, the "psychagogue" (cf. *Phaedrus* 271 c 10), who conducts the souls of the dead and guides those who must descend into Hades while yet alive (cf. Diogenes Laertius, VIII 31). He is also the bringer of political wisdom to men (*Protagoras* 322 c 2). In particular, Hermes is known as the guide of the hero Heracles in his famous descent into Hades (*Odyssey* XI 626), and he is often so represented on vases.

2   Heracles himself is a most versatile hero.[8] He is the chief founder of cities—witness the many cities called Heracleia. He is the great civilizer, "using music" (Plutarch, *On Music* XL 4), at which he is proficient, in this task. He is the guardian of boys' education, which takes place at the wrestling school, the *palaestra,* and the boys devote the cuttings of their hair to him. He teaches men letters; Plutarch jokingly calls him "most dialectical" (*The E at Delphi* 387 d). He is a partisan of virtue, having, according to a story told by Socrates (Xenophon, *Memorabilia* II i 21; cf. Plato, *Symposium* 177 b), chosen to follow Virtue rather than Vice as a teacher because of the happiness (*eudaimonía*) she had promised. But Heracles' greatest fame derives from the deeds or labors imposed on him by the unjust king Eurystheus. These include the killing of the snake-headed Hydra and of the Nemean Lion; his most awesome deed, however, is his descent, his *katábasis,* into Hades. His task there is to bring up to the light of day the triple monster Cerberus. He has Hades' permission to do this, but he is instructed to persuade the beast and make it more gentle, not to hurt it. On his way into Hades, so the story goes, he at first forgets his business and allows the shades to detain him in conversation. Before returning, he performs an incidental labor, a *párergon,* in releasing Theseus, his

emulator and the founder and lawgiver of Athens, who had been
chained down in Hades; however, he fails to free Theseus's companion Pirithous. While in Hades, Heracles is nearly washed
away by the underworld river.

This hero is, as it were, made for Socrates, and Socrates himself makes the comparison. In the *Apology,* speaking of his
search for a wise man, he says to the court: "And by the Dog,
men of Athens—for I must speak the truth to you— . . . those
who had the greatest reputation seemed to me nearly the most
deficient . . . , so I must show you how I wandered as if per-
forming certain labors . . ." (22 a 1). Every Athenian would of
course recognize the allusion to the labors of Heracles; most
translators put it into the text. In an interlude in the *Phaedo,* Socrates is called by Phaedo to take the role of Heracles in the battle of argument, with Phaedo taking the role of Iolaus, Heracles'
young friend (though Socrates playfully offers to reverse roles,
89 b–c). As they talk, Socrates plays with Phaedo's hair, which
he is soon to cut in mourning: as Heracles, the hair is his due,
and as Iolaus's friend, the intimacy is his right.

There are certain signs and indications that Socrates plays
this same role in the *Republic.* He "descends" to the land beyond, is caught in conversation in the house of Pluto, and, like
the phantom Heracles whom Odysseus meets on his own visit
to the shades—the true Heracles is among the gods (*Odyssey* XI
601)—he tells down there the story of his own descent. He
fights, moreover, the sophist Thrasymachus, who comes at him
"like a beast" (336 b 5)[9] and with whom he says he would as
soon quibble as "shave a lion" (341 c 1). A little before, Thrasymachus, laughing *sardánion*—"like one doomed," as the scholiast explains the word—had addressed him: "O Heracles! This
is that wonted dissembling of Socrates" (377 a 4). This is, of
course, a popular exclamation of wonder, but it sounds almost
like the lion's roar of recognition; by the end of the first book
the lion is subdued. And at one point, Socrates refers to the

wrong way to kill the Hydra, implying that he knows the better way (426 e 8).

3–4   But the longest labor begins after the "prelude" (357 a 2) of the first book.[10] In the nine books following, the running motif will be that old Heraclean theme, the relation of virtue to happiness, which is ever recalled, even in the midst of yet greater matters that are curtailed in its favor (e.g., 445 a, 580 b, 608 c); this relation is to be examined in a man who is wearing the Ring of Gyges (359 d 1), and as Socrates adds, the Helmet of Hades too (612 b 5), a magic cap that makes him invisible, stripping him of appearance and reputation and putting him in life on a level with the bare souls in Hades (cf. *Gorgias* 523 c). In the course of this argument Socrates will indeed teach his audience letters, using the great text of the city to teach them the small letters of the soul (368 d, cf. 402 a 7). He will also, as we shall see, found a city. He will face drowning (473 b). By the "soul-conducting" (*psychagogía*) of his rhetorical music (*Phaedrus* 261 a; Aristophanes, *Birds* 1555[11]) he will release his Theseus, blamelessly confined to Hades (391 c 9). But his longest effort will drag to light a triple monster having, like Cerberus himself, a bush of snakes for its lower part (590 b 1). For when he has plumbed in argument the remote depths of the tyrant's life, Socrates recalls once more "those first words because of which we are here" (588 b 2), namely Thrasymachus's claim that injustice under the reputation of justice is profitable. To conclude the case against him they "model an image of the soul in words" (588 b 10). It will, Socrates says, be a creature such as is found in ancient myth, a Chimaera or Scylla or a *Cerberus,* whose nature it is to have "many forms grown together into one" (588 c 4) under the outward guise of a man's shape. When this soul has been hauled up and cleansed of its accretions (611), the argument in defense of unrewarded justice is complete. Heracles has dragged forth the soul-monster from Hades; he has accom-

plished that exposure of human nature which is the first condition of its reform. And he has, incidentally, brought up a young
Theseus (the name connotes *nomothesía,* law-giving)—Plato's
brother, Glaucon, who is helping Socrates found his city.

Having ceased to enact a myth, Socrates closes the dialogue
by telling one, a recollection of one of the "myths which are told
about those in Hades." These are the very myths that keep tor-
menting Cephalus, because he is so close to death (330 d 7). In
it Er, of the clan of Pamphylos or "Every tribe" (614 b 4), is
charged by the souls to carry back to the living the long tale of
their thousand-year journey, of the ascent or descent that is their
reward or punishment. He actually tells only of the *end* of these
journeys, since, as Socrates significantly observes to Glaucon,
who has now listened the better part of a day and a night, the
story itself would take "a very long time to go through" (615
a 5). Socrates ends the dialogue by urging Glaucon to hold fast
to the "upward way" (cf. 514 b 4), so that they may do well in
the thousand-year journey "which we have just gone through"
(621 d 2). He must mean the ascent of the dialogue itself (e.g.,
473 a 5, 544 b 2).

This then is the setting of the *Republic:* Hades with its tales
and a deliverer willing to go down and able to come up—a most
appropriate setting, for down there, so it is said, justice is close
at hand (330 d 8, 614 c 3; cf. *Apology* 41 a; *Gorgias* 523; Sophocles, *Antigone* 451). In recounting the discourse Socrates will
then be playing that "noblest of games": "telling myths about
justice and other things" (*Phaedrus* 276 e).

II LÓGOS
A
We come now to the arguments, the *lógoi,* that form the broad
middle ring encircling the center. Just as the question concerning the connection of justice to happiness is answered by bringing to light the human soul in its mythical shape, so the soul itself, that is, its formal "constitution," is discovered by raising

and taking down cities. This is done "in speech" (*lógoi*) and not, to use a pervasive Greek opposition, "in deed" (*érgoi*, e.g., 382 e 8, 383 a 5, 498 e 4; cf. *Laws* 778 b). Let us first follow how these cities are constructed in argument.

At the beginning of the enterprise Socrates says: "Come then, let us make a city from the beginning *in argument*" (*lógoi*, 369 c 9, cf. also 369 a 5, 472 e 1, 592 a 11). The object is to find the nature of justice by looking at the largest human context to which it is applicable—hence the city founded in speech will have to be just. Socrates and his interlocutors first found a community of craftsmen, workers collected to ply their own trades so as to supply each other's wants, making the city as a whole (as opposed to its individual citizens) self-sufficient (369 b). In this city the full political weight of the Greek name for craftsmen, *demiourgoí* (370 d 6), "public workers," is realized. This city is, as we shall see, the most literal model for reading off the definition of justice that runs through the *Republic,* but just as Socrates is about to articulate that definition, Glaucon stops him. Here, he says, we have a city of pigs (372 d 4). He means that the citizens' whole being, like that of pigs, is absorbed in consuming and providing for consumption—there is no place or leisure for honor and nobility (cf. Aristotle, *Politics* 1291 a 18). Socrates, though still maintaining that this is the "true" and "healthy" city (372 e 6), yields to Glaucon, and giving up once and for all that self-sufficiency definitive of the natural city (*Politics* 1253 a 2), changes the "first city" (373 c 5; *Politics* 1291 a 17) by the addition of luxury and that soldier element which will procure wealth and maintain safety. He assents to the construction of this "fevered" city because in it one might see "how justice *and* injustice grow up in cities" (372 e 5); this city, then, will somehow contain the seeds of injustice also. He describes the natures and the training of the soldiers or "guardians," a subject to which we must return. At the end of this long argument (375–414) Socrates again reorganizes the city, this time by dividing the "guardians" into guardians proper, older men who

rule, and their "auxiliaries and helpers" (414 b 5), the younger
fighting men. This third, tripartite, city suffices for reading off
a similarly constituted soul and for showing conclusively that,
as in the city, so in the soul, justice will be profitable. Socrates
now considers the positive half of his task finished and is about
to go on to investigate how injustice comes about in cities and
souls (445–449, Book IV). He is interrupted. Three whole books
(V–VII) intervene, in which a fourth and very different city is
founded. Not until Book VIII does he return to the argument.
In Glaucon's figure, "like a wrestler he assumes again the same
position" (544 b 5) and goes on to account in order for the four
degenerate cities (544–592). When this argument, the complement to the genesis of cities, is finished, Glaucon once again
refers to "the city that we have just been founding and that is
preserved in speech only, for I do not think that it is anywhere
on earth" (592 a 10).

B

1 What is the meaning of the claim that the genesis of the
city, or the city itself, is only "in speech"? It means of course first
of all that no actual city of living men comes into being while
they speak or as a consequence of their discourse. But that is
mere fact. What is more interesting is that no such city *can* come
to be now or later, *by the design and intent of the argument itself.* These word constructions are not "constitutions," the practical patterns for working cities such as Plato and his pupils were
invited to write for Greek cities, nor are they even a model for
such patterns—they are instead contrivances for a different purpose, and intended to reveal themselves as such.[12] The dialogue
conveys this first of all in one significant fact: In the first generation no human being is *native to* or is *born into* any of the three
cities as people are in real cities that adopt a new constitution.
These cities do not, in the beginning, generate their own popu-
lations in a natural way; they are artificially constructed.

The first city is constituted by the collection, the second by
the addition, the third by the division of adults who are all of

one and the same generation; the institution of each city is simply the rearrangement of ready-made human material. This is reflected in the actual physical settlement of the third city, which is, at first, said to begin with the *separate encampment* of the guardians, who found, as it were, a separate city (415 d 8, *Critias* 110 c 6; *Politics* 1264 a 25 ff.). Hence the guardians' progeny will be born, quite literally, outside of the civilian city. Furthermore, this same third city first founded by *separation* is later said to be settled by the *expulsion* of all souls over ten years old (540 e 5), a contradiction that reflects the two irreconcilable geneses of the just city; in the books of the *Republic* relevant to the present context the city is understood as a planned re-constitution of available communities, while after the central books it is a radically new institution demanding a radical change in the character of citizens, to be achieved only by a lengthy process of education; it is a city essentially of children.

Now the re-constitution that in the early books brings about the third or guardian city, the city of separation, is secured by the circulation of one "noble lie," the "Phoenician myth," "our trick," which will persuade "especially the rulers themselves, and if not them, the rest of the city" (414 c 1). To be sure, as Socrates later admits, the founding generation itself can never be brought to believe the story, but he dismisses this crucial difficulty by high-handedly treating these citizens as the creatures of this argument that they indeed are: "Let this matter be left to rumor to carry about as best it can, while we arm our earthborn and lead them forth, under the leadership of their rulers" (415 d 6). Suppose then that the founding of this city of earthborn, parentless offspring was somehow accomplished because the myth had been somehow in practice accepted. The new citizens would now believe what the myth says, that their youth and education was a dream; that they were really formed like metals in the womb of the earth, their mother, who sent them up fully formed, so that they had never been infants; and that they are therefore all brothers, though of different metals. Those who have an admixture of gold must rule and those of silver must assist, for, as an oracle foretells, the city will fall when a man of brass or iron rules. The purity of the metals must be carefully preserved, and if a gold or silver parent has a child with an admixture of brass or iron he must consent to see it put into a lower class. That the earth is the common mother of citizens who are autochthonous, that is, "born of the land itself," is an old patriotic theme, and betokens their equality (*Menexenus* 237 c, 239 a). Socrates has put it to a radically new hierarchical use.

The "lie" in this myth of non-genetic inequality is not that men are of different metals or that the city cannot survive the wrong kind of ruler—all that might be true—but rather the claim that the citizens have no proper natural birth and no privacy, that is, no secrecy of soul. Under their flattering epithet "earthborn" (415 d 7), which intimates that they are Giants, or that they were molded by a god, are hidden the claims that they are elemental bastards of a sort, who have the earth as mother but no father, and that their soul can be accurately assayed like any mined ore. So too the continuation of the city depends on the citizens' belief that each generation is newly mined, like a public treasure,[13] from the earthly element on which the city rests.

But the curious character of this "needful lie" (414 b 9) is that it catches up, so to speak, with its perpetrators: the myth must not only somehow be *believed* at the outset if the city is to be founded, but *it ought in fact not to be a lie at all,* if the city is to breed true. For if men are *not* born from a common parent at the right time and with pure souls easily assayed, the guardians cannot control the new generation and insure the stability of the city. Its first natural birth will refute its foundations.

2   The scandalous institution of the community (*koinonía*) of women and children, the "source of the greatest good to the city" (464 b 5), is intended to achieve exactly this community of birth. All children born in the same year are to be ignorant of their parents and are to be called brothers and sisters, although such ignorance is likely eventually to lead to incest (461 e 2; Aristotle, *Politics* 1262 a 35). These children of the city will be tested and assayed all the time, but one of the conditions for stability is beyond the guardians' control: the timing of the mating. For as Glaucon wisely observes, the best are drawn by necessity to have intercourse with the best, but this necessity is "not geometric but erotic," that is, not rational but dictated by passion (458 d 5). Yet the guardians' control of breeding needs to be precisely "geometric." The Phoenician myth, in accordance with Phoenician greed (436 a 2), makes of men a Plutonic treasure to be dug up and refined at will; the scientific counterpart of the myth is to consider them a crop to be scientifically sown and harvested in accordance with the mathematical heavenly motions.

The geometry of these motions and their numbers as they affect breeding is, however, *not known* to the rulers. In Book VIII Socrates has just resumed the discussion of the degenerate cities, when he stops himself and prays to the Muses to tell him "how discord first arose," an allusion to the beginning of the *Iliad* (I 6) and the fall of the city of Troy. The Muses' response is a mathematical myth. A city so constituted as his, they say, can hardly be moved (546 a 1), but since everything that has a genesis also has a degeneration, this city too will not last forever. Note that in the order of argument the decline in fact follows immediately upon the beginning, with no account of the city's life and history intervening at all. This end must come (and may, as Aristotle points out, come on the day after the city's artificial birth, *Politics* 1316 a 17) because the rulers' reasoning, or rather their "calculating power, mixed with sense" as it is (b 1), will not be able to apprehend the "geometric number" that governs births. The Muses recite this fabulous number, which in fact no one has ever practically understood. Thus the generation of rulers is corrupted, and as a final consequence of their baser metal they neglect the study of "music" and themselves lose the power of testing souls. This is the *genetic* revolution that initiates the declining succession of Hesiod's ages from gold down to iron, a revolution radically different from the *political* revolutions the city undergoes thereafter (*Politics* 1316 a 14 ff.).

Human generation is thus an impenetrable mystery, and the city founders on the rock of the fact of bisexual generation. The human being, considered as the unstable union of body and soul, does not run *true to type* as does a plant (and, as Aristotle observes, where a child does resemble its parent in looks, that very fact immediately destroys the founding illusion of common birth, *Politics* 1262 a). If it is the nature of each kind to generate its like, human nature is un-natural; dwarf peas always bear dwarf peas, but golden parents may bear brass children. This is the insuperable problem that is again attacked in the *Statesman.* In this dialogue the Golden Age, the age of the direct divine rule of Cronos, is mockingly characterized by the fact that men grow directly from the earth and have no human birth (271), while in the Human Age the proper mixing of human "bents" (*trópoi*) by mating is the specifically human object of the political art (310). Later on Socrates quotes an old phrase[14] to emphasize the human geneses that will shape the city: "You do not think," he says, "that constitutions come out of 'an oak or a rock' and not out of the characters of those in the city?" (544 d 8). Very nearly the same figure is used by Vergil for the human race of the Golden Age of Saturn; they are indeed sprung from "trunks of trees or a rugged oak" (*Aeneid* VIII, 315); in the pre-political Golden Age men do spring up "naturally," according to their kind, like vegetables, and ripen backwards to ineducable childhood.

The dialogue itself tacitly underscores the impossibility of genetic control, both at the very beginning and at the end. For of those said to be present in Cephalus's house, five are full brothers; two of them, Glaucon and Adeimantus, are the sons of Ariston, and the three others, Polemarchus, Lysias, and Euthydemus, are the host's sons. The conversation itself will show how the sons of the "Best" (the meaning of "Ariston"—Socrates often alludes to the meaning of the father's name, e.g., 327 a 1, 368 a 4) differ profoundly from each other; something similar was known of the merchant Polemarchus and the orator Lysias (*Phaedrus* 257 b). The Myth of Er, moreover, which concludes the conversation, shows why generation is intractable; human natures are ultimately determined not on the hither side of life by other humans, but in the "divine place" beyond by each soul for itself (617 d 6). The coming to be of the city is therefore not in accord with the coming to be of human beings.

The enigma of reproductive generation is, however, secondary to the paradox of the city's foundation itself. For it seems that only those will be content to accept this constitution who have accepted the "dye" of its laws (430 a 3). The just city can only be realized by its own children: To begin it must already have begun. We see why the act of settlement itself is so curiously and doubly contrived. At one time, as was said, it seems to amount to the separation of those adults who might be fit to govern and who establish the ideal city by leaving the real city. But at another time the new city results from the removal of all adults whatsoever so that Socrates appears to found a city of children. This confusion corroborates the claim that the three cities that have been constructed are cities "in speech" only, not working plans for real communities.

3   The degenerate cities that are symmetrical with these three cities are, on the other hand, all too realizable—indeed, they exist. Socrates underscores this by mentioning, in this context alone, actual Greek cities, namely Crete and Sparta, the timocracies, where honor rules, as it does in the first of the less-than-just cities (544 c 3); the Athenian democracy needs no naming. Yet here too, in a different way, the argument is remote from the deed.

The argument to which Socrates returns in the eighth book had been merely initiated at the end of the fourth. Of the five bents (*trópoi*) of the soul, one alone is good while the other four illustrate the multifariousness of evil; to these latter correspond four cities. The interlocutors have "so far ascended in argument" (445 c 5) as to stand on a look-out tower whence to view the multiplicity of vice. This discussion of vice, when picked up three books later (544), continues to rise until, having traversed timocracy, oligarcy, and democracy, the interlocutors finally look down on the sinkhole of tyranny and the abyss of the tyrant's misery, an abyss which is 729 days, that is, two years of continual travel, beneath them (587 e). This is what should characterize all serious discussions of vice: They must certainly not bring about that of which they speak, but must become more detached from the matter the closer they come to its truth, just as the best judge of criminals should have the least experience of crime (409 a). The effect of this deliberate remoteness on the argument itself is that the degeneration of cities is presented schematically as an inevitable, irresistible, downward progression (which Aristotle finds implausible, *Politics* 1316 a 20 ff.), not so much of the natures as of the nurtures of successive generations. Here the argument represents, as it were, its own impotence to prevent evil. The situation is in fact quite desperate (*Seventh Letter* 325 d ff.); in a few years a fierce battle between the democratic faction and not one but Thirty Tyrants will be raging about the sanctuary of the very goddess whose feast is now being celebrated (Xenophon, *Hellenica* II 4, 11), and the tyranny will have destroyed the host's family; while yet a few years later a temporarily restored democracy will have killed Socrates (399 B.C.).

C

1 The facts of the host family's condition and politics determine the conversation in yet another pervasive way. The family ran a prosperous business in manufacturing and selling shields, and both Polemarchus and Lysias are known to have been de-

mocrats, though, we may suppose, of a decent and moderate sort. This is the clue to the peculiar treatment of the virtue that later gave the subtitle "On Justice" to the dialogue. It is not usually Socrates' way to inquire whether a thing is profitable or unprofitable before having inquired "what it is" (e.g., *Republic* 354 c, *Meno* 71 b, though see p. 85); but this is just what happens with respect to justice in the *Republic*. From the second book to the end the question is: Is justice profitable? The knowledge of what justice *is,* is really assumed. As Socrates, somewhat to Glaucon's annoyance, insists (432 e 8), when they come to find justice in the city they have constructed, they find there nothing more than they put in; the city is just because they have made it that way (433 a 1, 443 b 7). The working definition, which is not the *result* but the *assumption* of the argument, is that justice is "doing one's own business and not meddling" (433 a 8), a definition they have heard from many others and have themselves often given.

Justice so conceived is, to begin with, simply the negating opposite of the literal understanding of the names for various degrees of wrong-doing. There is *polypragmoneúein* (433 a 9, 443 d 2, 444 b 2), literally "engaging in many affairs" or being a meddling busybody, and *pánta poieín* (596 c 2), "doing everything" or being a jack-of-all-trades—Socrates' favorite description of the sophists' easy expertise (cf. 397, 596; cf. *Sophist* 233 d 9). And worst of all, there is *panourgeín* (409 c 5), "all-working" or being up to anything, simple shameless wickedness. It is the behavior of the man who takes full advantage of the impunity given by Adeimantus's Ring of Gyges, a man who has the wily Odyssean wisdom of the man of "many bents" (*Lesser Hippias* 365 e 2; cf. *Phaedrus* 271 c 2; the *Republic* cites both Odyssean virtues and vices). Positively, justice is acting in accordance with that conveniently ambiguous phrase *eu prattein,* either "doing right" or "being well," with which the *Republic* ends (463 e 4, 519 e 2, 621 d 2; cf. *Politics* 1323 b 31).

From this point of view the simply just city is, as Socrates himself says, the first, the self-sufficient city of "demiurges," the craftsmen who both know how to do their own business and do it (372 e 6, 428 b 12). In them virtue is indeed "wisdom," in the good old-fashioned sense in which *sophía* means what in English used to be meant by "cunning," namely craft and skill, and *areté* means the power to do work, the "virtue" of an effective agent (cf. 350 c 4, 353 e 1; cf. Aristotle, *Nicomachean Ethics* 1141 a 9).

We may well ask how a view so practical, almost banal, comes to underlie the dialogue. It is necessary here to recall that justice in the city is exposed by finding and analyzing out the other virtues of a good city and considering the remainder (427 e 13). Thus wisdom is found to be the rulers' virtue, courage that of the warriors, temperance the agreement of all on who shall rule (432 a). Justice is then found in each class as a residue. It is that virtue by which the class does its own work and nothing else. Clearly in this context temperance is somewhat redundant. In fact when Socrates turns from the city to the soul he makes no distinction between justice and temperance (443 d 4; compare *Laws* 696 d 11, where temperance is called a mere "appendage," and also *Charmides* 161 b 6, where Critias very knowingly, as he thinks, proposes the present definition of justice as a definition of temperance; see ch. 4). We may therefore say that justice, precisely because it is the one virtue that *all* three classes possess, stands out as a virtue unique and special to the craftsmen, "the popular and citizen virtue" (*Phaedo* 82 a 11), the practical virtue of non-rulers. (In fact it is pointed out in the *Statesman* [307 e] that rulers who possess this virtue too literally endanger the city.) It is the virtue by reason of which each performs "that to which his own nature is most fitted" (*Republic* 433 a 5), by which, we might say, a human being is ever at his best. In some cases this means quite simply quietly "minding one's own business," as must the lover of wisdom, for instance, in a city not fitted to his nature (496 d 6, *Gorgias* 526 c 4). Justice might therefore be termed the *private* public virtue, which turns *particular* natures to the general account (423 d). This is why its presence is the greatest good and its absence the greatest ruin to cities (443 c 4–444 b 8). It allows the city to assimilate even those men who are by nature private. Hegel, in his interpretation of the *Republic,* which is in this point the opposite of Aristotle's, understands and appreciates justice in precisely such terms, namely as the integration of the particular as particular, the confirmation of the individual in the Whole, "the being-for-itself of each part" (*History of Philosophy* pt. 1, ch. 3).

This virtue, understood not as a relation toward others but as decently self-serving self-respect, is therefore quite naturally discussed in just these terms under the roof of the kind of people who would constitute the multitude of the third city, the merchant and artisan class. This class would supply young warriors like the sons of Ariston with their armor and might occasionally send a philosophically disposed son like Polemarchus (cf. *Phaedrus* 257 b 4) up into the ruling class—though perhaps not his rhetorician-brother, Lysias. Socrates is speaking that politically saving "dialect of democracy" (*Fifth Letter* 321 d), which many people think they know but very few really master.

2   But Socrates never allows us to forget that this third, this guardian city is a dialogical phantom and that the justice in it is, for all its apparent practicality, a mere "idol" (443 c 4). For the true virtue lies, Socrates thinks, not in deeds concerned with the outside but in the inner disposition of "classes" (*géne,* d 3) of the soul and their ordering, the psychic constitution. We shall see that in the case of the true ruler, that is, of one so constituted as to be able first of all to rule himself, the distinction between "his own affairs" and "others' business" vanishes. For him that which is most common is also most his own "and with his private affairs he will preserve the common business" (497 a 5). In him, "doing his own business" will be turned into "knowing himself," which means "looking . . . at myself, whether I happen to be some beast more complicated than Typhon [Cerberus's father, *Theogony* 311] or a gentler and simpler animal" (*Phaedrus* 230 a; cf. *Timaeus* 72 a 5). True justice is concerned with that in man which is "truly about himself and his own business" (443 d 1; cf. *Alcibiades Major* 130 e ff.); the true ruler knows not only *that* he should do his own business but *what* it is. In Aristotelian terms, the practical or moral virtue turns into an intellectual one; in comparison with which the old justice is "somehow near to the body" (518 d 10). This individual character of justice is one of the reasons why, as we shall see below, the soul is the one and only subject of the dialectical method in the *Republic*.

3 For the true ruler, the philosopher king, the hope that justice might be conducive to happiness fails. This fact leads to a curious suspension of the main argument in the central three books. If justice can only with difficulty be proved to be profitable for the class of guardian rulers, because of the hard life they lead (419 a, 465 e 4), for the individual philosopher king, the ruler of rulers, this proof is altogether impossible. For those who already consider themselves to be living in the Isles of the Blessed (519 c 5), the descent into the city to take office cannot be made to seem like happiness (519 d 8), nor can it possibly improve the tone of their souls. They must be made to enter politics "forcibly" (520 e 2); in fact their reluctance is a guarantee of their suitability (e 4). Glaucon sees immediately that the main aim of the city constructions that constitute the outer rings of the argument, namely the proof that justice brings happiness—an argument still staunchly maintained for the warriors (466 b)—has been lost; he wants to know if the philosopher rulers are not being treated unjustly (519 d 8). Socrates' answer is an evasion (cf. *Politics* 1264 b 16); it is not their happiness but that of the whole city which is to be considered. When all is said and

done, the rulers at the apex of the *Republic* enter politics only out of pity, gratitude, and simple decency (516 c, 520 a–e).

III ÉRGON
A

1   Socrates is about to go on with the investigation of the unjust cities when he is again restrained, as once before on his way up to Athens (327), by a conspiracy of Polemarchus and Adeimantus (499). After some whispering a vote is taken, and the decree that has been passed is announced by Thrasymachus (450 a 3). Thrasymachus represents that "force" (*Phaedrus* 267 c 8) which boasts of its ability to rouse and soothe the multitude (though it is itself managed by Socrates) and now speaks for them: Socrates must expand and defend that principle, mentioned before with conspicuous brevity (424 a 1), which is to give the city both unanimity and a perfectly public character: "Friends own what is common" (499 c 5). Here is a new, a political reading of a common saying (cf. *Lysis* 207 c 10, *Phaedrus* 276 c 6, *Laws* 739 c 2), which may mean, significantly, two things: "What a friend owns is at the service of his friends," or "What friends own insofar as they are friends is communal by nature." They all particularly want to know about the equality of education for men and women (451 b) and the community of wives and children (457 b). Socrates reluctantly complies and faces the first two of the three waves threatening to overwhelm him (473 b 6).

When he has faced the flood, and gone on to describe such a city's relation to other Greek cities, Glaucon erupts: "But it seems to me, Socrates, that if one were to allow you to talk about such matters you would *never* remember what it is you pushed aside in saying all this, namely this question: *Is such a constitution capable of coming into being and in what way is it possible?*" (471 c). And he insists on this question even though Socrates stalls by getting him to admit that the object of their discourse was the discovery of justice and injustice and their respective merits, and that the "city in speech," having served that purpose, is none the worse for being impractical (473 a 1). But since Glaucon does insist (understandably, we cannot help feeling) on trying out their just constitution as a practical political pattern, he must not, Socrates stipulates, force him to show that "what they went through in speech can completely be in deed"; Glaucon must content himself with as close an approximation as is possible (a 5). This approximation will be reached by making the least possible number of changes to improve things now done badly in cities, changes that will effect a re-founding of a city in accordance with the constitution just discussed. There may be one or two or more such changes, but in any case there should be as few as possible (b 4).

So Socrates, like Odysseus, meets that third wave which will carry him to his Phaeacia (*Odyssey* V 313, 425). The *one* thing that must be changed, he announces solemnly, is this:

> Unless either philosophers rule in the cities, or those who are now called kings and dynasts philosophize genuinely and sufficiently, and these two—namely political power and philosophy—coincide, and the many natures of those who now pursue either way separately have been excluded by the force of necessity, there can be no end of evils, my dear Glaucon, in cities, or, in my opinion, in the human race (473 c 11).

He adds that he cannot see how any other city can be happy in public or in private.

Together with Glaucon he now prepares the ground for a new, a fourth, city. It is necessary to show why this "one change" may be said to produce a new city; is it not merely the third, the guardian constitution, put into effect? Both Socrates and Glaucon, at least, do seem to regard these two as different; Socrates calls the guardian city, as opposed to the fourth city, "the first selection" merely (536 c 8), and Glaucon refers to the new city as the better of the two (543 d 1). And rightly so, for as Socrates himself says, an actual city is never the same as its pattern, its *parádeigma* (472 d 9, 473 a). The guardian city and the philosopher city differ, then, as does a pattern from its institution. For although the warrior city has some features of the real Sparta, its radical features require a novel Lycurgus, a philosophical founder. The discourse on the possible city will be, among other things, a subtle consideration of the relation of pattern to effect, of theory to practice. In its course that which makes the pattern possible will prove to be that which makes it superfluous: the fourth or philosopher city will have no constitution separable from its philosophically guided life.

2   The philosopher kings, to pursue the difference between the cities further, can certainly not be regarded as part of the constitution of that just city which must have been known generally as "Socrates' city." Aristotle, in his critique of what "Socrates says" in the *Republic,* mentions the warrior class and the community of women, children, and goods, but omits all mention of the philosopher kings (*Politics* 1291 a 20, 1261 a 4). Aristophanes, too, in *The Female Parliament* (427), where the community of goods and women becomes the law of Athens, fails to seize the comic opportunity inherent in the subject of female philosophers. It is likely that this play was written before the *Republic,* but we may infer that people—Socrates in particular—had long been talking about such a city. In the dialogue there are enough passages parallel to the play to constitute an acknowledgment to posterity that Aristophanes' women's city is a parody of Socrates' already notorious city.[15] In fact the nod to the comedian is explicit, for, in facing his first wave, Socrates remarks that after the men's part has been played out it is only right to recite "the women's drama" (451 c 2); moreover, in going to meet his third wave he says, as if speaking from a familiar experience, that "it might overwhelm him with laughter and disrepute" (473 c 8); it is the philosopher kings who are the real news of the dialogue.

3   The most weighty evidence that the guardian city is not
identical with the philosopher city is the account Socrates himself gives of his city in the *Timaeus* when he recapitulates the
constitution that he had presented to his friends in a discourse
on the previous day. There is no reason to conclude that the dialogue *Republic* is that discourse. In fact while the *Republic* is
recounted on the day after the Bendideia, the *Timaeus,* very appropriately for a prologue to the praise of antique Athens, takes
place on the Lesser Panathenaea, a festival that occurred two
months later, also in the Piraeus (26 e); during the festival a
gown was sent up to Athena "on which the Athenians, her nurs-
lings, could be seen winning the war against the people of Atlantis" (scholiast on *Republic* 327 a; Atlantis is the subject of the
continuation of the *Timaeus,* the *Critias*). Furthermore, the dramatic year of the *Timaeus* seems to be earlier than that of the
Republic.[16] The city Socrates recapitulates in the *Timaeus* is,
dates apart, not the city of the central books of the *Republic,* for
although his account is said to be complete (19 a 7), there are
no philosopher kings. It is rather the third city, the guardian city
with all its notorious features that he sketches. We may infer
that Socrates proposed this city on various occasions and that
it was known as *his* city.

This guardian city therefore differs from the philosopher city
as the best pattern differs from its actual realization, as the impossible differs from the possible. Socrates himself explains to
Adeimantus, when he asks whether this guardian city they have
founded is the city suited to philosophy, that it *is* that city in
many ways but that in addition there "would always be needed
someone who had understanding of the reasoning [*lógos*] behind
the constitution—that same one who guided you when as a law-
giver you laid down the laws" (497 c 8). The difference between
the cities is therefore not constitutional, for the older guardians
will still rule, and rule so as to achieve the most harmonious
community possible. The difference is rather in the rulers themselves, in what they know and in what they will look to, in their

education. We shall see whether this may not outweigh any even more externally obvious formal difference.

B

1 The claim is, however, not merely that the fourth city is a possible city. It is something much more dramatic: that it is *actual,* that it comes into being while Glaucon and Socrates converse, that it is in fact a city "in deed," *érgoi.* This could happen only if one paradoxical condition were fulfilled: If there were some one adult who actually lives in the just city, and who, as a living citizen of the city, can bring up another within it and so initiate the "cycle" (424 a 5) of the reciprocating interplay between the citizens' education and their nature. This founder must be a first citizen not only in the sense that he possesses what Socrates calls "the constitution within himself" (591 e 1, 608 b 1) but also in the sense that he has such external relations—natural, as we shall see, to any truly educated human being (423 e 4)—as correspond with the constitution of the third, the fully differentiated just city, and its actualized version, the fourth or the "possible" city.[17] What would such a life and such a man look like?

To begin with, he would have to be brave and a soldier proven in battle, who put the safety of his comrades before his own (*Apology* 28 e, *Symposium* 220 d 5), past the age of fighting and over fifty years old (cf. *Republic* 540 a 4; Socrates is about sixty), but still spirited in the defense of philosophy (*Republic* 536 c 4), which he had steadily pursued from an early youth (*Parmenides* 130 b) to old age. He would have no private possessions (*Republic* 337 d 8, *Apology* 31 c 2), but would live with his friends as if all their goods were held in common (*Apology* 38 b 6, *Crito* 44 e, *Republic* 337 d 10). He would regard all promising young men as his sons to the neglect of his private family, and they would regard him as a father (*Apology* 31 b 4, *Phaedo* 60 a 7, 116 a 6). When he wished he would possess the persuasiveness to make gentler the enemies of philosophy so that they would accept its rule (*Republic* 354). He would be able to ascend in thought above the city, leaving his body behind (*Symposium* 174 d 5, 220 c 3). He would on occasion be willing, though not eager, to undertake political tasks (*Republic* 327, *Apology* 31 c). He would regard it as part of his charge to select and educate the best among the young for future rule, and he would prevent them from reaching too high too fast (*Republic* 506 d 7, 533 a 1). Finally, he would possess some special quality that would hold him to philosophy and protect him from corruption (496 c 4). Such a man would fulfill Socrates' last words concerning the possibility of the city, for, *without caring in the least whether she is or ever will be in fact,* "*he will do her business and that of no other*" (592 b 3).

The references after each statement above give passages in the Platonic dialogues where Socrates is so described. *He is a man,* the dialogues assert, *who is here and now doing the business of the just city.* Thus we see that the sum of Aristotle's criticism of Socrates' city, that its communality is really not the bond uniting a multitude but rather the bond of each good man with every other (*Politics* 1263 a 29), is deeply accurate, and what is more, that Aristotle's politics are ultimately not so very different: "Friendship seems to hold cities together; and lawgivers care more for it than for justice" (*Nicomachean Ethics* 1155 a 23). The reason that the corporate genesis of the third, the guardian city, is presented as an insurmountable dilemma is that that city was never meant to be a self-sufficient body politic, nor, for that matter, a single soul writ large, but something *between* these—*that set of relations,* correctly called friendship, which is essentially political (as we shall see) and which *a philosopher institutes between himself and his fellow-citizens whenever he is able.* When this kind of man comes to power, "our constitution, which we have told as a myth in speech, will achieve its consummation in deed" (501 e 4). As we shall see, Socrates *is* in power.

2   In the same way we must look at the nature and condition of the youth whom he will educate to be a helper and auxiliary first and later a successor and ruler. He will be a young man
of twenty (537 b 8), markedly spirited (357 a 3, 441 a 2, 548 d
9), and with some experience in soldiering, open to the influence
of music and with a strong bent toward mathematics. Now this
is a picture of Glaucon, "erotic" like Socrates himself (474 d 4;
cf. *Symposium* 177 d 8), a young man of about twenty, whose
manly courage and desire for victory are emphasized together
with his receptivity to music (548 e 5); he has already distinguished himself in battle (368 a 3), is delighted by mathematics
(528 e 7, 531 a 3), and is the son of the "Best." He is therefore
quite right to offer himself as a "helper" (474 b 1, cf. the
"helpers" of the guardian city, 414 b 5) and to say that "perhaps I could answer more fitly than another," for he is the reason why Socrates is taking so much trouble on himself (474 a
5); he is "responsible" (509 c 3) for Socrates' overcoming his reluctance to speak on the highest matters. And we must not forget that as the dialogue closes Socrates speaks to Glaucon—and
him alone—of the "upward road" as if they were again all by
themselves, as they had been when they "came down" at the beginning.

There is some additional evidence in favor of Glaucon as a
prospective ruler. Xenophon (*Memorabilia* III vi) recounts a
conversation in which Socrates persuades Glaucon, who is less
than twenty years old and wants to become head of state immediately, that he knows nothing of statecraft, nothing of rev-
enues, and nothing of military management, and that he should
perhaps first learn something about these subjects. Socrates,
Xenophon says, took an interest in Glaucon "for the sake of
Plato and Charmides"; he alone succeeded where everyone had
failed, and persuaded Glaucon to restrain his ambitions until he
should have become competent enough not to make a fool of
himself. We see that Glaucon must in fact have been very inter-

ested in politics and that Socrates was known to have been interested in him. The *Republic* even contains the counterpart in the Platonic mode of the Xenophontic dissuasion: Glaucon is persuaded that the mark of the true ruler is that he has no ambition to rule and despises the "political life"—the subtlest possible deterrent for a proud young man (520 e 4 ff.). Beyond this Glaucon's name had for Plato the tremendous advantage that unlike that of Critias and Charmides it was not tainted with political crimes. He may have died in middle age (he appears in the *Parmenides* when he is in his mid-forties). Scarcely anything else is known of him, except that he wrote dialogues (Diogenes Laertius, II 124)—and was Plato's brother. Perhaps his obscurity is actually a sign that Socrates succeeded with him more than with those notorious evil-doers—Charmides, Critias, Alcibiades—with whom he had sometimes talked in their youth.

3   The philosopher's city is coming into being while Socrates and Glaucon converse: *The primary political act is the "conversion" to a philosophical education of one youth by one man.* Because he engages in this kind of activity, Socrates can maintain in one and the same dialogue (*Gorgias* 473 e 6, 521 d 6) that he is not one of the "political men" and that he alone in Athens practices the "truly political art." Plato's own activities were in accordance with this principle (*Seventh Letter* 326 b ff.). The contrived *bodily* community of the guardian city (416 d) is here converted into a natural *dialogic* community. This is by nature a community of two; throughout the dialogue Socrates has *one* interlocutor, and when another enters, it is by way of interruption (e.g., 449 b 1, 487 b 1; cf. *Gorgias* 474 a). But minimal as it is, it is a true community as opposed to the artificial unity of the guardian city. For the latter is an artificially composed harmony of "one *out of* many" (423 d 6, 443 e 1), in musical terminology a *diapason,* the concord of the octave that goes "through all" the different tones. But it has no one natural source and indeed no discernible end beyond *subsisting* as a

unity. There is, as we shall see, no *eídos,* no idea of a city, while the community that underlies dialogic communication is, on the contrary, precisely *eidetic* and, unlike the guardians' community of bodily goods (416 d), indestructible. For the *eídos* that underlies speech is not a delicate adjustment of "one out of many" in which the many constitute and enter into the unity, but an indivisible one "by itself" and opposed to, or rather, dominating, all multiplicity: The relation of many sensible things to their *eídos* is that of "many . . . *under* one idea" (*Republic* 507 b 6). The *eídos* is the "*common thing,*" the thing public by nature *that belongs to friends.* The foundation of the fourth city, the establishment of that *Politeía* which is indeed rightly translated by *Republic*—that is, *Commonwealth*—consists in beginning that dialogue with which any Western education, an education that is the making of a free citizen, ought to begin. We shall see exactly how Socrates goes about this founding act. As Rousseau *half*-truly observes in his *Émile,* "Plato's *Republic* . . . is not a political treatise, as those who merely judge books by their titles think. It is the finest treatise on education ever written."

Readers will have noticed that this interpretation of the ideal city as a dialogic community subverts the notion of its real institution. Not only do I doubt that Socrates wanted his guardian city realized, but I think he knew that his one practical proposal for its founding in reality was quite impractical: Neither would philosophers be accepted as or consent to be kings, nor would kings turn philosophical. That throws a strange light on Plato's post-*Republic* attempt to educate Dionysios II of Syracuse into philosophical kingship (*Seventh Letter*). It was as if Plato had gone to Sicily on a venture about whose failure he himself has written the book.

C

First, then, let us see where and under what circumstances his dialogic foundation takes place.

The conversation of the *Republic* is held on the day of the Bendideia in the Piraeus, the harbor of Athens, which was united with the upper city by the Themistoclean walls (Thucydides, I 93); thus the dialogue may be said to take place within Athens. In the mythical dimension this place is revealed as Hades (p. 118); in fact it is a turbulent center of Athenian democracy. The cult of Bendis, a new Thracian import, is itself a symptom of dissolution, "a new workshop of turbulent revelry," as a comic writer seems to have described it.[18] Its celebration is to culminate that night in a torch-race and an "all-nighter" (328 a 8), an orgiastic affair which the young men are clearly waiting to join.

Socrates and Glaucon, both citizens of this democracy, will conduct their conversation, which occupies the central books of the *Republic,* within this setting. It is, in a strange way, the right setting, as the dialogue itself intimates. To show this let us look at the degenerating cities and citizen souls of Books VIII and IX.

There are four of them, in downward order: timocracy, oligarchy, democracy, and tyranny (544 c). But exactly as in the case of the just city, monarchy and aristocracy are regarded as being two names for one constitution (445 d 4); so a case may be made for taking democracy and its inevitable degenerate consequence, tyranny, together (cf. Aristotle, *Politics* 1292 a 18, where democracy is said to be analogous to tyranny; also 1286 b 17). For not only do they in fact alternate with each other in Athens at this time, but within Socrates' scheme they have this important trait in common, that they are both less than cities, almost non-constitutions, to which no definite kind of soul corresponds (557 c 1). This bracketing of the two gives us the following scheme:

3	monarchy-aristocracy	
2	warrior city	timocracy
1	craftsmen city	oligarchy
0		democracy-tyranny

It conveys a kind of inverse correspondence between the best and worst. The correspondence of opposites is evident in a number of ways: The just rulers, especially when the elders of the warrior city become the philosopher kings, make no distinction between their own and the public business (497 a 5), and in a perverted way neither does the tyrant, whose rule is a private nightmare publicly staged (573, 576 b 5)—for in private, in his soul, the tyrant is himself, like his city, almost absolutely tyrannized.

Like the just constitution, the democracy contains three classes, which again correspond inversely: The have-nots in the democracy form the lowest and largest class, the class most eager for revolution, while in the just city they are in the highest and least class (428 e 7), the unpropertied class most devoted to the preservation of the city. And again: The ruling class in the democracy cannot fight because of its luxuriousness (556 c 8), while those who have that strength and are the watchdogs in the just city are the very ones who become wolves to the human fold (415 e 2, 566 a 4). These cities are thus related by Socrates as extreme opposites which meet (576 d); he even describes them by the same term: The just city is called "the city of beauty" or "fair-city" for its harmonious unity (*kallípolis*, 527 c 2), and so is the democracy called, bitterly, the "fairest" of constitutions (557 c 4; the same of tyranny, 562 a 4) for the colorful variety of constitutions to be found within it. All the above characteristics contribute toward putting the citizen of a democracy into a perverse and yet peculiarly intimate relation to the just city, but it is the last circumstance mentioned that makes democracy practically the best base of Socrates' enterprise. (The ordering of constitutions in the *Republic* is made in abstraction from considerations of constitutionalism, that is, of legal frameworks; contrast the classification of the *Statesman*, 291 d ff., where democracy is "the best of all lawless constitutions"; also 303 a 8; cf. *Politics* 1289 b 9.) For, as he tells Adeimantus, it plays host to so many constitutions that "he who happens to want to found a city, *as we are now doing,* must go to a democratic city"; having picked a constitution he likes he may then proceed to settle his own city (557 d). This is precisely what Socrates does, for, as he himself points out, even as he is sitting in an Athenian prison, he never considered leaving a perverse Athenian democracy for a proper timocracy like that of Sparta or Crete (*Crito* 52 e 5); in fact, the perverse excellence of Athens is epitomized in this—that Socrates is taken seriously enough to become the center of a public scandal (ch. 3). Socrates' dialogic community, one might say, is one of the many *Athenian* constitutions.

D

    1   A consideration of the guardian city as it appears in the *Timaeus* will bring out the full force of Socrates' founding act. As I have shown, two things are required to bring the best city into being as an actual political body: that the breeding of the citizens should be founded in nature and that the vicious circle by which the established order makes citizens in its own image should somehow be broken. These very conditions are fulfilled in the *Timaeus* in a way totally different from that contemplated in the *Republic*.

    Although the guardian city and its institutions are said at various times to be according to nature (e.g., *Republic* 428 e 9, 456 c 1), it is the nature of the soul that is really meant—a most unnatural nature, as we shall see. The consequence of this unnatural psychic base is that the city no sooner ceases to be regarded as a mere pattern and begins to be imagined as having corporeal life, than it enters its road of dissolution. For it, change or "motion" (*kínesis*) is always "discord" (*stásis,* 545 d), since "a constitution in agreement with itself cannot be changed" (d 3). For it, being in the state of perfection, change is in fact unintelligible, since the question "how . . . then does our city come to have changed?" (d 5) is answered only by the impenetrable mystery of the mathematics of birth-governing celestial cycles (546).

Now in the *Timaeus* Socrates expresses this very wish: to see his city "put into motion" (19 b 8), like a person who sees some fine animals painted or resting and feels a desire to stir them. His hosts therefore must find a way to move his city without dissolving it. The entertainment that Timaeus, Critias, and Hermocrates provide for Socrates on the Panathenaea (17 a 1, 26 e 2), unlike the bitter feast Thrasymachus serves him on the Bendideia (354 a 10, 357 a 2), is truly amusing for him. They present to him the frame for his picture, as it were, by providing a mathematical hypothesis (see p. 272), a "supposed *eídos*" (48 e 6), which will serve as a pattern for that mathematically moving macrocosm into which the harmony of his animated city will fit consonantly. In the *Republic* the largest context (and one of strife) had been Hellas (470 e 4); now it is the numbered heavens. Whereas in the *Republic* the city was a soul writ large, in the *Timaeus* the city and the human soul is a cosmos writ small (24 c, 27 b, 30 d, 42 e ff., 69 b). The rulers of such a city would not need to do any intricate political geometrizing—contrast the forced, unnatural imitation of celestial circular geometry of Athens' enemy, horrid Atlantis, with the natural layout of beautiful Athens (*Critias* 111, 113 d; p. 70).

Obviously, in this setting the main political virtue would not be what might be called the "substantial" virtue of justice, which makes each man true to his own being, but rather the "relational" virtue of temperance, which keeps him in balance, "sound-minded" (*sóphron*)—"sane." This latter virtue is understandably dimly delineated in the local context of the *Republic,* for as Socrates says there (430 e 6), "temperance is a sort of cosmos"—an interior adjustment in tune with an outer order (cf. Theon of Smyrna, *Mathematics Useful for Understanding Plato* I: "For the harmony of the cosmos, the good order of the city, and temperance in private affairs are one and the same").

2   They animate the city itself *by translating it into history.* Its citizens are indeed earthborn, sown by the twin gods He-

phaestus and Athena, she the goddess of *wisdom* and *war* and he the patron of the *craftsmen* of the city. To this elemental genesis corresponds a natural end: the city sinks out of sight in a cataclysmic earthquake (*Timaeus* 25 c 7). Socrates had presented them with a theoretical myth (26 b 4, c 8), and a quasi-factual myth, a tale of antiquity, is the gift they return.

The city of the *Republic,* on the other hand, is only as old as "yesterday." It too has a source beyond itself, but this source is not *within* nature, visible or intelligible, but *beyond nature* (540 a 8). The true ruler must be in touch with this source. Thus the love of *attainable* wisdom is what is meant in this dialogue by philosophy (see *Sixth Letter* 323 d); Glaucon's question about the genesis of the best city turns into a question about the genesis of a philosopher (504 b). Socrates is going to answer this question with a practical demonstration.

3   Socrates' city, it is necessary to note, is mentioned once more, briefly, in a dialogue from which Socrates is absent, the *Laws* (cf. also Diogenes Laertius, III 52). There an old man, an Athenian stranger of Solonic, that is, of practical—as opposed to philosophic—wisdom (cf. *Republic* 536 d 1), sets up, in the course of a walk through Crete, a constitution. It is a constitution not only in the first sense of the word, in which it means the institution of rulers and ruled as in the *Republic,* but also in the second sense, namely a code of laws for the rulers to administer (*Laws* 751 a). He mentions the guardian city of the *Republic* in which "friends have all things in common" as a city inhabited by gods, a "pattern" for his own (739 e 1)—clearly he means an unattainable and impracticable pattern. The cities he *can* undertake to build are only the second and the third best (e 5; cf. *Republic* 445 c 5, where the best city is said to be unique, while the degenerate forms are several). The constitution that is then given, a conflation of monarchy and democracy (*Laws* 693 d), is meant as a practical political model for actual cities, and it was in fact so used. This city differs from the best city in its

essential characteristics: property, women, and children are no longer held in common (740), and a concomitant adjustment is made in the citizens' and rulers' education, which is no longer "*eidetic*" but rather "*aisthetic,*" that is to say, based on sense experience (817 e ff., 967). It is often observed that the word "philosophy" does not occur in the dialogue at all.

What it means to be a city of law is discussed in the *Statesman*, a dialogue where Socrates *is* present, and it is evidently discussed in his spirit. There it is called the "second sailing" (300 c 2), that is, that laborious rowing by which boats are moved when the wind fails (scholion on *Phaedo* 99 c); the phrase means not "second best," but rather "least worst" (Aristotle, *Nicomachean Ethics* 1109 b 1). The city of law is said to be merely the best of all those cities which are not true and genuine cities at all but only copies (*Statesman* 293 e 3); the "only constitution" is that in which the rulers are men of knowledge (c 6). The Eleatic Stranger, the chief interlocutor, mentions one aspect of the rule of law that particularly bears on the education of such men, that is, of philosopher kings, as it is set out in the *Republic*: Whatever, he asks, would be the meaning of a mathematics studied according to a "code of law" (299 e 4)? Clearly the liberal study of mathematics set out in the *Republic* is not appropriate to the rulers in the *Statesman*. Moreover, the one hope for the rule of law is, the Stranger says, its meticulous preservation under all circumstances (300 c), a demand totally incompatible with the radical subversion of the *status quo* demanded by Socrates' foundation (*Republic* 501 a). Thus the city meant to be a practical city, the Cretan city of law, is *essentially* opposed to the philosopher city. One might say that the former is grounded in the realm of the Cretan underworld judges Minos and Rhadamanthus (*Laws* 624 b), while the latter has its pattern laid up in heaven.

One more remark on the significance of Socrates' absence in the *Laws*: In his *Politics* Aristotle gives a critique of the *Republic,* in his usual way cutting through Socratic "brilliance" and "originality" (1265 a 12, 1291 a 11) to reach the sober political content of the dialogue. Consequently he strips away the "extraneous arguments and those about education" (1264 b 39), until he finally reduces the Socratic foundation to *one law*: "that the guardians shall not farm" (1264 a 9)—and the Spartans have already thought of that! Thus the *Republic* is made to emerge as an insufficiently detailed forerunner of the *Laws,* while the *Laws* is regarded as a *Republic* made practicable (1264 b 26 ff.). And Aristotle proceeds to underwrite this interpretation by pretending that Socrates, the man who never left Athens except on a campaign, is the much-traveled (*Laws* 639 d 9) Athenian stranger!

IV MUSIC
A
   1   a   I shall now show that, like Heracles, Socrates employs *music* to "civilize" his young guardian. He uses not the traditional music of the poets but his own restoration of true music; he shows how to apply seriously Damon's thesis that a change in the character of a city's music produces a change in the fundamental laws (424 c 5). Socratic music is, as we shall see, *philosophical music,* the music of truth. Its special force will lie in this, that its *lógoi* are at the same time *érga,* this coincidence being just what the poets cannot achieve; they, for all their speeches, leave no true deeds behind at all (599 b 3).

   By "music" the Greeks mean whatever activity is under the care of the Muses, that tradition consisting of the arts and skills which we call "arts and letters," and among these especially poetry and melodic music. To be "amusical" is to be an uneducated boor. Accordingly, the upbringing of the guardians of the third city, described in Book III, is to be "that discovered over a long period of time," namely gymnastic to strengthen the body, and music for the soul (376 e 2) to make it gentle and "well-arranged" (401 d 8). But this available music will have to be purified and purged. Since music, that is, poetry, is understood to be altogether "image-making and imitative" (*eikastiké, mimetiké, Laws* 668 a 6), the purging consists of condemning the poet's false and deleterious representations especially of gods and heroes, and of expunging the passages where he "makes images vilely in his *lógos*" (377 e 1). Children must be told myths that will be, on the whole, euphemistic lies—albeit beneficial ones—though they will contain some truths (377 a 4). Socrates gives a practical demonstration of this purgation in reviewing passages containing myths harmful to the tone of the soul (as Aristotle did later, he regards poets primarily as "myth-makers," 377 b 11; cf. *Poetics* 1451 b). When he has criticized the myths, particularly the Homeric tales "about gods . . . and demigods as well as heroes and about those in Hades" (392 a 4), among them the slanders concerning Theseus's presence there (391 c 9), he declines for the moment to go on to correct the *myths concerning men*. For these are the myths the poets are *worst* at telling, but we cannot correct them, he says, until we know how justice works (392 b; p. 155). We may accordingly expect such a correction of the myths of man later on. Socrates concludes by requiring not only the poets but all imitative artists to devote their works to "the image of the Good" (401 b 2).

b Not only are the stories of the poets, their *lógoi* (392 c 6), purged, but their mode of speech, their *léxis* (ibid.), which corresponds for them to the modes of melodic music, also comes under Socrates' review. His remarks make the whole dialogue itself the vehicle of a most fundamental reflection on the dialogic mode, for the form of the *Republic* is a subtle but precise example of the approved *léxis*. Socrates distinguishes two basic poetic modes. The first of these is straight narration, in which the poet himself is speaking directly while his characters speak in indirect discourse; for example, Homer says that "Agamemnon . . . said [to Chryses] that rather than release his daughter he would grow old in Argos with her." In the second mode the narrator drops out entirely and the characters speak in their own persons, as in all drama (392 d 5). Epic represents a mixture of these two basic styles (394 c 4). The first mode is honest enough, but the second mode is censured. It is bad because in it the poet, by hiding himself, hides the fictional nature of his work and evades all responsibility for its truth, leaving the actor (or reader) caught in an unwitting imitation. For the actor becomes, as it were, the character—all too often reprehensible—whose direct speech he declaims. But the guardians should be allowed to imitate only good men (395 d).

The *Republic* itself, however, has that form which is exactly designed to provide at once the most complete poetic responsibility, the greatest mimetic force, and the most worthwhile imitation. For the narrator, Socrates himself, is always present and responsible, and he keeps himself before us with the ever-recurring phrases "he said" and "I said" (393 c 11; contrast *Theaetetus* 143 c); nor is he an anonymous mouthpiece whose work we readers read, as we do the Homeric epics, without ever learning who the poet was. (We see here, incidentally, one reason why Hesiod, who not only identifies himself but even warns the reader that his source, the Muses, will sometimes lie [*Theogony* 22, 27], is if less loved by Socrates than Homer, yet more acceptable to him; *Republic* 546 e 1, 607 c 8.)

The first person teller of the dialogue is Socrates, backing his own words with the acts of his own life. At the same time the words and arguments are dramatically direct, in the sense that the readers can almost hear them as spoken. They may imitate them in the sense of rehearsing them and trying them out for truth; they can let the *lógos* turn into an *érgon* in their own souls. This text is almost an "unwritten teaching," having overcome the dead letter of the written word. Finally, the *Republic* as a whole—and this is a feature it shares with other dialogues—is just the required imitation of the activity of the "best of men" (*Phaedo* 118 a 16), for it is Plato's imitation of Socrates. It is, however, not merely a memorandum of Socrates' conversation but also an implicit commentary on it. For on occasion we can distinguish between what Socrates says and what Plato's dialogue says. The most striking example of this is the *Phaedrus,* which is so written that, even as we read it, it casts doubt on Socrates' assertion within it that the written word cannot teach (274 c ff.). We shall see that similar tensions, similarly inviting to thought, are written into the *Republic.*

   c   To turn back to the poet's music: In Book VII, when Socrates revises the guardian education to fit it for the philosopher city, even the music purged of all vice is explicitly and emphatically excluded from the formal plan of education as containing no "learning matter" (*máthema,* 522 a 8, 537, cf. 504 d 1) leading toward Being. For such music is learned merely "by custom" (522 a 4). It is an habituation of the soul that does not lead to knowledge; it is a training but not an education, a conditioning but not a journey to the source, for "the dialectic pursuit alone travels this way" (533 c 7). Consequently, the musical training is completed very early and actually *culminates* in gymnastics (cf. 376 e 6, 546 d 7, 591 c 5).

   2   a   We know from the dialogues, however, that there is yet another music, different from both the traditional and the purged music, the *philosophical music* mentioned above. Evidently it was Pythagoras who first appropriated the oldest of the Muses, Calliope, for philosophy.[19] Socrates gives her, together with the next sister, Urania, the same office in the *Phaedrus,* where Urania watches over those who make stories about the heavens and the gods, while Calliope cares for those who compose "human stories" (259 d 6). And in the *Phaedo* Socrates tells of a dream that has come to him often and in various shapes but always with the same message: "O Socrates, make music and let that be your work" (60 e 6); he has always taken this dream to mean that he should pursue philosophy, that being "the greatest music" (61 a 3; cf. *Republic* 499 d 4, 548 b 8).
   b   What then is this philosophical music, this "inquiring imitation" (*historiké mímesis, Sophist* 267 e 2)? In the passage of the *Phaedo* quoted above, Socrates says: "I myself am not a

myth-teller" (61 b 5). This is literally true, for he is not one who makes *imitations of what never was nor will be,* producing mere phantasms (cf. *Sophist* 236 c), though he is one who makes *images of what is.* The cities built "in speech" are, to be sure, Socrates' own myths; he speaks of "the constitution which we *told as a myth* in speech" (501 e 4). But otherwise Socrates, although he is willing enough to act out a myth, avoids *telling* myths of his own making. The "noble lie" of the guardians is a myth attributed to the Phoenicians (414 c 4). That anti-Homeric Descent to Hades, the replacement for Odysseus's false and tedious tale to Alcinous (cf. scholion on 614 b 1 and Note 11) which closes the dialogue is attributed to Er and only "saved" by Socrates (621 b 8); in other dialogues too Socrates avoids taking originating responsibility for myths (e.g., *Gorgias* 493, *Phaedrus* 244, *Meno* 81). Images, on the other hand, are undeniably his own mode; as Adeimantus ironically remarks at one point: "It isn't the usual thing, I suppose, for you to speak through images" (487 e 6).

c   An account of how such images as Socrates makes are formed is given in the *Philebus* (38 e). When someone goes about reflecting much by himself, many true opinions and accounts become written into his soul, as by an inner scribe. This scribe is succeeded by a painter who draws images illustrating these inner accounts, and if the accounts are true, then so are these images.

d   A Socratic image therefore differs from a myth in being the illustration of an inner argument and not the rhetorical supplement to a public conversation. When the dialectic attempt has ended, often in failure, the imagination, as Kierkegaard says, feels fatigued and reacts: "The mythical is thus the enthusiasm of the imagination in the service of speculation . . ." (*Concept of Irony,* p. 132; see ch. 3 Note 9). I think that the same faculty produces in all sobriety and in the service of reflection the images here called Socratic. Such myths are thus *preceded* by an argument, as nearly the whole *Republic* precedes the Myth of

Er, and dialogic passages precede the myths of the *Phaedo,* the *Phaedrus,* the *Symposium,* and the *Gorgias.* Images, on the other hand, are either *followed* by an explication of the interior argument that went into their making, or they themselves give plain hints how the participant in the dialogue should reflect on them. This reflection is of a very peculiar kind, and in inducing it lies the special strength of the Socratic image: Each such effort of unique production is accompanied by a reflection on the effort itself, for to study a Socratic image always means to study not only its content *but the general nature of "image" and "imaging" itself.* The study of Socratic imagery is then exactly what Socrates himself says "music" ought to be: the study of true Being *and* the analysis of its images; as he repeats twice, this is one and the same art and effort (402 b 7, c 7). The making of such images is, as we shall see, based on recognizing analogies, just as are metaphors (Aristotle, *Poetics* 1457 b 16). Aristotle thinks that the making of metaphors demands by far the greatest poetic gift, namely "the ability to see what is like" (1459 a 8). We shall see that it is also a great philosophical gift. In Socrates' images the "ancient difference between philosophy and poetry" (*Republic* 607 b 5) is reconciled. We shall inspect the great Socratic images of the *Republic.*

   e–f We see Socrates himself fulfilling the demand he makes of all poets, which is to "make an image of the Good" (401 b 1). His image of the Good is the "Sun Image" or "likeness" (*eikón,* 509 a 9, *homoiótes,* 509 c 6), which dominates the center of the dialogue. It is followed by that example of a "corrected" Myth of Man which Socrates had before omitted because the correction couldn't be made before the nature of justice was known (392 a 8). The myth that he now chooses to correct, tacitly but devastatingly, is indeed the most crucial of all stories concerning humans. It is the one dramatized by Aeschylus in the tragedy of *Prometheus Bound.* It tells how the treasonous immortal Prometheus, opposing the authority of Zeus, gave men fire (252), how he opened their eyes (447) and made them see, and how he made them come out of the caves they had been inhabiting, antlike (452), into the light of day to see the heavens and to become wise (476). As Socrates refigures this myth in his Image of the Cave (*Republic* 514), it turns out that the fire Prometheus brought was a counterfeit light (b 2); those few who know how to use it only abuse it by allowing it to project deceptions (b 8); men's eyes are as blind as ever (515 c 9); they continue to live deep in a dark cave and their wisdom is worthless (516 c 4–7; I might note here in passing that Prometheus undergoes critiques elsewhere. In the *Philebus* Socrates intimates that the true Prometheus is Pythagoras [16 c], and in the *Protagoras* the sophist Protagoras, while crediting Prometheus with having brought the other arts to men, claims that he omitted the political art, which Hermes brought later directly from Zeus, 322 c 1).[20]

g The *lógos* behind these images is absent in the *Republic,* but its terms may be recovered from Plato's oral "Unwritten Teachings," particularly the lecture—or several colloquia—*Concerning the Good* (see Note 28). In these terms, the terms of the Academy, the Image of the Good represents *the One* and the Image of the Cave *the Indefinite Dyad;* this interpretation will be pursued below in somewhat more detail. This, however, must be said at the outset: While it is a permissible enterprise to attempt to think what may be in the dialogues without being explicitly written there, it is a very external approach to discover in these texts some Academic formula, to think that the wisdom which never would or even could be written (see *Seventh Letter* 341 c–d) could nonetheless be recovered through an Aristotelian formulation. For Aristotle, here as always, proceeds soberly and seriously to profane the Academic mysteries in the interests of formulable truth. The mathematical nature itself of the "Unwritten Teachings" is evidence that there was a live community for whom the terms of the teaching were pregnant with semi-technical meanings, which, taken out of context, become exactly what Plato feared: somewhat fantastic fossils of truth. Plato himself appears, to be sure, to have spoken on some occasion to the public in the mathematical language of the Academy, and evidently for some students "mathematics had become philosophy, although they say that it should be studied for the sake of something else" (Aristotle, *Metaphysics* 992 a 32 ff.). Yet it is a remarkable fact of the tradition concerning the "Unwritten Teachings" that the arithmetical doctrine that must have been their central matter, the doctrine concerning the order or *táxis* of the *eíde* as discovered by dialectic (cf. *Philebus* 16 d–e), was fully divulged by no one, not even by Aristotle (see Note 35).

3   The particular object of Socrates' music in the *Republic,* which may be contrasted, for example, with the battering ram of his rhetoric in the *Gorgias,* is to work a gentle and orderly revolution of the soul in respect to the love of wisdom. This musical art is the ability to devise an inviting preview of the "marvelous way" such as, according to the *Seventh Letter* (340 c 3), must be given to any beginner. It is an art which Socrates once refers to as the "art of conversion" (518 d 3).

According to the stated plan of the philosophers' education, at twenty those chosen to study begin a formal sequence of mathematics culminating in a "synopsis," a pre-philosophical overview (537 c 2). At thirty, after another selection, the young philosophers enter upon the long road of dialectic, which again culminates in a synoptic vision, that of the Good itself (540 a 8; p. 239). Just as Socrates had first introduced Glaucon to the Good as the "greatest learning matter" (*mégiston máthema*) poetically, by an image, so he now sets out as a "hymn" the plan of study that will prepare Glaucon to reach the Good: "Don't we know," he says, speaking of the mathematical studies they have just surveyed, "that all these things are only the *preludes* to the *hymn* which we must study?" (531 d 7; cf. *Timaeus* 29 d 5; *Laws* 722 c 6). And a little later, playing on the double meaning of *nomos,* law or song, he speaks of the "law which the activity of dialectic fulfills" or the "song which it performs"

(532 a 1). Socrates will not turn this song into expository prose, since "no longer, dear Glaucon, will you be able to follow . . . , for you would no longer be seeing an image of what we are discussing but the truth itself, as it appears to me" (533 a 1). Socrates' music, as the art of conversion, is a poetic synopsis of the end, as well as the road, of the philosophical education. It is designed to turn Glaucon into the right course by showing him "what the business as a whole is. . . . For once he hears this, if he is indeed properly philosophical and worthy of the undertaking—a man divine—he is persuaded that he has heard of a wonderful way and that right now he must concentrate on it, or else life will not be worth living" (*Seventh Letter* 340 b–c). So this was the significance of the omission of music from the plan of higher education: *the presentation was itself to be the musical overture to learning.* We shall see that when the object of study is the "highest learning matter" the images and songs in which it is previewed demand the highest art.

4   Books V–VII, which contain the central images, are again, like the outer books, roughly symmetrical about the center. Upon the completion of the just city culminating in the discussion of the community of women and children (V, 449–471; VIII, 543 a), Glaucon asks his question concerning the possibility of this city. Socrates answers it by introducing the philosopher kings at the *exact numerical middle* of the text. This question and its answer encompass more narrowly the intellectual center of the dialogue (V, 471 c–473; VII, 540 d, cf. 466 d 8). The next inner themes are the definition and—here Adeimantus interposes—the defense, the temperament, and the proper age of the philosopher (V, 474 b–VI, 502; VII, 535–540). At the innermost core is Socrates' initiation of Glaucon into a philosophical education, effected by two great images, the Sun Image and the Cave Image, which are interwoven with explications and with each other, as shown in the following table.

507a ff. ⌐ Sun Image
509d ff. │ ⌐ explication of the Sun Image by the "Divided Line"
514a ff. └ Cave Image
517b ff. │ ⌐ correlation of the two images
522a ff. └ explication of the Cave Image in the "plan of studies"
533a ff. └ correlation of the explications of both images

We have before us a composition of intricate but clear texture.

B

1 Glaucon's introduction to philosophy will itself have a prelude. He will discover for himself the meaning of "opinion," *dóxa*.

Opinion in its various meanings determines the musical key of the different parts of the dialogue by its absence or presence. The outer ring of *lógoi* is explicitly spoken in a signature appropriate to the absence of the "good opinion" (*dóxa*) of mankind and its homonymous consequence, "reputation" (*dóxa*). Adeimantus had stipulated at the beginning (Book II) that the argument about justice must "remove reputations" (367 b 5), and Glaucon had provided the magic Ring of Gyges,[21] which will allow the wearer "to do anything"—that is, to be a complete crook, a *pan-oúrgos,* an "all-doer," without being either seen or blamed. At the end of the argument (Book X) the ring and also the concealing Helmet of Hades, which the argument had been, so to speak, wearing, can be removed (612 b 5), for even on the supposition that the opinion of men carries no weight, justice has been proved profitable, a source of happiness. At the center of the dialogue, however, where an *érgon,* a deed, is to be effected by the *lógos,* the argument, the opinion of mankind cannot be supposed away, for "the Many," *hoi polloí,* will have to be won to some sort of acceptance of philosophy if anything is to be *done.*

But it is really as the individual inner source of this public opinion, as the faculty of the soul Glaucon will soon learn to call *dóxa,* that opinion becomes of overwhelming importance at the center, for both the older and the younger lover of wisdom. For about the "greatest learning matter," the *mégiston máthema, Socrates himself has,* as he repeatedly says, *only opinion* (506 c 4, e 2, 509 c 3, 517 b 7, 533 a 4; cf. *Phaedrus* 278 d), although it is an opinion so well founded that Glaucon will not be able to follow him without a long course of study. So much the more will the "interest" on the capital Good, its "child" (Socrates plays on the double meaning of *tókos:* child and interest, as in our phrase "to bear interest"), which he presents to Glaucon, provide the latter only with opinion. But since the interest is not paid in counterfeit coin and the child is no bastard (507 b 5), we may infer that Glaucon will conceive not false but "true opinion." This is the beginning required if positive learning, as distinct from a preliminary purgative refutation, is to take place. Yet even the Good itself, that one thing which everyone wants in truth and without regard to "seeming" (*dóxa,* 505 d 8), will, as was said, have to be approached by way of opinion: "A man should remember that he is human not only in his fortune but also in his demonstrative knowledge," says an ancient commentator (*On the Good, Vita Aristotelis Marciana* 953 b, ed. Bekker).

2   As so often in the *Republic,* the conversation makes its own mode the object of reflection—in the case of *dóxa,* at its very inception; Socrates' opinions on the highest matters are prefaced by an inquiry into the meaning of opining.

The "third wave," the proposal of the philosopher king, has just closed in on Socrates (Book V, 473 c 6); he and Glaucon must now delineate that philosopher (474 b 5). Just as there are some who desire love, he says, and some who desire honor, there are some who desire wisdom, and all of it. Glaucon asks whether lovers of wisdom then include lovers of sights and sounds. Socrates answers with a distinction which he would have difficulty, he says, in getting anyone but Glaucon to admit (475 e 6): The just and the unjust, the good and the bad, are each one thing by itself, but "in communion with deeds and bodies and one another they are imagined in every way and appear each to be many" (476 a 4). Now lovers of sights love—and apprehend— beauty in its manyness and are asleep with respect to true beauty itself, being unable to distinguish this *one* from the *many*, but the philosopher loves the one true beauty. The thinking (*diánoia*) of the philosopher is knowing and is to be called knowledge (*gnóme*), while the lovers of beauty only opine and have opinion (*dóxa*, 476 d 5).

Furthermore, knowledge must be of something which *is*, and which is "that which is completely," and which is therefore completely to be known (*gnostón*), while "what is not" is entirely unknowable (*ágnoston*, 477 a 1). Now if there is something between (*metaxý*) complete Being and complete Nonbeing, then, as knowledge (*epistéme*) was said to belong to Being and ignorance (*agnosía*) to Nonbeing, so to this "thing between" must correspond something that is itself "between ignorance and knowledge" (a 10). This is found to be *opinion*, having an object and a power (*dýnamis*) different from both knowledge and ignorance (b 8; cf. *Symposium* 202 a). If he and Glaucon can discover what it is that, being more shadowy than Being but brighter than Nonbeing, lies between them, they will have found "that which is to be opined" (*doxastón*, 478 e 3). Then they will name it, "assigning extremes to extremes and means to means" (e 4). They will appeal to the lover of beauty in manyness and ask him if all these things he loves are not also sometimes ugly, and if the same is not true of things just, great, or heavy—that they will all be found at some time to be the opposite, so that they cannot be said to be or not to be one thing or another, but are tossed about in-between Being and Nonbeing. Lovers of such things should be called "lovers of opinion" and not "lovers of wisdom" (*philódoxoi: philósophoi,* 480 a 11). So ends Book V: Becoming, *génesis,* that "in-between thing," has not been explicitly named, but it will clearly have to play a central role in Socrates' subsequent presentation.

3 The foregoing argument cannot help but remind Glaucon of an earlier one (Book IV) in which it had been concluded that cities derive their constitutions from the individual constitutions of their citizens.[22] Socrates had then asked whether the three capacities of the soul—desire, spiritedness, and reasoning—belong to three different parts or whether each of these belongs to the whole soul (436 a 8). To show that they are indeed three separate parts, Socrates and Glaucon had posited a psychic correspondence between desires and the appraisal of their objects. If a man wants at the same time to drink and also wants not to drink because he knows that he ought not to, then his soul must contain opposing parts: a "bidding" and a "forbidding" part (439 c 6).

There are then, to begin with, two parts, the rational part (*logistikón*) "with which a man calculates" (*logízetai*), and the desiring part (*epithymetikón*) which is unreasoning (*alógiston*) and in which desire (*epithymía*) is located (439 d). Between these two, the forms (*eíde,* e 2) that are ordinarily recognized, Socrates inserts a pivotal third (e 3), the spirited part (*thymoeidés*). Glaucon, obviously listening to the *thymo*-part, thinks that it is more akin to desire than to reason. But Socrates points out that it can be auxiliary to the reasoning part, since it makes us feel high-minded anger or indignation (*thymós,* 440 e). Finally, these three parts are arranged within us as the "three terms of a musical proportion" (443 d 6), and *thymós* becomes "the in-between power" (479 d 8), which, while itself obedient to reason, can in turn govern the body (403 d, 411 e 6).

Glaucon had therefore been asked long before the present argument to distinguish the parts of the soul by means of their relative objects and to understand one of these parts as a mean between two extremes. If we juxtapose the results of both exercises we get the following result:

BOOK IV		BOOK V
logistikón	:	gnósis
thymoeidés	:	dóxa
epithymetikón	:	(agnosía)

For the middle parts this correlation is indeed tacitly but unmistakably made in the dialogue. For instance, a chief characteristic of the warriors, who as a class of the just city correspond to the *spirited part* of the soul, is the "preservation of law-abiding *opinions*" within themselves (433 c 7); in fact, as Aristotle points out, their *thymós* is the source of their discernment (*Politics* 1327 b 40). Moreover, in a timocracy, which represents spiritedness among the degenerating cities and is emphatically presented as lying "between" aristocracy and oligarchy (545 c 6, d 1), the chief characteristic of citizens is love of honor (548 c 7), which implies an interrelation of the *thymós* with the external *dóxa* called reputation. Spiritedness and opinion are the matching novel centers respectively of Socrates' temperamental and cognitive psychology.

4 The *logistikón*, on the other hand, is not quite coextensive with *gnósis*. Here we must stop to observe the name itself. In the traditional division of the soul into two parts, a rational and an irrational part, the first, as having reason (*lógos*), that is, the power of giving accounts (*Nicomachean Ethics*, 1102 a 30), was quite properly called *logikón*, a term evidently already used by the Pythagoreans.[23] Why then does Socrates call it the *logistikón,* connecting it explicitly with the verb *logízesthai,* to reckon or calculate (439 d 5), rather than with the *lógos* of *dialégesthai* (511 b 4, 534 c)? It is because the *logistikón* is a restricted power, a power of *planning,* whose specific work later does turn out to be calculation (cf. *Nichomachean Ethics* 1139 a 13), measuring, and weighing—in short, whatever corresponds only to the lower

level of the knowing power, to that power of mathematical thinking which Glaucon will discover later on as a mean between opinion and knowledge; it will be called *diánoia*. We must remember that the guardians as young puppy-philosophers have an admixture of *ignorance* in their knowing power, since they are said to apprehend the city's enemies as dogs do, by the criterion of their own unfamiliarity with them (376 b 5). Moreover, their service as soldiers and administrators requires a knowledge of *applied* mathematics, an ability to be correct about matters of sense. Hence this study forms a part, although a secondary one, of the philosophers' education (522 c).

The lowest capacity, on the other hand, the desirous part (*epithymetikón*), might well be said to correspond in a certain way to ignorance (*agnosía*), since the general object of desire, which is pleasure, partakes, as Socrates later shows Glaucon, of the object of ignorance, which is Nonbeing (585)—though, to be sure, "ignorance . . . is a void in the condition of the soul" (b 3) and not really a capacity at all.

It follows that the tripartite soul of Book IV both begins and ends on a level *below* the soul described in the central conversation, although it has a coextensive middle part. How is this new soul of the center to be understood?

5   At the very beginning of the articulation of the first soul Socrates had warned that nothing accurate could come from such "proceedings" (*méthodos*, 435 d 1) and that a "longer and fuller way" (d 3) would be needed, a requirement repeated at a crucial moment in Book VI (504 b 2). With the discovery of *dóxa* Socrates has started Glaucon on this longer way. The soul that now emerges is the soul as "the organ by which each man learns" (513 c 5, cf. 527 d 8), analogous in its passive openness to an organ of sense. The parts of this soul are specifically called powers when first introduced (477 b, c, e), and this describes them completely—they are nothing but the soul's *capability* of taking in, without modification, beings of a different degree, of

"having ideas" in the original sense; this is why in a crucial place (511 d 7) they can as easily be called receptivities (*pathémata*) in the soul. Compared to this learning soul, the three parts of the first soul sink to mere tendencies, dispositions, or appetites (cf. *Nicomachean Ethics*, 1102 b 30). Indeed, the alternate name of the *logistikón* is the wisdom-loving part (*philósophon*, 586 e 4), and the love of wisdom is often called an *epithymía*, a desire, in the central books (e.g., 475 b 4, 8; 517 b 6). And of course, the very name of the *thymós*, with its allusion to *epithymía*, implies a kind of reflexive, inward-turned desire, as opposed to the desire that goes out upon an object. This means that in a sense all the parts of the first soul function as desires, as activating human wants, and so it fits very well that the wisdom-loving part should not be coextensive with the knowing part, since when the soul truly knows, it no longer desires the objects of knowledge but has attained and moves among them (see Note 10).

Thus, once the learning soul has come into focus, the terms of the tripartite soul are used mostly to distinguish the temperaments of "lovers." The philosopher, for instance, is defined by means of a division of men into lovers of eros and wine, lovers of honor, and lovers of wisdom (474 c 8, cf. 435 e 7). Again, the degenerate cities are characterized by different prevailing appetites. When tyranny is discussed the three parts of the first soul are even explicitly connected to three pleasures or desires (580 d). This first, restlessly desiring tripartite soul is the *embodied* soul, a monstrous, precariously conflated unity (588 d). It turns into a single rising organ of love only at the sight of beauty (*Phaedrus* 249 d ff.), when it is under the influence of that divine madness which induces visions of the invisible (244). In contrast, the increasingly more receptive soul at the center of the *Republic*, although still using the senses, is more nearly the *soul by itself*, whose oneness, presumably similar to the unity of the Whole, is a subject, as Socrates says, for a more advanced inquiry.

6 The division of the soul is *the* pre-dialectical "exercise," the *gymnásia* (*Parmenides* 135 c 8, d 4, 7), of the *Republic*. Almost every reference to the dialectical process of dividing refers to distinguishing the parts or the objects of the soul (454 a, 476 a, 523 a, 580 d, 571 a–b, 595 a–b, 618 c). Division (*diaíresis*) is here not a very formal method, as can be gathered from the numerous names given to these parts: kinds, sorts, parts, affects (*eíde, géne, mére, páthe,* 435 b, c, e, 439 e, 441 c, 443 d, 442 b, c, 612 a 5). In the course of the central conversation a quadripartite learning soul will emerge, but Socrates indicates that more divisions might be made in a more complete study (534 a 7) and that the question whether the soul is ultimately "many or one in kind" (612 a 4, cf. 443 d 7) has not really been settled. An important aspect of this dialectic exercise is the finding of "the in-between" (*to metaxý*), which Glaucon immediately recognizes as analogous to the mathematical problem of "finding the mean." The ability to discover means, middle terms, is the chief gift necessary to the dialectician (*Philebus* 16 e 1). The soul becomes the object of this exercise, not only because, as we have seen, the philosopher's version of the definition of justice is "Know Thyself,"[24] but also because the politically indispensable art of leading souls (*psychagogía*), namely rhetoric, depends on a knowledge of the divisions of the soul (*Phaedrus* 271 d); in the *Republic* Thrasymachus is told to acquire this art. Socrates is teaching this rhetorician his own business, as it were. However, the undertaking remains a preliminary exercise because, as we shall see, Socrates must exclude true dialectic from the *Republic*.

C

1–2 Adeimantus, whose name means "Dauntless" but who has heard and is shaken by every current doubt (cf. 362 e, 419 a), interposes an objection (487 b): Socrates' argument about the excellence of philosophers is convincing in words, but in deed everyone knows that these people end up either scoundrelly or impotent, especially if they keep philosophizing past their youth. Socrates proceeds to win Adeimantus and the rest of the crowd—there are, besides Glaucon, eight named and several nameless auditors—"in deed" (327 c, 328 b). He does not deny the accusation, but he will justify his demand for the rule of the philosophers by an *image* (487 e 5) and its explication (489 a 4); the image is that of a mutinous crew and the good but powerless captain. There follows a series of images that show that the greatest of all sophists, the Many, *hoi polloí*, is in fact the greatest corrupter of natures and corrupts the best most deeply. This Public Sophist is like a great brute that the little private sophists know how to propitiate (492 a–493 d). Thus philosophy is left desolate and any little tinker may, as it were, take her to wife (495 e). There are, however, some good natures who are for various reasons incorruptible. Socrates here cites as one such reason his own "divine sign," the *daimónion* (496 c 4), that prevents him from false actions. When soon after he speaks of a "well-born and well-bred disposition" (*éthos,* b 2), one can scarcely help thinking of the Heraclitean saying that "*éthos* is a man's *daímon*" (Diels, *Vorsokratiker* Fr. 119). He who has such a nature will run to shelter as from a storm and will live—and die—in private. Thus such a man will do great deeds—but not the greatest, which can only be accomplished within a suitable constitution (497 a). Socrates is commenting on his own limited success in Athens.

Adeimantus's worries about the slanders of philosophy he has heard are allayed. They return to the question of the possibility of the ideal city, and now he wants to know whether any of the contemporary cities are suitable to philosophy (497 a 9). Not a single one, says Socrates, who, however, as we know, himself lives and acts, if limitedly, as a philosopher in Athens. Even the city in speech that we have just founded is deficient without the addition of a man, of a living law-giver (497 d)—the very one they were talking about when Adeimantus interrupted. This man's main problem will be how philosophy may be pursued in such a way as not to ruin the city.

The solution, as announced by Socrates, is that *not the young but those advanced in life must most devote themselves to philosophy.* Adeimantus remarks how serious Socrates seems to be here, but he thinks that most of his hearers will object just as earnestly, and Thrasymachus most of all. Socrates says reprovingly, "Do not make a quarrel between me and Thrasymachus, who have just become friends—although we were not enemies before" (498 c 9). Thrasymachus seconds this remark by his silence (cf. 450 a 5). It is no wonder, Socrates goes on, that the people are hard to persuade, for they have never seen a virtuous man rule in a similarly virtuous city. This is why no city or constitution will ever become perfect until either some necessity forces the lover of wisdom to take care of the city, or the true *eros* of philosophy falls on princes. This may very well happen; in fact it may already have happened or be about to happen if there is now some "barbaric place" (499 c 9) or if there ever was or will be a situation where a virtuous man rules: "The constitution we discussed has come into being and was and will be, *whenever this Muse is in power* in the city" (d 2). We must not attack the Many, for they will, under such circumstances, become gentle and will believe that no city can be happy which is not painted by an artist looking to the divine pattern (500 e 3). Such an artist will begin with a clean slate, painting on it a constitution whose model is *both* the just and the beautiful and the temperate itself *and* the actual condition of men (501 b), and the Many will accept him. So a conclusion has been reached: Our law-giving is difficult but not impossible (502 c). We have already seen to what extent Socrates is here whistling in the dark (p. 143).

Yet in this interlude with Adeimantus, Socrates completes the practical foundation of that other city, which is independent of the Many, his own dialogic city. Having been voted into office, he succeeds by his oratory in allaying the fear those present may have of the "philosophical clan" (501 e 3). His persuasiveness is due to his ability to present a living example of the uncorrupted lover of wisdom—himself. In defending what appears to both of them a crucial matter, the *lifelong* pursuit of philosophy, he even becomes, as he himself remarks in retrospect, a spirited orator who speaks "as an indignant man will" (*thymotheís*, 536 c 4). He is anxious for, and successful in, preserving a tenuous peace with Thrasymachus, the single sophist who represents that brutal public sophist, the people (cf. 336 b 5). Though when he imagines that their city may at this very moment exist in some barbarian spot, we may suspect some irony, recalling that the dialogue has by now been going on for well over ten hours; it is night, and we may hear the barbaric sounds of a Thracian orgy beginning to penetrate into the house, sounds of the celebration that the company had come to attend but which they will now miss as they sit through the rest of the night under Socrates' spell.

3   Socrates is now actually finished with Adeimantus. He will use him as an interlocutor only once more, in the discovery of the degenerate cities (548 d 8–576 b 10), for Adeimantus is the expert in accounts of the worst. However, they continue a little further. Socrates reviews the three waves he has faced and ends by daring to formulate the "possible city" boldly in terms of the revised guardian city: "*Guardians in the accurate sense, it must be ordained, are philosophers*" (503 b 5). These must be at once quick and gentle and able to undertake the "greatest learning matters" (503 e 4). Adeimantus wants to know what these are, and Socrates reminds him of their former study of the soul and its virtues and how they then said that a longer road must be taken to reach even better things (504 e). But what are these things? Adeimantus asks insistently. Socrates is annoyed that Adeimantus either does not understand or is trying to make trouble, "since you have often heard this—that 'the idea of the Good' is the greatest study" (505 a 2), for this alone is what everyone wants not *in seeming* but *in truth*. Although Socrates has already said that this Good cannot be either knowledge or pleasure (505c), Adeimantus presses to be told whether it is either of these or yet something else. A sarcastic exchange follows, in which Socrates denounces Adeimantus's unwillingness to hear, and Adeimantus scores Socrates' propensity for repeating the opinion of others (!); this ends in Socrates' refusing to talk to him about the Good (506 c 11). So Glaucon returns to the conversation and implores Socrates not to stop just as the consummation of the argument is ahead; they will be satisfied if Socrates speaks of the Good as he did before of the virtues (d 2). Glaucon does not seem to realize that they have, in fact, already gone a little way on the "longer path."

D

1   Socrates yields to Glaucon. He will speak, though not of the Good itself but rather of an "offspring," which is most like it (506 e). Socrates reminds Glaucon of the "oft-told" story of the One and the Many (cf. 476). Those many good and beautiful things are seen but not known, while the thing itself, by which what was many comes "under one idea" (*idéa*), is known but not seen (507 b 9). Now the artificer of the senses has made sight the most costly of the senses, since to work it needs a "third kind of thing" (e 1), light. The sun is of all the gods in heaven the one who gives us this precious light, and so the sense (*aísthesis*) of sight and the power of being seen (e 6) depend on him. The eye is, of all the organs of sense, "most like the sun" (508 b 3). This sun is the child of the Good, a child begotten "analogous to itself" (b 13). For the Good is "in the place of thought," that is, in relation both to thought and to things thought (*nous, noúmena*, c 1) what the sun is "in the place of visibility" (c 2), that is, in relation to sight and things seen. Socrates completes the analogy by likening that in the soul which knows in this way to the eye; as the eye sees things clearly (d 1) when lit up by the sun, so the soul knows or merely opines things in the measure that the idea of the Good gives or fails to give truth (*alétheia*, d 5). Glaucon is amazed. Adeimantus's question is now certainly answered; the Good cannot be either knowledge or pleasure (509 a 6). Socrates says that there is yet more to be seen in the image (a 9), for the sun provides not only visibility but also growth and becoming, *génesis* (b 3), though it is not itself Becoming. Analogously the Good is the source of beings, though not itself Being (b 7, 9). This image (*eikón*), which we shall call the "Sun Image" for short, is best seen in a schematic sentence:

$$
\text{As the} \left\{ \begin{array}{l} \text{sun} \\ \text{Good} \end{array} \right. \text{is responsible for giving} \left\{ \begin{array}{l} \text{light} \\ \text{truth} \end{array} \right. \text{in}
$$

$$
\text{the place of} \left\{ \begin{array}{l} \text{visibility} \\ \text{thought} \end{array} \right. \text{to objects of} \left\{ \begin{array}{l} \text{vision} \\ \text{thought} \end{array} \right. ,
$$

$$
\text{which are therefore perceived with} \left\{ \begin{array}{l} \text{clarity} \\ \text{knowledge} \end{array} \right. \text{by the}
$$

$$
\left\{ \begin{array}{l} \text{eye} \\ \text{soul} \end{array} \right. , \text{and the} \left\{ \begin{array}{l} \text{sun} \\ \text{good} \end{array} \right. \text{is also the source of} \left\{ \begin{array}{l} \text{Becoming} \\ \text{Being} \end{array} \right. .
$$

The image is now explicated in the "Divided Line." Glaucon is to take the "double kinds" (509 d 4), the visible (*horatón*) and the intelligible (*noetón*), and cut them, as he would a line, into two unequal parts. Then he is to cut each section again in the same ratio (d 7). Thus he will have, in the lower part, one subsection related to the other "in respect to clarity and lack of clarity" (d 9) in the same way in which images such as shadows and reflections are related to that of which they are images, namely natural objects and artifacts (510 a). To this whole lower part belongs "the opinable" (*doxastón*, a 9). Next, the lower subsection of the upper part is considered. Here the soul, using those things before imitated as images (510 b 4), proceeds "from hypotheses" not up to the beginning (*ep' archén*) but down to the end, while in the uppermost section she makes her way (*méthodos*) without any use of images but by the forms (*eíde*) themselves and through them alone, up to the un-hypothetical beginning (b 6). Socrates explains the lower of these subsections in terms of the work of the mathematicians, who assume certain hypotheses without giving an account of them and who deduce consistent conclusions on the basis of these. In doing this they may use the "visible looks" of things, that is, diagrams, but these are not what they are really thinking *about*.

The true object of their thinking is the intelligible look, the *eídos* (511 a 3), the look that "one may see in no other way than by means of the thinking faculty" (*diánoia*, a 1). Thus Socrates indicates that the term *eídos* is somewhat *ironic,* for it dissembles its true intentions by connoting seeing when it means thinking. In the top section this paradoxically named "intelligible look" itself, the *eídos noetón,* is attained by "the power of dialectic" (b 4), which uses the mathematical hypotheses as "hypotheses in deed"—or "in being" (*toi ónti*). This is a *double entendre;* the words mean *both* that the soul is now aware of the eidetic hypotheses as having so far been *nothing but hypotheses and* that it will now treat them as *hypotheses in the literal sense, as beings "supposed," that is, "put under"* so as to *underlie* the appearances. Then, having risen by means of these "up to the unhypothesized, unto the beginning of the Whole," dialectic descends, using nothing sensible, but only the hypotheses, the *eíde* which are now no longer mere suppositions (b–c).

Book VI closes as Socrates assigns four "affections" or receptive powers (d 7) of the soul to the four sections: thought (*nóesis*) to the highest, thinking (*diánoia*) to the second, trust (*pístis*) to the third, and image-recognition (*eikasía*) to the lowest;[25] these are to be "ordered analogously" to their objects (e 2). *Nóesis,* the activity of intellection, and *nous,* the faculty of intellect, are here both rendered by "thought" to contrast their perfect immediacy and fully achieved insight with the progressive and discursive way of dianoetic "thinking."

A table relating the Divided Line to the Sun Image will make the correlation clearer.

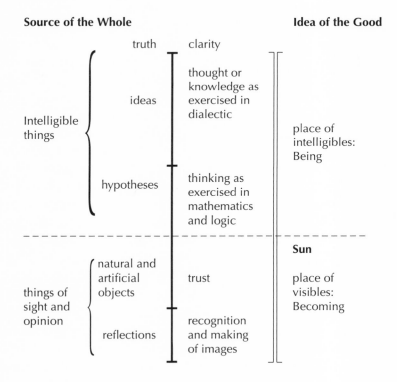

Source of the Whole			Idea of the Good
	truth	clarity	
Intelligible things	ideas	thought or knowledge as exercised in dialectic	place of intelligibles: Being
	hypotheses	thinking as exercised in mathematics and logic	
			Sun
things of sight and opinion	natural and artificial objects	trust	place of visibles: Becoming
	reflections	recognition and making of images	

2   a   In presenting the Sun Image to Glaucon, Socrates is requiring him to exercise his *dóxa,* his power to opine.

Of the two "doxastic" powers, the lower one, whose pregnant name is *eikasía,* is thrown in at the very end with conscious nonchalance; it will prove to be the most philosophically potent and pervasive of the four cognitive affections of the soul.

Ordinarily the verb *eikázein* means to "imagine," both in the sense of making an image and likeness, and of discovering a likeness or likelihood; in the latter sense it means to compare or conjecture. The noun *eikasía* means both the ability to make or see images, likelihoods, and conjectures, and the image, likelihood, or conjecture itself. For Glaucon the word would probably call to mind a witty and malicious amusement with which clever people spice their symposia, called "likenesses" or *eikasíai*.[26] The game consists of representing someone in an image, whereupon the victim might retaliate by making a "counter-image"—or by refusing to play. So Meno tells Socrates that he appears to be "most like" (80 a 5) a torpedo fish, while Socrates ostensibly declines to make a counter-image; of course the whole dialogue is an unflattering portrait of Meno. Alcibiades, in the one true triumph of his life, appearing in the *Symposium* as the god Dionysus himself, speaks of Socrates "through images." He compares him to one of the Sileni, the satyrs in the Dionysiac train, except that the image he makes, since it is "for the sake of truth" (215 a 6), shows this Socratic Silenus as being more sober than most men and far more divine than the god himself. Such images turn up also in Xenophon's *Symposium,* where Socrates curtly forbids the game when the *eikasíai* threaten to become injurious and false (VI, 8, cf. also VIII, 43). Socrates himself is, however, in the habit of introducing great matters under the image of a game or riddle (cf. 479 b 11, 521 c 5), and Glaucon will soon see that the "game of images" is an image of the most distinctive of human faculties.

In the meantime it must startle him just to hear "conjecturing" elevated into a power of the soul close to thought itself. But as he absorbs the meaning of Socrates' central image, he must notice that this Sun Image itself requires a peculiar application of his ability to see images. For he is, on the one hand, intended to imagine by means of the image what the Good is *like,* but he is also, on the other hand, required *to recognize simultaneously that the sun's world is but a likeness,* that his own visible world is a *counterfeit of Being.* Socrates had in fact prepared Glaucon for the fundamental importance of this power to recognize an image *as* an image when he had intimated earlier that to fail to possess it is to be permanently asleep to Being: "Look, isn't that just what dreaming is: when someone either in his sleep or while awake regards that which is like to something not as *like* to but as *the same as* that to which it is like?" (476 c 4). In taking in the Sun Image, Glaucon then learns to use his *eikasía* in *both* of the fundamental senses that Socrates, as the savior of the true and original meaning of words, has restored to it: first seeing analogies and likenesses, and then seeing them as *mere* images.

b   Now the next power, *pístis* or trust, comes into play. For as in seeing the sun's world as an image Glaucon has been forced to lose trust in the being of the visible world, so in seeing the sun as an image of the Good and "most like it" (506 e 3) he acquires a better opinion, a more believing *dóxa*, of this world, a trust that *life and government in the image of the Good are possible here,* in this world. Though his practically reasonable trust in the solidity of natural objects is intellectually shaken, another kind of belief is induced. The Socratic images of the Sun and the Divided Line serve here a purpose parallel to Socratic myth-telling (cf. 621 c 1, 3): The latter invariably means to rouse faith in virtuous living, the former intends to induce trust in cognitive effort. The question "whatever is the Good itself?" is, to be sure, "bidden goodbye for now" (506 e 1), and no explicit dialectical account of the Good is given at all. Instead the Good appears here as an object for *belief*, namely as the motive for study, the *end* and incentive to learning and doing. It is "that which every soul pursues and on account of which it does everything, *having a presentiment that there is* some such thing" (505 d 11). It is the one same, single thing which every human action, be it for show or genuine, intends not in seeming but in being, that which makes anything, including the virtues, *good for us,* namely "useful and profitable" (504 a 4). But above all, in this context, it serves to illumine the way of learning. In that function only is it the "greatest study," for as we shall see, in another sense it is no "learning matter" at all (p. 184).

We have now seen that the *explicit* consideration of the relation which human excellence and the human good have to the Good (*to agathón*) was dropped as soon as Glaucon re-entered the conversation (506 e) in order to concentrate his attention on it as an incitement to truth-seeking. But Socrates shies away from discussing the Good dialectically because that can be done seriously only after long preparation (see Aristotle, *Magna Moralia* 1182 a 27, who refers to the discussion of this question in *Concerning the Good*).

c An anecdote about the audience's reaction to Plato's "Lecture on the Good," that half-mythical event when he spoke to the public of the "Unwritten Teachings" of his school, is related by Aristoxenus in his *Harmonic Elements* (11, 30); it supports Socrates' reticence:

> They came, every one of them, expecting to get some one of the goods considered human. . . . But when his reasonings appeared to be of mathematical studies and numbers and geometry and astronomy and [when he said] at last that the Good is the One, I think it seemed to them very strange indeed; and then some sneered at it and others criticized it. Now what was the reason for this? That they knew nothing beforehand, but just like argufiers (*eristikoí*) were present to lap it up on the strength of the mere name.

Now Socrates himself has several such argumentative types, such eristics, on his hands—one of them Adeimantus, to whom he is careful to mention the "idea of the Good" as something Adeimantus *has* often heard of before, as something which is a cause of usefulness and profit and without which a man "cannot have the sentiments of a gentlemen" (505 b 3). Adeimantus reacts with a pat, eristic question worthy of the obtuse cleverness of a Meno: "But you, Socrates, do you think the Good is knowledge or pleasure or some other thing besides these?" (506 b 2; cf. *Meno* 70 a); clearly this is a standard, routine question about the Good (see *Philebus* 19 c). Here Plato shows a Socrates wiser in practice than Plato himself was when he lectured in public. For in the two dialogues dealing with the Good, the *Republic* and the *Philebus,* Socrates finds tactful ways to choose a responsive interlocutor from a small circle and to bring him slowly along. In the present dialogue he silences Adeimantus by suggesting to him that he has heard it all before; indeed, the incantatory use of the term "idea of the Good" (505 a, 505 e, 517 b, 526 e, 534 b), although it is made clear enough that the Good is not an *eídos* or *idéa* at all, sounds like a citation of a buzz word (cf. "Epicharmus" in Diogenes Laertius, VIII 14, 27). Meanwhile he gently brings Glaucon to face, seriously, the "awe-inspiring enormity" (509 c 1) of this Socratic Good.

But Socrates' indirection is not only a matter of avoiding public misunderstanding; it also has a positive pedagogic aim, which is to prevent Glaucon from pouncing precipitously on some bare truths that might turn his high spirits (c 1) into disengaged argufying. In providing Glaucon with images to reflect upon, Socrates instills in him a kind of artificial "recollection" (cf. *Meno* 81 c), which will enable him to "re-cognize" the *lógos* whenever he himself should come upon it.[27] This is, it seems, what the effect of any artfully wrought image ought to be—a slow or a sudden dawning of its *lógos*. Therefore in some way a dialectical account of the Good, formulable in terms not unlike those of the "Unwritten Teachings," must after all be latent here.[28] I shall try to work it out.

3   a   When Socrates has delivered his Sun Image Glaucon asks him to go once more through the "likeness of the sun" (509 c 5) in order to fill in whatever has been omitted before. Socrates' answer to this request is, as we have seen, the dividing of the line.

This Divided Line surely is the Sun Image schematized. It is the mathematical figure for the ascent of thoughtful speech (*lógos*) and the possibility of learning what is yet unknown. The choice of a linear figure is itself meaningful, for the line, as the unique connection of two point-monads, stands for the closest of all bonding relationships, that of like to like, for which the knower and the known are the acknowledged paradigm (see Aristotle, *On the Soul* 404 b 23, citing Plato; *Metaphysics* 1036 b 13 f., on the Pythagoreans); it stands as well for the possibility of incommensurable and hence irrational, that is, not directly expressible, relations. To understand this explication of the Sun Image, Glaucon will have to exercise his *diánoia*. We are now in the third section of the Divided Line, above "image-recognition" and "trust."

The word *diánoia* can be used quite generally for what we would call mental activity. For instance, Socrates himself says (476 d 5): "Why may we not call the mental activity (*diánoia*) [cf. *Sophist* 263 d] of one who knows, '*gnóme*,' and of one who opines, '*dóxa*'?" In its narrower meaning, the one pertaining to the third section of the Divided Line, *diánoia*, is the power of *thinking* or, as the phrase goes, of "thinking things through"; this thinking is the soul organ's restless scanning of things normally before us to find the articulations, distinctions, and comparisons proper to them. It means attending to, or searching for, that in things which can be grasped in thoughtful words, such as the Greeks call *lógoi*. This scanning involves a higher kind of *eikasía*, which might be termed "dianoetic *eikasía*."[29] For sensible things, when caught in speech, reveal themselves as mere imitations of something which the *lógos* is truly about; they show themselves as the "seen looks" (*horómena eíde*, 510 d 5) that copy the true but unseen looks (*eíde*) of the thing itself. Likewise in the *Phaedo* (100 a 2) Socrates intimates that those who look at things in terms of *lógoi* are less involved in images than those who look at them more literally with their physical eyes. In the *Sophist* (261 e) it turns out that this is because *lógoi* are manifestations (*delómata*) of being. The natural objects considered by the *diánoia* are therefore described primarily as images; in the dianoetic section, the soul proceeds by "using as images the very things before imitated," the natural objects that were imaged in the lowest section and trusted in daily use in the second section (510 b 4, 511 a 7). The originals of these new images are—somehow—caught in what speech *says*. Recall that the term *lógos* stands for the meaning as well as for the words that convey it. By entrusting its inquiry to this *lógos*, the *diánoia* is, in effect, "supposing" such originals; it is literally "hypothesizing" them so that they may serve as the basis of all distinctions, comparisons, inferences, and deductions. What are these originals?

In an inquiry by means of *lógoi*, certain results turn out to be primary and pervasive (522 c 8). Among these are the fact that a thing can always be called "one" and together with another, "two" (p. 234), that counting seems the inevitable concomitant of naming—the *lógos* "tells," that is, it counts, collects, and conveys. Furthermore, in different things the same "shape" can be discerned, which is caught accurately only in speech and only schematically in a spatial representation—the word "dog" and its definition have more precision that a generalized dog-drawing. Again, words are connected in a sentence and sentences in an account (all these are called *lógos*), and they have formal relations called "logical"—the *lógos* has inner necessities. Finally, behind the varied sensory shapes certain spatial regularities and pure assemblages of units can be discerned—these are the mathematicals, the "objects of learning" *par excellence,* which form an especially important province of the dianoetic realm. Arithmetic particularly is the subject of that indispensable pre-dialectical exercise to which Parmenides introduced Socrates in his youth (*Parmenides* 135 e) and which still resonates in the *Republic;* for the Platonic Parmenides the most important hypotheses to be investigated are, of course, the two suppositions concerning "the One," namely that it is or is not; for an older Socrates the inquiry into the nature of unity continues to be the fundamental learning experience (524 e, p. 227). However, any common name is in fact a dianoetic hypothesis as well; moreover any sentence is a dianoetic structure and as much the object of dianoetic inquiry as the mathematicals to which Socrates specifically assigns the dianoetic power.

   b   If for Socrates, the philosophical poet, the fundamental nature of the present discourse is *eikastic,* imagistic, for Glaucon, the mathematical enthusiast, it is *dianoetic.* Summarizing in his own words, but accurately, what he has learned from the division of the line, Glaucon perceptively brings out a central fact only implicit in Socrates' words, particularly in his naming of the *whole* upper part "intelligible" (*noetón*): The objects of the *diánoia* are in a sense the *same* as the *noetá,* the thought-objects, of the uppermost part—they are these *noetá* in the phase before the final *lógos* brings the thinker up to the *eidé,* the beings themselves. In fact he ends by treating the Divided Line as if the whole purpose of the division had been only to define the *diánoia.* For, observing that the very name of *dia-noia* suggests something in-between, or a mean, Glaucon defines it as "something between *dóxa* and *nous*" (511 d 4), as the intermediate and pivotal faculty *par excellence,* and so it is for an eager student. (See *Symposium* 203 e, where Eros as *daímon* is the divine intermediary between ignorance and wisdom; if this comparison were to be pursued, Eros would be revealed as the cosmic logician.)

   c   Socrates, of course, depends on the mathematical predisposition of his young philosopher when introducing him to the exercise of this *diánoia,* the lower noetic faculty (cf. 508 c 4, 509 d 11). In Book VII, Socrates takes the moment at which begins the long description of the formal mathematical education that is the "prelude" to dialectic (531 d 7) as an opportunity to engage Glaucon in a serious "methodical" (that is, upward-bound) dianoetic exercise. When Glaucon, accurately recalling the musical education of the guardians, perceptively concludes that this training cannot be the study that the future philosophers need, Socrates asks him: "O my marvelous Glaucon, what would be such a study . . . ?" Glaucon eagerly interrupts to ask in turn what study might indeed remain to them (522 b 6). Socrates now invites him pointedly to become his "fellow viewer" (523 a 7) while he himself makes "divisions," that is, distinctions, within himself about the studies that might lead toward Being; he is to say "I agree" or "I disagree," watching carefully that Socrates is "oracling" correctly. The discussion that follows shows Glaucon that arithmetic is precisely the study wanted, since it is "inviting to the *diánoia*" (524 d 3) and "arousing to *nóesis*" (d 5), and that all the best natures should be educated in it—to which Glaucon's slyly docile response is: "I agree" (526 c 7). Socrates proceeds to initiate him into the very study of "the one and the two and the three" (522 c–526 c) that Parmenides had once taught him. This is Glaucon's first and only step on the dialectical way; here and nowhere else in the *Republic* is undisguised direct philosophical work done—a "huge work," as he has begun to realize (511 c 3, 531 d 5). Glaucon intends to do it seriously, and when Socrates asks him whether he means to carry on as if demonstrating before others or in his own behalf, he wants to converse chiefly for his own sake. But, as Socrates says, suddenly speaking straight out to us who are reading the dialogue, "if someone else should be able to profit in some way, you won't begrudge him that" (528 a 2).

d   But why should Glaucon need to be especially invited to *this* dialogue, since they are already in the midst of one and have indeed come, as Polemarchus says in the beginning, just to converse (328 a 9)? Evidently there are various ways to converse. In fact three meanings of *dialégesthai* can be distinguished within this dialogue.

First it can mean a conversation in which anyone may and can take part. This, despite Thrasymachus's efforts to stage an exclusive rhetorical display, is its meaning in the "prelude" (357 a 2) of the dialogue, Book I. Second it can mean that great "power of *dialectic*" (511 b 4, 532 d 8, 533 a 8) in which the *lógos,* the account-giving power, leaves all sense perception behind and is moved "by the *eíde* themselves," advancing "through them and into them" (511 c 1). This activity is what is imitated by sight (532 a 2); as the soul ranges over *noetic* sights (whose merely figurative visibility the name *eídos,* "sight, look, aspect," indicates), so the eye sees things at once distinct and together. It is clear that Socrates regards the soul as truly moving, *both upward and downward,* only in dialectic, which is thus repeatedly called a way (*méthodos*), meaning a pursuit or a directed journey (533 b 3, 532 e 1, 3; 533 b 3, c 7; 532 e 3). In contrast, the conclusive motion of *diánoia* is *downward* (510 b 6, d 2) as in deduction; that of the lowest power, *eikasía,* is *back and forth* as in comparisons; and the next-to-lowest power, *pístis,* our ordinary mode, enjoys rarely disturbed rest. In the use of its lower powers the soul is therefore said to be bogged down and made sluggish (533 d 1, 611 c). The cause is its association with the body; the soul is never quickened with bodily life but only with the *lógos,* and its proper motion is a "heavenly journey" (cf. *Phaedrus* 256 d 8). But this dialectic is only *praised* in the *Republic* (532 a 1). Its actual *exercise* is nearly impossible to one who is not already practiced in dianoetic studies (533 a 9) and perhaps to any mortal, for dialectic is thought out-thinking itself. Accordingly the propaedeutic mathematical studies are carefully trimmed (536 d 6). They exclude not merely all "banausic," that is, applied, mechanical, elements, but also any explicit eidetic admixture; for instance, nothing is said of Plato's own arithmological teaching, the "eidetic numbers" (see *Metaphysics* 1080 a 12 ff.; see also Note 11 of ch. 13 and p. 235, herein), although, as we shall see, allusions to dialectical terms abound.

There remains the third, a middle *dialégesthai,* which happens to be the one that is characteristic of this central conversation. It is the mode usually referred to as Socratic dialectic. This is speech between two souls, though it must have a sensory clothing of sound, the audible dialogue. Such conversation is sharply distinguished from myth telling and hearing (e.g., *Protagoras* 320 c, 324 d, *Gorgias* 523 a, *Timaeus* 26 c), since the latter appeals to trust and imagination, while the former involves *diánoia* primarily. For *diánoia* supervenes as soon as sense perception is being carefully expressed in words; that attempt inevitably gives rise to dilemmas, especially to self-contradictions (524 e 3). Socratic dialectic is therefore often initially refutational. But in supplying hypotheses to solve these dilemmas, the *diánoia* brings in *noetá* and thus invites down the uppermost faculty of thought, *nóesis* (523 a 1). By itself *diánoia* is the faculty for observing differences, distinctions, and contradictions. As such it ranges over as well as betwixt and between its objects, ready to discover human perplexities as well as mathematical problems (530 b 6). Unguided, it can thus become "wayless," caught in *aporíai*, impasses (524 a 7). Therefore in those parts of a Socratic dialogue that are dianoetically dialectical one of the interlocutors must know more than the other, must be more advanced in dialectic, so that he will be able "to ask and answer most knowledgeably" (534 d 9, 528 b 8; cf. *Phaedrus*, 276 e 5).

In his dialogue with Glaucon Socrates exercises such a superiority even more than he does usually, since their conversation is synoptic and requires a large foreknowledge on his part—a dialectician must be *synoptikós,* comprehensive in his view. The introduction to arithmetic mentioned above displays precisely the required relation of the interlocutors: Socrates makes dialectical divisions "within himself" (523 a 6), which he then "shows" to Glaucon (a 9); Glaucon is to look on with him and to respond to Socrates' affirmations or negations with his own agreement or disagreement (cf. *Sophist* 263 e 12). But this dialogic superiority is evident most of all in the very naming of the powers of the soul with which Book VI closes. For these powers are, as it were, *named from above,* from a synoptic point of view. Anyone who has not left the first three sections cannot possibly know their true names: *Dóxa,* as used ordinarily, means the faculty of judgment; people rarely think that they have what to Socrates is "mere opinion." What they do think is that they know their own minds; and that the various provinces of *diánoia,* such as the arts and mathematics (511 c 6, d 3), are to be particularly highly regarded as producing nothing less than expert knowledge in their devotees (533 d 4). For Socrates, of course, *diánoia* belongs to a segment below knowledge (*epistéme*).

4 a Let me now take up again the invitation to reflection that is extended to Glaucon by the sectioning of the realms "as if" they were a line; he must wonder, as we have already done (p. 176), why this conversation has no dialectical treatment either of the Good or of the *eíde* under its aegis. This missing *lógos* is, however, absent in a different way for each of these dialectical objects. I shall begin with the Good.

The Good has no place within the realm of Being; it is "beyond Being" (509 b 9). Since it is that which is "un-hypothesized" it cannot be traversed by thinking in the same way as are the "hypotheses," the stepping stones of the *lógos* into Being (511 b 8). Consequently there is in this dialogue no power of the cognitive soul that corresponds to the Good as its object, as is signified by the fact that it is off the top of the Divided Line. Although within the context of the imagery of sight the eye of the soul is said to look *at* it, a distinction between movement "among" and "through" the *eíde* (510 b 8, 511 c 2) and movement "up unto" the Good (511 b 6, 533 c 8) is pretty generally maintained; the latter has about it something glancing and momentary; a glimpse of the Good is "scarcely" (517 c 1) achieved. Consequently this beholding is not quite knowing in the dialectical sense at all, for the idea of the Good is the result not of a unitary act of sight but is approached by "abstracting it from everything else" and "delimiting it by *lógos*" (534 b 9). Socrates repeats this several times: The Good as responsible source is known only *after* the eidetic vision, after dialectic dwelling among the forms; it is known on the downward return, so to speak, by a *syllogismós* or collection of *lógoi,* a *lógos* of *lógoi* (516 b 9, 517 c 1). It is, in effect, the most comprehensive of all those definitive "collections" (e.g., *Sophist* 267 b 1) that follow the distinction-making "divisions" of dialectic. The Good, the "greatest study," is a "learning matter" or a *máthema* only in a new and strange sense, for it is learned in the movement away from it. To confront the Whole as a human knower is to have to step back among the parts.

b   For those realms, however, that are on the Divided Line, Socrates' omission of *lógoi* takes on a different significance and form. It is essential to the following discussion to recall that the word *lógos* means not only account or reasoning but also the mathematical relation of *ratio,* a double meaning of great importance particularly in Pythagorean contexts (e.g., *Epinomis* 977 c 3). We are told that each of the unequal main sections of the line is again to be cut in the same ratio (509 d 7), but we are neither given the ratio itself—we are not even told whether it is numerical or irrational, that is, whether it is a ratio of commensurable or incommensurable lines—nor are we definitely told whether the greater or the less of the unequal segments is to be the upper one (see Plutarch, *Platonic Questions* 1001 d and p. 264). We can conclude nothing except that the two middle segments can be proved to be equal,[30] which means that *pístis* and *diánoia* are in some way coextensive. That is indeed necessary, since the realm of *diánoia* is particularly closely correlated to the realm of *natural objects;* I would go so far as to say that the dianoetic realm is the place of a future mathematical physics.

c   This absence of definite ratios is the more noteworthy because for the earlier tripartite soul the numerical ratios of the parts *are,* playfully, given: They form the musical progression of the "lowest," "middle," and "highest" place in the *diapason,* the concord that goes "through all" the tones, that is, encloses them all, the octave (443 d 6, cf. 432 a). If the "middle" is here taken to designate the mean through which the "first consonances" of music, the intervals of the fifth and the fourth, are compounded to yield this interval of the octave (produced by strings whose length is in the ratio of 2:1) then, since the string ratios producing the fifth are as 3:2 or 6:4 and those of the fourth as 4:3, the string lengths are as 6:4:3, the three terms of a "harmony." Here 4, a number said to represent the spirited element, the *thymós,* is a "harmonic mean," the *mése,* which is embodied in one string functioning both as the shorter (higher-pitched) string of the fifth and the longer (lower-pitched) string of the fourth (Theon of Smyrna, *Mathematics Useful for Understanding Plato,* musical section). The implied use of the so-called "harmonic proportion," that is, $a/c = a - b/b - c$, where b is the "harmonic mean" (so that $6/3 = 6 - 4/4 - 3$), may have a special significance here. Nicomachus in his *Introduction to Arithmetic* (II xxvi) says that Philolaos the Pythagorean regarded this proportion as the "geometric harmony" expressing the *cube,* which has 12 sides, 8 angles, and 6 faces, so that its characteristics are given in the terms 6:4:3.

The tripartite "embodied" soul is therefore here characterized as the basic solid, the cube. Aristotle (*On the Soul* 404 b 16 ff.) does in fact report a similar Platonic oral teaching about the soul: The noetic cosmos, called "the animal itself," arises "from the idea of the one and primary length and breadth and depth": so that in respect to the soul, which is similar to that animal, "intellect (*nous*) is one; knowledge (*epistéme*) is two, since it is uniquely and immediately related to one; the number of the plane is opinion (*dóxa*); and sense perception (*aísthesis*) belongs to the solid." Evidently the Academy too, in its Pythagorean moments, believed that the soul, descending from its dimensionless unity through the spatial dimensions reaches some sort of solidity as it meets the body.

We may ask further how this Pythagorean three-dimensional structure is related to the quadripartite knowing soul of the Divided Line that replaces, in the center of the *Republic,* the earlier tripartite soul, composed of reasoning, spirit, and desire. Although it is certainly not the same, there is an instructive relation between them which is best seen schematically:

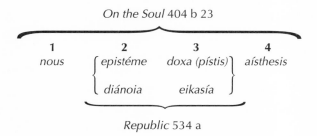

The dimensional soul will be seen to be the more comprehensive of the two since it possesses elements for apprehending both extremes of dimensionality, namely unit and body, where the former is the non-dimensional *source* of the whole soul, and the latter is its complete, full-grown *structure*. The soul in the central *Republic* has, as we have seen, no clear and separate capacities corresponding to these termini; furthermore, as the Divided Line shows, it has no dimensional progression, since the capacity for apprehension of solids (presumably assigned to the three-dimensional soul) occurs in one of the middle sections. On the other hand, it does have what one might call reflective depth or interior extension, a kind of imagistic cascade, which arises from the *eikastic* reduplication of *epistéme* in *diánoia* and of *pístis* in *eikasía* that takes place within its two major parts, *nóesis* and *dóxa* (534 a);[31] note that is is the *lowest* power that first apprehends the Whole, since it is the one that recognizes the image character of the ladder of Being.

In summary, it might be said that the Pythagorean dimensional soul is all-embracing or *cosmic* (as laid out in the *Timaeus*), and that is why some can say that "the soul is the place of the *eíde*" (*On the Soul* 429 a 27). On the other hand, in respect to the soul that goes with the realms of the Divided Line, it might rather be said that "the *eíde* are the place of the soul." For the knowing soul ranges all over this, its proper place, sometimes settling in one spot and then moving again, remaining always somewhat a stranger—in accordance with the similarity between knowledge and the pervasive, piecemeal *eídos* of otherness described in the *Sophist* (257 c 7). Later we shall see the significance of the fact just pointed out, namely that the soul of the *Republic* is not a cosmic harmony of number ratios (p. 218).

But though the *lógoi* of the Divided Line are indeterminate, this much about them is given: they are the *same* throughout, for sameness of ratio defines a proportion, an *ana-logia* or "recurrence of a *lógos*." How is Glaucon to interpret the mathematical fact that is here presented to his *diánoia*?

d We should, first of all, keep firmly in mind that this mathematical presentation is itself only a *simile;* Glaucon is to cut the realms "just as" he would a line (509 d 6). He has reason to think neither that the descending realms of Being literally have mathematical ratios to one another nor that the inexplicitness of the *lógos* in any way implies that the ratio of any two lengths is indeterminate (as would be lengths merely greater and the less, a ratio technically known as "indefinite," *aóristos, Metaphysics* 1021 a 4); on the contrary, the *lógos,* the ratio, here stands for the possibility of articulate human language, of rationality. Thus cautioned, let us see what the model will yield.

Immediately after the fundamental division of the line and description of the lower subsections has been made, Socrates reads off a first proportion (510 a 9; read proportions this way: *as* a *is to* b *so* c *is to* d):

Opined : known :: images : imaged object.

This proportion announces that the internal relations of the two lowest realms are the same as those of the whole, so that the relations connecting the whole are mirrored in even its lower parts. At the very end of the Divided Line passage he reads off yet another proportion (511 e 3):

Segments of line : truth :: affections of soul : clarity.

This means in mathematical terms that the affections of the soul are the *correspondents* of the realms of Being that the line segments represent (Euclid, V Def. 11: Given a:b :: c:d, *a* and *c,* as well as *b* and *d,* are said to correspond). Or, using analogical reasoning—that is, inferring the likeness of correspondents (cf. *Metaphysics* 1016 b 34, 1093 b 18; *Topics* 108 a 7)—we may conclude that known and knower are *alike* and *respond* to each other (cf. *On the Soul,* 404 b 18). Here the analogical method brings out the bond that "yokes together with the strongest yoke" (508 a 1), the linking of known and knower by the clarifying light of truth; this illumination can bind them because they are both "like the Good" (509 a 3), that "ruling source" of the "community" of knowns and knowers (cf. *Sophist* 248 a 11).

And finally, in concluding the explication of both the Sun and the Cave Images, Socrates forms two more proportions (534 a 3):

Being : Becoming :: thought : opinion.

Thought : opinion :: knowledge : trust :: thinking : image-recognition.

The first of these proportions signifies that the degrees of Being are the same as the gradations of knowing. The second, continued proportion displays particularly well the force of the mathematical form Socrates has chosen. For since the affections of the soul are coordinated with linear magnitudes, they may be "alternated" (Euclid, *Elements* V Def. 12). This means that the first is to the third as the second to the fourth—and that is exactly what Socrates has done here; he has alternated the original proportion of the segments which showed that

Knowledge : thinking :: trust : image-recognition.

The new longer form of the proportion draws attention to the close relation of each faculty in one main segment to the corresponding faculty in the other, a relation which mirrors that of the main faculties and again that of the realms of Being. The last ratio, which links thinking (*diánoia*) with image-recognition (*eikasía*), particularly justifies the notion of a "*dianoetic eikasía,*" a thinking use of images, while the preceding ratio shows that special relation between knowledge and trust which we experience in that unassailable finality or incorrigibility, analogous to the self-sufficiency of knowledge, that certain sense perceptions possess (523 b 1).

Obviously, by using the various Euclidean operations (Euclid, V Defs. 11–18) on these proportions, and by attending either to the sameness of the ratio relation or to the likeness of the correspondents in the alternated proportions, it is possible to obtain a variety of illuminating results. That this would be a legitimate enterprise is shown by the term Socrates uses when he dismisses further division of the line lest there be a surfeit of "multiplicate *lógoi*" (534 a 7), a punning reference to the "duplicate" and "triplicate" ratios, gotten by the compounding operation set out in the theory of proportion (Euclid, V Defs. 9–10).[32] Though we musn't overdo it, Socrates is saying, analogical reasoning is the way of philosophical ascent and descent.

All of these further results would be, however, only the expression of two fundamental similarities: First is that of the knower and the known, mentioned above, which Socrates has in mind when he tells Glaucon to "order them [the affections of the soul] analogously" to the realms of being (511 e 2). Second is that—really prior—similarity of each degree of Being to the next higher degree. It is by reason of this similarity that the successive realms of (1) images, (2) natural objects, (3) mathematicals, and (4) forms are described in turn as (1) "that which is made as something similar," (2) "that to which it is made similar," and (3) "that which was before copied and is now treated as a likeness" (cf. 510 a 10, b 4, 511 a 7); and (4) that whose original is beyond Being, for even the *eíde* themselves are, as we learn from other sources, formed in the likeness of the Good understood as the One since they are themselves each *one* (e.g., *Metaphysics* 987 b 18 ff., where the formula is "being/one," *on / hen*).

This four-stepped ladder of similars is what makes the upward transition, the dialectical road, possible. It is, we should note, completely articulated only in the Divided Line; the Sun Image has merely two undifferentiated realms, the intelligible and the visible. The Divided Line does, as we said, preserve this original homogeneity of the larger realms; images and natural bodies are not found in *differently constituted* realms, for both are sensibles and either have their own body or use an alien one. For reflections are "in water" and "on smooth bodies" (510 a 1), so that the difference between a body and its image is not really that between the plane and the solid dimension or between merely visible and palpable things—images are palpable through their solid medium. Similarly, mathematical hypotheses and *eíde* are *equally* intelligibles; we may think of the multitude of mathematical objects (say, circles) as images cast by their one defining form (circularity) onto a mental space supplied by the imaging intellect. Thus what differentiates the realms internally is not a different material, but rather the reflective distinction of like to what it is likened to, understood as that of the genuine to the counterfeit. For the parts of the line are mainly meant to specify the image-original relation first grandly set out in the Sun Image.

e   Glaucon will, then, see that the *lógoi* relating certain aspects of the Whole are one and the same throughout, that one *lógos*, one ratio, is pervading the Whole, expressing its self-similarity, its iterated likeness (*homoiótes;* cf. *Sophist* 231 a 7, *Statesman* 285 b 6). In conveying this notion to Glaucon mathematically, Socrates is signifying that he is presenting him with such *hypotheses* about Being and Becoming as will make thinking itself possible—and by this he means thinking consistently, namely "in a manner that preserves the sameness of the *lógos*" (510 d 2; Socrates takes the adverb *homologoúmenos* literally;

ordinarily it just means "concordantly, agreeably with . . ." See Aristotle, *Topics* 108 b 8). But if the characteristic dianoetic direction is *downward* to conclusions by deductions that win agreement (*homología*) because the *lógoi* in different souls have remained in concord, the discovering *diánoia* moves *upward* by an *analogía*. It is this latter analogic ascent that is chiefly required in any Socratic search and is therefore suggested to Glaucon in this part of the dialogue: "Make an analogy . . ." (524 d 9, cf. 509 b 2). An explication of this means of learning is given in the *Statesman*: The teacher chooses as an example some thing about which the learner has right opinion to "lead him up to" (*anágein*) something unknown, that is, the teacher shows the learner an example, a *para-deigma,* "something to be shown beside" some unknown. That paradigm is able "to lead [the learner] up onto" (*epágein*) this unknown. And then this unknown may become known to the learner by a recognition of the analogy (277 d 9; here Socrates, in the reflexive mode characteristic of him, explains "example" by giving an example as an example, just as in the *Republic* he explains "image" by an image). The sun, as an image of the Good, is just such an example, and since the Good is far above the sun, the "bringing up" (*epagogé*) of Glaucon will be a true ascent. In fact it will be an ascent—though only provisional—to the source of all examples, to that *parádeigma* which is no longer example but exemplar.

We might summarize this exposition from a different point of view by saying that the Divided Line tells the story of recollection mathematically, by presenting through proportions that "affinity" of all nature (cf. *Meno* 81 d 1) which makes it possible to move with a sense of recognition in unknown places. Aristotle will reduce this upward, or inward, journey to the "logical" procedure of induction (*epagogé*), of which he makes Socrates the inventor (*Metaphysics* 1078 b 28).

f   The first and original affinity, the Sun Image implies, is that which the Good as progenitor has with the sun as the offspring made in its image. In other words, the Good itself possesses an image-making power that it passes down to the *eíde* and that they pass on in turn (cf. *Phaedrus* 250 a 6). This power might be called "downward *eikasía*." By making our world a cascading progression of likenesses, it is originally responsible for our own ability both to *make* ourselves, our thought, like to the highest things by an effort at "likening" (*homoiósis, 500 c 5; Theaetetus* 176 b 1) and to *recognize* likenesses or to make analogies. It is, we might say, ultimately responsible for our "upward *eikasía*" and for the pleasure of recognition that the play of eikastic thinking over all the realms gives us (cf. Aristotle, *Poetics* 1448 b 8). It is a power so unobtrusively indispensable that without it we would never "know ourselves" even in the most superficial sense of having confronted in a mirror our own looks, the *eídos* or look of our own face!

g   We can now see precisely why the criticism of poetry in Book III turns into a reprise of that radical "ancient quarrel between philosophy and poetry" (607 b 5) in Book X. This quarrel, which already engaged Pythagoras, who descended to Hades to watch Homer and Hesiod suffer for their lies (Diogenes Laertius, VIII 21), is now given a precise cause. In the light of the Sun Image, poets are usurpers and perverters of the power of the Good. They are more despicable even than that sophistic charlatan who, having carried a mirror through the world, claims to have "made everything" (596 c 2), when he has really only mimicked the lowest effects of the power of the Good. For poets make artificial images, using a perverted power of *eikasía,* a "low" (603 b 4) sort of generation called *mimetic* or imitative (602 a 11), which produces images of good and bad things indiscriminately (604 e 1; *Sophist* 233 c, cf. also 267 a) and distracts the listeners from Being (605 a 9). Such *mimetic* products are not natural likenesses but are separated from the true source of images by the interposition of a human maker, who "makes images vilely" (*Republic* 377 e 1). Poetic *mimésis* makes distorted, artificial imitations.[33] "Artists," to speak in modern terms, arrogate to themselves an unauthorized function of "creativity." Socratic *eikasía,* on the other hand, makes honest likenesses of Being as it is given (p. 271). Like it or not, Socrates is just that harsh—in behalf of truth seeking.

5 a We must now go on to see exactly what conjectures about the Good the Sun Image allows Glaucon to make on reflection, even though he cannot yet reach a full and sure *lógos.*

In the image the Good is presented in three successive capacities, a triplet proved to be fundamental by its recurrence in the *Philebus* (20 b 8). It is presented first as the *father* of the sun which rules the earth (508 b 12), then as the *light* which is responsible for knowledge (e 3), and last as the nourishing *source* of Being (509 b 7).[34] The first of these might be called its cosmogenic function, by which the potent male Good generates the sun as a male offspring to be lord of the visible world and an intermediate source of the world of Becoming, analogous to the Good itself as ruler of the world of Being (508 c 4, 517 c 3); the obvious question that arises here is whether the sun also has a mother. The Cave Image will deal with that (p. 212). However, although the sun resembles its maker in its brightness, its continual risings and settings clearly mark it as a part of the world of becoming and passing away, while at the same time they intimate that the Good is also a *source of motion* (cf. Alexander on Aristotle's *Metaphysics* 988 a 11 ff., ed. Hayduck, p. 59). In its second capacity the Good is several times called the "responsible cause" (*aitía,* 508 e 3, 517 c 2) and *aítios,* "that which is to be called to account" (516 c 2) both for the passive state of the "beings that are known" (*nooúmena,* 508 e 1, 509 b 6, d 8) and for the active knower (508 e 2), that is, for the soul in its receptive act of knowing (509 b 6); this *aitía* is, however, more beautiful and more honorable than either of its effects. In its third capacity, the Good is called king and lord (509 d 2, 517 c 4) and "ruling source" of the Whole (*arché,* 510 b 7, 511 b 7) or the "*arché* itself" (533 c 8), "in power and seniority exceeding the nature of Being" (509 b 9); it gives things both the "state of being" (*to einai*) and their knowable nature as beings or "beingness" (*ousía*, 509 b 8). The latter two capacities are reduplicated by the sun insofar as it is the source of natural growth and visibility.

Socrates presents these functions in the order that will bring Glaucon up by analogy from the visible many to the invisible One (507 b 2). In the order of logical generation, however, the listing should clearly be reversed, since Being itself must precede the confrontation of active and passive beings, and this split must in turn come before the birth of a world that is both perceptible and perceived by sense. The grandest, most inclusive, most politically relevant, function of the Good is therefore its rule (*arché*) over beings; next it acts as the responsible cause (*aitía*) for teachers and learners, while its most personal function, finally, is that of a father. But in truth neither order holds, for the Good itself is not hierarchically ordered, since it is itself the source and beginning of all order—"the *arché* itself" (533 c 8).

b   The diagram below shows the parts of this order; all its terms except one are taken from the text:

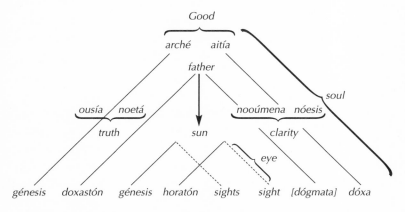

This scheme shows the Good as presiding over and bonding a kind of pervasive duplication: The Good as the cause of knowledge is responsible for the unifying confrontation of knower and known (right side) and thus originates the soul, the agent of thought (*nóesis,* 508 d 4; cf. *Sophist* 248 c 11, e ff.; as was said, *nóesis* is here rendered as "thought" because it is completed thinking, perfected *diánoia,* and the noun "thought" is homonymous with the past participle of "to think"). The Good is as well the direct source of beingness (*ousía,* left side), which is also the "place of thought" (*tópos noetós,* 508 c 1, 509 d 2), the place provided for the soul, since it contains the "things made for thought" (*noetá,* the *-tos* ending signifying the *capability* of being thought; cf. *Sophist* 248 d 4). Finally, as generating source, the Good puts forth the sun, a sensible secondary source that reduplicates the whole structure of Being on the lower level of sense and Becoming (*génesis*).

The lower part of the diagram, where Becoming is located, brings out an aspect of the Sun Image that is of fundamental importance to the human place in the Whole. The soul, although primarily a knowing soul directed to Being (508 d 6), is, insofar as it is embodied, also involved with the world of Becoming. For some aspects of sense "invite thought" (523 b 1). Furthermore we do have opinions, that kind of unthinking set mental reaction significantly expressed in the phrase beginning "I feel that . . ." which is mostly concerned with worldly Becoming. Human speech, too, is accommodated to Becoming, since in its negations it is capable of the same involvement with Nonbeing that Becoming itself has (477 a; cf. *Sophist* 260 b 10; p. 301). In other words, the human soul as the moving agent of knowledge has a faculty, *dóxa,* by which it ranges over Becoming and has a place there. This place contains "that which is made to be opined" (*doxastón*), and the name of these things, as apprehended by the soul, has been added in the diagram—they are the "matters of opinion" (*dógmata*), a word denoting both ordinary private opinions (cf. *Republic* 538 c 6) and their political codifications, the decrees and ordinances of the city.

Thus from the point of view of the human soul, Becoming belongs to Being as one of its gradations (just as the representative of the Good, the sun, is not above but within this world); hence its faculty, *dóxa*, has a certain kinship with knowledge (*Meno* 86 a). But from the point of view of the body, Becoming is the place of sense perception (*aísthesis*, 507 c 4, e 6) and, most characteristically, of "things that can be seen" (*horatá*), the organ of whose perception is the eye, which is "most like the sun" (508 b 3). Hence Socrates has *two* names, *doxastón* and *horatón*, for the segment and realm of Becoming (509 d). So also each human being has two instruments or organs: that "by which" it sees and opines, the soul; and that "through which" it sees and senses, the eye (*Theaetetus* 184 c 6; cf. *Timaeus* 28 a 2). Becoming is then, as part of the cognitive universe, *within* Being, not an external accretion to it.

c   Seen in another way, however, the diagram brings out not the unity of the Whole but a certain downward doubling, effecting a differentiation, or rather proliferation, from one to many that Socrates had recalled when he introduced the Sun Image. Whence does it arise? Although no source beside the Good is mentioned, the language of the image persistently implies that something *already there* is capable of "taking" the gifts of the Good in various ways. The Good "provides" (*paréchei*, 503 e 1, 509 a 7, cf. b 3, 517 c 4) what is to be known with that truth of which the things known "partake" (*metéchei*, 511 e 3, 4); it "gives" this power to the knower (508 e 2), makes intelligibility "to be present" (*pareínai*, 509 b 7) in things, and causes being "to be added to them" (*próseinai*, b 8).

One might be tempted to think of some underlying "material" (with which Aristotle, speaking in his own terms, does indeed equate that in Plato's teaching, which "takes," that is, receives, the Good, *Metaphysics* 988 a 11). The Good, however, does not actually differentiate some available stuff, but rather *binds* something already disposed to come in a two-fold way. For instance, just as the "yoke" of light yokes two different things, vision and visibility (507 c 6), so the truth is the bond by which the Good binds the disparate knower and known. This dyadic disposition appears also in other ways, for example, in the "double *eíde*" (509 d 1, 4, 6) of the visible and the knowable and their two-fold subdivisions (534 a 1; compare the two *morphai* of Parmenides' "double philosophy," Diels, *Vorsokratiker* 1. fr. 8, 53 and p. 218, 6). It shows up also in the world's aptitude for being divided which is expressed in the "taking apart into two" (*diaíresis*) that complements the unifying bond of analogies (534 a 6). We have here an intimation of that secondary dyadic principle, so often mentioned by Aristotle under the name of the *Indefinite Dyad,* the Duality which in Plato's arithmological teaching is the second and secondary *arché* complementing the Good understood as the One.

Although it is only an intimation, it is one that must attend on any presentation of the Whole, because even this second principle has "a certain likeness to the whole" by reason of which it "contains all things" (Aristotle, *Physics* 207 a 19). As Speusippus explains:

> For they held that the One is higher than Being and is the source of Being; and they delivered it even from the status of a principle. For they held that given the One in itself, conceived as separated and alone, without the other things, with no additional element, nothing else would come into existence. And so they introduced the Indefinite Duality as the *principle of Being.*[35]

This second—or rather, first—principle or *arché* of Being is discovered and described in the *Sophist* in pursuing the source that makes sophistical speaking (commonly known as "Double Talk," *Dissoi Lógoi*) possible (chs. 10–11). A difficulty had arisen over the necessary two-ness of Being. This two-ness had been a consequence of the very fact that plays so pervasive a role in the Sun Image, namely that there is both knowing and something knowable; therefore Being, as both known and knowing, possesses a knowing and living soul and is thus in motion, while as knowable it is steadfast and at rest (248 d ff.). Being thus seemed to contain *both* Motion and Rest, and this resulted in a quandary: For it couldn't *be* both at once, so that it had to be "some third thing" embracing these indefeasibly incompatible two. But that was impossible too, for now Being *was not* either Rest or Motion, and these in turn *were not* beings (250 ff.). The solution to this quandary was found in the nature of the Other (*to héteron*), which goes "through everything" (255 e 3), bonding all beings as each other's other. Now, instead of saying that Being *is not* Motion and Rest, we say that it is merely *other* than they (without, however, being some third thing); since each of the two indeed *is,* and, instead of saying that Motion and Rest *are not* beings, we say they *differ from* Being Itself—and from each other. In this way the deliverances of speech were justified and the *lógos* was saved. But more importantly, a potent super-*eídos* had been established, an *arché* of relationality (p. 299).

The *eídos* of the Other is described in the *Sophist* as effecting a kind of distributive Nonbeing, for every being is *not* the other being, but *is* that other's other. The Other is pervasively relative (255 d) and cut up into many, indeed indefinitely many, duplicative parts (256 e, 257 c). But these are exactly the terms associated by Aristotle with his report of Plato's Indefinite Dyad (*Metaphysics* 987 b 19 ff., 1087 b 13 ff.).[36] Plato, he says, made "the other-nature" (cf. *Sophist* 256 e 1, 257 c 7) a dyad because the numbers "outside the first," meaning the One and the Dyad, can be "begotten from her just as from a matrix" by the One as begetter (*Metaphysics* 987 b 34). Thus neither the One nor the Dyad are numbers; they are principles of numbers. The first begotten true number (*arithmós*) is the eidetic Two (1082 a 11), that is, Being (see Note 35 and ch. 13 Note 11).

This "two-making" *arché* is precisely one of those "responsible causes of division" of the *Sophist* (253 c 3) which is there being sought. It also appears to be, as has been said, one source of that confrontation of knower and knowable that the Good sustains with its illuminating truth. Clearly, then, such an *arché* is in the background of the Sun Image. We shall see, however, that in the context of the human good, which is the concern of the *embodied* soul, it will appear not as a second source of Being but as something opposed to that Good, as the source of evil. But for the human *knowing* soul Socrates has coined a special term—it is "like the Good" (*agathoeidés*), or "well-formed" (*Republic* 509 a 3), and so are all its situations; it is exempt from acquaintance with the bad version of the second *arché*, whose name is Matter, Matrix—of which more below (p. 213).

   d   We must now take a last look at the role of similarity or *likeness* in the Sun Image, not merely insofar as it permits ascent by analogy, but as a constitutional principle. In the conversation of the dialogue *Parmenides*—which is, incidentally, recounted to Adeimantus and Glaucon—young Socrates had tentatively presented the notion of pattern and likeness (*parádeigma, homoíoma*) as a solution to the problem of the participation (*méthexis*) of the many sensible things in the one invisible *eídos* (132 c 12). He thought that the *eíde* might be "patterns in nature" (d 2), patterns which "the sensible things become like." Hence they are "likenesses," and "their participation in the *eíde* is nothing but this being made in their image" (d 4). Parmenides shows him that his solution is impossible. The *eíde* cannot be "in nature," that is, among things, as patterns since, likeness being reciprocal, the pattern would be indistinguishable from its copy—they would be mutually like and would require yet a third *eídos* above them to be like to (e 7). This version of the so-called "third man" criticism (see Aristotle, *Metaphysics* 990 b 17) amounts to showing that patterns, merely by being designated as patterns, are not necessarily above their copies in the scale of being and need have no originating power. Such patterns cannot be the desired *unique* sources of multiplicity. (This same criticism is in fact made by Aristotle of the Platonic *eíde*, *Metaphysics* 1079 b.) At this stage young Socrates does not even suspect that the problem might have to be considered on a higher level, namely that of the participation (*méthexis*) of the *eíde in* each other as they form communities *with* each other, and even beyond that, on the level *of the Whole they belong to all together* (129 d 6). Therefore he does not see that his image solution might after all be applicable. For, as we shall see, on the highest level there is a place for such a solution.

One aspect of the higher *methexis* problem, the problem of the several "communities" that the *eíde* have with each other, was, as we have seen, considered in the *Sophist* (254 b 7). There the solution to the question how Rest and Motion can retain their identity and yet both together *be,* was given in terms of the Other. This *eídos* extends throughout all the *eíde* so as to relate each *eídos* to every other as that specific other's other; hence each becomes intelligibly capable of being together in a diverse community of beings (256 a 10). That is why Otherness is the bond of Being which enables the *eídos* Being to encompass all the beings.

If the point of view taken is not that within but that "beyond Being," then young Socrates' theory of Pattern and Likeness performs just such a function as Otherness did within Being, and does so in a way more plausibly. For within Being, the reflexive *eídos* of the Other (reflexive because it makes everything another's other) is, as was said, the *source of community,* the "bond" that runs "through everything" (*Sophist* 255 e 3, cf. 253 a 5, c 1), while another major *eídos,* the Same, is responsible for the separate and independent oneness, identity, and self-sameness of each being (254 d 15). But the *bonding of the all-inclusive Whole* is achieved precisely because of the *likeness* of each being within it to a pattern beyond and so to each other being; it is exactly the progressively failing power of "being like" that manifests itself within Being as that peculiar case of Otherness called "being an image of." For an image is only partially like its original (*Sophist* 240 a 8). The fact is that Parmenides' objection to Socrates' pattern theory of participation falls as soon as the pattern is really of a different order and sufficiently *beyond the reach* of being-bound thought, as the Good indeed is: the Good is *not* "Beinghood" but yet *beyond* Beinghood, exceeding it in seniority and power (*ousía, Republic* 509 a 3, b 8). Note that while it was impossible for Being to be "some third thing" (*Sophist* 250 b–d) beyond its constituent *eíde,* the Good is to be imagined as precisely such a "third kind" of (non)thing (*Republic* 507 d 1, e 1). From the highest point of view, then, that of the Whole, not Otherness but Likeness is the bond; in terms of the knowing soul, not *lógos* but *analogía* is required. It is a token of this that the knowing part of the soul, which in the *Sophist* is compared to the Other (257 c 7), is said in the *Republic* to be "*like* the Good" (509 a 3).

This cosmic bond, by which the Good makes everything one, has a mathematical image that takes the form of a proportion: "And the most beautiful of bonds is that which makes itself and the things bound together as much as possible *into one.* Proportion (*analogía*) accomplishes this most beautifully. For when the middle term of three numbers . . . is such that as the first is to it, so it itself is to the last, . . . then necessarily all will turn out to be the same. They will all become *one* with each other" (*Timaeus* 31 c 2; cf. *Metaphysics* 1016 b 34). We can now see a second reason for the equality of the middle sections of the Divided Line (Note 30): The three-term proportion (i.e., a:b :: b:c) "makes one" or unifies by means of the power of the "in-between" (*metaxý*)—the Divided Line represents a harmonized *Whole.*

Socrates had already described and named this beautiful union, the true home of the philosopher, in that "persuasion to the rule of philosophy," which precedes the presentation of the Sun Image to Glaucon (487 b ff.) and is addressed to Adeimantus and the others. His language then was in terms of man and god; in keeping with his purpose he gave, as it were, an anthropomorphic view of the realm of Being:

> For surely, Adeimantus, he who has his thinking truly set on beings has no leisure to look down into the affairs of men and, engaging in fights with them, to be filled with envy and malice. Instead he looks at such things as are ordered and always stay the

same, and seeing and contemplating them as they neither do injustice nor have injustice done to them by one another—all being contained in a well-arranged whole (*kósmos*) according to
lógos—he imitates these and makes himself as like [to them] as
possible. Or do you think there is any way that he who associates with what he loves can *not* imitate it? And so the philosopher, associating with what is divine and well-arranged, himself
becomes as divine and well-arranged (*kosmios*) as is possible for
a man to be (500 c–d; cf. *Theaetetus* 173 c ff.).

Socrates is throughout employing the word used of the ideally
ordered visible world, *cosmos,* and the man who becomes like
a god is presently called a *demiurge,* who, like the divine artificer in the *Timaeus,* uses a divine pattern in making his work of
art, the city (*Republic* 500 e 3; see *Timaeus* 28 a 7). We see that
the interior order of the world of Being is to be imagined as analogous to a *cosmos,* a beautifully regulated visible world, having
a *táxis,* a hierarchy or rank-order. The Good is to be understood
as the comprehensive source of this order, which is here presented in the familiar language of Pythagorean cosmology: Justice is a reciprocal matter, the parts of the whole are related "according to *lógos,*" that is, by ratios, and participation in the
order is by imitation and likening (cf. *Metaphysics* 1075 a 12 ff.).
We may conjecture that this is a popular presentation of that
táxis (whose terms are also borrowed from the Pythagoreans)
which comes about when the Good is understood as the One
acting as the simultaneously unifying and articulating principle
of the *eíde.* Together with the Dyad, it generates *Being,* the eidetic *Two* comprehending Motion and Rest. The rank-order that
thus arises is that arithmological structure of the *eíde* which is
the prototype of all ordered associations, ordinal and cardinal
(see *Metaphysics* 1080 a ff.).

   e Socrates had introduced the Sun Image with a reference to "the things said earlier and often spoken of at other
times" (507 a 7), namely the many and how they participate in

the one idea that is "what [truly] is" in these many things (476 a 7, d 1, 507 b 5). Yet within the image he goes, as we have seen, beyond the oneness of each *eídos* to a still higher point of view, the way to which is sung in the "hymn of dialectic." There he says that "when someone tries by dialectic, apart from all sense perception but by means of the *lógos*, to set *out upon that which each thing is itself* (*ep' autó ho éstin hékaston*), and does not leave off before he grasps by thought itself *that which is Good itself* (*autó ho éstin agathón*)," then he has come to the culmination of the knowable (532 a 5, cf. 507 b 5, 7).

The repetition of the phrase in which "Good itself" is substituted for "each thing itself" is clearly meant to catch Glaucon's attention and to convey to him something—actually the most pertinent thing in the dialogue—about the nature of the community governed by the Good itself. For upon having grasped what *each thing is in itself,* one would expect to learn what *all things are together,* and it is in place of this expected phrase that "Good" occurs. This sentence then hints how the Good as the "source of the Whole" (511 b 7) will have to be understood—insofar as thought can attain it: It is not simply a different *being* but precisely the *oneness* of all beings (cf. 244 e ff.).

It is the All as that Whole which comprises what each partial whole is as well as what it is not, that bonding container within which *different* things are *at one.* It is "the source which *is* the Whole" (*he tou pantós arché,* 511 b 7)—the Greek phrase is, surely intendedly, ambiguous: it can mean either "the beginning *of* everything" (objective genitive) or, more radically, "the source which *is* the Whole" (subjective genitive). The latter is the more significant reading, for as the encompassing source the Good is indeed the fit pattern of all community, and in the *Republic* especially, of the political community: "Using it as a pattern" (*parádeigma*), the rulers are "to order the city and private men and themselves" (540 a 9). Dialectic turns out to be the—eminently political—*study of idea-communities* (cf. *Sophist* 253 d). Socrates has, in his own efforts, not only composed the quarrel between philosophy and poetry, but he also composed the quarrel between philosophy and true politics, for he has shown, in speech and in deed, that the lover of wisdom best knows and most desires genuine community.

f   Nothing more direct is said here or in any other dialogue about that primary dialectical aspect of the Good—that it is the One. However, there *is* a dialogue in which Adeimantus and Glaucon are shown (on some occasion that must have occurred long after Socrates' death) the reason for Socrates' silence. This is the *Parmenides,* in which Antiphon, their younger half-brother, who has given up philosophy for horses (as well one might after listening to this relentless pre-dialectical exercise), recites from memory—that is to say, without drawing any personal consequences—an old conversation. In it Parmenides performs a demonstration exercise for the then very young Socrates. He generously takes his own notorious One (137 b 4), namely that One about which he himself says that "it is," while others say that "it is not," and shows Socrates what follows from either assertion. The dialogue ends—as some think, too abruptly—with the conclusion: "Whether the One is or is not, it and the others, in relation to themselves as well as to one another, all in every way are and are not, and appear and do not appear.—Most true" (166 c). The dialogue has shown that when the Parmenidean One is conveyed in speech—as indeed it must be, for Parmenides says in his own poem that it is necessary both to *say* and to think it (Diels, *Vorsokratiker* Fr. 6)—such speech leads, dialectically, to its own denial (cf. *Philebus* 15 d), while that denial itself cannot stand firm but flips back again into its opposite. Everything possible to speech has been said about this One and has had the wrong consequences, so that nothing remains for Parmenides but to fall silent: "Most true" also means "Hopelessly false."

Young Socrates is listening; he must know that one hypothesis, the very hypothesis that is *apparently not possible* to rational speech, has been omitted, namely the self-contradiction

that "*the One is not-one.*" Now that is precisely the crucial possibility whose dialectical expression, "*Nonbeing is,*" appears,
with apologies to Parmenides, in the *Sophist* (258 d). "Father"
Parmenides, having confronted in his life his own One, which
is just Being uncompromised by negation, and having allowed
its difficulties to emerge in speech, will in his dialogic death engender a new order of Being-and-Nonbeing. It will call for a
new One, beyond Being, which is not really conveyable in the
mature Socrates' customary conversations. Perhaps it is not yet
quite present to him, although he intimates it to our imagination. As far as this greatest matter is concerned, Plato himself
thinks that "it can never be just said, as are other learning matters (*mathémata*)" but requires *long* and intimate conversational
intercourse, upon which it will be suddenly apprehended (*Seventh Letter* 341 c 5): The *Republic* is Socrates' longest recorded
conversation, but it is not long or intimate enough.

　　g One last additional observation: What is characteristically Socratic about the Sun Image (on which the Divided Line
is a gloss) is that it is reflexive, an image of imaging. But more
than that, in presenting the sun as an image of the principle of
wholeness, Socrates shows not only how imaging itself comes
about but also how that particular kind of philosophical imaging which makes the Whole reappear as embedded within itself
is possible—how we can see the Good from within recursively,
as a likeness of itself. This aspect of the imagery of the *Republic* is reflected also in the central visual image of the closing myth,
the Myth of Er.

　　The place in the Myth of Er where the souls choose their lives
(616 b) is not immediately clear to the imagination. There seem
to be two irreconcilable images;[37] the first one consists of the
whole of the cosmos, which has a shaft of polar light passing
through the *heavens* as well as the earth (b 5); the second consists of Necessity sitting at the *earth's* pole (or thereabouts)
whirling a spindle tipped with a spindle-whorl that represents a
planetary system hung on chains let down from the heavenly

light encircling the whole (c 4). Now if we recall what a spinning woman actually looks like, these two disparate images become *somewhat* more coherent. We may imagine the situation
about like this: Necessity sits spinning. Between her knees she
has a long distaff at the top of which a cloud of white wool is
fastened; it feeds into the thread as it is spun. This thread is
twisted into yarn by the spin of the whorl-weighted spindle,
which is tied to the end of the thread; onto it the finished yarn
is wound. In the figure of the myth the axial shaft of light represents the distaff, the chain of heaven is, perhaps, the thread
that is being spun, and the whorl of the spindle of Necessity is
a miniature planetary system, an orrery, a *model of the Whole,*
within whose sight the souls of the dead choose their future
lives.

Thus the imagery of the final myth of the *Republic* is the cosmic complement of the Sun Image and the Divided Line with respect to the location of the human soul. (See ch. 8.) For in the
final vision the soul is again both *within* the whole seeking its
proper place in the world and also *without* viewing the whole
as if it were a likeness of itself. I think for Socrates this eikastic
power of the soul is the wonder of wonders.

E

1   Book VII begins with this invitation to Glaucon: "Now,
after this, liken (apeíkason) our nature concerning education
(paideías te péri) as well as the *lack of education* to the following sort of condition" *(páthos,* 514 a 1).

The sentence is dramatic. "After this" indicates that what
has immediately preceded—that is, Socrates' naming of the affections *(pathémata)* of the soul, the last of which is *eikasía*—is
the necessary prelude to what is now to come; the word *páthos*
has a tragic flavor, and the placing of the preposition "concerning" *(péri)* after its noun is a poetic device meant to convey the
drama (see *Poetics* 1459 a 2). Glaucon is now to use his power
of *eikasía* to *see* (514 a 1) the dark drama of human nature in

an image. This image will show what human beings are and do *within* the Whole.

Behold, he says, men living as in a cavelike underground habitation (*oíkesis,* 514 a 3) whose entrance is turned toward daylight. From childhood on, their legs and necks are fettered so that they can only see straight ahead into the cave and are unable to turn (*periágein*). Their light comes from a fire burning behind them. Between this fire and themselves runs a road, alongside of which a screen wall has been built. Behind this wall men pass back and forth carrying artificial objects that show above it. To Glaucon's exclamation "What a strange (literally "out-of-place," *átopon*) image and what strange prisoners" (515 a 4) Socrates replies with quiet irony: "Like us" (515 a 5). And, he goes on, these prisoners see only their own and each other's shadows, which are thrown on the wall they face, together with the shadows of the things carried about by the people behind the wall. If they converse it is about these shadows, which are as truth to them; the echo of words spoken behind the screen wall seems to them to be the speech of these shadows. Now suppose a prisoner was released and forced to stand up and turn around, and was compelled to answer questions about the things formerly behind him. He would be perplexed, at an impasse (*aporeín*), his eyes would hurt, and he would regard the ventriloquistic shadows as having more being than the things now before him. And if someone dragged (e 6) him up the steep road and out of the cave by force to look at the light of the sun, his eyes would be so pained that at first he could see nothing. But after a while he would be able to see, first only natural shadows, after that the effigies (*eídola*) of things as they are reflected in water, and at last the things themselves. From these he could raise his eyes to see the moon and the stars at night, when the sun itself is absent. And finally he would see the sun in its own place; after that "he would infer" (*syllogízoito*) that the sun was responsible (516 c 2) for the seasons and years and was caretaker of everything. Then if he recalled his former habitation he would feel that he was now happy. The honors given down there to those who were good at observing, remembering, and giving oracles (c 8) about artificial shadows would be nothing to him and he would do anything rather than live like that (e 2). But if he had to join the competition, his eyes being still full of darkness from his sudden descent, he would make himself ridiculous (cf. 509 c 1). Men would then say that by ascending upwards he had ruined his eyes and that it was not right to attempt to go up. And as for anyone who tried to release another, if they could catch him they would kill him (517 a 6).

This image (*eíkon*, 517 a 8) "must now be attached" to what has been said before: Glaucon is to liken the situation that appears through sight to the cave-like habitation: the power of the sun to the light of the fire, the ascent of soul and its visions in the place of thought to the forced climb of the prisoner into the light of day. In a table:

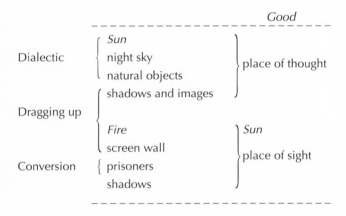

2   This correlation of the Sun and Cave Images seems, though brief, explicit enough, from the conjecturing about shadows at the bottom up to the happy movement of the soul in the upper realm. Yet Socrates expresses a certain reservation. If you interpret the ascent, the going up (*anábasis*) in the former to be

the upward way (*ánodos*) in the latter, Socrates says, "you will not fail to fulfill my expectations. But perhaps only god knows if that is what truly is" (517 b 4).

Let us look anew at the interrelation of the two images. The Sun Image as interpreted in the Divided Line shows how the Good has everywhere prepared places for the cognitive soul to learn in. There is directed upward motion with returns to and reprises of these stations but no straight linear ascent—the word *anábasis* is never mentioned. The Cave Image, on the other hand, deals with the actual habitation of human nature, that is, of the embodied soul, and with the painful steps and stations of its slow ascent. Furthermore, in the Divided Line the Good itself is not actually represented but is to be caught by *analogy,* while in the Cave Image the sun *represents* the Good and an underground fire is in turn contrived to represent the sun. This means that in the schematic correlation of the two images our visible world comes, curiously, to occupy different levels:

		Sun Image	Cave Image
Being	:	intelligible realm	sensible world
Becoming	:	sensible world	underground realm

Thus the Good is off the Divided Line, *beyond* the realms of Being and Becoming, while its representative in the Cave Image, the sun, is, of course, *within* and part of the world. And finally, while the Sun Image, again as explicated by the Divided Line, represents only different degrees of the capacity to learn but not the incapacity of ignorance (cf. 585 b 3), the Cave Image is explicitly about *both* education and *lack* of education (514 a 2); it is very much concerned not only with "mindlessness" (*aphrosýne,* 515 c 5) and "want of knowledge" (*amathía,* 518 a 7) but even with positive deceit. For those who carry effigies, "idols" (*eídola*) back and forth are like puppeteers who manipulate their "marvels" (514 b 6—Socrates plays on the double meaning of *thaúmata:* puppets and marvels); they are indeed engaging in that elaborate kind of manipulative dissembling which the orator shares with the sophist and the whole tribe of imagineers (*Sophist* 268 b, cf. 260 c 8).

3 At the very beginning of their conversation Socrates and Glaucon had determined that ignorance (*ágnoia*) must necessarily be assigned to Nonbeing, knowing (*gnósis*) to Being (478 c 3), and opinion (*dóxa*) to an unnamed intermediate, partaking of both and later identified as Becoming. It must be in order to recall this scheme that the main segments of the Divided Line are at one point called respectively "knowable" (*gnostón*) and "opinable" (*doxastón,* 510 a 9). Thus it is obvious that wherever Becoming occurs *Nonbeing* is implied. But since Nonbeing is not explicitly named in either of the images, Glaucon should conjecture that it is present somewhere somehow, in the manner appropriate to "that which is not." Socrates himself suggests the following new correlation, in which the levels of the "sensible world" in both images are made to coincide so that the soul's upward trek out of the cave into the sun's realm is matched with the raising of the *bodily* eye and the world outside the cave is matched with the place of *sensory* sight (532 b 6), while the cave is where caves belong: *to the underworld.*

		Sun Image	Cave Image
Being	:	intelligible realm	
Becoming	:	←———— sensible realm ————→	
Nonbeing	:		underground realm

4 a To put in a word the effect of seeing the Cave Image in this new juxtaposition with the Sun Image: The Cave Image is evidently intended to complete the image of the Whole so as to take into account human badness in all its organized obtuseness and to assign it its place within Being—or rather Nonbeing

(*Seventh Letter* 344 b; the Neoplatonic Plotinus, *Enneads* I 8, in fact locates evil in Nonbeing). This is why its presentation ends with a brusque reference to that most telling crime of ignorance, the execution of Socrates (517 a 6).

The introduction of this factor, namely human ignorance and its consequence, badness, as well as their management, which is called *politics,* comes out clearly in the table that outlines the Cave Image (p. 209). In contrast to the main segments of the Divided Line with their two subsections, each realm here has a *third* part: in the lower realm the screen wall with its puppeteers and in the world above the starry night sky with its moon, bright with reflected solar light (cf. 617 a 1). We may interpret the puppeteers as representing the politicians and their retinue, bearing about their laws and ordinances, their peculiar kind of doxastic image-making, their decrees (*dogmata;* see *Statesman* 303 c). Here we must recall that political deceit is practiced in any city, even in the just city, though there it is done nobly, for the public good (p. 125 and *Republic* 414 b 8, cf. 382 d). The heavenly bodies will then be the cosmic counterparts of the civic decrees, modeling the "laws of nature" (*Timaeus* 83 e 5), which are best studied in the nocturnal sky—although, Socrates thinks, better yet not observed by sight at all but deduced by reason (529 a).

b   When Socrates first introduced the sun, the source of the visible world, as a son, Glaucon had immediately inferred that as a parent the Good was a father (506 e 6). The Cave Image now provides the answer to the obvious question: Who is the mother? It is *Nonbeing,* the realm in which things are nothing in themselves but only in relation to another; in the terms of the *Sophist,* it is the realm of the Other (257 b) which bonds beings in the realm of Being, but whose human effects outside that realm are just the opposite: negativity, lack of community, and consequent privacy in the literal sense, namely privation, as well as alienation and ignorance (pp. 292, 296; *Republic* 478 c 3; the Greek word for a private person is, neatly, "idiot"). These effects in turn lead to injustice and to all sorts of evil (444 a 1, b 8).

Nonbeing is not easy to imagine, for in its elusiveness (*Sophist* 237 b 10) it is experienced only as a bewilderment of the eye— that positive apprehension of darkness which is felt after the descent into the infinity of human evil so feelingly described by Socrates (517 d 5, cf. 445 c 6; 517 e 3). The cave represents Nonbeing under the guise of a *womb*, where, as in the Phoenician myth, the "earthborn" race gestates (414 c). From the point of view of the human soul struggling with a body and with other men, the Good is at work throughout the whole only "in a certain way," not directly (516 c 1). For its light never penetrates into the cave, where a counterfeit takes its place; to the lighted realm of Being on which shines the true sun, the Good, there is opposed a dark realm of Nonbeing (cf. *Sophist* 254 a); between these realms is the steep road of birth and becoming (*génesis*) along which men "come into being" as learners. Socrates' cave is the very image of that Indefinite Dyad whose nature is womb-like, murky, material, unsubstantial, bad (p. 212). But we must not forget that this second world-making principle is bad only from Socrates' present perspective, the human condition, where Nonbeing is on the loose, so to speak, not involved in the order of Being. From the ontological view taken in the *Sophist* it turns out to bond beings and to enable speech, and from an even higher, a meta-ontological perspective, so to speak, it participates as Indeterminate Dyad in the generation of the ordered realm of Being; there it is an indispensable second principle with its own dignity.

c   Socrates, however, does have a vivid figure of his own for such life as goes on in the cave. Before, he had forbidden the poets to slander the underworld; now he himself commits such a slander against our terrestrial underworld. Earlier, in his critique of poetry, he had struck a line from the *Odyssey* (XI 489), the one in which Achilles as a shade among shades laments, saying that he would rather be "a serf on earth slaving for another portionless man" (386 c 3) than a king among the dead; now Socrates himself puts this very censored line into the mouth of the man forced to descend once more into the cave, our human habitation (516 d 5)!

Just as in the *Phaedo* there is presented to the imagination a place rather to be taken "as truly the earth" than the hollow in which we live (110 a 1), so in the *Republic* Socrates points to a place to be taken as truly the underworld, a truly shadowy and obscure Hades (508 c, 517 d). It is a new realm distinct from the underworld he will describe in the *Phaedo*—that "invisible Hades" (*Aídes aidés*) of *after*-life, which is sightless rather than dark, a place purified of all sensory vision (79 b 7, 80 d 5, *Cratylus* 404 b 1), and as such after all a "divine place" (*tópos daimónios*, 614 c 1). This novel Hades is the realm of living souls; it is Socrates' *mortal Hades*. It therefore adds to the intelligible and the visible places a third, a murky place—the cave itself seen as a terrestrial underworld. Its inhabitants live in a dream-like isolation reminiscent of the mindless flittings of the shades in the traditional Hades (533 b 8, 476 c 4; cf. Heraclitus, Diels, *Vorsokratiker* Fr. 89). Some go completely to sleep, having, as Socrates puts it, "arrived in Hades before they have woken up here" (534 c 7). Like the shades in Homer's Hades they are incapable of touching each other (*Odyssey* X 494; XI 204), for they are shackled, and of talking with each other, for their faces are always fixed on shady, manipulated images. They live in a manner familiar enough among modern image watchers.

Aristotle had his own cave story, reported by Cicero (*On the Nature of the Gods* II xxxvii 95). We may conjecture that it was a counter-image intended to combat Socrates' scandalous view of human life. For the inmates of Aristotle's cave, which is a well-furnished underground apartment but is nevertheless a *natural* cave, need only a chance to catch a glimpse of the upper world, a glimmer of its sun by day and its stars in their regular courses by night, to know right away that theirs is indeed a world ruled by gods. Aristotle, contrary to Socrates, implies that this splendid world, whose divinity is immediately apprehended by anyone with unjaded vision, is precisely our own *present habitation,* toward whose beauty our senses have grown dull.

What is most characteristic of Socrates' mortal Hades is the willfulness of its inhabitants, who resist and mock their liberator (517 a). Again Aristotle's cave image is instructive, for he makes its inhabitants prisoners by nature who must wait for the "jaws of earth" to open before they can come up. But for Socrates' men the way is open; the Good has prepared other and better places for the soul, and there is no necessity to sit below; these cave men seem to cherish their chains. In an engraving of the "Antrum Platonicum" of 1604 A.D. the huddled prisoners very tellingly wear no visible chains at all. Perhaps, then, the most important aspect of the cave is that *it is not a natural cavern* but a "cavelike underground chamber" (514 a 3; *Axiochus* 371 a 8), clearly an artificial prison made by men for men. The position of the prisoners itself indicates stubborn perversity; they are facing the wrong way round and have a perverted view; that is why those who can be released must first of all be "converted" (518 c 8). The cave is the human city always and everywhere, a prison compound; genuine community is to be achieved only by escaping and looking beyond it.

d   Glaucon should have no difficulty in recognizing this place, earth-hell—Socrates' novelty isn't so new after all. He has some acquaintance with Pythagorean doctrine (531 a 4), and the notion of the world as a prison and life as a living death are both well-known Pythagorean teachings (cf. *Gorgias* 493 a), as is also that of the "descent into Hades." Pythagoras himself is said to have "told how he descended (*katábas*) to look on the way of life of those who have gone below, to see how entirely different were the lives of the Pythagoreans" ("Pythagoras," Diogenes Laertius, VIII 38).[38] In fact the dialogue of the *Republic* as a whole has a Pythagorean atmosphere, for the lectures of Pythagoras were said to have taken place by night (VIII, 15; compare the "nocturnal council," the governing body of the *Laws*, 961; also Plato's "night clock" made specially to tell nighttime, Athenaeus, *Dining Sophists* IV, 174 c); it must be well into the night when the central part of the *Republic* is spoken. What is more, its very form has a Pythagorean cast, since it seems to be that of a Pythagorean exercise: It was evidently part of the discipline of a Pythagorean to attempt, before starting the day, to re-collect within himself in its entirety whatever conversation he had had the day before.[39] This would provide an additional reason why the dialogue is told by Socrates as having taken place not just recently, but "yesterday" (327 a 1), and it would explain why he does not address it to anyone: For all we know, he speaks it within and to himself, and Plato, even more truly than Alcibiades, who claimed to have "opened up" Socrates, is revealing his soul to us (*Symposium* 216 d 6). Certainly if we are to take seriously the form of the *Republic* as a report of a conversation that lasted the better part of a day and a night, we shall find it to be a somewhat incredible feat that needs to be accounted for by some power such as a special mnemonic discipline would give. In the *Republic,* we may infer, Socrates is shown as a master of the Pythagorean practice that provided a congenial discipline (*áskesis*), useful for preparing the soul by a kind of habituation for that inward recovery of truth to which Socrates gives an underworld origin in the Myth of Recollection (*Meno* 81) and which appears to be most persuasively displayed in mathematical investigations (82; see Note 27).

F

   1   a   After the cave image Socrates considers with Glaucon the actual education of the philosophers. He begins significantly with a question: "Would you like now to see in what way such men will come to be born [in the city] and how one will lead them up into the light, just as some [presumably Heracles[40]] are said to have ascended from Hades to the gods?" (521 c 1). The sequence of learning, which follows closely the *páthos* of the cave drama, has three stages: "conversion" by a teacher returned from above (*periagogé,* 515 c 7, c 8, d 4, 521 c 6), the "haul" of the soul toward being, effected by mathematical studies (*máthema psychés holkón,* 515 e 8, 521 d 3, 527 b 9, 533 d 2), and the "divine sights" revealed by dialectic (*theíai theoríai,* 517 d 4; note that *theoría* is here still used in its literal sense of spectating, viewing).

Conversion is what we are witnessing in the dialogue itself. Since it precedes all education and is more the effect of finding a teacher than of engaging in a study, it is not part of the explicit study plan. Nevertheless there is an "art of conversion" (*téchne tes periagogés,* 518 d 3). Since this first act is largely a matter of making the soul recognize the shadows on the wall *as* mere shadows, it is clearly an *eikastic* art; it is *Socratic music,* the persuasive imagery of truth. As we have seen, it may be said to take the place of that traditional habituating music which was to be used in the moral education of the warrior-guardians but was so emphatically excluded from the advanced education of the philosophers (522 a 4). Note that in the image (as in fact) the city will try to prevent such conversions and will call them corruptions (517 a). Thus it appears that these philosophers-to-be are not born and bred in the just city. Their upbringing seems in fact to be conceived against a hostile background that can hardly be the education provided by the guardian city. Hence Socrates must be setting out the education of the *founders* of his city.

b The long haul into the light of day is accomplished chiefly by the hauling study of mathematics (522 c 5–531 d 6). The program appears to be that of Pythagorean cosmogenic mathematics (530 d 8).[41] In arithmetic, "that lowly little thing" (*phaulon*),[42] the "one" and also the "two" and the other numbers are investigated; in plane geometry the surfaces of (mathematical) bodies and in solid geometry the bodies themselves are studied; in astronomy these bodies are put in motion; and finally, the audible relations of moving bodies are studied in harmonics, which is mathematical music. In this way the cosmos that is imaged in the Myth of Er, with its heavenly bodies sounding a harmony as they revolve, is constructed. There is only one difference between this Pythagorean cosmos and the Socratic study, but one so deep that it is very hard for Glaucon to grasp, since he loves physical science, especially astronomy. He immediately identifies Socrates' phrase about "seeing the things above" with "looking into the [sky] above" (529 a 2). Socrates has to rebuke him: That kind of astronomy, the "visible music" of the Pythagoreans (Theon of Smyrna, *Mathematics Useful for Understanding Plato,* "Astronomy"), in truth makes its students "look downward altogether" (a 7). Socrates demands that in the serious study of mathematics, that paradigm of every learning matter (*máthema*), not only all practical applications, but even every suggestion of an admixture of sense experience should be set aside. Only those true motions and numbers and figures which are grasped by nothing but the *lógos* and the *diánoia* should be studied (529 b). Glaucon, who follows well enough through the early part of the discussion, the part concerned with demonstrating the dianoetic power of arithmetic, is somewhat puzzled by the non-physical "dimensional" studies that follow (526 d ff.). Yet it is indeed the extended effort of actually doing a program of pure mathematics that is needed to complete the conversion from sense (533 d 3). But this is still before him.

Ancient commentators, such as Plutarch, Theon, and Proclus, have a standard way of referring to the use and meaning of the mathematical course of the *Republic*. They simply assert the elevating effects of such studies. One of the reasons why there should be this effect is of far greater consequence than the others, since it amounts to a genuine interpretation of the sequence of subjects. There is a strong ancient tradition, mentioned above (p. 203), that attributes to Plato and the Academy the theory that the whole of Being arises, as it were, in a mathematical way: From the One and the Indefinite Dyad spring the Ideal Numbers; from these the sequence of dimensions is educed, until first the mathematical solids are attained, and then the sensible world itself is brought about.[43] The "dimensional soul" discussed above belongs to this context. Now aside from the internal difficulties of this cosmogenetic mathematics (which Aristotle discusses at length in the *Metaphysics* 1080 b 24 ff., 1085 a 8 ff.), and its somewhat stultifying estericism, there is an almost insuperable difficulty in interpreting the mathematics of the *Republic* along the lines that served to elucidate the Cave Image. For in the *Republic* mathematical objects are only one set among the images that reflect the realm of Being and comprise only a part of the realm of the *diánoia,* a part fitted into a scale of increasing *genuineness,* and lying between natural objects and Being. In the theory mentioned, however, the mathematical structure comprises the whole of things arranged in a scale of increasing dimensionality and bodily *concreteness.*[44] While its scope is more global, its progress is the inverse of Socratic mathematics, which is away from sensory solidity.

It therefore becomes necessary to go to the dialogue itself to see why the young philosophers must study Socrates' mathematics, aside from its—admittedly—purifying effect, the conversion of the merely embodied soul into a primarily knowing soul (527 d 8). We may expect that, as usual, Socrates is quietly presenting Glaucon with something astounding.

So it turns out, for, upon inspection, the mathematical order Socrates is talking about is indeed a *reflection* of Being, and this means that it is *an inverse of the realm of Being.* Glaucon must use his imagination to see why this is so. A diagram picturing the realms of the Divided Line in solids will show what he needs to see (p. 220).

The whole realm of natural objects is here pictured as a cone with the sun at its vertex. It casts a reflection or shadow (510 a 1) which, like most natural images (as distinct from more deceptively independent artificial ones), is tied to and opposite or inverted in relation to the original, for it reverses sides and it inverts height, so that the image of a tree stands on its crown. Thus it "produces a shape (*eídos*) that yields a sense perception the opposite of the usual view" (*Sophist* 266 c 3; here, toward

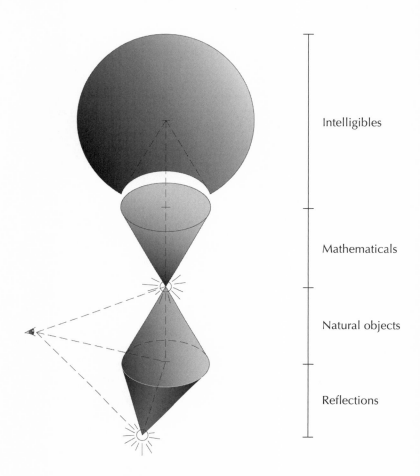

the bottom of the ladder of Being, *eídos*, Socrates' "invisible look," is used in its normal sense of "visible shape"). This natural fact may now be applied to the imaging of the noetic realm, so that the beings of the uppermost sphere may be imagined in the same way as invertedly reflected in the dianoetic objects. In the diagram mathematics is therefore represented by an inverted cone having its dimensionless vertex, which represents the elementary study of the unit, at the bottom, and opposing its base to that of the conical sector of a sphere which represents Being. I choose the sphere to represent Being in order to indicate both that mathematical objects are only a small part of all the possible dianoetic images of being and that, unlike the advance of dimensional mathematics, the dialectic ascent within Being does not end in an upper limit but culminates in a kind of point source and beginning which is *at once* central and encompassing.[45]

We must now attempt to extract the meaning of this inversion of the dialectical order in Socratic mathematics. One observation seems warranted right off. Such mathematics does not lend itself well to institutionalized research. Socrates does not seem to be announcing the study program of the future Academy (not to speak of a state education), especially since "no one unversed in geometry" was allowed to enter there to begin with, and the members were evidently left by Plato to engage in all sorts of advanced study with great freedom.[46]

Let us look, then, at the elements of Socrates' presentation in their order. To introduce "the study concerning the one" (525 a 2), Socrates draws attention to a finger, a finger that is simply one finger, the fourth, and seems to have nothing contradictory within itself (523 d 6). In it, sight sees everything "poured together," confused, indistinct, and for this very reason self-sufficient; the finger is "absolute" for the sense of sight (524 d 10). But as soon as two other fingers are brought in, one greater than the first (the middle finger) and the other smaller (the pinkie), sight reports that the original finger is now both big and little; the other senses will report similar oppositions. At this point, the soul in its perplexity calls on the "counting capacity" (*logismós*, 524 b 4) and the *diánoia* to determine how many objects it is really dealing with, and thus arises the distinction between the visible and the intelligible worlds (524 c 13). For the *diánoia* separates out the big and the little as being "each one, both together two" (524 b 10), a formula that, though it does not solve the problem, states it precisely, that is, "arithmetically": *Two* different items, namely the Great and the Small captured in speech, can be together in *one,* namely the physical finger. "The whole of number" is gotten analogously (525 a 6)—whenever something is no more one than the opposite of one (i.e., a plurality) it is an assemblage of so-and-so many things taken *together*. That assemblage, in which a *multitude* of unit-things become *one*, defines an *arithmos*, a "numbered collection."[47]

The second study is, as Glaucon knows, "next in succession" after this philosophical arithmetic. It is geometry (526 c 8). After plane geometry, which is the study of the "second increase" (the second dimension), must follow the study of solids taken "by themselves," perhaps meaning as dimensionally complete (528 b). Fourth comes the study of astronomy, which deals with systems of solids in visible motion. Since there is at least one other kind of motion, the one concerned with motions relative to the ear, a last sister study is required, namely harmonics. In pure harmonics consonant numbers are studied; these are the numerical relations presented in a theory of numerical proportion dealing with simple and compounded ratios (that is, multiplied ratios: e.g., 6:4 cp. 4:3 gives 6:3 or 2:1—the octave). Such relations bear on human *génesis*, as we know from the "marriage number," that eugenic fantasy formula which is to govern the matings of the "fair city" (546). At the end of this course of philosophical mathematics the "community . . . and kinship" of these studies must be synoptically grasped, and what is characteristic of them must be collected (531 d 2). Upon this basis dialectic is finally to be laid, "just like a coping stone" (534 e 2).

The elements of this *mathematical* study in the order in which they appear are, then:

1   the sensible undifferentiated one,
2   the big and little by comparison,
3   the "hypothesized" ones, the units that add up to two, and every other number,
4   the dimensional structure of the geometric cosmos,
5   the community of all these mathematical objects seen synoptically.

Although the *dialectical* way is not explicitly described in the *Republic* (533 a 1), we have by now collected enough of its elements to name them in the order in which they would become the center of attention:

5 the community or cosmos of *eíde* seen in a preliminary synopsis,
4 the lowest ranks of *eíde*, which are close to the sensory cosmos,
3 the eidetic number-assemblages going back up to the eidetic Two and its constituent eidetic ones,
2 the Great and Small and other super-*eíde,*
1 the One.

The dialectical objects are, as can be seen, in fact encountered in the reverse order of those that have a similar name in the mathematical sequence. For the mathematical studies ended with a community of consonantly moving solids that had first been set out in terms of their elements of "growth" (the progress of dimensions), then "by themselves" (solid geometry), and finally in their "consonances" (astronomy and music). So, in reverse, the dialectician must try to see both "which *eídos* is consonant with which" (*Statesman* 285 b; *Sophist* 253 b, where harmonics had just been used as the type of such knowledge) and whether any eidetic elements extend through all the others: "for he who can see things together is a dialectician" (*synoptikós—dialektikós*); note that it is indeed the final phase of the mathematical development that provides the required training and testing of the synoptical ability (*Republic* 537 c).[48] After this initial synopsis, this comprehensive "seeing together" (of which Socratic music is a foretaste and which is required for making the right "divisions") it is necessary to survey first those *eíde* that are lowest in the eidetic hierarchy, the ones closest to the becoming of the natural world. Then it will be possible to see the order, the *táxis,* of the communities of *eíde* and to rise among them, attaining the highest *eíde* (*Sophist* 254 d 4). These higher genera (*géne,* sing. *génos*) contain more of being but belong to ever smaller, or rather prior eidetic assemblages or numbers. Finally Being itself, the greatest *génos* (243 d 1), the eidetic Two, will be reached, together with the two great *géne* it comprises, Rest and Motion (250). At this point it will be possible to recognize that the *eíde* that run through all the others are beyond Being and ought not to be called *eíde* but *archai.* Thus two sources appear beyond the objects that were discovered as the hypotheses of mathematics and then as beings of dialectic: *the Other* (259 a–b), called by many names, of which the chief are the Indefinite Dyad and the *Great and Small* (e.g., *Metaphysics* 987 b 20, 1087 b 5), and *the One,* the "not-to-be-regarded-as-hypothesized/suppositionless beginning/source" (*arché anhypótheton*), the "initial principle *of,* which also *encompasses, Everything/All*" (p. 204). In the One everything again rests without opposition, just as once before, at the beginning of the road and at the opposite extreme of Being, the finger combined *in fact* that which is incompatible *in words.*

Socrates himself emphasizes the opposite ways of mathematics and dialectic at crucial points. The segment of the intelligible, he says, is cut "in such a way that in one part of it the soul is forced to search from hypotheses, using the things before imitated as images, and journeying *not toward the beginning* (*arché*) but toward the end, while in the other, the one that leads toward the non-hypothetical beginning, *she goes [up]* from hypotheses and [proceeds] without the images used in the former section, journeying by means of the *eíde* and through them" (510 b; also c, 511 a, 533 c). The mathematical way is thus, taken in itself as a whole, a *deduction,* moving down from beginnings, just as do its demonstrations. But, at the same time, as a learning process, it is an "elevation (*epanagogé*) of what is best in the soul to the sights seen among beings" (532 c 5). Mathematics is, however, as Socrates gently and tacitly informs a too enthusiastic Glaucon, not knowledge of Being itself but only an approach to it (527 b 9).

How can Socrates imagine that these two motions take place at once? To begin with, Socrates shows no interest whatever in that straightforward deduction of mathematical fact which is the pride of mathematicians, and which, because of its logical rigor, becomes for Aristotle the paradigm of "apodeictic," that is, demonstrative, knowledge (*Posterior Analytics* 71 a 3). This form of proof, which mathematical systems like Euclid's *Elements* primarily employ, is called "synthetic." Socrates, remarkably enough, implies that synthetic proofs are to be left to all the non-mathematical arts, which deal with "*geneses* and *syntheses*" (533 b 5). His own approach is "analytical" or, what will be shown to amount to the same thing, "hypothetical" (cf. *Phaedo* 100 a, *Meno* 86 e).

The discovery of analysis as a formal method of proof was attributed in antiquity to Plato, who was supposed to have imparted it to his pupils as a means for finding solutions to problems of mathematical construction.[49] As Pappus, the ancient commentator on Euclid, explains, it differs from synthesis, which leads from agreed-on assumptions (or suppositions) to conceded consequences, in the direction of its movement: "For in analysis we assume that which is sought as if it had already come about, and we inquire what it is from which this has resulted, and again what is the antecedent cause of the latter, and so on, until by retracing our steps we come upon something already known or *belonging to the class of the first principles*. And such a method we call 'analysis' as being 'solution backwards' [*anápalin lýsis*, that is, *re-duction*]." Pappus goes on to distinguish two kinds of analysis, theoretical and problematical. In the former we assume a hypothesis and trace out its consequences until we come to something admittedly true or admittedly absurd—this second case is known as a *reductio ad absurdum* or negative proof. In the latter we assume a solution or a construction as if it had been found, and trace out its consequences until we come to something either known to be possible or the reverse.[50]

Analysis is therefore a means both of returning to and reflecting on those beginnings that Socrates calls *hypótheses* (e.g., 510 b; "sub-position" is the precise rendering of the Greek word *hypóthesis*). It is also a means for achieving agreement (533 c 5) concerning the consistent consequences of any suppositions that happen to be offered and, occasionally, for the reduction to absurdity of a position by refutation. Whether or not Plato was really first to recognize in this dialectical way a formal mathematical method, he himself certainly attributed it to Socrates who regards it as his very own mode of conversing, which, "while he is the man he is," remains his *only* way, as he himself says somewhat hyperbolically (*Theaetetus* 197 a 1).[51]

Consequently the most familiar form of analysis in the dialogues, which people find "not unpleasant" (*Apology* 33 c 4), is that non-mathematical *reductio ad absurdum,* the Socratic refutation (*élengchos*). It is used for silencing professional argufiers, "eristics," by disposing of their dangerous absurdities, and for producing in those who are well-disposed that perplexity of soul (*aporía*) which is the beginning of serious inquiry; its complement is Socratic ignorance, Socrates' ironic self-denigration (*Republic* 354 b 9). Accordingly refutational argument occurs in the *Republic* only in the first book, where Socrates uses it to effect the forcible conversion that the violent Thrasymachus has brought down on himself as a "prelude" to the real inquiry (cf. 349 a 10, 354); thereafter Socrates uses the gentler way of his analogic "music." We must now see how the mathematics he proposes is also, in some sense, "analytical," consisting as it does of "conversion-aiding arts," the devices that at some point induce reflection on suppositions (533 d 3).

To begin with, the mathematical enterprise is analytic in the same way as is any Socratic "search" (*zétesis*), in which the object is always assumed as something known of which the con-

sequences will emerge in the course of the inquiry (cf. *Meno* 80 e
ff.). Socrates regards mathematics as just such a search (523 a 2,
524 e 5, 528 b–c, 531 c 6); in fact it differs from any Socratic
conversation only in the greater disembodiment and commonness of its objects, commonness in the sense both of generality
and of *apparent* triviality (522 c). Thus the question "What ever
is a finger?" is transformed in the course of the mathematical inquiry into the question "What ever is a one?" (523 d 4, 524 e 6).
Socrates gets Glaucon to admit that the power of counting finds
in a finger opposites that are "each one, both together two,"
precisely as earlier he had gotten him to agree that since the
Beautiful and the Shameful are opposite, they are "two, and
each one" (524 b 10, 476 a 2). In other words, Socrates is interested not so much in getting on with the specific mathematical science as in returning again and again to its hypotheses; a
sign of this is the preposterous name he gives to "arithmetic,"
which he calls "the study of the one" (525 a 2), as if number science consisted of nothing but its beginning principle, the unit,
that "source of the whole of number" (Aristotle, *Topics* 141 b 9;
p. 221) which is traditionally not even regarded as a proper
number (cf. Euclid, *Elements* VII Defs. 1–2).

But Socrates intends his young philosophers to practice analysis also in a more technical sense, namely as "problematic"
analysis. Each of the two final, theoretically physical, sciences is
to be studied, in Socrates' strange phrase, by "rising to problems" (530 b 6, 531 c 2). To see what the nature and purpose
of such problems are—besides supplanting observation—we
must look again at the order of Socrates' mathematical course.
Theon, for instance, observes that non-sensible harmonics, since
it is the study of pure number relations, that is, of *lógoi* and
analogíai, should naturally follow immediately after arithmetic
and before geometry in the mathematical order (*Mathematical
Matters Useful for Reading Plato,* ed. Hiller, p. 17). It is therefore not surprising that Socrates thinks it necessary to justify his
own different ordering, in which harmonics is the capstone, by

an appeal to the very men whose preoccupation with matters sensible and experimental he immediately after disowns; harmonics is to be understood as cosmic music, the sister science of astronomy, "as the Pythagoreans say, and we, Glaucon, agree" (530 d 8, 531 b 7). For by accepting this ordering, Socrates obtains a final propaedeutic study that is both non-sensible *and* cosmic, namely the *unheard music* of the *unseen heavens* underlying the "eye's sky" (Socrates' pun: *horatós—ouranós*, 509 d 3).

Now we can see just what it means to "use problems" in astronomy, "bidding the things in the heavens good-bye" (530 b 7). According to tradition it was Plato himself who raised that truly epochal question of astronomical hypotheses, setting this as

a problem for those interested in these matters: By what hypotheses of regular and ordered motions can the appearances associated with the motions of the wanderers [the planets] be saved? (Simplicius, *Commentary on Aristotle's On the Heavens* 292 b 10).

The young philosophers will, presumably, work on just such problems, contenting themselves with "saving," not too exactly, the more basic appearances such as the daily revolution of the stars and the yearly anomalies of the sun. Here "saving the appearances" means learning to observe them *as appearances of rational patterns closer to Being*, that is, in terms of mathematical hypotheses, and at the same time to dismiss them *as mere appearances*, "bidding them good-bye." Using, then, the visible heavens as a nicely made but not very important example (259 d 7 ff.), they will, I imagine, be set the following problem: to construct a rational—arithmetical and geometric—cosmos such as might be "hypothesized as a model" by some mythical demiurge who wanted to bring our visible world into being (*Timaeus* 48 e 5). Note that on this level a mythical demiurge rationally forming some *given* material in real space is a requirement of cosmic genesis, since any mathematical hypothesis just by itself is not a "pattern-cause" (*paradeigmatikón aitión*), it will not have the power of a true source or cause and will never produce the sensible world by itself; there exists, the Pythagorean's hopes notwithstanding, no strict deductive account of the sensible world from the purely mathematical cosmos alone.[52] In terms of Socrates' Divided Line, mathematics does not, by itself, make the material world—though it makes it rationally structured.

The profits from working such problems will be many: The students will learn to make images that will exceed the visible original in truth. They will learn to make dianoetic hypotheses about the whole of appearance and to deduce their consequences. In attempting to "save the appearances" by underwriting them mathematically they will learn what a mere appearance is and is not. They will get used to living with their mathematical cosmos as a preparation for dwelling with the invisible and bodiless *noetá* (see *Sophist* 246 b 7, *Statesman* 286 a 5). It is unlikely that this study will much resemble the spherical geometry presented in those dull *Sphaerics* (like that of Theodosius) which are supposed to be realizations of Plato's "pure" astronomy. We must rather imagine that the young philosophers will be asked to study an armillary sphere in order to reflect on matters such as the human significance of suggestive astronomical terms like "obliquity," "error," "anomaly." They will find these studies "useful . . . in the search for the good and the beautiful" (*Republic* 531 c 6), since they provide the terms of the rationalizations that insinuate equality, symmetry, consonance, and order into a discordant cosmos. They will have remade the world on a higher level. Then their time will have come to leave mathematics for the pursuit of dialectic, which begins by "taking up (*anaírousa*) the hypotheses" (533 c 8), in the senses both of "removing" them and of "raising" them to a higher mode. (Just so will Hegel use the word *aufheben:* to cancel or supersede and to lift up or preserve.) Now they will take up first their synoptic hypotheses. This means that they will try to see through their stereometric and cosmic mathematical models into that array of lower *eíde* that most immediately governs the world of appearances and human excellence within it. These are the *eíde* that the dialectician encounters first (500 c, 484 c–d, *Gorgias* 508 a) and which, while least in being, are longest in their defining *lógos* and, one might say, most concrete, for example, *eíde* of animals and arts (e.g., *Statesman* 267 a–b).

I have mentioned stereometry because we are told, quite incidentally, that static geometry is to be pursued in problems as well (530 b 6). Here again the order of studies proves interesting. The first geometry of the curriculum was naturally plane geometry (528 d 3). Next, skipping solid geometry, Socrates brought in astronomy, but, right away, with an air of significance, he asked Glaucon to "draw back" (528 a 6) so as to let him deliver a speech in praise of the study of that missing third dimension which seems "not yet to have been discovered" (b 4). Solid geometry, the study that comes between earth measurement and the motion of the skies, aiming at the objects that lie between heaven and earth, is, he now implies, in some special way the city's business; it is a political affair, which ought to be carefully supervised and which, even less than the other studies, is to be pursued for merely private purposes (b 6 ff., cf. 525 c 2). He might, however, have stopped himself even sooner, for he had at its very inception disrupted the dimensional development of his mathematical world. That was when he introduced the "second increase," when a line generates the plane, even though he had omitted any mention of the first increase, when a point generates the linear dimension.

This one-dimensional study, however, so conspicuously missing in the *Republic,* is solemnly introduced in the *Laws* (820 a–b), where it is presented precisely as the necessary prerequisite of stereometry, that is, of solid geometry. It is the study of *irrational* lines, the special interest of the young mathematician Theaetetus, who is Socrates' lookalike and his best interlocutor (*Theaetetus* 147 d ff., 144 d 8). Theaetetus is also credited with the first cogent presentation of all the regular solids called "Platonic,"[53] with which Timaeus fills the cosmos (*Timaeus* 53–54). We happen to know what *the* classical problem in solids is. It is the problem of doubling the cube. According to legend it was originally raised by Minos, the underworld judge, and later again by the Delians, whom Apollo had ordered to double his altar; they were said to have brought it to Plato for solution.[54] Socrates himself uses the plane version of this problem to display the natural knowledge of a little slave boy whose education consists simply in knowing Greek, and who is nonetheless able to find, under Socrates' supervision and yet through the recollection of his inborn knowledge, the side of the double square; it is the "irrational" diameter, which happens to be the mean proportional between the side of the unit square and the side of its double, a length inexpressible in terms of the unit side, though, of course, commensurable with it when squared, since the squares are as 1:2 (*Meno* 82 b ff.). We might conjecture that as the doubling of the square, done in the sand on the earth, is a boy's introductory problem, requiring for its solution only the learner's sound and willing nature (for the slave boy needs to know no geometry but must only attend to Socrates and consult his own soul), so the doubling of the cube, applicable to the solid world of bodies, is the citizen's problem, requiring both the right nature and some sophistication. It may therefore represent practical politics. For the stereometric problem is solved by finding *two* mean proportionals in continued proportion,[55] sometimes called "powers" (*Theaetetus* 147 d 3, *Timaeus* 31 c; we would say "roots"); this procedure again gives a side irrational vis-à-vis the unit length, though commensurable when cubed (Euclid, *Elements* X Defs. 1–4). Stereometric analysis then might represent the advanced work of finding ways and means *to reconcile that which has no common measure by going into a higher dimension,* the one that represents bodies mathematically (cf. *Epinomis* 990 d 8); mechanical, that is, might-and-main, approximations are evidently unacceptable for the philosopher kings-in-training, who must learn to solve problems dianoeti-cally. This is perhaps why Socrates mysteriously tells Glaucon not to allow his children, who will eventually have charge of the city, to be like "irrational lines" (534 d 5); he means they should not be like that which has failed to rise to the higher dimension in which commensurability and consonance are possible. "Higher dimension," I am intimating, might well stand for "higher on the Divided Line," closer to the Good.

There is indeed something obvious in taking problematic analysis as the paradigm of practical planning, and, accordingly, Aristotle in the *Nicomachean Ethics* compares deliberation to the analysis of diagrams since in both cases there is a search for solutions (1112 b 20). Such a use of mathematics can be quite dangerously reductive when it substitutes schematism for wisdom (as we moderns well know), but it surely provides brilliant practical models for solving complex problems (see *Meno* 86 e). What Socrates is concerned with, however, is how mathematics can serve as "the haul of the soul from Becoming to Being" (521 d 3).

Thus he concludes his exposition of the philosophers' mathematical education by suggesting to Glaucon that "the experts (*deinoi*) in these matters can't seem to you to be dialecticians" (531 d 9; Theodorus, the good-natured but philosophically dim mathematician in the *Theaetetus*, is a prime example). This distinction between expert mathematicians and dialectical philosophers is ever his theme; for instance, he observes that "inasmuch as they themselves [the mathematicians] don't know how to use their discoveries they turn them over to the dialecticians to use—if they have any sense at all" (*Euthydemus* 290c3). Socrates characterizes the helplessness of the mathematicians' arts: "They *dream* about Being, and cannot behold it as if awake, [at least] as long as they use hypotheses that they leave undisturbed, unable to give an account of them" (533 b 8). For Socrates, mathematics will always remain a dreamlike and "phantastic," that is, imagination-bound, enterprise. For instance, in the *Philebus*, where in the course of the investigation of the human good he constructs just such a "bodiless cosmos" (64 b 7) as was described above, using principles like the One, the More and Less, and Number (23 c), he always attributes his knowledge of these to a god, a myth, or a dream (16 c, 18 b, 20 b, 25 b). For him mathematical objects are shadows or reflections on the surface of Being, catching its mere spatial reflections. They are, to be sure, more immediately accessible to the human understanding than Being itself and certainly more rational than embodied shapes, but they have no substance of their own. They are interesting because they are in turn reflected within the sensible world, which they order by shape and number. Mathematical objects are "the middle things" (*Metaphysics* 987 b 15, 1090 b 31), intermediate between the lower and higher realms. For they differ from sensory objects in being eternal and immutable and from the *eíde* in having each a plurality of instances, while every *eídos* is unique. That is why their study is indeed capable of hauling the soul from Becoming toward Being. For the mathematical part of the dianoetic realm contains the shapes and numbers and their relations that can, as was said, rationalize the natural world below because they are reflections not only of the intelligible beings above but surely, as logical systems, also of the ordering structure, the *táxis* of Being. Thus mathematics mediates between the realms, since its study, which deals with *pure but quasi-visible objects,* is preparatory for dialectics, which moves among *pure and invisible beings.*

It might be useful to give one example of an attempt to "take up" a mathematical hypothesis in the double sense of canceling it and raising it to its eidetic original. Out of the many hypotheses of mathematics, that is, its assumed elements, such as units, numbers, ratios, proportions, "the odd and the even and figure and the three kinds of angles" (510 c 4), let us choose the most fundamental objects, the element *one* and the first number, *two.*

At the risk of some repetition, let me begin with a familiar perplexity (p. 221). The senses of sight and touch elicit from us merely the words "a finger," but in comparison with other fingers, a bigger and a smaller, we have to say of the same finger that it is both large and small. However, "large" and "small" are contraries and evidently not capable of being simply thrown together; they are incompatible. We therefore say that the finger comprises both of these intellectual objects intended in speech—which are therefore candidates for being *eíde*—in such a way that they are "each [an incompatible] one, both together [a *de facto*] two" (524 b), that is, *two* contraries *at once* in *one* finger. Thus arises what Euclid calls the first "multitude composed of units," the first number, two (*Elements* VII Def. 2). Since each one sensory object includes oppositions "infinite in multitude," every other number can arise in this way (525 a); each unit of sense reveals itself as numerous.

But here we must stop to notice that actually the components of the finger distinguished by speech are not like pure, homogenous Euclidean units at all, but are qualitatively disparate *eíde*, namely Great and Small. So mathematics, having taught us to analyze a situation by discerning and counting units is no longer adequate to collecting these into one unitary number, the finger-complex. For mathematical units can, though each is one, be together as two, but how can Great and Small be together in our finger? This perplexity, it turns out, mirrors in the sensory realm a situation in the realm of *eíde*.

So now let the inquiry concern not some one thing in the world of sense, but the greatest single noetic object, the *eídos* Being itself. In the *Sophist*, after a survey of the possible opinions (242 b 10 ff.), it is decided that Being must comprise two "most opposite" *eíde*, Rest and Motion (250 a 8), neither of which is by itself *Being* but both of which *are* indeed Being. Hence that Being appears as "a third thing beside these" (b 7). If we now try to apply the hypotheses of mathematical unit and number to these opposites comprised by Being, that is, if we try to "count up" Being, we see again, just as we learned in the sensory case, that these elements discerned by dianoetic thought are not countable; you can't mix even ordinary apples and oranges. To count up units it is, to repeat, necessary that they should be *mere* or pure units "capable of being thrown together and indifferent" (*symbletaí kai adiáphoroi,* Aristotle, *Metaphysics* 1081 a 6), units capable of addition (*Republic* 526 a 3). But Rest and Motion have no such common ground, being irreducibly different; from the perspective of the Whole (where there is no relativity of motion) nothing can be at once at rest and in motion.

Furthermore, if we did make such a reduction we would get mere abstractions and lose exactly what we are after in dialectic, which is "the thing itself," in its fullness, in its very nature. Being is not, therefore, a counting-number, the result of adding two mathematical units, but a community of incomparable eidetic monads which are themselves neither prior nor posterior to their common number, namely Being, the unique Two (ibid. 1081 a ff.; see ch. 13 Note 11 for a condensed exposition). We can see how the mathematical hypotheses of the unit one and the number two, having taken us up into Being—for without the ability to count we could never have ascended to its dialectic—must now be superseded by being raised to a new kind of one, an eidetic unit. Thus we rise to dialectic by learning, using, and leaving mathematics behind: The aspects of the appearance called finger became enigmatic to us when we used our counting ability inherent in speech, and the *eídos* called Being became clearer to us when we again tried to count mathematically and met eidetic units instead. Finally, the mathematics is left still further behind when we recall that the mathematical one, the atomic, least and indifferent unit (525 e ff.), is the total inverse of the dialectical One which as the Whole is the source of Being in its fullness and the differentiated *eíde* under it (p. 220, 511 b 7; on these disparate functions of the Platonic One, see *Metaphysics* 1084 b 13 ff.).[56]

This dialectic which supersedes mathematical thinking is not often practiced in the dialogues, for they cannot leave the realm of *diánoia* and its analytic *lógoi.* Ordinary speech is at a permanent impasse about Being (*Sophist* 250 e 5), and whatever solutions are offered to its enigmas must be somehow misstated. For example, in the *Sophist* one problem concerning Being is formulated in terms of the mutual Not-being of each of its constituent eidetic units (251 d ff.): Rest is not-Motion and Motion not-Rest; the brute negativity of this definition is removed by discovering that the negating Nonbeing there at work is merely Otherness, "the Other" (254 e ff.). But then it will, along with its correlative "the Same," appear, when presented in speech, to be a hypothesis exactly like the other three *eíde*, Rest, Motion, and Being. The Same and the Other will therefore be counted with these three among the five greatest *eíde* or *géne* (255 c), although they both have (as I have already claimed for the Other, p. 224) the nature not of beings but of principles that are "beyond Being," of *archaí*. In the context of the *Republic* the more important of these *archaí* is, I think, that whose eidetic name is never mentioned there, "the Same." For this is precisely the Good, whose dialectical name is also the One: In the *Republic* it is imaged, and it is given that name most fitting for an inquiry into justice. But it is not further delineated; it is not, for example, described as the encompassing wholeness of Being or as the source of the oneness and *self-sameness* that renders each being "one and the same" with itself and thus makes it just what it is. For these are the dialectical terms of that longer, imageless, journey toward the "greatest study" (505 a 2).

To return to the pedagogical purpose of Socratic mathematical study. It is, then, to reflect on its own elements, its hypotheses, above all on that Promethean gift of number (Aeschylus, *Prometheus Bound* 459); this study is a *preparation*, a propaedeutic, for dialectic, the ascent of thinking into the realm of the intelligible *eíde*. Often this examination involves a reflection on its own language, its *lógoi*. As so frequently, Socrates' very example is chosen to express the reflexiveness of the inquiry, for the hand with its fingers is a pointer, and Socrates is pointing at this pointer. The purpose of such reflection is, in turn, to bring the soul up to that highest internal "power of dialectical conversation" (*he tou dialégesthai dýnamis,* 533 a 8, cf. 511 b 4; *Parmenides* 135 c 2). In such conversation the soul, freed from all the senses (*Republic* 532 a 6) and raised even beyond the intermediate dianoetic *lógoi* (see *Phaedo* 99 e 5), confronts being immediately by means of its own noetic *lógos* (*Republic* 511 b 4, 532 a 7, 534 b 9, c 3), which is simply its power of having a direct relation, a "ratio," so to speak, to Being.

c–d The activity of this higher *lógos,* dialectic itself, is naturally beyond Glaucon's present reach and no part of the preliminary survey. To set out on the dialectical road would be to see "no longer an image . . . but the True itself" (533 a 3); the "most serious matters" are withheld from Glaucon, and so from any initial reader of the dialogue. (Here we may perhaps discern the admission of a rift between Plato himself and his Socrates: Socrates withholds the highest matters from pedagogic care, Plato from self-protective caution—so he says, *Seventh Letter* 344 c.) Instead, Socrates chants his "hymn" in praise of dialectic (532 a 1), and with that Glaucon must be content until he is ready for the long haul.

The *Republic,* however, in which for pedagogical reasons philosophy is allowed to appear as the *fulfillable* love of wisdom, does not resolve for us this question: Has even one human embodied soul ever been able to withdraw entirely into the noetic realm to move "by means of the *eíde* themselves through them and into them"? Has even one soul ever addressed itself in wordless speech to invisible sights? Or is the human limit perhaps reached when, while reflectively exercising our power of provisional thinking and speaking, we have a sudden flash of trust in those hypotheses that appear to make most sense of these activities? We know that Socrates looked to others as if he were lost in the realm of thought (e.g., *Symposium* 174 d, 220 c) and that Plato described a moment of entry into that realm (*Seventh Letter* 341 c, 344 b), but beyond that we are on our own.

Glaucon has now been given a preliminary synopsis of these extendedly synoptic studies in which the young rulers are to prove their aptitude for dialectic (537 c); he has also been given an intimation in images of the ultimate sights of dialectic. After this Socrates addresses him as a fellow law-giver. He rehearses with him what he, Glaucon, would do "if he were ever to nurture in deed those whom he is now nurturing and educating in speech" (534 d 3, 8, 535 a 3, 537 c 9).

Together they review once more the virtues to be tested for in the natures of the future philosophers. At this point Socrates again brings up the danger to the puppies (539 b 6, cf. 498) in taking up dialectic too early. He vividly describes the aggressive questioning these yapping young philosophical dogs engage in; they are both more acute and more dangerous than full-grown watchdogs. The philosophical city, as Alcibiades' mentor well knows, is always playing with fire in indulging youthful dialectics. Hence in his *Seventh Letter* Plato himself gives a much more severe account of the preliminaries required to test the readiness of a mature tyrant to engage in philosophic inquiry (340 b, 344 c).

2   a   So they come to the final question, which Socrates obviously considers of acute importance in the serious execution of his educational program. He has raised the matter before with some intensity (536 c 4). It is the question of age, the fitting of the progress of study and practice to human growth.

Its significance can be gauged by reference to Plato's last dialogue, the *Laws*. There the purpose of study is to engender piety rather than dialectic, and the objects of study are the gods revealed in astronomy (966 c) rather than the Good attained by dialectic. There also the definite and written assignment of ages to studies is said to be useless (968 d). Evidently such a schedule becomes feasible—indeed, crucial because of the dangers of premature exposure—only where there is to be a genuine ascent of the soul. What Socrates is here talking about might be called the "biological," the rational life development of the *embodied* human soul and its proper program of nurture (*Republic* 492 a). Why this is so sensitive a matter is made plain in the discussion of the human natures suitable to philosophy, a discussion which both immediately precedes and again follows the central section where the great images of Sun and Cave are presented (490–496, 535–536). Since a human being is a conflation of body and soul, the soul must, at least in the beginning, live its life in conjunction with the body, exposed to or even dominated by its influence.

The best natures, Socrates thinks, will also be well set up in body (535 a–b), in addition to possessing vigorously those virtues that are "somehow close to the body" (518 d 10), perhaps self-control and the like. Such vigor, however, is particularly sensitive to disrupting influences (491 b ff.). The schedule of studies clearly takes account of this obtrusive parallel life of the body: gymnastics occupies the years of the most rampageous sexual vigor, practical politics occupies the prime of life, and the later years, when the body fails and it is no longer possible to learn many things at once (536 d 1), are given to the contemplation within sight of the single highest hyper-being.

The ages Socrates assigns to each stage of growth (539 d 8) are best seen in a chart fitting them to the ascent of the Cave Image:

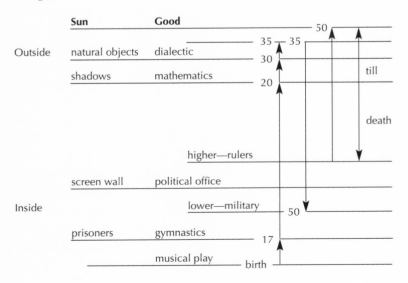

After fifty, Socrates says, the time has come for the philosophers to behold the Good itself and, using it as a pattern (540 a 9), to order well (*kosmeín,* b 1) the city and to educate others to live in it as its guardians. Thereafter they will spend their lives in philosophy whenever possible, but when their turn comes they will descend and govern, considering it "not as something fair [i.e., beautiful] but as necessary" (b 4).

This last phrase recalls one last time that for the philosopher kings there is suspended the chief thesis of the dialogue, that justice brings happiness. They tend "their own business," which is to govern, merely because they see the necessity of preserving their city, or from a Cephalus-like, that is, unreflective sense of duty (see 331 d 2), or perhaps from some pedagogic affection for their young.

But they lose more than they gain by their governance. For as Aristotle has clued out, only incestuous love is not explicitly forbidden in the "fair city" (*Politics* 1262 a 35); all other kinds of lovers are prohibited from being together, except on occasion as a reward for valor, because of the disruptive strength of the pleasure involved. Hence the *kallípolis,* the "fair city," most deliberately contains for its rulers nothing fair (521 a), that is, nothing permissibly and humanly lovable, for which a philosopher might willingly descend from the realms of contemplation; witness the amusing fact that the city is called fair insofar as its citizens are involved in the study of solid geometry (527 c 1, 528 c 7). In this city *geometric* is substituted for *erotic* interest (546, 458 d 5; note Plutarch's phrase on the business of the Academy: "to become happy through geometry." *Dion* 14, 2; *Epinomis* 992 a 4). In the just city, "love" means primarily the ascending love of truth, *philosophía* (e.g., *Republic* 490 b 2), and human *eros* is allowed only a subordinate and utilitarian part in it (459–460, 468 c, cf. 521 b 4). Yet such *eros* alone can be imagined as sufficiently strong to bring the philosopher *down* by his own desire—unless it be that he passionately loves to teach elementary geometry (which is, however, thinkable).

It is indeed necessary that the commerce of friendship should replace the intercourse of lovers, that *private* love should be absent here, where the dialogic community is displayed as the fundamental *political* community. Thus in the *Republic* the Good and not the Beautiful is the central theme. In compensation, as it were, Plato wrote another dialogue, the *Phaedrus*, later subtitled "About the Beautiful." It is set, in contrast to the *Republic*, outside the walls of Athens, and in it love ranks above politics and the lover of wisdom is identified with the lover of beauty (248 d).

Glaucon too receives compensation at another time for the austerities of his philosophical apprenticeship as a ruler of the "fair city." It is to him that the speeches made about *eros* at a famous party are recounted in the dialogue *Symposium*. He hears them in circumstances that are the suggestive counterpart of Socrates' "going down to the Piraeus" that opens the *Republic*, namely Apollodorus's "coming up from Phalerum," Athens' harbor in earlier days (172 a 2, c 3).

b What is most remarkable about the age chart itself (p. 239) is that the rulers' education, although instituted by and for the city, leads them initially and recurrently straight out of and beyond it. Hence practical experience with the city's life comes to them late and episodically. In terms of the Cave, it is conspicuous that no mention is made of an initiatory look behind the scenes of the puppet theater, of something that might be construed as a political apprenticeship. The counterpart of this lack of practical training is the absence from their studies of any "political science," of any theoretical abstractions from practical politics. In the dialogue called "Constitution" (*Politeía*) *the study of constitutions has no place.*

One reason for this omission lies in the nature of such patterns: The pattern of the just city is not really an *eídos*, a being responsible for what is in the world, but an *ideal*, a model significantly located *not* in the "hypercelestial place" (*Phaedrus* 247 c 2) with the *eíde*, but in the sky (592 b 2, cf. 529 d 7) with

Cloudcuckooland. A model (*parádeigma*), unless it be a caus-
ative model (*paradeigmatikón aítion*), is only a *schéma* or a
mímesis, having the mode of being that belongs to a work of art
(501 a 9, *Laws* 817 b 4). The polis-pattern of the *Republic* is of
the latter sort; it is neither a practical handbook for rulers such
as the "Mirrors of Princes" popular in the Renaissance nor a
textbook for civil servants such as the treatises on administration currently used in courses on government. If it were prospective young rulers could be urged to study this book called "The
Constitution" as a source of constitutional and administrative
law and of the practices that spring up around these. They might
undergo some indoctrination, as do our students of government,
and the intellectuals among them might acquire a suitable mind-
set, that is, an ideology.

But the *Republic* is a book altogether different from a pattern book of politics or a textbook of governmental science. Its
salient political advice is that the young philosopher kings are
to look to the one effectively responsible pattern which is that
originating "beyond Being"; the practical political teaching of
the *Republic* is that governing below is learned by looking up.
Even in the thick of affairs the rulers will try to govern "in the
light of the Whole" (540 a 8). The ability to do this, irreplace-
able by any administrative technique or political procedure, is
called human wisdom (*phrónesis,* 433 d 1, 521 b 8), the one
virtue *containing* all the political virtues (*Symposium* 209 a 6).
Were it visible, says Socrates, it would be the loveliest of all the
virtues (*Phaedrus* 250 d 5). "The best thing is that not laws
should be in power but a kingly man with human wisdom"
(*Statesman* 294 a 7);[57] his practical wisdom would be under the
aegis of the unifying Good.

We moderns tend to seek our political safety in procedure,
and so a polity relying on humans, not laws, rightly makes us
nervous, no matter how wise the ruler. Plato's *Polity* of course
contains plenty of fundamental law: the constitution of the
castes, the severe discipline imposed on the ruling caste, the

arcane eugenic formula, and above all, the public education of
the philosophers. Regarded—falsely, as I have tried to show (p.
124)—as practical political proposals rather than as incitements
to reflection, these must be objectionable to an American citizen. But that a community of learning, such as the city of the
Republic turns out at its heart to be (p. 142), is best maintained
not by people who have been trained in administrative science
but by people who have been educated to act from philosophical reflection—that seems to me to be both benign and eminently
practical. And then, what political community is not in some
central aspect a community of learning?

c Having come to the end of life, the philosopher kings
will at last be allowed to depart permanently to the Isles of the
Blessed, and the city will honor them with memorials and sacrifices—if the Pythia permits, as divinities (*daímones*), otherwise
as happy men (*eudaímones,* 540 c 1). Socrates, speaking from
beyond the grave, as it were, is ending the conversation with a
sly reference to himself. He has indeed just advocated (seeking,
to be sure, the permission of the Delphic oracle) the introduction of "other new divinities" into the city, exactly as the indictment against him was one day to state (*Apology* 24 c 1, cf.
21 a 6); he was indeed apparently honored in Athens after his
own death very nearly as he here prescribes (Diogenes Laertius,
II 43; Xenophon, *Apology* 15). He has, moreover, outrageously
implied that to be an *eudaímon,* a happy man such as he is, is a
greater thing than to be a mere *daímon,* a lesser divinity (see
Symposium 202 e 1). For to be happy is "to turn the soul to
that place where is the happiest part of being," the Good (*Republic* 526 e 3).

d And now Socrates and Glaucon are emerging from
their wonderfully central philosophical digression back into the
context of that city which had been developed for the whole
company, the "city in speech," the just or guardian city. Socrates himself recalls this city, a revolutionary community of men
and women, by a smiling rejoinder to Glaucon, who had allu-

sively praised Socrates' ancestral craftsman's skill as a "maker of men-statues" (540 c 4; cf. *Euthyphro* 11 b 9); he reminds Glaucon that he can shape women too, for they are to share in this city (540 c 5). Socrates now founds this guardian city, still in speech, instituting it quickly and with charming offhandedness: All inhabitants over ten years are to be driven out "into the wilds"; this forced emigration will leave a clean slate for the lawgiver (541 a 1, cf. 510 a). The just city will start as a community of children!

Glaucon recalls accurately where they were when they digressed. Socrates, like the wrestler he is—he had assumed, we recall, the role of Heracles, who is the master of all wrestlers (p. 119)[58]—is to put himself into his former position so as to continue to wrestle with the account of the city in its degenerating forms (Books VIII–IX).

With his mordantly realistic deduction of these failing polities from the deteriorating characters of their citizens, Socrates is on the way back from his central conversation with Glaucon. As he passes to the periphery of the *Republic*'s concentric circles (p. 117), he mounts a reprise of its initial issues—whether justice is in itself a good (Book IX) and poetry by its very nature bad (Book X)—a return in the light of the ontological center.

Socrates, by descending with Glaucon into the mythical setting of the Peiraic underworld, has shown him that he lives his life as one imprisoned in a mortal Hades. But this demonstration is itself a release, the first step of the rescue. Unlike the poets, who fail to wrest from Hades the shade they desire (*Symposium* 179 d, Orpheus is the example), Socrates, a new Heracles, knows the way to bring his new lawgiver, his *nomothétes,* young Theseus, back up into the world of light.

Yet Glaucon's later life is almost a blank for us. He seems to have done little in his time, and no reputation, either good or bad, has survived him; certainly he founded no new Athens. We may be sure that this fact, presumably already evident when

Plato was writing the *Republic*, is meant to reflect on the dialogue. It forces us to ask whether in the face of it the labor of Socrates must not be considered altogether lost. Then we might remind ourselves that the city he was founding is a dialogic city, a community of conversation and, moreover, that while Socrates is speaking to Glaucon, the dialogue itself is speaking to us. Consequently it may happen that Socrates' articulated thoughts (*lógoi*)

> are not fruitless but bear seed whence other such thoughts grow in other haunts, thoughts able to extend to what is immortal and forever and which cause the one who has them to be happy (*eudaimoneín*) as far as is possible for a human being (*Phaedrus* 277 a).

7

WHY JUSTICE?
THE ANSWER OF THE **REPUBLIC**

There are, I suppose, many books concerned with the question "What is Justice?" but few with the question that you have posed for yourself this year: "Why Justice?" What might be the reason for that?

Human language has an exceedingly strange and thought-provoking characteristic. To put it in a somewhat jaunty way: I find it thought-provoking that certain terms don't provoke thought in certain of their aspects. "Good" is a good word. "Decent" is a good word. "Fair" is a good word. "Just" is a good word. By a "good" word I mean one that has positive connotations, in the sense that we incline toward its sense, that we're for it. Is there anyone in whom the word "justice" raises a negative attitude?

To be sure, people get disgusted with what they regard as the established notion of justice or with its administration. In the book from which I will be borrowing most of my thought for this talk, there is even a real-life character—he happens to be serendipitously called Thrasymachus, "Bold-in-Battle"—who argues outright that perfect and complete injustice is better than justice, and that injustice is a virtue and justice a vice. But although this sophistical wild man is eager to say something really spectacularly scandalous, he also has a genuine intention: He wants to argue that the common sense about justice, that it is somehow protective of the weak, is all wrong and that true justice, called for its shock value "injustice," ought to be understood as preserving the natural order of things in which the strong do what they will and the weak suffer what they must. Thrasymachus's unjust justice is, however, still what is good in Thrasymachus's eyes, at least until Socrates shows him that it doesn't work as intended. In fact arguments of Thrasymachus's kind show that even the principle of doing what comes naturally begs for moral approval.

My point is this: In literature as in life, justice is taken to be something good, and there are two questions about "good" that are hard to ask. The harder one is "Why is good better than bad?" When Satan leaps over the wall into Milton's Paradise he utters to himself the words "Evil, be thou my good," perhaps the most disastrous utterable sentence imaginable; it is Thrasymachus's argument that injustice is better than justice on a cosmic scale and raises the question how the bad can get the name good.

The more approachable question is "Why should a particular notion or thing, commonly held to be good, in fact be good?" I take that to be the sense of the question you have proposed to yourself for the year: "Why Justice?" It must mean "Why is justice a good thing?" albeit it was framed by someone who was reluctant to tangle with goodness. To me it is pretty clear that, although it is a tricky and difficult business to tackle the question "What is Justice?", it is a topic that learned judges, scholarly ethicists, and concerned citizens do in fact talk about. In the normal course of social and private life, however, "Why Justice?" is a conversation stopper. It can't help but raise the possibility of undermining our bedrock of agreement. For if you ask the question in good faith you must think that there might be a totally corrosive answer, as when someone asks: "Why come to this lecture?" and the answer comes "No reason at all."

So there are, at least in my experience, not many books that deal with the question "What's the good of justice?" But there is one that deals with it preeminently. It is the mother of all books on constitution-making, on governance and education, on psychology, on the routes of moral decline, on the role of the arts in human life—you name it. There is, I have no doubt, much wisdom to be gained from life without the benefit of books, but if you are committed, as all members of a college presumably are, to learning by books, then this is the one you need to have studied before and after all the others, whether you belong to a department of philosophy, politics, psychology, education, literature, art, music, mathematics, or science. I'm perfectly willing to defend this bold and presumptuous claim in the question period.

The work is, of course, Plato's *Republic*. It is a conversation carried on by Socrates with Plato's two young brothers, Glaucon and Adeimantus. There are others present, among them the aforementioned Thrasymachus and the people in whose house the meeting is taking place, an old arms merchant and his son. The house is in the Piraeus, the traditionally most democratic part of Athens. The conversation is very long; it extends through much of a day and night, and is presented as being retold by Socrates himself—who thus takes responsibility—in ten parts or books. It is Socrates' longest conversational session.

In the first book the old host and his son and some others, including Thrasymachus, are involved by Socrates, the incorrigible raiser of questions, in a slightly bad-tempered and inconclusive discussion about the nature of justice.

Then the two brothers get tired of this exercise and say they really want to be told about something different. Glaucon in particular states his wish very clearly: What I want to hear is praise of justice in and by itself. He calls to aid the myth of a ring that renders the wearer invisible. No one, not even the most completely just person, would not take advantage of doing every sort of injustice if, wearing the ring, he could do it with impunity and without loss of reputation. Together the brothers ratchet up the conditions: Let a just person lose everything by possessing this virtue, even the reputation of having it; let him find himself in the greatest misery: Would he still be happier for being just? Is justice an unconditional good? Can Socrates tell them the answer to the question "Why Justice?" when it is framed in the most extreme terms? What does justice inherently, apart from external and circumstantial advantages, do for its possessor?

Here, some way into the second book, begins that city-building for which Socrates' Republic is famous, or infamous, with its caste system, its censorship of the arts, its curious upside-down structure in which the lowest, politically least powerful class is the richest and freest, and the rulers the poorest and most constrained. This is the civic community which gives the dialogue its name, "The Constitution," in Greek *he politeía,* the supposedly perfectly just city-state.

Here I must draw your attention to a circumstance about which the dialogue is perfectly open and natural, so natural that many readers simply overlook it. All three participants in this constitution-making have tacitly agreed on a huge assumption, an assumption that I expect most of you to find quite alien once it is enunciated. They all take it for granted that justice is primarily an individual and not a political or social matter. It is not political or social justice they primarily care about, but justice as a human *virtue,* an individual quality. I think you might agree that when we talk about justice today we are almost always thinking of something systemic. Not so these three.

Thus I conclude that, however this book is commonly understood, it is not primarily and ultimately a book about politics at all. Rousseau says in his *Émile* that, rightly read, the *Republic* is a book about education. But I think that it is a book about education only because it is a book about psychology.

Let me stop for an aside here. Most books which I have studied that have some real magnitude about them share this characteristic: You can't readily classify them, as you always can a textbook, in respect to their true topic; in fact discerning what the true subject of a great book is might be said to be the chief interpretational labor. That holds for Plato's *Republic,* for Aristotle's *Metaphysics,* and for Kant's *Critique of Pure Reason.* One might almost say, hyperbolically, that the more naked the topic, the less deep the work.

But back to the *Republic.* Socrates needs a special device to turn from personal to public justice. He proposes, speaking anachronistically, a kind of magnifying glass. Things are easier to discern, he says, in the large. So let us look for justice in the small but complete civic community called a *pólis,* a city state. We ourselves will build, in words of course, such a city to our specifications, and then we'll be able quite easily to read off the nature of human justice.

This procedure is fraught with fascinating assumptions. One is that Socrates knows exactly where they are going, that he knows the ultimate principle of justice. The other assumption is that a political community is the soul writ large, or put less magnificently, that psychology precedes politics or that individuals are prior to society in the sense of shaping it in their own image. As soon as you hear it you will recognize how radically unconventional this notion is—and was, I can assure you, among Socrates' contemporaries. To us the idea that we are shaped by our political situation and determined by our social context is so much a given that anyone who lays claim to an original independent humanity is going to be accused by someone of naiveté or bad faith.

At this point I should say what I mean by psychology, which is a Greek word signifying "an account of the soul." We are used to thinking of psychology in association with the diagnosis of psychic pathologies and their therapies. You consult a psychologist when something is wrong, though of course there is also much theoretical study of the psyche. But in the Platonic context, psychology refers to the constitution of the soul, to what Freud, who is in certain respects close to Plato, calls its topography, its hierarchical layout, its functional parts and their relations of domination.

Socrates now builds the city that is to display justice writ large, that is to say, political and social justice. When completed it is constituted of three castes. The largest caste consists of the makers and consumers of commodities, craftsmen who are each other's customers, who accumulate wealth and please themselves in their way of life. We are after all in the house of a wealthy armorer and his son, who live well and freely. The middle caste is the military, whose proper virtues are courage combined with the willingness to take orders. This unlikely combination of daring and obedience, which lends to the warriors of all ages a complex pathos, distinguishes the guardians of the city. They live under a strict discipline, without luxury or wealth.

And finally some of these guardians form a small governing elite, the philosopher kings. Once these are evolved, the other guardians become their helpers and auxiliaries. To give those of you not very familiar with this book a taste of the way it is composed, let me say this: If you open it to the exact numerical center as counted by the traditional numbering of pages you will come on Socrates' introduction of these rulers shaped by the love of wisdom. To me this numerological device betokens that Plato regards them as central to his work. Socrates presents them as likely to be his most shocking suggestion. The description of their education, which Rousseau thought was the true subject of the *Republic,* forms the philosophic center and high point of the *Republic.*

The city, the *kallípolis,* the "beautiful city" as Socrates calls it, has now been constituted. It contains what a well-working community requires: people who produce and consume, people who guard and defend, people who administer and govern. Where in it is justice to be found? For, recall, the object of the exercise was to find large-scale civic justice on the hypothesis that it would be analogous to the personal virtue of justice, and that through this magnification we could then answer the question "Why Justice?"

Socrates now gives an answer to the question "What is political justice?" that might seem almost repellent in its dry simplicity. He says that justice is "doing what is one's own," "doing one's own thing." He means what we call "sticking to one's last," not exceeding one's competence. The producers and consumers are to do just that and not to get mixed up in the military life. The guardians and defenders are to submit to the Spartan discipline and training—some of the features of their life are in fact adopted from Sparta—necessary to the guardians of a community's security, and the philosophical kings are to do what they least want but are most fit to do, that is, govern the community. To Socrates one criterion of being fit to be in charge is not wanting to be, of having something more desirable to do. You will recognize an early, perhaps the earliest, example of Kant's test for genuinely moral action; acting against the grain, acting against inclination.

Socrates' oddly homespun notion of justice is probably influenced by the Greek word for an evildoer, *panoúrgos,* someone who does anything and everything. But there is, of course, also his aversion to a political system that invites irresponsibility and chaos.

However that may be, this notion of justice must now be located in the human soul. And here Socrates' topographical psychology comes in. The soul, he says, is composed of three parts or aspects. For how would the three parts of the city arise except from the individuals who have these characteristics? The guiding principle of this psychology is one that has become completely natural to us, so much so that in common speech we locate the different parts in different regions of the body: We think with our head or brain; we feel in our hearts or breast; we have desires like hunger and sex below the belt. The guiding principle is that each work or effect is to be attributed to its own faculty. (This faculty psychology goes in and out of favor, but con-

WHY JUSTICE? THE ANSWER OF THE REPUBLIC   **253**

temporary brain studies tend to support it: The psychic function we discern in folk psychology seems to be in fact located in different though interrelated brain centers.)

Socrates proceeds to read these faculties off the city—no great wonder since this city was artfully constituted to mirror the soul. Consequently it has a largest and—this is Socratic prejudice or wisdom, take your pick—lowest part, the desires and appetites. No need to describe this unruly province whose needs are bent on satisfaction, on possession and consumption, and which is willing to labor to supply these wants, be they culinary, sexual, or even just abstractly greedy, as in mere money-making.

Let me leap from this part, which is sometimes just commonly human, sometimes mob-like, to the highest and, in Socrates' estimation, smallest, least diverse, and least sprawling part. It is the one that calculates, considers, decides, reasons—in short, thinks. It is to the development of this part that the central books of the *Republic* are devoted. Here is one way to summarize the educational aim governing the program of liberal studies then set out—a program that for two and a half millennia prescribed the education of those who were free in the sense of being able to do what we call non-vocational learning, learning not immediately connected to crafts, trades, or professions. This aim is to see in all the free arts and sciences a unifying principle at work, a principle at once of illumination, development, and unification, which Socrates calls "the Good." You can see why it informs the education of the philosopher kings, whose chief business it is to hold the community together. One might say that the aim of a traditional liberal education is to contemplate what makes the intellectual world a community and to bring this vision into the worldly city.

To return to the parts of the soul. We have mentioned a lowest and a highest part. Now comes the middle or mediating part. I think of this as Socrates' very own contribution to constitutional psychology. The reservoir of lower appetites was called *epithymía. Epi* is a Greek preposition here signifying "motion toward." The desires naturally move people toward acquisition and possession. Socrates calls this discovery of his, this middle part, *thymós*. It has the same root as *epithymía* but without the outward motion. It stays internal, within the soul. *Thymós* is etymologically related to "fuming" in the sense of raging, storming, and also to the German word *Mut,* high spirits, courage. *Thymós* can be translated as temper, temperament, spirit, spiritedness, indignation, righteous anger, shame.

Socrates thinks of it as a part of the soul closely allied to and willing to be helper and auxiliary to the capacity for thinking. He gives an example. The eyes are sometimes captivated by low desires, by the appetite for seeing violent and horrible sights. Our slasher movies are a good case in point. Socrates tells of a man drawn to the viewing of a heap of dead bodies whose *thymós* berates his organs of sight for their wretched desire. The man feels indignation at his own shameful appetite.

As the lowest part of the soul dominates the life of producers and consumers in the city, so the middle part is, of course, characteristic of the soldiers of the city, who, for all their spiritedness, are inclined to obey authority, held in Socrates' city by the philosophical rulers. What I've just said implies that if the city as a constitution is a magnified soul, then the city as a human community mirrors the predominance of the different parts of the soul in its castes. Thus each individual member of a caste has the specific psychic characteristics of that caste. In fact Socrates thinks that all political corruption begins with *individuals* who fail to be true to their character, who fail to do their own, their proper thing; thus vice is psychological pathology.

The answer to the question "Why Justice?" is loud and clear in all I've reported. Socrates himself gives it in the last, the tenth book, returning to that very question, the one Plato's brothers really want answered: "Why Justice?" Why is justice an unconditional good?

The answer is that as the just city was one which respected the competence of its castes and submitted to the discipline of educated thought, so the just soul is one that lets no part of it-self get out of control. It allows scope to its needs and appetites and respects its righteously indignant spirit but bends all these propensities to the educated decisions of thought. This justice of the individual soul is what we call being "well-adjusted." It is psychic health. Nothing external can do it serious harm or much good. It is a pretty nearly impregnable *pólis,* an internal psychic community, integral and uncorrupted.

Let me put Socrates' answer in my own terms: Well-directed human effort has its hierarchies or, as we say, priorities. First comes the doer, then the deed—although Aristotle would dis-agree with this dictum, since he thinks that you become a doer by doing. Socrates, however, thinks that you do well by think-ing well. First attend to the adjustment of your own soul, par-ticularly the regulative liberal learning of your intellect, then project your internal economy on the world as social and polit-ical justice. The other way around is headless.

8

IMITATIVE POETRY: BOOK X OF THE **REPUBLIC**

A mindful reader of the grand finale of Plato's *Republic,* the myth of the soul's fore- and afterlife in the cosmos, might well feel scandalized. Twice in the work Socrates has inveighed against myth-making and vision-inducing poetry. First, in Books II and III, he excluded from the just city he is founding those poets who, like Homer the epic poet and Aeschylus the tragedian, show Olympian gods and great men misconducting themselves. That was a *moral* critique of poetry. Now in the same tenth book which ends with that myth, he has shown that all of imitative poetry celebrates a low grade of Being we should not get mixed up with. That constitutes a *metaphysical* condemnation of poetry. What could possess him to go into a grand poetic mode himself? What could his justification be?

I imagine that when you studied this and other Platonic dialogues you sometimes talked about Socrates' propensity for poetry and parables and how they are put in the service of dialectic. But after reading the *Republic* you might have felt that in using this poetic mode he is, simply and shamelessly, contradicting himself. Self-contradiction is, so Socrates thinks, the corruption of reason. Then how is he to be saved? I will give it a try, but I will have to start from several parts of the *Republic* in turn.

Imagine Socrates' discussion with Adeimantus and Glaucon as a series of topics arranged like concentric circles (see p. 117). Socrates leads the two boys—and his readers—on a path that follows the diameter of these circles into the center of the dialogue and then out the other side. The outside segments, the beginning and end, are concerned with the encompassing question and its concluding answer: Can Socrates show that a just life is in itself, apart from all external rewards, better than an unjust one? Then follows, on a series of inner rings, first the constructive part of the dialogue, the constitution of a just political community, together with a consideration of the role of poetry in the education of its citizens and an inquiry into the constitution of the soul, whose parts are discovered to be analogous in kind and relations to the classes of the polity just constituted. From this constitution, this civil framework, the dialogue known in English as the *Republic* takes its Greek name, *Politeía*, which in fact means "Constitution." It is, I will say by the way, because Socrates discovers the soul itself to be a kind of civil community that we can speak of a personal and interior justice, a proper psychic adjustment. All this happens along the entering side of the diameter.

On the exiting side, toward the end in Book VIII, instead of the constructive building up in Book II of the just city stage by stage, we find its destruction—its decline and fall, phase by phase, and the progressive deterioration of the soul that goes with each regime, from a still honorable timocracy with its predominant warrior caste down to the vilest tyranny and its hopelessly self-enslaved tyrant. Then, in Book X, follows the second consideration of imitative poetry and imitation in general, especially in painting. Socrates does not make the connection explicit, but he implies that imitative activity in general is one cause of the fall of the soul from perfect adjustment.

At the center of this diameter—and I mean the *numerically* exact center (473)—is Socrates' somewhat outrageous suggestion that for the just city actually to come about philosophers should be kings or kings philosophers. Then follows a sketch of these philosophers' education, the outline of a liberal arts curriculum such as you in your Integral Program and we at St. John's College follow. To give this philosophical curriculum a basis in the Being of this and of a higher world, Socrates presents a version of what we might call his metaphysical polity (Book VI), the ontological constitution of the world (meaning its classes or levels of Being). He presents this philosophical framework in an abbreviated form, first as a mathematical diagram—the famous "Divided Line"—and then, a second time, as a picturesque parable, the famous "Cave Image." He is talking to two very bright young men, Plato's brothers Glaucon and Adeimantus, but great as their aptitude is, Socrates doesn't think they are yet quite up to the long dialectical way required for the serious ascent of thought which they will need to pass through the Socratic world of graduated Being.

As we've seen, Plato has arranged the dialogue as a sequence of topics symmetrically disposed about a center, and this disposition has just the effect on the second consideration of imitative arts that I intimated before: On the way into the dialogue poetry is considered from the moral aspect, whether it strengthens or weakens moral fiber, but in the reprise, past the ontological center of the dialogue, its analysis is based on the levels of Being that Socrates has established. And so, as we exit the dialogue, he juxtaposes the grandest picture directly with the deepest critique of the very idea of depiction. That juxtaposition makes this myth more questionable than any of the numerous Socratic myths in other dialogues. Those myths manage to escape Socrates' moral strictures. In the first critique of poetry, he in fact allowed for a certain purified poetry, such as might encourage the steadfast interest and sober cheerfulness needed for philosophical inquiry. He might well claim that usually his visions and tales do just that—they put auditors in the frame of mind to carry on with philosophy. Sometimes they complement his inconclusive dialectic by presenting a consoling vision of a beautiful homecoming for the searching soul, and sometimes they circumvent an apparently insoluble perplexity by providing a solemnly mythical foundation for carrying on *as if* knowledge were attainable. Almost always they give a representation of the disembodied souls in their other-worldly home being rewarded or punished for their this-worldly conduct. These myths are therefore morally pure, cleansed of all the excruciating amoralities of epic and tragic tales, and Socrates is simply giving examples of the poetry that is permissible in the just city of the entrant side of the *Republic*.

These myths, all the myths told at a distance to Book X of the *Republic* and out from under its influence, are philosophically not so very problematic. But the exit myth of the *Republic* is placed, as I said, right next to a critique of image-making *per se* and thus of all imaginative poetry, a condemnation that is much more radical than was the earlier moral critique. Socrates has just condemned image-making *on principle,* and so it seems he shouldn't here be engaging in it. The grander the myth, the worse, the more paradoxical, his proceeding, it appears. I don't know, however, of any of those other infamous paradoxes—for example, that virtue is knowledge or that philosophers practice being dead or that there are invisible forms—that can't be resolved by thinking a little more vividly, I mean less formulaically. And so it will be with this one. It will be a while before I get to the solution I intend to offer for this paradox, not because I imagine I can keep you on the edge of your seats with suspense but because, without the proper preparation, I cannot make the solution particularly interesting.

Let me now retell the final myth in terms that will bring out what I think it means. It has various separable aspects. The straightforward one is that Socrates—having shown the two youngsters Glaucon and Adeimantus that justice is good not only as a political virtue but as a human way of being, since it is in fact nothing less than the healthy condition of the well-constituted soul—now wants to bring back in abundance the external rewards of which the just man had been stripped for the sake of the experiment. This superabundant bonus reminds me of the Book of Job, in which the Lord, having accepted Job's self-judgment, finally blesses him and gives him twice the earthly possessions he had lost and more, fourteen thousand sheep, for example.

Socrates, however, adds to this earthly restoration a reward in the larger realm, the life surrounding this life here. He repeats a tale first told by a mysterious man called Er, whose father "was of the clan Everytribe." Er presents an image of the soul after its earthly death as it wanders in the cosmos. This cosmos Socrates has adapted from the ancient astronomical cosmology to fit the requirements of that true rational astronomy which is a part of the philosopher's education. That is to say, this cosmology is to be mathematically beautiful but not necessarily observationally correct. And so it is—a glorious design, both like and unlike the astronomers' heaven. There seems to be a luminously immaterial containing structure, the cosmos, and within it a smaller, somewhat more embodied astronomical model imagined as a shaft-like pole, on which are fixed, as on revolving concentric spindle whorls, the orbits of the eight ancient planets. This inner image is the Spindle of Necessity, and hither come all the souls after their judgment and after a long period during which they suffer terrible penalties for their crimes or enjoy the delightful rewards for their good deeds. So far the myth is a simple tale of retribution or recompense in hell or heaven whose setting is a mythified rendition of Greek astronomy, in which an astronomical planetary system is placed around an imagined pole transversing a cosmological container.

But after a thousand years of such journeying, when the souls get to the Spindle of Necessity (p. 206), the tale becomes very strange. Around the spindle sit the three Fates, singing of past, present, and future, and in their sight a wonderful ritual is enacted. Lots are thrown on the ground, and the souls are told to pick them up; these lots determine the order of choosing. The souls are to choose a pattern of life from a multitude of patterns set out before them, every kind of life, including that of animals. They are to choose their *pattern of life,* Er specifies, but they do not choose the corresponding *ordering of the soul,* because the soul must adapt as it lives through the chosen life pattern. Each soul chooses according to the experience it has gained in its previous life together with the lessons learned—or missed—in the thousand-year journey. So the soul with lot number one chooses a tyrannical life out of greed and stupidity. And Odysseus, who has the last number, gets the life left over, that of a peaceful retiring man; it is just what he wanted anyhow because he has had excitement enough to last a lifetime. The choices are then ratified by the Fates. The souls camp in a scorched plain by the River of Oblivion. All drink, but some greedily drink so much that they forget everything. Then they are swept up to be reborn onto the earth's surface.

There is much to think about in what might be called the parable part of the myth. What can be meant by saying that we choose our life pattern before we are born? Is this prenatal choice of fate an odd form of predestination? Does the parable mean to signify that we are or that we aren't responsible for our lives? Let me offer my understanding.

What is meant by *a* life, a pattern of life? Well, we are born into pre-given circumstances—into our nation, class, family—and with congenital aptitudes—aptitudes for thinking or doing, for being biddable or obstreperous, for easy success or hard work. Most of us are shaped, with or without our cooperation, into a nameable pattern, which is the answer to the question: "What is he?" "What is she?" The answer might be: "A parent," "A teacher," or, God forbid, "A tyrant." These are recognizable life-patterns. The Myth of Er says that we are born into them. But it also says that we choose them. Isn't that paradox

very close to our experience? People of student age, like yourselves, struggle to "find themselves," to discover what they were,
from way back, intended to be. At the same time this discovery
feels like an assertion of freedom, like a free choice, a choice,
however, within the limits of the available options. Your soul is
not entirely pre-formed; you yourself order it as you discover
your lot in life. Even when your life has assumed its practically
permanent shape, so that you can only fleetingly imagine yourself in a different pattern, it is still a daily choice expressed as a
continual affirmation or at least acceptance of that life. In this
understanding of the myth, to have drunk too much of the waters of oblivion means not only to be unaware of the analyzable
complex of prescriptive pattern and free choice that make up our
lives, but to have forgotten as well that this lifetime is also a
preparation for the choice of the next life. In this-worldly, non-
mythical terms that means: Today's deed is in effect the choice
of tomorrow's life. Our next life begins every morning, and our
past days partly determine the next day's choice, which is nonetheless free as well.

The interpretation I have just given seems to me to be an example of a characteristic Socratic mode, of Socrates' mythical
modus operandi, so to speak: He depicts the soul in its pre- or
post-mortal realm, in its life before birth and after death. But he
means no *pre-* or *post-*, no before or after at all; he means *here*
and *now*. Another example of this mode occurs in the *Phaedo*
when Socrates says that a philosopher is to practice dying and
that his proper business is being dead. Yet it is pretty clear that
the death that comes at the end of life is of little interest to him,
although he is to die that very day. The dying to be practiced and
the death to be achieved are to take place in *this* life: He is talking about the soul's daily ascent into the realm of thought, the
daily exit from earthly living.

Why does he express himself in this solemn way? I don't think
it is only a guru's rhetoric. I believe Socrates really thinks that

in philosophizing we here and now transcend our this-worldly condition.

I called this interpretable aspect of the myth its *parable* part. But the myth is also a great *vision*, a cosmic image, which I have briefly described. In truth it is indescribable. Intensely visual though it seems to be, we don't succeed in picturing it as a coherent whole. In this scintillatingly indefinite spatial character it resembles the ultimate vision at the end of Dante's *Paradiso,* which is a spatially impossible yet brilliantly visual image of the union of the human form with the three divine circles of the triune god. In both images the imagination is baffled by trying to fit a sensory shape into a supersensory container; in Socrates' image that means fitting the merely mathematical model into its meaningful mythical frame.

This is the moment to leave that particular image, the Myth of Er, in order to consider imaging and image-making in general. Let me recall to you how I am moving within the layout of the *Republic.* In the first half Socrates seized the occasion for a moral critique of Homer and the tragedians, in the interest of the right ordering of the soul. Let us set that critique aside for now. At the end of the dialogue Socrates tells an exit myth, a great vision, the one I have just described and partially interpreted. This vision, an image of the luminous cosmic container with its astronomical content envisioned as a spindle attended by the spinning Fates, follows closely upon a condemnation of all imitative and image-making arts. Both the mythical image and the previous critique of imagery occur in Book X. The critique and condemnation, in turn, depend on the center of the dialogue, where philosophy comes seriously on the scene. The second half of the conversation is reflected through this philosophical axis; I mean that the ordering of the soul is from now on seen against the backdrop of the gradations of Being.

These gradations are set out in Books VI and VII, first in that mathematical diagram which sketches the way the grades are related and then in a parable, the Myth of the Cave, that tells the story of the human ascent through the grades of being. I shall briefly review the mathematical model.

Socrates imagines a line, probably an upright. (See diagram, p. 173.) He divides it once in some arbitrary ratio that we might exemplify in natural numbers, say as four is to twelve. This division represents the realm of things to be seen (visible things) and distinguishes it from the realm of objects thought about (intelligible objects). Which of these segments is the larger he does not say. From the point of view of the multitude of objects within it, the visible part would be larger; from the point of view of fullness of Being, the intelligible part is greater. Let us choose the latter perspective, so that the lower segment (visible things) is also the less in size. Now we take this lower segment of four units and subdivide it in the same ratio that four has to twelve, namely one to three, and in the same way we subdivide the larger, upper part, namely as three to nine. So the whole and both parts are each subdivided in the same ratio: 4:12::1:3::3:9; each first term is a third of its corresponding term. Notice that in this kind of division the middle parts of the divided line are equal; each is three in our example. This can be proved to be generally true whenever we divide the subsections in the same ratio as we divided the whole. (See p. 357.)

Now Socrates assigns to each segment first a realm and grade of Being and then the capability of our soul by which we learn about it. Let us take the middle parts first, those equal ones of three units that span the visible and the thoughtful realms. To the visible part he assigns all the solid things we find in nature, all visible bodies. Our soul's relation to these he calls "trust" (*pístis*). We live among these things, confident that they are what they seem to be and behave accordingly: the ground under our feet will support us, and the sun will rise tomorrow. In the upper segment of three he puts all the mathematical objects which are the paradigm shapes of, and the counting numbers for, the visible things. Here also occur (I think) the words and their logical relations with which we name natural kinds or classes and express the rational relations that hold among them. The capacity of the soul for this segment is called "thinking things through" (*diánoia*). The two segments represent the ratio that physical space has to geometric space and that nature has to its science—a pretty good one-to-one fit. It was the equality of the segments and our intellectual familiarity with their objects that made me take these middle segments first and together.

Now attend to both the highest, largest and the lowest, least segments. The highest segment contains what Socrates calls the forms, the invisible "looks" (*eíde*) to which he assigns the completest being. These open themselves to dialectic; they are truly knowable. The forms are closest to an "idea," as he calls it, which is beyond all these beings: the Idea of the Good. It is the ultimate principle, which is not only the cause of all beings coming into Being (as the sun is the cause of all Becoming on earth) but is also the source of that illumination which makes all beings visible to the soul, that is to say, intelligible. It is, moreover, the unifying principle that makes all beings cohere as a community of Being. Here, incidentally, is the reason why the philosophers should rule in the *Republic:* They alone have contemplated the Good as the ultimate principle of community, the principle on which political communities depend; thus the culmination of philosophy is an approach to the source of togetherness.

That is a lot of prime philosophy in very few words, so I'll say a little more about the forms shortly. Let me descend now to the lowest segment, worth only one unit but stuffed with indefinitely many items. Here, at the bottom of the line of beings, Socrates locates every kind of image: shadows, reflections, pictures, and, as we will see, poetic myths. It appears that we have a special capability for dealing with images: Socrates borrows a word for it that means literally "likenessing" (*eikasía*), dealing with images, recognizing them. "Likenessing" engages with what are, after all, just the shadows and likenesses of the solid natural things—very thin beings, deprived of complete dimensionality and of independent life. But these more solid natural things, for all their bodily thickness, are themselves only the images of the more intelligible mathematical and logical objects above them, which in turn are only space-like depictions of the wholly intelligible, non-spatial, invisible forms.

An example of the way one object, a clearly definable object, would appear in the four segments might help. Take a sphere. First let an irregular, flat (i.e., two-dimensional) yellow disk appear in a painting. It is meant to be the image of a melon; there's nothing more to it—for all its appeal it lacks a dimension and the sensory qualities of solidity. Next there is the natural melon, a three-dimensional body, really there, and having the incidental virtue of ripening into lusciousness. But it is really one of a myriad of imperfect instantiations of a mathematical sphere. This sphere in its perfection presents the understandable spatial structure of the fruit. Of course there are many mathematical spheres differing in size and location, but all are identical in structure. Yet none of them show what it means to be a sphere. They are only examples of sphericity, of the form *Sphere,* the invisible form, which *is* what it *means to be* a sphere.

This much is clear, I think: The metaphorical light cast by the Good, which both illuminates and bonds all beings, is an image-causing light. The grades of Being cascade from the top as a series of originals and images; each higher realm casts its images into the next lower realm. This lovely view of a Whole bonded and made knowable by the image relation has some grave difficulties, the chief of which (in my opinion) I'll mention right away. In the realm of sensory visibility, and even in the realm of the spatial intuitions of geometry, the likeness relation that bonds original to image is not so very obscure (though some thinkers have found ways to make it so). But when we rise to the forms it becomes highly questionable. Is the form of Sphericity a shiningly perfect Sphere? Does dialectic deal simply with unique ideal instances? If so, there's trouble: We need yet another form to account for the roundness, the ideal sphericity of the first form. One modern solution to this problem is to understand the *form* of sphericity as a *formula:* $x^2 + y^2 + z^2 = r^2$, where x, y, and z are symbols standing for any triple of numbers whose added squares are equal to the square of a given fourth. The formula's image will be the graph of all spheres with center 0 and any given radius. But there's one thing this formula itself can never be said to have: fullness of Being. It's just a grouping of symbols held together by a complicated convention—a "formula," a formlet, not a form. Socrates would turn in his grave at this solution.

Let me, however, turn from this difficulty, which I felt compelled to mention only so that you wouldn't think that I subscribe to Socrates' world uncritically. (I will say, as an aside, that I subscribe to it critically.) So back to the point.

That point here is that the Divided Line represents a world with several lovely features, for instance, that it is a hierarchy. A hierarchy is an ordering in which, though not all levels are equal in standing, all are equally within the community of the Good. That's what hierarchies do: they discriminate but they also validate. Another fine feature is that in presenting our universe as a cascade of images, descending from the intelligible realm into the sensory realm, the Line represents the whole as accessible to learning, for progressive learning needs a direction and the progression of the Line shows which way is up. Not only does it indicate the direction of ascent, it also shows the means, which is—what else—by way of image-recognition. Recall that image-recognition, "likenessing," was the capability of the soul belonging to the lowest segment of the Divided Line. I once took a little boy to a children's play called, I think, *The Haunted Forest,* a play full of monsters. He was shivering with its delicious scariness, and by way of comforting me he said "It's not really real, it's only a story." *That* was image-recognition; not only did he recognize the figures on the stage as representing dragons, but he also saw that they were *merely* representations of dragons. In a more sophisticated way it takes place on every level; in the largest sense it allows us to see all visible or sensory appearances as recognizable images of an original and originating Being. So here a device that Socrates is fond of employing is once more at work: a seemingly lowly, innocuous element, image-recognition, turns out to be pervasively potent. It may, as I said, ultimately fail on the level of the forms understood as the true originating entities of all lesser beings, but it is nevertheless a powerful incitement to, and a first exercise in, philosophizing. So it is no wonder that the ladder of beings, in which the levels of Being are bonded as image to original, is a preface to the philosopher's curriculum in Book VII.

Now I will leap back into Book X, where Socrates mounts his really uncompromising attack on the imitative arts. I won't enter here on a question that didn't vex him but occupies modern estheticians: Are literature and the visual arts in fact characteristically imitative? Socrates takes that for granted.

The condemnation of the imitative art follows the divisions of the Divided Line quite straightforwardly. Where I chose a sphere, Socrates chooses a bed. It isn't clear that either mathematical objects or artifacts have forms such as were acknowledged in Plato's Academy. Probably Socrates has chosen a bed partly to be funny—it's certainly very late at night toward the end of this long, intense dialogue—and partly because at this point he wants us, after all, to think about artifacts, particularly those produced by craftsmen and reproduced in the imitative arts.

He then asserts the following: There is the unique single form, the true Bed, the Bed Itself. It is not made by a craftsman nor visible to the sensory eye. Then there are the beds we actually sleep in, the beds in the realm of solid objects that we trustingly fall into. Finally there is the painter's bed, a re-presentation itself easily reproducible, a mere likeness of the bodily bed. It is not made by an expert furniture maker, and it is really good for nothing. So there are three beds: the divine Bed, the carpenter's beds, and the painter's canvas plus a whole stack of museum postcard beds.

You'll notice that Socrates omits one of the Divided Line's four segments, the second one from the top, the mathematical bed. But it is easily supplied. I think it is the blueprint or designer's specification of the bed, the bed-diagram.

In Socrates' hierarchy the painter's imitation bed is the third and least degree in the gradation of Being and at a second remove from truth. The ultimate imitator, the painter (or poet), knows nothing worthwhile; Socrates compares his activity to that of a cherished but unhealthy harlot. He uses pretty strong language to describe how far from the truth sought in philosophy an involvement with the image-making arts takes us. He claims that in those arts we are doubly enmeshed in the lower parts of the Divided Line. We are implicated in that fall from being which absorption in mere imaging brings about, and through that involvement in imaging we are yet more enchained by the cherished but deleterious pleasures of the senses—for pictures and poems arouse the senses even as they refine them.

Let's look at a famous picture bed, the one in Van Gogh's painting *The Bedroom* of 1888 (see the next page), which is probably sold on postcards by the thousands. I'll take it for granted for the moment that most of us share the sense that this bed, which we admittedly cannot sleep in, is more, not less, of a bed than the one we do fall into at night. How can that be?

Recall that in my account of the Divided Line I took together the least and the greatest divisions, the segments of images and forms, because they were left dangling when the two middle segments had been brought together through their equality. Then, to carry out the mathematical metaphor, it is true that in a proportion the outer terms compounded are equal to the middle terms compounded, or in modern language, the product of the extremes equals the product of the means. (If $a:b::b:c$, then $ac = b^2$.) So the extremes somehow get together on one side to balance the means. If you put images and forms together you get some compound as telling as nature and its science together. Well, I won't insist on this *jeu d'esprit*.

What is of more consequence is the thought behind this leap from the image up to the form: Why should a painting or a poetic myth not image the truths of Being directly? Why might a painter or a poet not vault to a direct, non-dialectical contemplation of the forms? We call that overleaping of reason "intuition," literally, "insight."

This thought—that the artist might vault in his imagination directly into the highest realm—is both ancient and modern. The Neoplatonist Plotinus says:

> When someone looks down upon the arts because they are concerned with imitating nature, it must first be replied that the things of nature too imitate other things. Next you must know that artists do not simply reproduce the visible, but they go back to the principles [i.e., the Forms] in which nature itself had found its origin; and further, that they on their own part achieve and add much, whenever something is missing [for perfection], for they are in possession [of the form] of beauty.

And closer to us, Schopenhauer says:

> All our previous reflections on art were based throughout on the truth that the object [intended] in art, whose representation is the artist's purpose and whose knowledge must consequently precede his work as germ and origin, is an *idea* [i.e., a form] in Plato's sense and absolutely nothing else: neither the particular thing, the object of ordinary apprehension nor a concept, the object of rational thinking and science.

"Particular thing" and "concept" are Schopenhauer's way of describing the middle parts of the Line, the natural things apprehended by the senses and the reasoning about them done by the understanding. The artist reaches directly for the Platonic "ideas," the Forms, and then brings them down in images.

Well, if the artist can do it by the *leap* of his inspired craft, why not Socrates who can, if anyone can, actually *mount* dialectically through the segments? Plato never allows Socrates to give this explanation, but that must be what he is doing if he is not to be in flagrant contradiction with himself. Socrates and Plato in conjunction, then, are philosophical poets who, having climbed the ladder of Being, are able at crucial junctures to overleap the middle rungs and do it more knowledgeably than any artist. Having taught themselves image-recognition on all levels, they know how to engage in image-making, in capturing and bringing down into appearance the highest beings. They are able to express the forms in that least and lowest grade of Being, the realm of images. They are able to imitate Truth directly.

The Myth of Er seems to me to bear the marks we might expect to see in such a philosopher's image. Since it imitates the highest degree of Being, the invisible, nonspatial realm, it is rightly spatially incoherent, just as is Dante's theological image of the invisible God who has made humanity in his image.

Beyond the knowable realms of the Divided Line is the sunlike Good, an encompassing principle of genesis, intelligibility, and above all, unity, wholeness, and community. In the myth its

272 THE MUSIC OF THE REPUBLIC

image is the luminous cosmic container, a light pole from whose tips extend light-straps binding together the circumference of this hyper-heavenly cosmos. Contained within the light is the world of rational astronomy with its heavenly planetary music; this planetary music is the highest mathematical study prescribed for the philosopher kings in Book VII. The earth's sphere, the place of variable appearance, is hard to locate clearly in this picture: it must be at the center, but there also in the image is the Spindle of Necessity. This cosmic hyper-place—whose location is oddly identical with the earth we live on—is the destination of disembodied souls. There they go for judgment, and thence they shoot up to the terrestrial surface with their chosen life.

To the geometrical segments of the Divided Line were assigned the cognitive capabilities of the soul in general; to the mythical cosmic place come the individual souls to meet their self-chosen fate. On the Divided Line we meet our soul as it learns; in the Myth of Er we see our soul as it chooses. For the *Republic* is that book in which philosophical inquiry, the satisfiable desire to search out Being, from bottom to top, is brought together both with doing right and with living well on earth: Learning, knowledge, goodness, and happiness are shown as being inextricably involved.

Accordingly the *Republic* ends with Socrates' injunction to follow the way up, the way of philosophy, so that we may practice justice with thoughtfulness—meaning with some knowledge of what it *is*—and thus live happily. That is what the Myth of Er teaches, he says, and if we trust it, then—and this is the final phrase in the dialogue which I shall give you in Socrates' own Greek—*eu práttomen. Eu práttomen* means both "we shall do *right*" and "we shall do *well*." And so *the* question of the *Republic* is answered: In being just we will indeed be doing well for ourselves.

9

TIME IN THE **TIMAEUS**

In the dialogue named after him, Timaeus has the divine Craftsman, who is making the heavens, say:

> He thought of making a certain movable image of eternity, and,
> at once with ordering heaven, he made an eternal image going
> according to number, that which we have named Time (37 d
> 6 ff.).

This is, I believe, the second most often quoted sentence in the
literature on time—just second to Augustine's "What, then, is
time? If nobody asks me I know; if I want to explain it to him
who asks, I don't know" (*Confessions* XI, 14). The Timaean
passage is not only the precipitating definition for Plotinus's
theory of time (*Ennead* III 7) and for that of all his Neoplatonic
successors, namely that time "falls out" of eternity. It is also a
favorite quotation for time-romantics and physicists alike—for
the former because of its cosmic grandeur and for the latter because it says what they have for centuries thought: that the cosmological frame of the world is also its fundamental clock.

Before analyzing its sense, I must say that neither Plato nor Socrates speaks this sentence but Timaeus, an astronomer (27 a 3) and a person of whose existence we are uncertain. Plato has presented him as sharing some opinions of the Pythagoreans, among which is the notion that time is the revolution of the embracing star-bearing sphere or even of the whole heaven itself. It hardly matters, however, whose views are behind those of Timaeus, as long as they are not taken to represent Plato's theory of time. The dialogues never make time thematic. There are, to be sure, early versions of still-debated time-puzzles concerning the being and intelligibility of the "phases" of time—namely "is," "was," and "will be," and the moment of temporal transition, the "sudden instant" (*Parmenides* 141, 151 e ff.).[1] There is also the myth of reversed time, the Age of Cronos, the father of Zeus (whose name is often identified with *Chronos,* Time), an age in which human beings are earthborn in the prime of life, nurtured by the earth and ruled by the god; there follows the age of unwinding when humans are human-born as infants and toil and govern themselves while the epoch declines into chaos—until the god's time takes hold again (*Statesman* 268 d ff.). But as I said, there is no extended treatment of time in the Platonic dialogues, and though the Timaean myth cannot be regarded as a *lógos,* a rational account of time, it may supply the reason why Plato has offered none.

For Timaeus's "likely story" or, more literally, "veri-similar myth" (*eikós mýthos,* 29 d) is presented as a feast to Socrates in return for the account of the best city and its citizens that he had given the day before. Timaeus is going to provide a cosmic container for this polity. And just as Socrates in the conversation of the previous day—a conversation that is certainly close to the one recounted in the *Republic*—founded political discourse, so Timaeus will provide the mode of discourse proper to cosmology and mathematical physics in general, the myth or story that is at once likely *and* like. It is, in short, what we call a model, which is both in itself rational and true to its original.

Timaeus is not only presenting a model of the cosmos but also supplying the reason why such a model can plausibly be a likeness of the real heavens: *because the heavens are themselves an image modeled on an eternal paradigm.* They are rationally and beautifully crafted by an artificer-god who, in making the great heavenly image, looked to this aboriginal, atemporal, intelligible model. Here is the first account of model-making in physics, showing the two defining features that this activity still has today: It frankly produces nothing more (or less) than *plausibly* rational artifacts, and they have the character of *mathematical* images. Its underlying assumption is that the physical universe embodies a mathematical model; it is this model that the scientist discovers and expresses in human-scale diagrams, models, and formulas.

That is why the Timaean story of the origin and nature of time is not the Socratic, and therefore not a central Platonic, theory. Socrates, and Plato behind him, try to rationalize Becoming in its instability and the appearances in their variety by the "hypotheses" called *eíde,* forms, the beings that make possible stabilizing and unifying language and thus all inquiry. For Socrates (and Plato through him) it is an unsolved problem just how the world of irregular appearances participates in the world of forms, while another question is hardly even broached: how the soul lives through and orders Becoming; what psychic temporality might be.[2] Timaeus, however, has mathematical-mythical answers to these questions, especially the latter.

As the Greek word *kosmos* signifies, the Timaean cosmos, in contrast to the Socratic world of the senses, is a place of beautiful order, as good as possible, a place of geometric shapes and numbers. For it originates as the work of said divine Craftsman, who "orders heaven" (*diakosmón ouranón,* 37 d) by making a "movable image" (*kinetón eíkon*) which imitates within the stuff of the world of becoming a model (*parádeigma*) of Being. If one is bent on speaking of a Timaean "theory" of time, then one should say that what is there presented is Plato's theory of astronomical-physical time. Thus Plato supplies through Timaeus a quasi-theory of world-time, external time, but he leaves the inquiry into soul-time, internal time, for the future.

Yet that claim leaves one marvelous circumstance out of account. If time is the numerable motion of the heavens, it might indeed be thought to be the most exterior thing imaginable. But the outermost embracing frame of Timaeus's cosmos is made of soul-material. It constitutes what we call the celestial equator and the ecliptic circle that is oblique to it. In this encompassing psychic frame, Being or the Same, and its Other or Nonbeing, are blended in numerical ratios and then shaped into the circles that contain Becoming. The Craftsman makes these cosmic arrangements so that the soul may not be junior to the body but may be its ruler (34 c ff.). That is to say, Plato acknowledges in his cosmic story that temporality outside of a numerally disposed soul is practically unimaginable; it is in effect unthinkable. Time needs to be imagined and thought as psychically contained. It is in fact from this mythic vision of intrapsychic world-time that the Neoplatonist Plotinus will derive his ontopsychological theory of time as identical with the fallen soul (*Ennead* III 7).

Now to a closer look at the quotation. Time is an *image* of eternity. That means it has the dual image-features of being at once *like* and also *not* the original (see p. 100). The difference-feature of the image is expressed in a pun: The word for eternity, *aión*, looks like the privative of *íon*, the word for "going." Eternity is the stable "ungoing," while its movable image goes, and it goes "according to number." That is as much as to say that the heavens are a cosmic clock. Timaeus says that the god designed the sun, the moon, and the other five stars—together called the "planets" (literally, the "wanderers")—and placed them in their circular orbits so that time might be generated. From them comes the definition and guardianship of the numbers of time, and by them time is distinguished into its parts, the days and nights, months and years—the units of time. In another place Timaeus speaks of the stars as the "instruments of times" (*órgana chrónon*, 41 e 5, similarly of the earth and moon,

42 d 4). The heavenly bodies are the indicators or, one might say, the moving dial, of the clock. (Although the Greeks had no circular analog-dial clocks, they were well acquainted with circular measurement of time through the chief diurnal clock they did possess, the sundial, whose upright shadow-throwing indicator was, significantly, called the *gnomon,* the "knower.")

The similarity-feature that links the heavenly clock to its eternal paradigm is the steadiness of its circular celestial motion, a motion of which Aristotle will show in the *Physics* that it is the most stable, continuous, and regular motion there is (264 b 9 ff.). The celestial motion is *standard* motion.

As time has parts marked by the orbital motions of the instruments of time, so time generates two forms (*eíde*): "the was" and "the will be." These apply properly to the two "motions" (phases) of time and the becoming that "goes on" within time (38 a 2). But, Timaeus says, we use speech wrongly when we apply these tenses of the verb "to be" to Eternal Being; they belong only to Becoming and the things that are borne about in the world of sense. He says that his discourse is not the opportune moment (*kairós*) for precise speaking about time, and that is, I imagine, why he omits the grave consequences of the obverse of his prohibition: If the tensed forms of "to be" are not to be used of Being, the tenseless form "is" is not to be used of Becoming. Herein lies one of the most serious, if not the most serious, perplexity of time: the impossibility of speaking intelligibly of the human present, which is enmeshed in Becoming and therefore evanescent. In any case, Timaeus implies that the "phases" of time—past, present, future—arise with human speech about time, and they will indeed henceforth be human-centered.

Here is a crucial point: Time is *not* natural passage. The heavenly bodies are mobiles and move, and their going gives rise to the epiphenomenon of time and its numerable parts. It is *we* who name this moving image "Time." What can be seen here at its origin is the baptism of *motion as time,* which befits physics and bedevils philosophy. It is Timaeus who performs it, by representing the heavens as a cosmic clock.

10

INTRODUCTION TO THE **SOPHIST**

THE PROJECTED TRILOGY

The drama of the *Sophist* is part of a continuing conversation. Three of its participants had talked the day before: Socrates who is known to the world as a philosopher; the brilliant young geometer Theaetetus who so uncannily resembles the ugly Socrates; and Theaetetus's elderly teacher Theodorus. A young friend of Theaetetus who shares not the looks but the name of the elder Socrates is a silent bystander in both conversations. In the earlier conversation, recounted in the dialogue *Theaetetus*, the mathematician proves unsuccessful in his attempts to answer Socrates' question: What is knowledge? The dialogue ends with Socrates urging his partners to resume their talk the following morning: for now Socrates must go off to answer the charges brought against him by Meletus, charges of impiety and corruption of the youth.

The conclusion of the *Theaetetus* leads us to expect another conversation between Theaetetus and Socrates the next day. Instead, as we see from the opening of the *Sophist*, something very different is about to take place. Theodorus has modified the terms of the appointment by bringing along a Stranger, whom he recommends to Socrates as "a very philosophical man." Socrates seizes on the possibility that Theodorus has not recognized the Stranger correctly: Perhaps he is a god in disguise! Theodorus brushes off this suggestion. The Stranger is not a god, though he is godlike, for that is what he, Theodorus, calls all philosophers. By speaking so confidently—one might say, so unreflectively—of the Stranger's philosophical nature, Theodorus unwittingly poses the question that will haunt the conversation: Who *is* the philosopher? Socrates intimates that true philosophers always appear in disguise, sometimes as statesmen, sometimes as sophists, while at other times they appear to be "in a totally manic condition." This last guise drops out of sight. By calling attention to the possibility that Theodorus is deceived, Socrates shifts the focus of yesterday's inquiry: the search for knowledge becomes the hunt for the purveyor of ignorance—the sophist.

The trinity sophist-statesman-philosopher suggests a triad of dialogues: *Sophist, Statesman, Philosopher.* We have the *Sophist* before us. The *Statesman* also exists, and its conversation takes place right after that of the *Sophist.* But there is no Platonic dialogue named the *Philosopher.* We are left to wonder: Has the philosopher's nature already been implicitly revealed somewhere in the course of the two existing dialogues?

THE PLOT

In the prologue to the dialogue the Stranger takes Theaetetus as a partner in the hunt for the sophist. To prepare for this difficult task, they first track down the fish-hunting angler. In this way the search for the sophist begins (216 a–221 c).

1   *Getting.* The sophist turns up within five divisions of the "getting" art, the art of acquisition. Among other things, he is an angler-like hunter of rich kids, a sham virtue salesman, and a professional athlete in contests of words (221 c–226 a).

2   *Separating.* The sophist is then found a sixth time as a practitioner of the homely art of separating, which includes spinning, combing, and cleaning. In particular he is shown to be a philosopher-like cleanser of souls, who refutes others with a view to removing opinions that impede learning (226 a–231 b).

3   *Making.* Confronted by what seems to be a disordered heap of possible determinations of the sophist, the Stranger and Theaetetus decide to focus on one aspect of sophistry, the sophist as debater. Debating turns out to be a kind of making: the art of making spoken images of all things. This art of imitation has two forms: likeness-making and apparition-making, the making of true and of distorted images. But it is unclear in which division the sophist belongs (231 b–236 d).

A   The very positing of an image-making art entails a number of difficulties; to articulate and resolve them is the task of the remainder of the dialogue. The existence of images presupposes that Nonbeing *is.* But Non-being appears to be unutterable, indeed, unthinkable. If the hunt for the sophist is to be brought to successful completion, the Stranger and Theaetetus must find some way to say that Nonbeing *is* and Being *is not*—even if this involves committing a kind of intellectual parricide against the Stranger's teacher, Parmenides (236 d–242 b).

B   The turn to the question of Being occurs at the exact center of the dialogue. The Stranger begins his inquiry into Being with a critical examination of claims men have made about it: He must show that Being is as difficult to come to terms with as Nonbeing. Six claims in all are shown to be wanting. The claim that Being is two and the Parmenidean claim that Being is one are dealt with first. The Stranger then turns his dialectical powers against another pair, the Giants who claim that everything that *is* is body and the Gods who, ever at war with the Giants, insist that only the invisible forms *are*. Out of the conflict emerges yet another claim about Being, which the Stranger himself advances and then appears to demolish: Being is Motion and Rest together. The final claim about Being refuted by the Stranger is that none of the "kinds," including Being, mix together with any others (242 b–252 c).

C   The Stranger's critique of this last claim serves as the introduction to the dialogue's pivotal moment. The Stranger and Theaetetus resolve to examine the ways in which the greatest of the kinds—Being, Rest, and Motion—mix and do not mix together. But they no sooner begin their inquiry than they are forced to introduce two more kinds—the Same and the Other—and with this the solution to the problem of the sophist comes into view. For the Other is Nonbeing by another name, and it turns out to be the case, not only that the Other *is,* but that Being and beings participate in it and hence in some sense *are not* (252 c–259 d).

D   What remains to be shown is that these conditions obtain in the case of speech, the medium of sophistry. The Stranger and Theaetetus examine the structure of sentences as well as the relation of speech to opinion, thought, and appearance in order to determine that and how Nonbeing makes its appearance within the realm of human speech and thinking (259 d–264 b).

E   The Stranger and Theaetetus are now able to track down the sophist a seventh time: within the class of apparition-making, that is, the making of images that do not preserve the true proportions of their originals. The sophist is shown, among other things, to be a shrewdly knowing imitator of what he does not know—a false image of the wise man rather than a true lover of wisdom (264 c–268 d).

REAL-LIFE SOPHISTS AND THE SOPHIST'S KIND

A fair-minded reader might wonder: Who in real life is the dark and wily operator that the Stranger and Theaetetus are pursuing? There was in fact in the Greece of Socrates' time a tribe of travelling professors who gave themselves the honorific title "sophists," "wisdom-pliers," borrowed from the legendary Seven Sages of an earlier generation. Plato often brings them into his dialogues; the two most famous ones, Gorgias and Protagoras, have dialogues named after them, as do a number of minor sophists. When they appear in a dialogue, they are treated with real respect personally, though their activity, the selling of expertise—particularly of rhetorical techniques and of philosophical opinions—undergoes a politely devastating critique, usually unbeknownst to themselves.

In the *Sophist,* however, no particular sophist is under attack. Instead the Stranger and Theaetetus investigate what in the nature of things makes such a being possible anywhere and at any time: In order to function profitably as a "trader of learnables" without quite knowing what he is doing, this persuasive expert in everything and nothing relies on the fact that nature is riddled with Nonbeing. Moreover, the Stranger allows it to appear that along certain lines the philosopher and sophist engage in like activities, though they diverge along others, as an aspiring lover of wisdom must diverge from a confident professor of wisdom. The sophist will appear as a universal expert, and the philosopher as a perpetual amateur of sorts. The sophist is the philosopher's lasting preoccupation, because he is, to a certain extent, a mirror image of the philosopher.

FATHER PARMENIDES

The figure who is in fact attacked by name in the dialogue and whose teachings undergo a devastating critique is, remarkably, the Stranger's own teacher Parmenides. Parmenides was the first to inquire into Being and therefore might be thought of as the first philosopher, as the veritable father of philosophy. His insight into Being and Nonbeing was as follows: Being *is* and is the One and is the only thing that *is*, while Nonbeing is not even thinkable and ought not be uttered.

Parmenides unveiled his insight in an epic poem, quoted three times in the *Sophist*. It begins as an account of the young Parmenides' blazingly grand initiation by a goddess into the heart of Being, the One and All, and then sets out a "Way of Truth." Strangely enough, it also sets out a "Way of Opinion" (now lost) —strangely because opining is strictly impossible if only Being, along with its Truth, *is*.

As we are told in the Platonic dialogue that bears his name, Parmenides, with his associate Zeno, visited Athens when he was sixty-five and Socrates was a boy. Their conversation is set some time before the middle of the fifth century. Parmenides initiates young Socrates into the way of dialectic, the way of asking brief questions and refuting the answers; he generously uses his own One as the object of refutation. In the *Sophist*, which takes place more than half a century later, Socrates slyly causes the disinclined Stranger to employ a similar style.

In the dialogue, the Stranger reluctantly commits philosophical parricide in pursuit of the sophist and his kind. If the sophist is not to have an impregnable hiding place in the impenetrable thicket of Nonbeing—a defense he gladly appropriates— Parmenides must be shown wrong in his principal insight, and Nonbeing must indeed be accessible to thought. It is part of the philosophical pathos of this inquiry that the elusive sophistic kind is merely netted, while the actual man who fathered philosophy is, as it were, done in.

THE WAY OF DIVISION

Socrates appears in the *Sophist* only in the beginning, to pose the question about the naming and nature of three human kinds: Sophist, Statesman, Philosopher. Why do Socrates and the Stranger, along with the teachable young Theaetetus, care about the first of these types, the sophist? How does this pseudo-

philosopher manage to give rise to this grandest of philosophical conversations? How is the Way of Division particularly good
for pursuing the sophist? Can we call it a method? Does it seek
definitions? What does it actually find?

In the world of Socrates and the Stranger—the stay-at-home
philosopher and the traveling one—and of Theodorus and Theaetetus—the seasoned old mathematician and the promising
young one—the question of expertise, art, and know-how is
bound to loom large, just as it might nowadays in a group of
teachers and students. Which subjects are solid and which trivial? Which teachers are genuine and which fake? The pursuit of
the sophist gives the Stranger an occasion to chart human expertise—to show who gets things and who makes them (a shaky distinction, as our term "making money" shows), and in what mode
and with what motive. The reader will see that part of the en-
suing fun comes from name-assigning subtly shading into name-
calling, and that in this project no pretensions are honored, for
louse-catching is parallel to generalship. In short, the Stranger
mounts a tongue-in-cheek critique of the inventory of human em-
ployments, while Socrates, we may imagine, stands by smiling.

Presumably Socrates is no less amused by the delineation of
the sophist who, at several crucial points, comes perilously close
to being the same as the philosopher. In particular, Expertise as
a whole is rather surreptitiously divided into three parts—a
proper employment of the Way of Division calls for two—and
in this central part, termed "separating," the Stranger tracks the
sophist into the kind of soul-cleansing-by-refutation-of-error
that is usually attributed to Socrates. Thus the sophist appears
like the philosopher—at least as like as a wolf is to a dog, the
Stranger says.

So the sophist is represented as a sort of rogue philosopher,
a wild beast that ranges over the chart of arts. What is this wildness of his? He runs away; he is a hunter who is himself to be
hunted; he plunges deep into a thicket that seems pathless; he
tricks his pursuers into a series of impasses, yet he himself runs

all over within his thicket; he confuses the proper forkings of paths. Thus he turns up in many lairs—seven times, in fact. Not only does he have the expertise of *getting* money in bewilderingly different ways, he also *makes* everything—the whole world!—by his imitating art. Here, within the form of imitation, he is finally collected in the Stranger's net—the genuine sophist, finally, but surely not conclusively, caught.

These trackings of the sophist give the Stranger a chance to practice with Theaetetus and to show Socrates a brilliant working case of a way not entirely new to him (*Phaedrus* 266 b), the way of making divisions and of collecting the results into a long descriptive name.

The Way of Division addresses the question "What is it?" by pursuing the question "Where is it?"; in this case the "it" is an activity requiring expertise. The way proceeds by cutting a given field into two, rejecting one side, and attending to the other, and then again and again cutting the remainder in two, until the object sought is boxed into a small enough territory. Then all the names of the branches are collected, and a long descriptive title results. Sometimes the division is thought of as a left-hand and right-hand cut, and sometimes the slippery sophist has to be caught "with both hands" because he escapes into both sides of the cut at once. Sometimes, too, as if to undercut a false rigor in applying the method, a third division is slipped in, as was the case for the division of Expertise itself. The whole scheme, with all its aberrations, begs to be diagrammed not only in order to be seen clearly, but so as to invite reflection on the emphatically spatial character of this kind of thinking. That is why the reader is asked to inspect the diagram on page 286.

A reader might get the impression that the actual divisions are comically redundant exercises and, moreover, are quite confused. To be sure, they are sometimes hilarious spoofs of self-important professional titles. They are surely duplicative, but that is because the sophist is full of duplicity and never stays caught. One of them may indeed seem like a mere exercise, the

The Sophist's Thicket (231D–E)

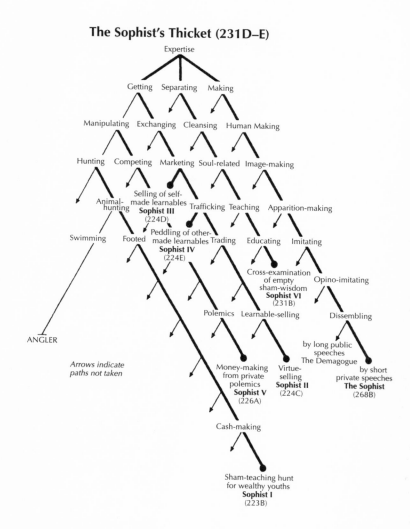

one where the Stranger and Theaetetus practice dividing by catching the angler (who, unlike his cousin the sophist, once caught, stays hooked), though even these divisions bring to light something about division-making. But above all, the divisions are never pointlessly confused; even the dislocations are playfully subtle and suggestive.[1] Besides not being mere exercises, there are two more things the Way of Division is not—or is not yet.

Although the Greek word for our term "way" is actually *métho-dos*, division here is not a full-blown "method of classification," a rigorously jigged procedure. Aristotle will apply division to the natural kinds of the animal kingdom and turn it into the method of classification by genera and species. But in the *Sophist* it is yet informal, tentative, and fresh. It has not yet hardened into a confident but dry procedure.

Nor in the same vein is it yet a "method of definition," if we mean by defining producing a word-formula to match an already current word. In fact the participants invent words, "titles," to fit fields of activity never yet distinguished or named. And when Socrates asks at the beginning about the "naming" of sophist, philosopher, statesman, it is not the terms as such he cares about but the human kinds behind them—whether they corresponded to the number of names.

That is why the method, especially when applied to the sophist, serves the cause of philosophy so well. For who can help thinking beyond and behind the Stranger's dividing activity to wonder what he must know beforehand to make his divisions and to catch the sophist who is all over the fields of expertise? Clearly the Stranger must know—somehow or other—everything, just as the sophist claims to do. In particular, he must have some prior knowledge of the kinds and forms that give things their recognizable shape. In this dialogue we are not told how the Stranger comes to recognize these ways the world has of sorting itself out. Instead the point is first somehow to locate these kinds and forms themselves and then, by way of division, to reveal and bring them to light—to make them explicit by marking them off. In this way the Stranger lays the basis for understanding how the kinds or forms come to mix, to "interweave" with each other in a coherent and cohesive way.

All the divisions "specify" descents on the one hand and leave the lineage of the "other hand" indeterminate. On the diagram the thin arrows pointing to nothing illustrate these indeterminacies. For each division that is pursued, another, with all its ramifications, is left in the dark; it leads into a disregarded thicket of possibilities. The very first division illustrates this point: Expertise is opposed to Nonexpertise. Surely there is a lot more of the latter in the world, but we hear no more of it; it is entirely uncharted. For all we know, the sophist has escaped into these blank branchings as well, and there he remains entirely uncaught. Even farther into the background, though very much a floating presence in the dialogue, recedes the unifying title of Expertise and Nonexpertise together: Power, potent possibility (*dýnamis*).

Now these unbalanced dualities, one of which is definitely marked off while the other is left in indefinite opposition—consider the "infinite judgment" of later logic, in which the predicate bears the prefix "non-"—imply a lurking presence that will become central to the dialogue: the Other. It turns out to be one of the "greatest kinds." For in these divisions the "other" fork leads not to a well-marked alternative—Amateur, for instance, would be a definite alternative to Expert—but just to Non-expert, a mere other, necessary for marking off the positive side but nevertheless merely a *non*-being. The discovery of Non-being as otherness, the deepest and most consequence-laden discovery of the *Sophist*, is thus foreshadowed by the way of division itself, though it is explicitly confronted only later, within one of the actual divisions, when the sophist is tracked into "image-making."

THE INTERWEAVING OF FORMS AND KINDS

The Way of Division depends on the fact that we naturally and without much reflection discern forms and kinds. Every thing looks like other things and is recognized by us through the shape or form it has in common with them. We can hardly imagine coming across something that does not "look like" anything else at all. Thus any individual angler has the aspect or form (*eídos*) of Angler. But individual things are not alone in sharing a form. The forms themselves prove to be akin, to share a kindred nature and to belong to a more inclusive kind (*génos*). These higher forms or "greatest kinds" are introduced by the Stranger not as "concepts," as objects formed by the mind, but rather as the most comprehensive beings that reveal themselves to us when we come to reflect on our speech about the way things are.

The most positive result of the Stranger's parricide is the view that the forms or kinds are not radically separate from one another but constitute a community (*koinonía*). The Stranger at one point provocatively refers to this community as an "interweaving of the forms." The image of weaving occurs regularly in the *Sophist,* although it is not until the *Statesman* that, as a figure for the statesman's art, it replaces angling as the dominant image of the conversation. Weaving first comes up in the *Sophist* in the context of the Stranger's hunt for the sophist within the kind he calls "separating." It is alluded to without being explicitly named. The descent into separating curiously reveals the sophist as a cross-examiner of empty sham-wisdom and therefore as entangled with the philosophic nature. Sophist and philosopher appear to be interwoven.

The image of weaving suggests that the interwoven elements retain their self-identity while being interrelated and incorporated into a greater whole. Such interweaving among the forms is the necessary condition for the possibility of all discourse. Discourse is the interweaving of names; and if this fabric or texture at the level of names were not somehow a reflection of the interweaving of beings, then speech and Being would have nothing to do with one another. Philosophic inquiry would be impossible. Interweaving follows immediately from the identification of Nonbeing as otherness: The forms have the power of relating to one another, of participating in one another's natures, without sacrificing their distinctive identities. At the heart of all this community, participation, and interweaving is the power of the Other. This is the power by which a being is what it is only by being other than *and therefore related to* everything else. With the interweaving of the forms, we come upon the power and art that distinguish the philosophic nature from all others—the dialectical science that studies how a one wends its way through a many. For the second time in the dialogue, the hunt for the sophist, through the image of weaving, leads straight to the philosopher.

IMAGES AND NONBEING

The sophist's expertise appears in five comical yet ominous varieties within the kind of "getting," the acquisition of money and power through the purveying of sham-knowledge. In a sixth case, as a kind of "separating" that purifies the soul, this expertise achieves a dangerous dignity: sophistic refutation and Socratic questioning seem indistinguishable.

Even so, the sophist somehow remains uncaught. For this too can be said about him: He is, more than anything, a know-it-all, who has a "certain opinion-producing knowledge" about all things. The way to understand how a human being could know and display knowledge of everything is to see him as a maker of all things, a kind of artist of Being. Thus the sophist's art appears with a third lineage, that of "making," for which the Greek word is, conveniently, *poíesis,* "poetry." He is among those who mime things or paint them, or who make *images* in words.

But the sophist, we are told, will laugh at this all-out attempt to corner him. Taking advantage of Parmenides' teaching, he will claim that images have no place in the world, for they are curious hybrids. Here, in the first analysis ever of the nature of an image, we are shown that an image involves an interweaving of forms. Being and Nonbeing are intertwined in an image because in its very being an image is genuinely a likeness, though it is equally not what it pretends to be. It certainly *is* an image, but precisely as an image it *is not* the original. Anyone who paints the world in words is mixing Being with Nonbeing—including the philosopher.

But there are images and images. Some preserve the proportions of the original and are truthful likenesses; others are distortions—phantasms and apparitions of the original. The sophist is naturally identified as a producer of such apparitions. He is not only an image-maker, an "artist" in our sense—a dubious enough status—but he is something more and less: a con artist. His facile duplications of the world are full of duplicity and shamming. He gives "phantastic" accounts and induces, for profit, deceptions and false opinions in the soul. Just as an admixture of Nonbeing makes possible that first fall from genuineness seen in images and imitations, so it is responsible for another and further fall into positive falsity. To hold a false opinion is to think that what is not, *is* and what is, *is not;* to speak falsely is to say that what *is not* the case *is* the case and the reverse.

But again, the sophist will not stay cornered as a maker of false verbal images. He cunningly appeals to the great Parmenides himself, who denied that exactly this was possible: to think and to say what *is not.* If the sophist is to be caught as a maker of counterfeit accounts, Father Parmenides must be gotten out of the way.

NONBEING AS OTHERNESS

The sophist as a kind can be grasped only if falsity is possible. But the False in things and in words, that which makes them pseudo-things and pseudo-accounts (*pseúdos* being the Greek word for "falsehood"), is shot through with Nonbeing: Just as imitations *are not* what they seem to be, so false sentences say what *is not* the case. If Nonbeing is unthinkable and unutterable, as Father Parmenides asserted, then we may conclude that all speech must be granted to be true for those who utter it. Perfect relativity reigns.

Parmenides' dangerous single-mindedness cannot be overthrown by the mere counter-assertion of the paradox that Nonbeing after all somehow *is.* Nonbeing has to be given a meaning; it has to be rendered specific and placed among the articulable kinds. The Stranger helps Theaetetus to discover the great and comprehensive kind that does indeed make Nonbeing sayable: *the Other.* When Nonbeing is specified as otherness, it becomes a powerful principle for regulating the slippery relativity that is the sophist's refuge.

The Other controls relativity in two ways. First it is itself the principle of relativity which turns the swampy *relativity* of "everything is true for someone" into a firm source of *relationality*. The Other does this work by being chopped up and distributed through all beings or, in the dialogue's other metaphor, by being thoroughly interwoven with Being. Every being, every thing, is not only the same with itself but also other than all the other beings. Each being is related to all the others by the reciprocating principle of otherness: It is the others' other without being the less itself, the less self-same.

So the Other acts as a sort of divisive bond that enables speech to mark off each kind of thing from all the others without consigning any of them to mere non-being or consigning itself to saying nothing. As the Other, Nonbeing does indeed become speakable, for it is a kind among kinds. In fact the Stranger's Way of Division relies continually on this power of the Other when it selects certain kinds and sets aside the other or non-selected kinds.

Nonbeing interpreted as the Other thus ceases to be mere nothingness and becomes instead the source of articulated diversity in things and in thought. Parmenides has been superseded.

But the sophist's relativity has not yet been completely controlled. The Stranger has shown that Nonbeing, far from being unutterable, is in fact a necessary ingredient in thought and speech. To catch the sophist, however, another step is needed. The sophist does not just speak; he speaks falsehood, makes pseudo-arguments, offers imitation-wisdom. Though the Other is Nonbeing positively understood, it is still negative enough to help account not only for the diversity of kinds but also for differences in their dignity. An image or an imitation, because it has a share in Nonbeing, is not merely other than its original but also less. It is less in genuineness and may even fall further, into falsity. The sophist can no longer claim that there is no intelligible discrimination between true and false.

The Other as positive Nonbeing thus has a double function: First it establishes a world of diversity through which the multifarious sophist ranges, with the Stranger in hot pursuit. And second, the Other plays a role in establishing the hierarchy of genuineness in which the sophist is caught and marked by the Stranger as one who truly deals in falsity.

11

NONBEING ENFOLDED IN BEING: THE **SOPHIST**

Parmenides' discovery of Being as One and as the one and only truth is, I think, the primordial event of First Philosophy. But in naming Nonbeing so as to proscribe it as unthinkable and unsayable, he establishes it—an unintended consequence—as an outcast. The next step in the ancient story is then the reversal of its outlaw status and its integration into the community of Beings, a step taken in Athens, the city of reconciliations. Here primeval wildness is domesticated by kind compromise, the self-perpetuating chain of retributive killing is broken by reasoned judgment, the defiling outcast is invited to his protected place of sacral annihilation.[1] Here Nonbeing finds its place.

A Stranger has come to Athens from Elea, Parmenides' town. He is a devoted pupil of his great teacher, whom he calls Father. Yet he is about to commit what he himself thinks might look like parricide (*Sophist* 241 d): He will show that Nonbeing *is*, and *what* it is, and why it must *be*. But this is not, in fact, the obliteration of his philosophical father at all, but a vast extension—one might say a doubling—of Parmenides' domain, Being.

NONBEING ENFOLDED IN BEING: THE SOPHIST **295**

Two figures are the more forcefully felt for their absence from this great event. One is Plato, the concealed author of the dialogue called the *Sophist,* in which a visiting Stranger revises the Parmenidean doctrine; with characteristic generosity Plato assigns to an anonymous Eleatic visitor the credit for what is, I think, one of the most consequence-laden discoveries in the life of ontology. The other figure is Socrates, who poses the problem and recedes into silent presence, turning over the conversation to two boys. One of these is another Socrates who does not, however, seem to resemble Socrates in anything but name, while the other is another Socrates not only in his facial features but also in a likeness of nature; his name is Theaetetus. Being other than another and being like one another will be the theme of the dialogue.

Socrates' dialogic life span is framed by Parmenidean associations; they are, so to speak, its *termini.* It matters not at all whether their truth is mythical or factual, but it is at least possible that Plato's dialogue between a very old Parmenides and a very young Socrates had a factual origin. In it Socrates learns dialectic and the generosity of self-refutation, for Parmenides uses the occasion to expose the logical contradictions of the hypothesis of the One. Now, in Socrates' old age and soon before his death, comes another old man from Elea, once again to refute Parmenidean doctrine. It is probable that Socrates sets this course going. Certainly the question he puts, "What is a sophist, a statesman, a philosopher, and are they one or two or three kinds?" (217 a), will make a critique of Parmenides' proscription of Nonbeing necessary, as we may imagine Socrates well knows. For the Eleatics were, from antiquity, thought of as having sophistical affinities, partly because as ingenious dialecticians they sometimes argued from words rather than meanings—sophists are, as their name proclaims, "professors of wisdom," who travel the world selling the art of the word divorced from truth—and partly, we may think, because the doctrine that rejects Nonbeing in behalf of truth turns out to make error indiscernible. And so it is hard to imagine that Socrates has not perceived this perplexity and that it is not the sly agenda behind his posing of the question.[2] But then he bows out, perhaps to mark the fact that he has instigated a new phase in the inquiry into Being which is beyond his life's mission.

Like Parmenides' epic poem, Plato's philosophical prose drama is fraught with humanly significant circumstance; neither abstracts its message from persons and settings. Now of the three types Socrates proposes for inquiry, the statesman will become the subject of the dialogue by that name, the sophist is pursued in the present work, but the philosopher has no dialogue of his own. I think that is because sophists and philosophers are identical—the Stranger keeps coming close to saying so (231 a ff., for example)—except for two differences: One is just the fact that a sophist can divorce himself from the place he is in and the people he faces and above all the life-affecting, almost sacral character of dialectic (253 e) to ply his peculiar expertise for the sake of reputation and money, while the philosopher never forgets his human circumstances and the seriousness of his enterprise—which is why Parmenides' poem and Plato's dialogues survive while the sophists' speeches and arguments are largely gone.

The other difference is precisely in their relation to Nonbeing (254 a), which will be considered below. But we may conjecture right now that once the typical sophist's affinity for Nonbeing has been brought to light, the philosopher too is sufficiently elucidated—as that rare sophist who acknowledges Nonbeing without taking cover in it. As I said, I cannot imagine that this outcome is not in Socrates' mind as he sets the conversation going or, rather, that Plato would not smile to have us think so—though ultimately for Socrates the philosopher is immeasurably beyond the sophist (*Statesman* 257 b).

The discovery of a new, legitimating name for Nonbeing, a name that has shed the dreaded negative—for that is how it will be saved—is then a by-product of the pursuit of the sophist-type, though it is the high point of the conversation. Here is what the Stranger finds.

The sophist is an escape artist who will finally seek shelter in the thicket of Nonbeing. But to begin with he is a type who assumes numerous shapes and lineages in the universe of human expertise.[3] He is, above all, a purveyor of "learnables," a whole world of them. So the question arises whether these are the genuine article or fakes, whether he is a teller of truths or of enchanting simulacra of truth—falsehoods. If he is the latter, the sophist is an imitator and possesses in truth only the art of imitation, by which he can mirror or otherwise copy anything more or less accurately and give this image out for the real thing and sell it off (234 c ff.). So if the Stranger can say what an image is, he ought to be able to catch the sophist.

Therefore the Stranger gives an analysis of "image," the first ever to articulate the proper place in the nature of things of this strange structure that plays so overwhelming a role in contemporary life.[4] *An image,* along with all sorts of "seeming," *is a composite of Being and Nonbeing* (240 b–c). An image *is* truly a likeness and is really *not* its original. And the analysis can descend to speech, the domain shared by sophist and true dialectician: False speaking *is* real utterance, but it *is not* saying—saying what is the case (236 e).

But now the Stranger has landed himself in big trouble. The sophist will certainly not stand still to be captured by this characterization (239 e ff.). He will forthwith escape into the thicket of Nonbeing where no one, least of all an Eleatic, can pursue him. There is something savage about these suave talkers—the Stranger says they are to philosophers as wolves are to dogs (231 a)—but they are smart. The sophist has turned the Stranger's very analysis into a hiding place, since Nonbeing is an inaccessible, unnameable region—it is what is not. But if Nonbeing is not, the sophist is not to be captured as a faker and a teller of falsehoods. (In Greek the word for fake and false is conveniently the same: *pseudés*.)

Meanwhile the Stranger knows very well that he has given an analysis forbidden by Parmenides. He himself quotes from the ancestral poem, and it is through him that we have these lines:

> This should not ever prevail, that nonbeings are,
> But do you restrain your thought from this way of inquiry.
> (*Sophist* 237 a, repeated at 258 d)

Therefore the time has come to illuminate the "darkness of Nonbeing" (254 a). The sophist must burst the paternal restraint and show how and why Nonbeing *is*. Note, however, that he has chosen for refutation lines that speak of "nonbeings," in the plural. Nonbeing itself, he will assert, has no number (237 d), but a first consequence of admitting it as thinkable at all will be the appearance of a multitude of derivative nonbeings (or rather not-beings). So he has picked a fitting passage. I can here imagine Socrates quietly listening, noticing with a smile how subtly the Stranger is shifting from Parmenides' Being, which is One and All, to Socrates' Being, which is one among many forms that are all beings by "participation" in this greater form (*eídos*).

For, remarkably, the Stranger seems to be perfectly familiar with the Socratic-Platonic forms and the dialectic they invite.[5] But perhaps it is not too surprising, since these forms are "beings to be thought" (*noetá*), but not in the sense of being thoughts, meaning some thinker's own ideas, or, as we say, "subjective" (*Parmenides* 132 b). They are in themselves, by themselves, whether any human reaches them by thinking or not. To a pupil of Parmenides, used to hearing that Thinking and Being are the same, it should be, if anything, a lesser effort to accept that there are thinkable beings whose common character is intelligibility.[6] In any case, the Stranger speaks of the forms familiarly, and is friendly to the "friends of the forms" (248 a).

These forms make it possible to collect an infinite variety of appearing things in this world under a finite number of kinds, for they hold still for thought when all the appearances are changing; they are what each mere appearance truly is and what is expressed in unifying speech. The Stranger, however, is not here interested so much in the relation of the forms to the world of the senses, but in a more advanced problem: the relation of the forms to each other. The reason is plain: It is his—somewhat technical—task to introduce Nonbeing into the realm of Being that comprises the forms. That is how Nonbeing is to be domiciled in Athens—as a form.

In preparation the Stranger launches into a dialectic of Being (249 d ff.). He shows that among the "greatest kinds" (*mégista géne*) of the beings that constitute Being (which here names the whole intelligible realm) some mix with each other while others do not. For example, Rest and Motion can hardly take part in each other; in fact they are utterly distinct, though both *are,* and so they both mingle with Being (which here names a single form). There are thus three great kinds, related as stated. "Stranger: Then each of them is *other* [first appearance!] than the remaining pair but itself the same as itself" (254 d).

He then shows that neither Being nor Rest nor Motion can *be* the Same or the Other, though they do participate in sameness (that is, self-identity) and otherness. So first the Same and finally the Other are added as a fourth and fifth to the greatest kinds (255 c–d). The Stranger pays particular attention to distinguishing the Other from Being; they are *not* two names for one kind. They must be distinct, for if the Other were identical with Being, there would be some participants in Being such as Rest and Motion, that would as beings remain *utterly* distinct, while as participants in a *separable* Other they can indeed be related, namely as each other's other.

The Other turns out to be a most wonderful form. It runs through all the forms (255 e), making each other than the other—it is the very principle of *bonding diversity,* of *relation-*

ality. For each being is what it *is* by reason of its own selfsame nature, by the Same, but it is *related* to all the others by mutual otherness—it is bonded to each of them as that other's other.

And now comes the moment. If all forms participate in the Other, then any one form, say Motion, is *other* than Being, and if it is other, it *is not;* it is in that respect a not-being, though also a being, since it partakes of Being as well (256 d). Nonbeing, alias the Other, is a form among forms (258 c) that makes all the beings not-beings insofar as they are neither Being nor the other forms. And even Being itself is not the other beings (257 a).

So here is Nonbeing as a form, one of the greatest, under its new name of "Other." It has not only been saved; it is even in a certain way grander than Being, for "Being is many, while Nonbeing is unlimited in multitude" (256 e). Why is Nonbeing innumerable? It is, as Otherness, "all chopped up—just like knowledge" (257 c)—recall that the dialogue begins with the ever-branching divisions of expertise. Of each form it is true that it is what it is (whether that be a unitary nature or a somewhat complex structure), but it is *not* each of the forms and communities of forms that it confronts—of which there are so many as to be incalculable.[7] But what is the nature of that ubiquitous "not"?

Nonbeing makes not-beings. The Stranger is not consistent in his usage, but while the more general "non-" (*me*) is always used for Nonbeing, the more definite "not-" (*ouk*) is used in certain crucial places (e.g., 256 a, c) to negate the beings as each mingles with Nonbeing.

I think the usage signifies two things. First, the Stranger wants to indicate what will turn out to be the most consequence-laden effect of his indentification of Nonbeing as Other. The first step in his refutation of Parmenides, right after he quotes the prohibition against thinking that not-beings are, is to show the silencing effect of taking Nonbeing to mean "Utter-non-being" (237 b), *nihil absolutum,* absolute nothing. It is its naming as the Other that saves it from the utter inability—which Parmenides does indeed assert—to become sayable. Hence when the Other is suffused over beings, it is important that it not behave like Utter-non-being. Theaetetus would indeed probably hear "not-being" as utter denial, as sheer opposition, cancellation of being. Yet he must learn not to take relating *otherness* for abrupt *opposition*. So "not-" used in certain places is an attention getter: Nonbeing both bonds *and* negates beings, but its negations are not annihilations.

Second, the Stranger is about to return to language, and "not" is the particle used for negating declarative sentences. Recall that this exercise, grand though it was, had as its object catching out the sophist who is an image maker in words (234 c) and who, while uttering falsehoods and giving out knowledge both fake and false, claims that there is no false speech (260 d). The Stranger has, to be sure, achieved far more than the grounding of *false* speech; he has elucidated all *negative* speech.

The crux of his solution is (1) the establishment of Nonbeing as the Other, (2) the demonstration that forms are interwoven and commune or mingle with each other in various determinate combinations (which I have neglected here), and (3) the peculiar universal relational mingling of the Other, which makes each being an other's other.

Now in addition, there is (4) its mingling with opinion and speech:

> If it doesn't mix with these, then it's necessary that all things are true; but if it does mix, then both false opinion and speech come about. For to opine or to speak things that *are not*—this, I suppose, is the false, insofar as it comes about in both thought and speech (260 b ff.).

All of these results work together right away to help the Stranger dispose of a difficulty of negative speech that has occupied philosophically inclined logicians into our times: What is it that is intended in negating sentences? Are they about nonexistent objects, and if so, how can they be? The Stranger wants Theaetetus to understand that when he speaks, for example, of something as not-beautiful, it is not simply nothing, but something other than beautiful that he is speaking about. Consequently every well-formed sentence is a connection made between beings, true if it says that things are as they are, false if it says that they are other than they are because the connection is falsely made.

All such speech is thus (1) about something, namely, beings (262 c), (2) positive or negative in that it speaks either of a being or its other, the not-beings, and (3) true or false in connecting beings truly or falsely. I believe this is the first time the logical term "quality" is used of this property (263 b).

Should anyone be inclined to ask why Plato had to take us into the august dialectic of Being to explain falsehood, the answer must be along these lines: Speech is *about* something, and what it is about are the beings of thought. Since that is, of course, what thinking is about, human speech and human thinking are, except for the fact of sensory utterance, identical: "The soul's inner conversation, when it arises without voice, has been given just this title by us—'thinking'" (263 e).

Hence any deliverance of speech will have to be explained by reference to thinking *and* to the intelligible forms. But whereas the universal form of mutuality, the Other, makes a bond of diversity among the forms, when it descends into speech it makes possible not only true negations but also false attributions.[8] Thus worldly otherness, the Other fallen into appearance, is not always benign.

A coda will enumerate the benefits of ranging Nonbeing among Beings. The sophist, that "hard-to-hunt" kind (261 a), is now well and truly caught, but who cares about that type? He may be an irritating imitator (though real sophists tend to be rather nice people in the dialogues), but his capture is really incidental to something greater: the enfolding of Nonbeing within the sphere of Being, so that one may say not only that Nonbeing *is* but also *what* it is, namely the Other, or Otherness. That enfolding and that naming have a number of wonderful consequences:

1 For those who want to think about the realm of intelligible beings, this dialogue, by letting us range Nonbeing among the forms, makes a whole out of a heap.

2 In the face of the current explosion of image-making and viewing, and of the postmodern theory of images that breaks their connection to an original in favor of an infinite self-mirroring, it might be profitable to recall an analysis that bonds the image, albeit negatively, to the original of which it is a likeness.

3 "Professors of wisdom" also abound in our time, and the tracking of the sophist into the lair of Nonbeing is a salutary exercise in understanding the contemporary type.

4 Nonbeing is the antidote to nihilism, since the enfolding of Nonbeing in Being turns negation, whether of things or in words, away from being an irruption of nothingness to being an intimation of difference.

5 Since "diversity" is a contemporary social preoccupation and "the Other" a pervasive intellectual interest, it has to be a concern to recall the aboriginal Western analysis of these notions in terms of domesticated Nonbeing.

12

ON TRANSLATING THE **SOPHIST**

In 1995, I was asked by the series adviser Keith Whitaker to do a translation for the nascent Focus Philosophical Library; Plato was suggested as a possibility. The Focus Press under its editor Ron Pullins publishes fresh translations, intended to be very reasonably priced and to be used by American students. The project was appealing to me both as a teacher in a school dependent on good and accessible translations and as a dean in need of intellectual recreation.

I had what turned out to be an inspired idea, that of seeking collaborators among my colleagues, figuring that the pleasure of becoming so really intimate with a dialogue as only a translator is would be enhanced by the close partnership of common work, and that three heads could better solve the problems and detect the mistakes that would surely dog a lone translator. Peter Kalkavage and Eric Salem agreed to becoming a trio. We chose the *Sophist* because we had all three begun to recognize it as the most ontologically future-fraught of all the dialogues, and we welcomed the challenge of preserving its originary freshness.

What follows is a report, under various headings, of the things we think we learned and of the advice we might venture to give our fellow translators.

COLLABORATION   One feature of the sophist is that, wherever you are, there he is not; he is forever trying to escape into trackless, impassable thickets. ("Impasse," incidentally, is one of our translations, very nearly literal, of *aporía,* "waylessness.") But those who deal in knowing also display an opposite fault in the dialogues: that of position-taking. They occupy positions in defense of which they throw up outworks (*próblema* is the Greek word for such a defensive outwork) and employ various apotropaic stratagems. Evidently Socrates and Plato consider that to have a universal escape route in all arguments or to occupy entrenched positions is unworthy of the philosopher's mission.

And so it is for the translator's task. Those who work together on transferring Greek meanings into English words have to be focused on what the Greeks call the *prágma* and what Hegel calls *die Sache.* They have to eschew both escape and entrenchment, and they must be objective—intent on the object at hand.

Yet while ego is out, there is a strong human element in a collaboration put in the service of a dialogue. It demands and develops friendship. The three of us all bring slightly different strengths: One is perhaps more alert to Greek grammar, another to the philosophical resonances of terms. All three of us, having undergone the most effective part of our education as teachers at St. John's College, are relatively fearless in the face of ignorance and fresh in our deliberate amateurism.

The way we worked is that each of us presented a translation of one Stephanus page in turn every third week, which all of us together then raked over as with a fine-tooth comb, the original translator explaining but not particularly defending a choice. Often we let somewhat daring or awkwardly accurate readings stand, waiting for that reading, close to the final one, in which we would attend particularly to idiom and flow while erasing false inspirations.

I think we have become persuaded that in putting a rich Greek text into English there are so many facets to be attended to that three heads are indeed better than one. We do, in fact, have grand predecessors to look to: You will recall the legend about the seventy-two scribes, six from each of Israel's twelve tribes, who produced, in the third century B.C., the Septuagint, the earliest extant Greek version of the Hebrew Bible. They worked in separate cells and came up with identical translations, presumably inspired by the text itself. We might say that the Platonic text acted on us in a more modest ex post facto mode in a similar way—one version would suddenly, after some trial and error, click for all three of us.

Our advice to collaborators: Cotranslating is a form of intimacy, best entered into by those who have the same object firmly in their sights while viewing each other with affectionate respect.

READERSHIP   We thought it essential to keep in mind for whom we meant this translation of the *Sophist*. We meant it for the people whom we imagine as standing around as spectators and auditors in this as in so many other dialogues. They are presumably tacitly engaged, like the silently present young Socrates, Theaetetus's friend, who shares our Socrates' name, as Theaetetus shares his looks. Another way to put it is that we thought of our students as they prepare for a seminar by silent reading. Some are quite innocent of the issues, some have, or think they have, insider knowledge, some read casually and disengagedly, and some are intensely serious.

Consideration of our audience brought up the delicate question of colloquialism. One device that would keep the conversation casually speechlike was contraction, and we used it a lot, but not in places that we thought were meant to be stuffy, high flown, or solemn. We looked for idiomatic equivalents, but avoided slang (though we had a great time devising some raucous interim translations, such as "wise guy" or "weisenheimer" for the Sophist himself). While we were well aware that every idiomatic translation will, in time, betray its date, nothing dates more quickly than slang, which even in its day fails, like all truckling under to fashion, to have real appeal for students.

In the course of thinking about drawing readers into the dialogue, we often had occasion to consider what is probably a real difference between the ear of a young contemporary Greek and that of one of our students. The well-brought-up Greek (and not only an Athenian), being nourished on Homer and the tragedians, whose language was no one's spoken Greek, could savor artificialities and archaisms that our students would find simply off-putting. A couple of generations ago, some English-speaking students would have absorbed enough of Shakespeare and Milton to appreciate such echoes, but we couldn't count on that. So we put everything into plain, current English, sometimes allowing ourselves the merest whiff of high poetry or archaism.

We tried, in our students' behalf, to put ourselves into the interlocutors' sandals: What is being said, what is being heard, what is being felt, and what is being thought? We called on our experience as teachers to guess at the dialogic backdrop of anxious agreement, triumphant dissent, and shamed realization that young Theaetetus contributes. But, above all, we clung to our main hypothesis as trusting readers of the dialogues: that each speech uttered has a discernible meaning contributing to the drift of the conversation and that the translation should preserve that motion.

Our advice here is: In translating, fill out imaginatively not only the conversation within the text, but draw in the external participant, the reading student.

PREDECESSORS   Of course, we took all the help we could get from earlier translations. We used Robin for his intelligently chosen readings, Campbell for his linguistic annotations, Cornford for informational help.

The two translations we had always at our sides were the Loeb version of Harold North Fowler (1952) and Seth Benardete's rendition in *The Being of the Beautiful* (1984). Fowler, though old-fashioned in diction and uninspired in terminology, was almost unfailing in making sense of puzzling passages and turns of phrase. We consulted Benardete, whenever we ran into trouble, for his meticulous attention to every word and because of his linguistic ingenuity. His version is a crib for the better sort of folk; it becomes intelligible if you read it as essentially in Greek and accidentally in English. Since, however, we were determined to translate not only *from* Greek but also *into* English, we only rarely borrowed phrases from him, though we took many hints as to meaning.

Heidegger translates numerous passages of the *Sophist* in the lecture notes published in 1992 under the title *Platon: Sophistes*. These versions are a reminder that in certain respects the translator into German is to be envied. Some of the forms that have to do with Being go more directly into German than into English. *To eínai*, for example, becomes in German "das Sein," while in English the infinitive cannot normally be nominalized; also *to on* readily goes into "Seiendes," and *ta ónta* is rendered as "das Seiende," which functions, like the Greek neuter plural, as a collective noun. Probably most provocative and least helpful to translators who intend to be as naively true to the text and as agendaless as possible are Heidegger's terms for *ousía*, which he renders in uninterpreted and interpreted versions, as it were. In the former, *ousía* is plain "Sein." In the interpreted version, *ousía* is rendered as if it were *parousía*: "das Anwesende" or "das Vorhandene," that is, "the present" or "the at-hand," in accord with his idea that Greek thought suffers from the aboriginal flaw of thinking of Being as if it were a thing.

We puzzled a good deal over the proper translation of *ousía*, being loath on principle (namely the principle that translation should be as far as feasible into an existent language) to invent noncurrent abstract substantives. But we finally decided on "beinghood." We chose it over "beingness" not only because it sounded better to us, but because it had more concreteness, as in neighborhood or manhood: we were mindful that *ousía* means something like "real estate" in ordinary Greek. We had decided to make up a word to begin with because we had an unresolved sense that *ousía*, which in the *Sophist* is usually contrasted with *génesis*, had a peculiar weight, and we wanted the reader to be in a position to attend to that interpretational problem.

I was relieved to see that even German could not deal with the crucial little adverb *ontós*, which for our private amusement only we translated as "beingly," but more soberly, for public consumption, as "in its very being." Thus the phrase that concludes the ultimate collection of differentiating terms reveals *ton óntos sophistén*, "the Sophist in his very being."

Let me return to the advantages of translating into German with two examples. First, we had long discussions about the translation of *stásis*, the specific other of motion. We settled on "rest," knowing full well that "rest" is wrong insofar as it means lack of, or cessation from, motion. "Standstill" or "stationariness," or stillness, as designating a condition coequal with motion, seemed too strained, and we consigned them to the glossary. German is lucky in being able to form "Ständigkeit" quite naturally, as Heidegger in fact does (579).

Second, in 244 c 4, when the Stranger begins his critique of Parmenides' *hypóthesis* of the One, we were pretty much forced to use the English word "hypothesis" with all of its scientific baggage. Schleiermacher uses the Germanized version of "presupposition," that is "Voraussetzung," but Heidegger eschews both and brilliantly writes "Ansatz," with the observation that Parmenides's One is not a supposition to be consequently confirmed but a beginning, an *arché*, an "onset"—which is exactly what "Ansatz" may mean.

Nonetheless with all the felicities to be gotten especially from the German propensity for easy prepositional compounding, I was continually grateful that it was our lot to be putting Plato into English, particularly American English. In our idiom we could achieve a plainness and a playfulness that must be, when all is said and done, more pleasing to Socrates, as he listens in, than a lot of linguistic incense.

I think our general advice to fellow translators would be unabashedly to cannibalize and unabashedly to set aside previous translations.

APPARATUS   Since we were left very free by our press to decide on supplementary materials, we thought long and hard about our obligation to the text and to the reader.

We come from a school—meaning both a way of thinking and an institution—that has the greatest misgivings about standing between a reader and the book. The extratextual stuff in a volume is, of course, meant to facilitate the approach to the translated text; but really, how can it? Take an introduction. If it says the same thing as the work, it will, assuming that the work is of the highest quality, say it worse. If it says something else, it will keep the reader from the work by that much time. We have a strong faith, based on our common teaching experience, that good books don't need approaching; they need facing, immediately and directly, at least at the first reading.

We compromised that faith, partly because, by the end of our labor, we were simply so full of thoughts that we couldn't contain ourselves, and partly because we know perfectly well that well-instructed students skip introductions and come back to them much later, if at all.

So we decided to keep it short, simple, and straightforward. We avoided historical backgrounding on the principle that Plato would have felt about our doing it much as a landscape painter might if we took his painting and provided it with a broad frame extending the scenery, so as to give the viewer an enlarged setting. We didn't want to deface the dialogue or distract or prejudice our student readers in this way; I should say that at St. John's evidence of familiarity with introductions is a suspect virtue. But we did set the dialogue briefly in its sequence—

Theaetetus, Sophist, Statesman, and the mysteriously missing *Philosopher.* We gave a succinct plot outline of the hunt for the Sophist, geared to a new and, we think, quite spiffy diagram of the infamous divisions that play so large a role in the *Sophist.* We pointed out some aspects of the dialogue that had become particularly pregnant for us, such as the generic nature of *the* Sophist here pursued (as opposed to the named individual sophists Socrates politely persecutes in dialogues like the *Gorgias* and the *Protagoras*). We had a little section on Father Parmenides and the strange and wonderful fact that he, the Stranger's own teacher, attracts the main attack of the dialogue. Then we told briefly what we understood about such deep matters as the relation of Image to Nonbeing and of Nonbeing to Otherness. And we left it at that. (See ch. 10.)

Since we made use of the printer's full typographic menu, we had a little note on that. We were very sparing with footnotes, using them mostly to supply what we thought an ancient contemporary reader might have known, or where we thought we detected a joke or an allusion obscure to a current reader.

Our energy went into the glossary, which we put in back, to be used or not. We arranged the Greek terms and our reasoned translations in meaning-clusters. (You will find something similar in Hope's translation of Aristotle's *Physics* and *Metaphysics,* except that we transliterated all our Greek in the hope that students might learn to accent and pronounce correctly words like *phrónesis* and *poíesis* and *mímesis.*) We avoided the alphabetic order so as to prevent the impression that we—or the partners of a dialogue—are ever looking for dictionarylike definitions. We also hoped to provide students with what we thought of as the prototerminology of a coming ontology—or perhaps better a *me*-ontology (*me* expresses negativity), an account of Nonbeing: the *Sophist* is a spawning ground of metaphysical terms-to-be.

EDITING   The translator's final reading, of course, tries for absolute correctness. But we have to warn the trustful that having a perfect disk is no protection. Something will get screwed up, there will be unexpected glitches, and, as we learned to our sorrow, it will be in the most carefully construed first sentence. No matter how good and accommodating the editor, there will be howlers. Our advice: Trust no one but yourselves and demand to see final proofs.

REPLIES   Theaetetus plays to the Stranger by regularly uttering a budget of stock replies signifying slight hesitation, passive assent, positive agreement, or requests for clarification.

After a while, we began to suspect that the rotating litany of responses might not be entirely mechanical. This apprehension made it incumbent upon us to keep a list of our considered renditions of *nai* (yes), *pos* (how so?), *pos gar ou* (of course), *hoútos* (just so), *panu ge* (entirely so), *pantápasi men oun,* and a dozen others, so that in later readings we could make all the replies consistent. In that way, we would give readers of the translation a chance to discover patterns we only suspected. *Pantapasi men oun,* for example, for which we did borrow Benardete's phrase "that's altogether so," occurs in the dialogue as a strong assent to a summary claim and concludes the dialogue as Theaetetus's last response to the final collection of divisions that catch the true and ultimate Sophist as the expert of the non-genuine. Theaetetus is clearly assenting not only to the definitive, but also to the global character of this final determination of a human type and profession.

PARTICLES   We were similarly anxious to render particles fairly consistently. The dialogic life is in them—*they* indicate inflections of the voice, gestures of the body, and even motions of the soul.

The dictionary, or even Denniston's *Greek Particles,* though they must be consulted to give the limits of usage, cannot do it all. The translators must savor the speech in its context and judge whether it is marked as an inference or a new departure, whether eagerness is being displayed, smiles are suppressed, eyebrows raised, or hands thrown up. We were mindful that typographic and punctuational devices were not available to a Greek composer of living speech, and we used italics, dashes, colons, semicolons, and exclamation points liberally to render the force of particles or of emphases indicated by sentential order. I might mention here that capitalization helped us a great deal in translating a dialogue full of terms for forms and kinds designated in Greek by the definite article and a verbal or adjectival substantive such as *to on* (Being), *to me on* (Nonbeing), *taúton* (the Same), and *tháteron* (the Other).

Our advice to translators is to be—within the limits of natural English—consistent, careful, and ingenious in rendering apparently little and apparently automatic elements of the dialogues; they may be more revealing than one realizes at first.

TECHNO-HUMOR   At the end of Bacon's *New Organon*, there is to be found a prescient catalogue of one hundred and thirty "histories" of special investigations that are one day to constitute the sphere of human expertise. It is a strange and wonderful fact that the first such comprehensive ordering of extant technical know-how (that I know of) is found in the *Sophist*— and that it is a send-up. The Stranger, who is not an overtly funny person, engages in what might be called techno-humor at the expense of experts.

As readers of the dialogue, of course, we thought a good deal about the reason why a comprehensive classification of human know-how or technique—we translated *téchne* as "expertise" (but sometimes as "art," as in "arts and crafts")—should be the approach of choice to the delineation of the Sophist. We were alert to the startling conjunction of apparently disjunct themes that governs a number of the great dialogues, as the *Phaedrus*, for instance, seems to yoke the unlikely pair of love and rhetoric; we wondered if the *Sophist* presented a similar case.

We soon saw, however, how much sense it made that the Sophist, whose nature is presented here as that of a faker and a know-it-all, should be tracked into the branches of human activity and that in that great decision-tree he should reappear in seven places, sometimes among the lowly but genuine crafts and sometimes among the high-sounding but dubious ones. It also made sense that the hunt for this elusive creature should be the occasion for presenting to the world the new dialectic art of division and collection and all its problems—chief among them what might be called the problem of heuristic direction: At what moment in this dialectic enterprise, at the beginning, end, or in between, does new insight arise?

But as translators, it was not so much our business to have theories about the inevitable implication of expertise and shamming or about the problems of classification as to render the divisions faithfully into English. And there we were in a pretty good position. As I have said, all three of us come from a college that has distanced itself from specialization, and we were alive to the tragicomedy of defining human beings as the professors of a profession. (Our English version of *sophists* was, incidentally, "professor of wisdom.") Not that all of us aren't ourselves certified members of the world of expertise. I myself, for instance, began my working life in a profession that the Stranger might have ranged, looking to the three great branches of human expertise called "getting," "separating," and "making," under getting, specifying it as a hunt beneath the soil for fragmented old artifacts carried on by means of pickaxes. We call it archaeology. Recall that the sophist is first found in the right-hand branch of animal hunting on land, specified as the sham-teaching hunt for wealthy youths.

We tried to preserve the neologic high jinks of some of the divisions. Thus the Sophist is found a second, third, and fourth time in the getting part of expertise as a psycho-trading virtue-seller, and in the manipulating part both as a seller of self-made learnables and as a peddler of other-made learnables: "psycho-trading" renders *psychemporiké* and "learnable-selling" *mathematopolikón*.

We had not long worked on our second project for the Focus Philosophical Library, a translation of the *Phaedo*, before we became aware of the varieties of Platonic humor. In fact Peter Kalkavage began retrospectively to refer to the *Sophist* as a one-joke dialogue, dominated by the techno-humor of the otherwise ponderous Stranger that I've just described. The *Phaedo,* because in it Socrates not only speaks but even makes speeches, is, we discovered, infused with a very different, far more subtle humor, which we are doing our best to preserve. It is the sort of hilarity or jocundity in the original Latin sense, the subdued joyousness and even merriment of the ultimate moment, that belongs to a man going blithely to his death without having lost his firm, even hard grip on the earthly condition. We have come to think of it as the tone of the lightness of Being. It keeps his companions in an ambivalent state of sorrowful exhilaration, suspended between tears and laughter.

The secondary partners, too, are very different in the two dialogues. Theaetetus is, at least vis-à-vis the Stranger, a somewhat stuffy boy, while that comradely pair Simmias and Cebes are pretty lively, each in his way.

Does bringing out the humor of the dialogues in translations need a justification? I should not imagine so, but I might mention once more that all three of us learned much of our way of reading Plato from Jacob Klein, who in his interpretations was especially alert to the mimetic character of the dialogues. As imitations of Socrates and the conversations he conducted or attended, they were bound to be playful, as Socrates was playful with a playfulness that is the kindly counterpart of his notorious dissembling, his irony. Thus Socrates' humor is not usually comedic in Aristotle's understanding of comedy as the imitation of what is laughable, that is, low and absurd but relatively harmless. The techno-humor of the *Sophist,* however, comes far closer to comedy than does that of the other dialogues, with the proviso that, for all its laughableness, the sophistic craft is not so harmless.

In any case, our advice to colleagues who plan to translate Platonic dialogues is to be prepared not only to laugh themselves but also to be the cause of laughter in others.

FAITHFULNESS   It was clear to us from the beginning that looseness, paraphrase, and interpretative adumbration were intolerable in the translation of any Platonic writing, but especially in a dialogue like the *Sophist,* which is so close to the brink of technical metaphysics and yet so carefully refrains from letting philosophy become a *téchne,* an expertise. It does so by going at what Aristotle will later codify as the "perplexities," that is, the problems of Being in an oblique and human way. It is oblique in concentrating, as I have said, less on ontology than on "me-ontology," the account of Nonbeing as the ground of imitation or pretense, and it is human in pursuing the Sophist as a human type as much as it pursues sophistry as a profession. In this morning-twilight of philosophy, meticulous accuracy is especially necessary. So we spent, as I have said, much time on words, determining for ourselves whether they were terms of a trade or not—yet. *Aporía* and *méthodos* are examples. Both have come to be fixed as terms of philosophy: "perplexity" and "method." But we aimed to preserve, at least in some places, the unfixed original meaning: "impasse," that is lack of passage, and "way," which preserve the playful spatial analogy that is so prominent in the Stranger's reflections on the motion of thought.

We aimed at faithfulness, however, not only in words and terms but also in sentences. The obvious problem is always sub-literalness—the risk of producing a contortedly accurate pony. We thought that it was a part of faithfulness to render the various levels of elegance, clarity, and emphasis of the speeches—and the Stranger surely has his obscure and clunky moments, at least as we heard them.

The faith of translators who mean to be faithful must be that, meaning-element for meaning-element, it is possible to turn Greek into English and that this must imply that *usually*—it never pays to be too rigid—one Greek word goes into one English word or typographical symbol, one phrase into one phrase, one clause into one clause, and one sentence into one sentence—in other words, that it is possible to get equivalence without sublinearity. It also implies that one can find an English word order that renders the emphasis of the Greek sentence and English connectives that maintain the Greek flow. One of our last readings was addressed, as I have mentioned, to the attempted eradication of all signs of translaterese. Our trust was that if we stuck faithfully to the Greek, barring simple mistakes and omissions, we would get English that said exactly what the Greek said and with something like the original naturalness and deviations from naturalness. In other words, we had the faith that we might overcome the charge expressed in the Italian pairing *traduttore/traditore:* We hoped that a translator need not be a traitor to the text.

Our best advice to others is not to give in to current hermeneutic theories concerning the essential untranslatability of one language into another, but to suppose, as a starting hypothesis, that even if it is not possible to say exactly the same thing in any two languages, yet we can think and say practically the same thing as our ancient intellectual progenitors—from which it is evident that the translator's hypothesis is no negligible commentary on contemporary philosophy.

REQUIREMENTS The last item on my list of observations concerns the crucial question "What do translators need to know and be good at?"

The three of us did not think that we were required to possess a full-fledged interpretation to have a go at a translation. What we needed, instead, was a lively sense of intimations, a sense born of a belief in the unfailing significance of the text. In other words, we came to Plato's philosophic plays with the trust that every word (or nearly every word) was deliberately placed, but that some terms and turns were special sign-posts to implied meanings. We tried to be alert to oddities of language and emphasis as well as to *hápax legómena* (linguistic singularities which we treated as occasions for literalness, even if it proved awkward). On another level, we listened for high points and crucial junctures, which Plato's most responsible speakers and, of course, Socrates himself, often signal by a throwaway reference to that one more "little" addition.

None of us are, this is the moment to say, great believers in esotericism. We are much too possessed by a sense of the pedagogic generosity of the dialogues—a sense that a discreetly fierce energy is devoted to carrying interlocutors, bystanders, and readers beyond themselves into realms reachable only by circuitous and indirect means—to believe that the author would be deliberately obscure in order to screen out the non-elect. The matter is difficult enough as it is. On the contrary, we are told as much, but no more, than we need to make us want to think onward. This is why the dialogues are fairly easy to read the first time and get harder to understand as, with each reading, more signals are picked up.

There certainly exist occasionally esoteric writers like Newton who, "to avoid being baited by little smatterers in mathematics . . . designedly made his *Principia* abstruse" (Portsmouth Collection), and authors who touch guardedly on theological or political issues in intolerant times (though they never do seem to escape persecution). Socrates' dissembling and Plato's subtlety, however, are not of this self-protective sort but are pedagogical devices for drawing the learner in. At least, that is our experience. The dialogues work on the principle that "a cat may look at a king" or, rather, "a boy may look at Being." And in any case, they display hardly any attempt to mask the fact that not everything that goes on in these conversations will be of comfort to respectable parents. So the translator's first requirement is a belief in the many-layered accessibility of the text and an alertness to those signs and signals that the English version should preserve for readers to puzzle over.

A second requirement we put on ourselves was to attempt consistency but to shun method. An intelligent consistency is, we thought, the guardian spirit of open minds. So as much as possible we tried, as I have said, to choose the right word and to stick with it even in fairly routine phrases. Thus *phaínetai* is almost always "it appears," and *dokeî* "it seems." At the same time, we tried to remain open to significant nuances and strange turns within the dialogue, though our avoidance of methodical translating bound to a particular interpretation of Platonic philosophy applied mainly across the dialogues: In taking up the *Phaedo*, we saw once again the truth of the teaching that each dialogue is a fresh world of discourse and is to be faced without preconceptions regarding "Platonic thought." That observation is particularly true as between dialogues in which Socrates guides the conversation and those in which he only listens in or is, finally, even absent (*Laws*).

As far as preparation is concerned, since none of us can really read Greek as a living language, we were glad to see that we could do pretty well on a lot of Greek reading experience to give us a feel for the intention and on enough grammatical expertise to tell us when we needed to do careful parsing. We found that besides Liddell-Scott we needed to have at hand Roget's *Thesaurus* to help us to the word we were looking for.

But we think that, all in all, the main requirement for translators of Plato, and our advice to them, is to believe in the semantic plenitude of the Platonic texts and to produce an English version that, like the Greek, says more than the translators know.

13

PLATO'S "THEORY OF IDEAS"

My subject for tonight is, as announced, "Plato's 'Theory of Ideas.'" Whether that subject actually interests you, or you think that it ought to interest you—you will, I imagine, regard it as a respectable lecture topic. Yet I must tell you that every term in the project is wrong-headed. Let me explain.

First, Plato's Theory of Ideas is not a subject at all, that is, not a compact mental article to be presented on an intellectual platter. Plato himself refrained from making it the direct theme of any of his dialogues. Instead, the ideas appear in the context of conversations, incidentally and in scattered places. He gives the reason directly in a letter (*Seventh Letter* 341 c):

> There is no treatise of mine about these things, nor ever will be; for it is not sayable like other kinds of learning, but out of much communion which has taken place around this business, and from living together, suddenly, like a light kindled from a leaping fire, it gets into the soul, and from there on nourishes itself.

It follows that my lecture (like all the similar scholars' efforts) is something of an outsider's attempt to short-circuit a required initiation, an attempt that betrays my inability to participate wholly in the truth I am conveying as a molded matter. Nevertheless there is much in Plato's works that invites such an exposition of his doctrine—much explicit and provocative argumentation and many promises of a communicable way to insight.

I have another reason for thus boldly ploughing in. Last summer (1978) there died that man, that teacher in our school, St. John's College, who, as it seemed to many of us, best knew the way into the Platonic dialogues. His name is Jacob Klein. While he was alive, I, for one, resting secure in the fact of his existence, postponed a bald confrontation of my own with this ultimate philosophical matter. But now, I thought, the time had come to be bold in acting on the advice Socrates gives to his friends in the course of the last conversation of his life. When he is asked where they will find someone to charm away their fears that philosophy is impossible once he is dead, he tells them that not only among the Greeks, but also among the barbarians—that, of course, includes us—there are many good people who can do this for them. But then he adds (*Phaedo* 78 a):

> You must search for him in company with one another too, for perhaps you wouldn't find anyone more able to do this than *yourselves*.

We speak of "Plato's Theory," and let me now say something about that. Its chief source is, to be sure, the works of Plato, and he is its ultimate master.[1] Yet within his works, his dialogues, it is not Plato but his teacher Socrates who originates and maintains the theory. Plato presents Socrates as having a lifelong hold on it, though he speaks of it from continuously changing aspects. There is a "middle to late" dialogue, the *Parmenides*, in which the elderly author imagines a boyish Socrates—a wonderful turnabout—and in which Socrates' originating claim is elicited by the father of philosophy, old Parmenides, himself (130 b). In the *Sophist,* a "late" dialogue, an old Socrates, just a few weeks away from execution, listens silently while a Stranger who is a disciple of Parmenides brings the theory to its height with the solution of one of its deepest difficulties. And in a "middle" dialogue, the *Phaedo,* Socrates, in the last conversation of his life, addresses the theory more directly than anywhere else. Plato, at least, wished the world to think of *Socrates'* "Theory of Ideas."

More accurately, however, he would not have had us think of a "theory" at all. By *a* theory we usually mean a conceptual construction designed in principle to yield satisfying explanations for every problem brought to it.[2] A theory ought to be falsifiable, which means it should be capable of being made to reveal its incompleteness or inconsistency by strenuous formal reasoning so that it might be discredited and discarded if necessary. Thus its author must present it in the most impregnable form possible. Scholars find difficulties aplenty in the Theory of Ideas. But here is a curious circumstance: they are all anticipated in their boldest form in that very dialogue, the *Parmenides,* which represents a boyish Socrates as first proposing the ideas.[3] Can you think of another philosophical theory that is presented at its very beginning in terms of a series of devastating difficulties, never to be explicitly resolved?

The point is that the Ideas are not a theory. Socrates calls his bringing in of the *ideas* a "supposing" (*Phaedo* 100 b); the Greek word for a supposition is *hypóthesis.* A hypothesis is, literally, an underpinning, a prop.[4] It comes to him and he comes on it at every departure and at every turning. It is a basis he acknowledges so that he can carry on as he must—not a conclusion presented for verification, but a beginning that becomes the end of the inquiry. It is first of all the condition that gives him heart for a search, by making it possible for him to frame a question that has in it the arrow to an answer. One might say that it allows him to make a suspect of the unknown (*Meno* 86 b).

Thereafter, however, the idea-hypotheses—for the hypothesis is not the proposition that there are ideas but is each idea itself—are to be used as stepping-stones to their own conversion into something not merely supposed, but truly beheld, "seen" (*Republic* 511 b). Such suppositions are surely not fruitfully accosted by formal hammer-and-tongs argument, though they are, of course, amenable to careful and critical inspection.

I keep calling these Socratic suppositions *ideas*. The word "idea" is a transcription of a term Socrates himself uses, *idéa*. Nonetheless it is an infelicitous term. Ask yourselves what we usually mean by an idea, for instance when we say, "That's her idea of a good lecture." Clearly we mean an opinion or a mental image or a concept, often in opposition to the "real" thing. This modern notion of an idea, the result of an earth-shaking intellectual upset (with ancient roots), is that of a mental representation, something before or in the organ of ideas, the mind. The use of the term would cast my exposition into a false, albeit familiar, frame, and I would only make things worse were I to insist that Socrates' ideas are "real," and worse yet, "really exist."

Socrates' own chief word is *eídos*. Like the word *idéa* it is built on the simple past stem of the word "to see," which signifies the act of seeing once done and completed. We can collect the many meanings of *eídos* that flow continuously from the broadly ordinary to the narrowly technical: shape, figure, face, form, characteristic, quality, class, kind. But when we dwell on the multiplicity of Greek usages, we are standing the matter on its head, for they are all revealing divergences from the dead-center meaning. *Eídos* means sight, aspect, *looks,* in that eerily active sense in which a thing that has looks or is a sight *presents* itself to our sight and our looking. "Looks," then, and, not idea or form, is the most faithful rendering of *eídos*.[5] But it sounds too curious, and so I shall speak simply of *eídos*. The plural is *eíde*. *Eídos,* then, is the word Socrates chooses for his hypothesis. For that choice he might, for this once, be called a "Greek thinker" (for by and large he is just a thinker), someone who cherishes and yet overturns the wisdom of his language, which associates seeing and knowing: "I know" in Greek is built on the stem of "I saw." *Eídos* is a choice full of witty depth, for the first of all those notorious Socratic paradoxes is surely that the *eídos* is *invisible*.

So let me convert the falsely familiar title "Plato's Theory of Ideas" to "Socrates' Hypotheses of the *Eíde*." I shall pursue the *eídos* under seven headings, for it shows as many aspects as there are beginnings to Socrates' inquiry. Indeed, that is what makes his hypotheses compelling: that so many roads lead to the *eídos*.[6] These are the headings:

1   Excellence and Commonness
2   Speech and Dialectic
3   Answers and Questions
4   Opinion and Knowledge
5   Appearance and Being
6   Same and Other
7   Original and Image

1   EXCELLENCE AND COMMONNESS

"Philosophy" means literally the love of wisdom. Therefore it begins in desire (*Republic* 475 b, *Symposium* 204 a, *Phaedrus* 244 ff.), in desirous love, in erotic passion, the most acute of all passions. That is what we might call the *young* beginning of philosophy.[7] It is the love that arises when another human being appears "all-beautiful in aspect," "in *eídos*," as the Greek phrase goes (*Charmides* 154 d). We might say that it arises when someone suddenly becomes *visible* to us. For beauty, Socrates says, has the part of shining out eminently and of being most lovable, and of coming to us through sense, through the most acute and comprehensive of senses, the sense of sight. Beauty *is* brilliance, attractive visibility. Beauty is sight par excellence, and a sight is that which, without going out of itself, draws us from a distance. But such a sensual sight, such a bodily "idea" (*Phaedrus* 251 a), which draws us from afar, affects us with an exciting and utterly confounding sense of its being a mere penetrable veil, a mere representation of some divinity beyond. That is why we speak of such love as adoration. It draws us not *to* itself but *through* itself—the enchantedly attentive fascination with sensual looks goes over into something directed to the other side of that surface. Desire through distance is called love, and if what beckons is on the farther side of surface-sight, it is called philosophy. For, Socrates says, there is a road whose first station is the beckoning irritation aroused by one beautiful body and which leads us to have an eye first for all particular beauty and at last to sight beauty in its self-sameness (*Symposium* 210 a). And that sight we are to view, the very source of visibles, is beyond sense and is the *eídos* itself.

There is another beginning in what is extraordinary and captivating, and though its visible aspect may be a little duller, its luster is lifelong (*Phaedrus* 250 d). It has to do with what is outstanding, excellent. Some time or other all of us are overcome by admiration for the fullness of being of certain people and their deeds, or even of an animal or a tool (*Republic* 353 b, 601 d). Such potency of being, such proper goodness, is called in Greek *areté,* which means effective excellence, potent capability (*Laches* 192 b). It is more than ordinary usefulness or humanity or sincerity. It is rather a kind of superlativeness—its name may be related to *áriston,* the best. It is competitive, "agonistic," as the Greeks say, and uncommon, although we speak rightly and yet paradoxically of a "standard" of excellence. Excellence and how to engender it is a topic of pervasive fascination. It interests parents and citizens, the good, the crafty, the curious, and the corrupt—perhaps them most peculiarly (*Meno*), them and the young.

But again, as in the case of beauty incarnate, every outstanding human being and every fine deed appears as a mere instance, a mere exemplification of excellence. It is spurious for being only an instance and not the thing itself, deficient in being abstracted from the complete complex of virtues, deformed by being bound to a particular setting. We all know that even the best founded hero-worship eventually loses its edge and luster as the admirer gains perspective, whereas the desire to see excellence and to be excellent is a longing for an ever-bright, undeformable shape, looming behind the tainted earthly example.

The beautiful and the best, the fine and the good—through these is the enthusiastic first access to the *eídos*.

But there is also a very sober beginning, one whose implications Socrates himself was a little put off by in his first youth, feeling its meanness (*Parmenides* 130 c). For besides the high and shining *eídos* of what is beautiful and excellent, there is also a common *eídos;* or better, everything, from a small bee to a grand virtue, displays or "has" an *eídos* (*Meno* 72). *Everything* we see, everything that appears in any way at all, looks (or sounds or smells) *like* something—excellences, elements, animals, tools. Everything wears the aspect of being *of a sort.* Unless it has the looks of something, we cannot see it, for it has no coherent shape to draw us to it; we cannot point to it or name it. To see is always to *re*-cognize; just imagine trying to focus on something—I shouldn't even say "something"—that is truly unique and looks like nothing. Whatever wears a look at all wears that look in common with other things. One look presides over numerous things, and that is why we can "identify," that is to say, make out the sameness—of things, of people, elements, animals, tools. It is not in their multifariousness and difference that we lay hold of things but "by their being bees" or beds or excellences (*Meno* 72 b). Socrates is far more interested in this common look than in what we call individuality, that inarticulable deviation from the common which he never thinks of as a source of particular fineness. He pursues the common *eídos* because it is *more* revealing than are the world's idiosyncrasies.

For we do not learn of this *eídos* by looking at individual things; on the contrary, we can look at these only because they display this *eídos,* this look. For example, Socrates would agree that equal objects—scratched lines, say—are needed to call up in us the thought of equality (*Phaedo* 75 a). But they do that only because they take part in the *eídos* that makes them look equal to us, even though they are but uncertainly, passingly, approximately equal. From these scratches we could never *gather* the sharply precise idea of equality, any more than we can identify goodness by watching human actions even from now till doomsday. That look of things which not one of them has fully or purely but which is common to all—that is a wonder to Socrates.

And so both outstanding and common sights point to an invisible *eídos* beyond.

2 SPEECH AND DIALECTIC

We have a surpassing strange power of reaching the things that share a look, all of them, at once: we can say the word, their name. When the eye sees a sight the tongue can utter a sound that is the sensual appearance of a word, of speech (*Third Letter* 342 b). One word reaches, picks out, *intends* what is the same in many things. One word presides over many things (*Republic* 596 a). A word is *not* a symbol for Socrates, for it does not stand for something by reason of some sort of *fit*, natural or conventional, between it and the thing; rather it reaches toward something utterly other than itself. It has meaning. Socrates thinks that what words mean is precisely that common *eídos*. In fixing on speech he discovers what the panoramic familiarity of daily seeing leaves obscure: that the visible world, particularly the natural world, comes compounded of more and more encompassing visible sorts, rising finally into totally invisible kindred groups. The Greek word for a visible sort is, of course, *eídos* and for a kindred group, *génos*. The Latin word for *eídos* is *species*. Socrates discovers the organization of the world by species and genus,[8] and that things can be placed, defined, by thinking about the meaning of names and connecting them properly in speech. All the world seems to be at the roots akin (*Meno* 81 d), and that kinship is articulable in complexes of words.

Such connected speech is what the Greeks call *lógos*. It is, first of all, inner effort, movement, attention, intention; indeed, it is the same as thinking (*Sophist* 263 e). It is always an activity of discerning and picking out on the one hand, and comprehending and collecting on the other; in fact that is what the verb *legein* means: to select and collect. Socrates thinks that such speech can reveal the interconnections of the world, but only if it "looks to," has reference to (e.g., *Republic* 472 b, 532 a) the interweaving of the invisible *eíde*. Meaningful and true speech is speech in accordance with the *eídos* (*Phaedrus* 249 b); names reach for the *eíde* singly, and sentences reach for their interconnections. Socrates calls such reaching speech *dialectic*, "sorting through" (266 c).

But he gives that word another sense also, a wider one. Dialectic is serious and, if necessary, uncompromising conversation with oneself or with another—that is, argument. I might say that if the enthusiasm of love is young philosophy, argumentative dialectic might be called the very youngest philosophy, because bright children make lovely dialecticians. Dialectic, however, not only reveals the articulated unity of the world. It also can shake our easy acceptance of its oneness. Speech can rake up the obtuse self-contradictoriness of things. Such self-opposition comes out when speech is used in one of the most aboriginal ways, in "telling," as the old term goes, in counting. Take this fourth finger. It is smaller than the middle finger but larger than the pinkie. It is both small and large. It has both looks at once. They dumbly coincide in the thing, and yet we can tell them apart and count them as each one, and two together in the thing. Whoever takes the deliverance of words seriously will find this provoking—provoking of thought (*Republic* 523). Socrates can account for this

revelation only by supposing that the *eídos* Greatness and the
eídos Smallness, which are each one and forever separate *be-*
yond the finger, can be fused *in* the finger. Even if the finger is
confounding, the *eíde* are pure and intelligible. The *eídos* saves
the *telling* power of speech.

3   ANSWERS AND QUESTIONS

Socrates asks questions of himself and others, and he urges them
continually: Try to say the answer. His questions are not quite
the usual kind, namely, requests for information or invitations
to acknowledgment. Nonetheless people see a charm or a dignity enough in them to try to respond. Socrates' kind of question is preeminently framed to elicit speech. He asks after that
in things which can respond, which is answerable, *responsible*.
The Greek term for what is answerable in that way is *aitía*, the
"responsible reason." Socrates thinks that such a responsible
reason—we sometimes say "cause"—cannot be some external
linkage of events. It is a trivializing answer to the question "Why
is Socrates sitting in prison?" to say that he is flexing his joints
in a certain way and a certain place. Although he is too modest
to say so, he knows he is there because of his peculiar kind of
courage. Similarly, if the question is "What makes this face beautiful?" the answer he insists on is that it is beautiful not by a certain incidental shape or color, but "by beauty." He calls such answers unsophisticated but safe (*Phaedo* 105 b). They are indeed
so simple-minded as to seem at first futile. They are answers for
those whose ambition is not to go onward but inward, for their
safety is in keeping us to the question, in directing us through
its words to a word. To accept that things are beautiful by beauty
means that the cause is not to be evaporated in inquiry but kept
in sight and pursued; that granted, the answer can then be safely
elaborated (*Phaedo* 105 b). For it poses a new and deeper question: What is beauty—or excellence or knowledge? I should say
here that Socrates does not go about idly asking what scholars
like to call the "What is X?" question. His questions are not

one function with variable objects, but each is asked differently in each conversation, for each is set differently into Socrates' life and each reaches toward a unique being. We all know that the answer to the question what something is can take many forms. Socrates sometimes begins by showing people that they quite literally don't know what they are talking about and can't mean what they are saying—a charming but dangerous project for the young to listen to (*Apology* 33 c, *Republic* 539 b, *Philebus* 15 a). Sometimes he proposes a startlingly revealing, seemingly paradoxical and dubiously convertible identification, for instance that excellence is knowledge. And once in a while he does what, persuaded by Aristotle (*Metaphysics* 987 b), people think of Socrates as doing first and preeminently: he looks for a definition by genus and species and differentiae. So, as Jacob Klein used to say: There is no one method for interpreting all the dialogues.[9] Yet it is equally the case that Socrates *is* always after the same end, on a trail of speech for which the one-word answer, the *eídos,* is a trail blaze. The trail, however, runs asymptotically toward its goal, approaching it without meeting it. The goal is the *eídos* named in the simple-minded but safe answer to a Socratic question. Ultimately the *eídos* toward which the word points cannot be attained through speech but only by itself and through itself (*Cratylus* 439 b), since it is not speech that determines the *eídos* but the *eídos* that founds speech (*Parmenides* 135 c). For *lógos* is utterly diverse from *eídos,* since its very nature is to be merely *about* being; it might be said to climb along the eidetic structure, articulating, so to speak, the lattice of an almost impenetrably crystalline complex.

Yet meanwhile the question that is steadfastly answered as it itself directs, focuses the soul on the *eídos* as responsible cause.

4 OPINION AND KNOWLEDGE

Socrates comes to grips with the strangest of human scandals: that we are able to talk without speaking and to believe without acting. Human life is peculiarly capable of intoxicating heights and excruciating falls, and it is these heights and depths we most avidly chatter about and have powerfully ineffective beliefs about. Indeed, public talk about them is obligatory. —It is an incantation to keep the spirit of excellence from fading. It consists of certain partial lopsided truths whose deficiency is obscured by their familiarity. Socrates calls such speechless talk, such logos-like utterance without present thought, *opinion*. (Our favorite phrase signal that an opinion is coming is "I feel that . . .") He thinks further that it is because we do not know what we mean when we talk of excellence that we fail to be excellent. By "knowing" he does not mean being familiar with certain arguments and definitions or having some sort of competence or canniness in getting what one wants (*Lesser Hippias* 365 d). He means that our souls are alight with, are filled with, what truly is. He means a knowledge so alive and rich that it goes immediately over into action without leaving room for the mediation of a wavering or perverse will. So Socrates' first interest in knowledge is practical, but I should say here that a knowledge vivid enough to pass immediately into deed will also be an end in itself, a realm in which to dwell beyond all action—another of the great Socratic paradoxes (*Phaedo* 66 b, *Phaedrus* 247, *Republic* 517 b).

To be cured of being caught in mere opinion we must know how this state is possible. Socrates finds only one explanation plausible. What we have opinions about cannot be the same as what we think seriously about (*Republic* 477). The name may be the same, but we cannot have the same thing in mind when we just talk and when we truly speak. We are using our powers so differently that they amount to different powers and must have different objects. That is not really so odd an idea. We seem to switch gears when we pass from pontificating to thinking, and the matter we have gone into deeply is no longer what it was when we "knew" it superficially, just as the friend well-known is a different person from the friend of first acquaintance. The superficial glance is reflected by a surface that masks the depth in which thinking becomes absorbed.

That first aspect of the world which is the object of opinion, whose whole character it is to seem and then to vanish before closer inspection, Socrates calls *Becoming,* because it is always coming to be and never is what it is quite stably. It is what is before our eyes. Our first fascination *is* with the shifting, inexact, contradictory appearances before our eyes, or with the obtrusive, baseless opinions of our fellows, and these are our unavoidable beginning (*Phaedo* 74 a). But as the visible surface is penetrated and those opinions are searched into, a new world appears, now to the eye of the thought; it is steadfast in being such as it is; it has a powerful "suchness;" it is shapely, unique. Socrates calls this world *Being.* He understands it to be all that knowledge demands. For in knowing we have a sense of being anchored, based, rooted in something stable and lucid for the eye of the soul (*Phaedo* 99 d). It is the world of the *eídos* as that which is to be known; it is the knowable *eídos* (*Republic* 511 a).

And however I have made it sound, Socrates does not regard the knowable *eídos* as a mere contrivance to grant himself knowledge. Rather he thinks that we are, all of us, capable of the experience of going into ourselves in thought, led on by the beckoning *eídos*. It is a process so vividly like the raising of a memory that he calls it—making a myth of it—recollection, the calling-up of a primordial memory (*Meno* 81, *Phaedo* 73). The way to the *eídos* is by an inner passage through our souls, not by the penetration of external things—or rather, the two ways are one.

I should add that the *eídos* is knowable, but it is not knowledge. It confronts the soul and is not of it. To put it in modern terms: It is a presence *to* the soul, not a representation *within* the mind. Or I might put it this way: Being is for us irreducibly aspectual. We look *at* it and move *among* its articulations, for it has a power of affecting the soul and being known (*Republic* 511, *Sophist* 248 e). We may even, speaking figuratively, comprehend it, but as mortals we cannot pass *into* it. For Socrates philosophy, the human desire for being, remains forever *philosophy,* an unfulfilled longing.

5 APPEARANCE AND BEING

The *eídos* is steadfast and lucid. Not so the world that envelops us; it is shifting and opaque. Yet the Greeks call what appears before our eyes the *phainomena,* which means "what shines out," "what shows itself," for the things that appear glow and ensnare us in their kaleidoscopic spectacle. That is why we are all lovers of sights and sounds (*Republic* 475 d). I should note here that although I cannot help talking of "things," the appearances are not things in any strict sense since they have no "reality" (which is but Latin for "thinghood"), no compacted, concrete, "categorical" character. Socrates sometimes uses the word *prágmata,* "business," "affairs," for our world. The "phenomena" sparkle busily, but it is all surface.

The systematic illusions and the serried variety of appearance can, however, be mastered by various sciences, for example, sciences of perspective and classification, but there is still a recalcitrant residue. That incorrigible phenomenality shows itself as a twofold multiplicity. First, there are always a diverging many of a kind, many beautiful things, many just acts. Second, no beautiful thing and no just act is that way perfectly, unbudgeably, purely, but each changes as our perspective on it changes in time or place. Appearance *as* appearance is scattered and shimmering, fragmented and iridescent.

But most of all it is *not* what it shows, or to put it more plainly: Appearance is appearance *of* something; it points beyond itself. What is it whose refracted form is shown to us in appearance? What appears must be for that very reason in itself invisible. This invisible *eídos* is what Socrates thinks of as the being behind appearance, and appearance is Becoming regarded as a manifestation. This *eídos,* since it is a being from the Realm of Being, is all that appearance and Becoming are not: not scattered, but one; not multiform, but having a single look (*Phaedo* 78 d); not mixed, but pure (66 a), not passive, but potent (*Sophist* 247 e); not elusive and illusory, but steadfast and true; not for busy show, but the thing in its verity, "the very thing" (*to autó prágma*); not self-contradictory, but self-same (*Phaedo*

78 d, *Cratylus* 386 e); not dependent and *of* something, but "it-self by itself," absolved from subservience, or "absolute," as later commentators render Socrates' deliberately naive term "by itself"; unique, immortal, indestructible (*Phaedo* 78 d), outside time, and beyond place (*Phaedrus* 247 b). Most simply, Socrates calls the *eídos, the* Just, *the* Beautiful.

Whatever has this characteristic of potent, shapely, and, one might also say "specific," self-sameness is called a being. It provides such "beinghood" (*ousía, Cratylus* 386 e; *Meno* 72 b) as appearances have, and it does this by somehow "being by," having presence (*parousía, Phaedo* 100 d), in them. The eidetic beings are responsible for the fact that the question "What is it?" asks not only *what* the thing is but also what it *is*, where *is* refers to the Being that accompanies every "whatness," all quality.

I should observe again that beings are not "real," for they are not things and do not move in the categories true of things, nor do they "exist," for to exist means to be here and now.[10] But they are not unreal or nonexistent either. They *are,* in the way described, and as they appear they give things their looks, their visible identifying form (*Phaedo* 104 d).

6   SAME AND OTHER

The Being that all the beings named above have in common is not Socrates' discovery. It comes to him from those so prejudicially called Presocratics, in particular from Parmenides, who entered the sanctuary of Being in a blazing chariot. Thus it comes to Socrates already fraught with established controversies and difficulties. Even he has an inherited legacy of "problems," that is to say, of questions posed in terms of his predecessors' inescapable doctrines. Questions posed in this way, as problems, notoriously have resolutions that pose more and tighter problems, and so the tradition of professional philosophy is set. Socrates does not entirely escape this unfresh beginning.

This is the problem Socrates takes up when still almost a boy: The Being Father Parmenides discovered *is* and is nothing else.

It is, one and only, without distinction or difference. For to distinguish is to negate, to say, "This is not that," and we cannot, Parmenides learned, think or intelligibly speak what is not. There is no permissible sentence that does not articulate, audibly or latently, an "is," an assertion of the truth of Being. Such austere attention to what speech *always* says is not primitive. Listen to a modern poet, W. H. Auden:

Words have no word for words that are not true. ("Words")

What Parmenides says—that what is, is, and in merely being is all one—is compelling since we have no immediate speech with which to say it nay. But it is equally monstrous, for it negates both our multifarious world, the one in which we are at home, along with the very possibility of articulate speech itself. Because Parmenides' grand insight brings all articulating speech to a halt, his zealous follower Zeno had taken the clever way of attacking the opposition who continue to talk and say that Being is not one but many. He understands this to have to mean that Being is *at once* like and unlike itself, self-contradictory, unthinkable. Socrates knows that the visible world, at least, *is* like that, and yet he knows that thoughtful speech cannot bear such self-contradictions. So he offers a supposition that saves both at once: the integrity of that which speech is always about, this "is" that is the bond, the copula, of every *lógos,* and *also* the manifest multiplicity and inconsistency of appearance and its gathering in speech. He saves Parmenides from sinking into the white silence of Being.

Socrates' supposition is the *eídos,* which is not Being itself but *a* being. His resolution is that Being is many but not confused. The *eíde* are each self-same, as a being should be, but they are also diverse from each other. The appearances somehow "participate" in these beings in such a way that the diverse beings intersect in them and are superimposed. Thus the appearances become self-opposed; the *eíde* save at once the purity of being

and the alloy of becoming. "What wonder?" says young Socrates dismissively of the Parmenidean problem with multiplicity
(*Parmenides* 129 b); it is the dismissive triumph of those who
have resolved another's perplexity. An older Socrates will say
that philosophy begins in wonder, for his solution, that there
are several and diverse beings, of course poses new problems,
and wonder never ceases. The most telling of these problems is
that each being is also a non-being—at least it is a *not*-being; it
is *not* what the other beings are; thus Zeno's problem with the
self-opposition of the world of appearance has merely been
raised into the realm of Being. A few weeks before the end of
his life Socrates is present at a great moment in the course of philosophy, when a visitor from Parmenides' country presents, by
way of resolving this higher problem, a momentous elaboration
of Socrates' supposition which, while turning it almost irrevo-
cably into a theory, advances it greatly. For if Socrates had
shown how we can come to terms with the self-opposition of the
world of appearance, the visitor will show how we can account
for false and fraudulent speech, and even for spurious being.

The Stranger's bold solution to the problem of negativity is
this: All the *eíde* are beings, and that is taken to mean that they
all take part in Being itself; they belong to a highest *eídos,* the
eídos Being. The Stranger boldly claims that there is also another previously unheard-of *eídos* that ranges in a peculiar way
through all the *eíde.* It is indeed Not-being, but Not-being rightly
understood, understood as a being (*Sophist* 258 c). He calls it
the *Other.* The *eídos* of the Other runs through all beings and
makes them other than each other—not what the other is. By
being scattered through all Being, it is the cause of its pervasive
negations, distinctions, and differences. It is a wonderful principle that relates by opposition and unifies by diversity, for since
all have otherness in common, their very community makes them
different. It makes all beings confront each other. It is the very
eídos of relativity. It is not a new name for Nonbeing that the
Stranger contributes but a new view of the world as articulated

and bonded through difference. It is a world in which the fact that we take one thing for another and speak falsely, as we surely do, is accounted for (see pp. 291, 302).

The Stranger also mentions in passing another principle, evidently not itself an *eídos* among *eíde,* but comprehending, surpassing, and beyond all Being. He calls it the *Same (Sophist* 254 e) in antithesis to the Other. It is that which gives the *eídos* of Being its very own nature, and from it all the beings derive their steadfast abiding in themselves, their being what they are through and through; the Same gives the *eíde* their self-sameness. It is the culminating principle. Depending on how it is approached, it is also called the Good, because it gives beings their vividness and fittingness (*Republic* 509 a), and in Plato's "Unwritten Teaching"—recall that he declined to write down the most central things—it seems to have been called the One, because it is the first and final totality. Socrates speaks of it explicitly, though in metaphor, only once, likening it to the sun because it gives the *eíde* their luminous sightlikeness (509 b; p. 169).

Aristotle told a story of Plato's famous lecture on the Good, which he gave at his school, the Academy. People came in droves, expecting to hear about something fascinating and useful to themselves, perhaps about health or wealth or power. But it was all about arithmetic and how the *eíde* are a certain kind of number, ending up with the just-mentioned revelation that the Good is the One. So they got disgusted and drifted off (Aristoxenus, *Elements of Harmony* II 30). Mr. Klein used to add—as if he had been there—that only one person stayed, comprehending and critical. That was Aristotle himself.

What Plato spoke about then was what is called dialectic in the last and strongest sense, thinking by and through the *eíde* (*Republic* 511 c, 532), attending to their grouping, mingling, hierarchy, and "intertwining" (*symploké, Sophist* 240 c). Such dialectic, the ultimate use of the *lógos* and the philosophical activity proper, appears in the dialogues but once, namely in the

Sophist, and scholars have not often succeeded in recovering it. I should say that there is a chapter in Mr. Klein's book on Greek mathematics which engages in true dialectic and tells how the *eídos* Being can be understood as the number *Two.*[11]

8   ORIGINAL AND IMAGE

There is one greatest, almost overwhelming perplexity about the *eíde* that Socrates knows about from the very beginning (*Parmenides* 131 c). How can an *eídos* do the very business for which it is submitted to us? Is not the *eídos* unit,

> being each one and ever the same and receptive of neither becoming nor destruction, still steadfastly the same? And thereafter, must it not be posited either as scattered and having become many in the things that are becoming or as yet whole but separate from itself, which would seem to be the most impossible of all—that one and the same thing should be in one and many (*Philebus* 15 b)?

Then how *can* the *eídos* be the source of the appearances around us, how can it have truck with what is always changing and multiple? This question can be called the "lower participation problem," since it deals not with the community the *eíde* have with each other but with that which is below them. It is the question closest to us: How do we understand the working relations which the *eíde*—once we suppose them to *be*—have to the variety, the passages, and the contradictions of our world of appearance whose Being they are and for which they are responsible?

Socrates uses a number of terms to name this relation. He speaks of the "partaking," the "participation" (*méthexis, Phaedo* 100–102) of the appearances in the *eídos,* but, of course, he does not mean a partaking as when people take up a part of an awning they sit under (*Parmenides* 131 b). He speaks of a *community* of the *eídos* with the appearances, of their being *named* after it, of the *presence* of the *eídos* in them (e.g., *Phaedo* 100 c, d, 103 b). These terms signify that the two realms are strongly related, but they do not reveal what the appearances can have in common with beings or why they merit being named *after* them or how the beings can be *with* them.

But Socrates does use one group of words that tell more. He speaks of participation through similarity, likeness, imaging, imitation (*Phaedrus* 250 a, *Phaedo* 74 e, *Timaeus* 39 e, and above all *Republic* 510 b).

That our world should stand to the realm of *eíde* as copy to exemplar (*Parmenides* 132 d, *Timaeus* 48 e) has a certain high plausibility. It conveys a falling off from the fullness of being, an imitative, derivative mode. It suggests that one original *eídos* will have many image-appearances and that each such appearance cannot to stand free, but will be, like any image, attached to some material medium (*Timaeus* 52 c). It indicates how every appearance could be doubly dependent, on the *eídos* for being *visible,* and on our sight for being *seen.* If the appearances are somehow mere images of the *eíde,* their inferiority, multiplicity, materiality, and sensuality become comprehensible—and so does the fact of their inescapably beguiling looks.

Yet there are apparently devastating difficulties with this primordial imitation, of which the one most open to formal attack is this: If the *eídos* is what is originally beautiful, and beautiful things are copies, and if the likeness of copies to their originals comes from their sharing the same quality, then both have the quality of being beautiful. Then the *eídos* of beauty is beautiful, as the *eídos* of justice is just, and Socrates does not scruple to say exactly that (*Protagoras* 330 c, *Symposium* 210 c). But that way of speaking—that beauty is beautiful—is an insupportable redundancy, called "self-predication." Furthermore, if the function of the *eídos* is to account for the fact that anything is beautiful, then another *eídos* beyond will have to be posited to account for the fact that the *eídos* itself has been said to be beautiful. Aristotle calls this dilemma the "Third Man," because behind the man and the man-like *eídos* of mankind there must appear a third-man-*eídos* (*Metaphysics* 990 b).

But in truth, these terrible perplexities, whose various versions and issues Socrates knows about (*Parmenides* 132 d, *Republic* 597 c), miss the point. When Socrates so often chooses to employ the nominalized adjective "the beautiful" rather than the noun of quality "beauty," he is not simply misled by the fact that in Greek, as in English, the former phrase sounds as if it meant a beautiful *thing*, since it is an adjective turned into a substantive. When he speaks that way he means to make us face the self-same "suchness" of the *eídos*, to divert our desire from beautiful things to a better but invisible beauty, to convey its greater desirability, to persuade us to "look to" it. The turns of speech that call the *eídos* verily beautiful, through and through beautiful, *the* beautiful itself, are, I think, philosophical rhetoric. They try to lever us into new ways of being enchanted, enchanted not by that which appears as beautiful but by the very condition of our seeing and saying that it is beautiful. The *eídos* beauty is certainly not ugly, but no more is it adjectivally beautiful; it is rather such as to be itself the sole source of the attributes in others. The word "beautiful" does not *describe* this suchness, but it *reaches* for it.

How then can beautiful things be images of beauty if it is not, as seems indeed to be impossible, by likeness in the sense of sameness of quality? It is because imaging is the deepest capability of Being, the accompaniment of the pervasive otherness that haunts it, the Nonbeing that dogs every being. Each being confronts another as its other, and its own otherness is mirrored in the others.

For the image nature of an image is not really caught when we point out similarities between it and its original, say of conformation and color. The closest we can come to articulating the nature of an image is to say that an image is, in truth, not what it images, and then again it somehow is. For example, we

are apt to say of a little statue of Socrates looking like a pot-
bellied satyr, "That's Socrates," while we know it is not. We mean
that he is in some sense present in the clay—"re-presented," but
not in truth, since an image is that which *in its very nature* is *not*
what it *is*. It is an interweaving of Being and Nonbeing (*Sophist*
240 c).

Among the beings, the *eíde*, each is self-same and truly what
it is, and also other than and not what the others are; its not-
being is with respect to the other beings; the interweaving is not
a mingling. But Becoming, Socrates explains, is an *amalgam* of
Being and Nonbeing (*Republic* 477 a). The appearances mingle
within themselves such non-being and being as those great *eíde*
lend them; they have neither steady self-sameness nor fixed difference, and yet they are somewhat enduring and sometimes distinct. They are *in their very nature* not what they are. In that
sense they might well be called images of being. So here is a
formal way of conceiving the claim that appearance images
the *eídos:* Appearance is a fused incorporation of Being and
Nonbeing. But it must be said that it in no wise solves our greatest problem: how the *eídos* drops down from the context of Being to become entangled with Nonbeing in a new and world-
making way—how there can be an *eídos* incarnate (*Phaedrus*
251 a).

Socrates ascribes to us an initial power—most startling to see
in children—of image-recognition (*eikasía, Republic* 511 e), by
which we recognize at once the fact of a counterfeit and the original lurking in the imitation (510 b, p. 173). In its developed
form it is a sense for what Jacob Klein once called the "duplicity of Being," and it provides the initial, the youngest impulse
of philosophy.

I have said what I think Plato's Socrates thought, but I do not
want this lecture to be what is, wonderfully, called an "academic" exercise, so I must now say what *I* think. But before I
do that, let me make mention one last time of the name of Jacob

Klein, to whom this lecture is most surely dedicated in loving memory and who—so good a teacher was he—taught me nothing but what I could straightway recognize as my own.

Socrates himself says of the *eíde* that they have become buzzwords (*Phaedo* 100 b); there are even people known, a little absurdly, as "the friends of the *eíde*" (*Sophist* 248 a). That kind of thing comes from being drawn and fascinated by Socrates' sights without having ourselves seen them. What is more, Plato does not reveal, indeed conceals, in the dialogues the answer to the question: Did Socrates himself view the *eíde*? Did anyone ever? In short, *are* there *accessible eíde*?

Therefore our attention is naturally turned to the Socrates through whom we hear of these matters and to his trustworthiness. And I find the man who is commemorated in the dialogues trustworthy beyond all others. I trust his slyness and his simplicity, his sobriety and his enthusiasm, his playfulness and his steadfastness, his eros and his dignity. Yet it is not mainly his character that I trust, but his presuppositions, and I think that they must have formed him more than he did them.

I make Socrates' presuppositions out to be these: that there is that in human life which stands out; that there are heights and there is a way to them, an ascent; that what is desirable is at a distance, by itself and in itself, and therefore sightlike and yet invisible, and that there must be a means for reaching it; that this mediating power is speech, which first arouses that irritably articulate wonder at common things which is called a philosophical question; and first and last, that where there is a question, an answer has already been at work, and it is our human task to recollect it.

These presuppositions are not at all obvious or necessary. Our specific human work does not have to be thought of as arising from enthusiasm about the extraordinary or marveling at the common, as Socrates says philosophy does (*Theaetetus* 155 d). It can come from a cool, sober sense that the ways of the world should be exposed and explained, its myths dismantled and its depths made plane; that not what is best but what is individual, not what is common but what is ordinary, should preoccupy our efforts; that we should not view but master, not play but work, not suppose but certify, not ask but determine, not long desirously but draw limits. I am describing the self-controlled maturing of philosophy that is responsible for all that we call modernity. I do not think for a moment that we should play truant from this severe and powerful school. But I do think that Socrates' suppositions are that beginning which can be forgotten but never superseded.

14

"TEACHING PLATO" TO UNDERGRADUATES

In my experience, spirited young students are apt to be leery of Socrates both for his trick-laden dialectic and for his sense-denigrating preachments. Every once in a while, it is true, a student is immediately captivated by arguments that will show themselves, on examination, to be more subtle than sophistical and by a view of the world that turns out, after all, to give its due to the life of the senses, be it sensory or sensual. Such a student is not in need of teaching but of companionably common inquiry. I am thinking here more of those sturdily if crudely resistant students who just don't like the needling old bully with his totalitarian politics, his yes-man partners and his indifference to current moral mantras. If their teacher feels about the same way, the class will unprofitably expend itself in the discovery of Socrates' semantic chicaneries, self-contradictions, paradoxes, and other paralogisms. Such a teacher might be urged to adopt that intellectual version of a Christian virtue, the textual principle of charity. It requires that a text should be given its best chance to make sense. But in general, it seems to me good to stay away from teaching what you are hell-bent on despising.

Therefore the preliminary notions about teaching Platonic dialogues I'll set out here presuppose a teacher who is somewhat well inclined toward Socrates while appreciative of the resistance felt by independent young students. This would indeed be an element of a hopeful beginning. So also would be a willingness to relinquish the idea of "teaching Plato"—an impossibility on several counts, set out below. Here, then, ranged under seven headings, are some thoughts that might help in reading Platonic writings with students new to them.

1 SOCRATIC CONVERSATIONS   As I recall seminars about Platonic dialogues, it seems to me a good sign when students don't think of themselves as "reading Plato" but as engaging with Socrates. In almost all the dialogues usually read with undergraduates, Socrates is the guiding partner of the conversation, and in those in which he is only a silent presence, like the *Sophist* and the *Timaeus,* he is the instigator or the occasion for the conversation. By making Socrates their opponent students show that they aren't supposing themselves to be studying Platonic doctrine but that they are involved in a Socratic inquiry. After they've read quite a few dialogues they might try, speculatively, to distinguish Platonic elements behind the Socratic presence. But in the beginning it is task enough to follow Socrates by joining in his conversation rather than to learn Platonic doctrines torn from their roots in a live inquiry.

2 DIALOGUE   Socrates is usually found in a dialogue with one person; that is to say, he converses with people seriatim, not in a free-for-all. Meanwhile the others—they might range in age from boys younger than American undergraduates to old men—sit and listen; some will come forward to be engaged by Socrates, some are silently, but, as the dialogues intimate, attentively just present. Are these the only listeners and interlocutors? Sometimes a student, fed up with the long parade of "Certainly's," "What else's," "Of course's," produced by Socrates' all-too-amenable partners, will burst out to this effect: "Don't they see that he's misleading them?" "Well," a teacher might say, "he didn't fool you, did he?" And then a light dawns: Socrates' most welcome partner is the responsive reader, this student here and now, one of us who belong to those "tribes of barbarians" to whom Socrates bequeaths his arguments, his *lógoi*, on his last day (*Phaedo* 78 a).

3   DRAMATIS PERSONAE   Dialogues are, Aristotle intimates (*Poetics* 1447 a 10), akin to mimes, those sometimes farcical prose-plays about common life. Thus they imitate the utterances of "characters" who have not the large-gauge fatedness of tragic figures but rather the humanly complex character of ordinary people. Students are welcome to clue out what these characters are from what the persons in the drama say, and then, conversely, to interpret what they say—and what Socrates talks about with them—in the light of their characters. It is, I think, a fine imaginative exercise, inviting careful attention to the dialogue, to figure out what Socrates really thinks of his partners. Some of them, as we know from outside sources, went spectacularly to the bad later on: Meno (portrayed as a villain by Xenophon in his *Anabasis*), Critias (the leader of "The Thirty," Athens's worst tyranny), Alcibiades (whose ready treasons are recounted by Thucydides). While nothing is more disruptive to involvement in the dialogues than canned background and factoid biography, it seems to me sometimes permissible to show students these ancient accounts, so that they can meditate on this question: Do the seeds of practical corruption appear in philosophical discussion? Can Meno's unteachableness in the *Meno*, Critias's Atlantean visions in the *Critias*, and Alcibiades' impetuous invasion in the *Symposium* be read as warnings and judgments? Can we tell who a human being is by how they join in a Socratic inquiry?

But generally background information is a conversation stopper and the death of dialogue. There is a principle of trust that great books desire us to adopt. It says that if the author thinks we need to know something he'll tell us. Anyhow, students should learn—indeed it comes easily to them—either to tolerate occasional information gaps or to get discreetly footnoted texts.

4 NARRATIVE PERSONS I began by inveighing against the notion of "teaching Plato." Plato himself seems to do his best to forestall it; he disappears far behind his work. The *Theaetetus,* for example, is read by the servant of one Eucleides to his friend Terpsion from a scroll in which Eucleides himself has recorded a past conversation told him by Socrates. What Eucleides has done is to turn Socrates' account, which was evidently in indirect discourse, into a mime, a little drama. In the light of what Socrates says in the *Republic* (393), that narrative in indirect discourse is more responsible than dramatic miming (since in direct discourse the narrator always speaks in his own voice rather than imitating someone else's speech), Eucleides' proceeding is very curious: As Plato is somewhere behind the persons of the drama, in a place not easily pinpointed, so Socrates is not present on the scene in which his words are read as if he were in fact speaking them. I am not saying that our students should be expected to figure that out completely—I haven't. But they should be allowed to discover some of the narrative subtlety of the dialogues, which is, I think, intended partly to keep us all from inelastic formulations and from premature attributions of doctrine.

5 INQUIRY Socrates says in the *Apology* (33 a) that it is false that he ever was anyone's teacher. In fact he mostly asks questions, and with these questions he often undoes what opinions the acknowledged educators have produced. Living through a Socratic dialogue ought therefore to be an education in living with disequilibrium and inconclusiveness, of bearing up under the sting of the gadfly Socrates (*Apology* 30 e). Yet it goes against a dutiful professor's grain to allow students to leave class knowing less than when they came, and they may certainly resent it. Here is the moment of truth for both: Is this class a place where products of previously-owned knowledge are distributed under warranty to satisfied customers, or is it a place where the soul—intellect and spirit—is touched?

But, of course, Socrates' conversations are only in part forceful refutations of common opinions followed by all too tentative replacements. There is a lot of definiteness in Socrates, and some of it is doctrinal. The most assertive Socratic "dialogue" is actually a speech, Socrates' *Defense,* the only piece into which Plato inscribes his own, albeit silent, presence. (Students might, incidentally, be told that the Greek word *apología* has nothing apologetic about it.) I would not put Socrates' passionate self-justification first on the list of dialogues to be read. It is an explicit counterargument to perennial claims that philosophy is a craft like any other and may be divorced from the morality of the practitioner. Therefore, to appreciate both the charges for which the Athenian court executed Socrates and his defiant defense, students should have some prior experience of actual Socratic philosophizing.

Almost all dialogues include long dialectical sequences, inquiries conducted by means of question and answer with a twofold aim: to discover whether Socrates' interlocutor knows what he is talking about and to discover something true about the issue at hand. In other words, this dialectic usually reveals at once the partner's ignorance and establishes a platform for launching the search for positive truth.

It seems to me good to direct students to think themselves into the interlocutor's mind: to determine whether the answers come attentively or carelessly, are spontaneously or grudgingly given, are the result of free consideration or of sophistic affectation. Thus, students might be asked to reflect on what they themselves mean by their "yes" and their "no." They will, of course, also wonder what turn Socrates' partner missed and why, and what deeper purpose there might be behind Socrates' "eristic," his debater's skill. It goes without saying that they are free to recoil from the enterprise. In that case they should be encouraged to say very clearly what repels them, so that they will be examining their rejection of Socrates' examined life.

What is the teacher's positive part in all this? I think it is to display not dead but live seriousness, one sign of which is pedagogic playfulness. Accordingly, the teacher seems to me to have a double task. One is to keep the class elastically tethered to the text. That requires bringing alive the above-mentioned hermeneutic principle of charity: It is practically impossible to stick with a text one cannot even pretend to appreciate. The other task is to demonstrate, to act out, the inquiry as an extra-textual concern, to give the question independent life by finding phrasings and examples that go to students' souls—and funny bones; a class that does not, now and then, break up in laughter cannot be reading Socratic dialogues. In the course of such a class, the students, who had first learned that *they* were the truly intended participants in a Socratic dialogue, might now find that Socrates and his youngsters are in turn the watchful bystanders and on occasion the apt contributors to *their* discussion, *their* inquiry. It hardly needs saying that lecturing to a class on these readings is a plain perversion of their spirit.

6 TEACHINGS Socrates' activity in his dialogues is neither merely corrosive of common opinion nor just a never-to-be-completed inquiry into the ultimately unknowable. There are, as I suggested, lots of doctrines in the dialogues, plenty of positive claims. Although a studious teacher might cobble these together into a system, it would be, to my mind, premature—and a preemption of the Neoplatonists' achievement—to weld Socratic hypotheses and Academic doctrine into a systematic whole for inexperienced students. When reading the dialogues with young students it is, I think, better to leave these positive opinions, these necessary hypotheses, *in situ,* in their "zetetic" context, that is to say, enmeshed in a living search.

There seem to be two kinds of direct teachings in the dialogues. One advocates the philosophic way of life and details the virtues of those who follow it: faith that an inquiry leading to substantial, non-factual knowledge is possible; the understanding that this inquiry requires a desire to know that is different from common curiosity; fearlessness in that pursuit even onto a contempt of death; concern amounting to love for one's own political community and especially for its young; eventual rejection of the senses either as sources of pleasure or of information.

I can't imagine that students aren't best off meeting these virtues in their talking embodiment and themselves talking about them, even imagining themselves as responding directly *to* Socrates. For example, they might ask him: "What do you mean when you say that 'the unexamined life is not livable for human beings'? [*Apology* 38 a]. Why aren't we better of living naturally, instinctively?"

The other kind of doctrine is what after Aristotle we will come to call metaphysical, perhaps even epistemological. Every student of classical philosophy knows that Socrates believed a number of paradoxes and philosophemes: Virtue is knowledge. Philosophers practice death. The soul is immortal. Learning is an activity of introspection. Being is its proper object. There are beings, items of Being, called forms or kinds that are responsible for our ability to collect many appearances under one word. The forms are also responsible for the existence of this earthly multitude of sensory appearances, which are to be regarded as unreal and deceptive.

Well, the trouble with culling these claims from the dialogues is that it is with them just as it is with Socratic politics: If you peer at his public philosophy with the microscope of a doctrine-collector, it looks as if Socrates were an ardent anti-democrat, albeit one with a hilariously acute insider's eye for democracy's foibles, as shown in the *Republic* (562–3). But if you take a longer view it turns out that he thinks his own activity of city-founding finds its natural home in a democracy. That's what he says, again, in the *Republic* (557 d), and that's where that mother of all political dialogues takes place—in the stronghold of Athens' democracy, its harbor city.

And so it is with the metaphysical axioms. They all transform under a larger view, and students ought to have the opportunity to discover that mutation, even as they go to town on them. Take one example, a principal stumbling block for lusty youth: Socrates' rejection of the senses. Well, it turns out that philosophy, the "love of wisdom," has its affective beginning in erotic attraction, the most passionate of loves (*Phaedrus* 251 a), and its cognitive start in the recognition of images, the most apparitional of appearances (*Republic* 510); the "love" part of philo-sophy is thus sensual and the "wisdom" part is sensory in its individual human origin. And thus or similarly are all the paradoxes qualified. Students can be gotten to delight in the discovery of such subtleties if their attention is opportunely drawn to them. Opportunely—that implies that there must be plenty of time, time to bumble about, to miss the point, to come back to it on a new route. Compacting knowledge to save time is to philosophizing as turning the oven a hundred degrees too high for quicker results is to cake-baking: cinders with a raw center.

7 TALES Most of the dialogues undergraduates are likely to be reading have a climactic myth, a great visionary tale, a brilliant word-picture as their center or their finale. Students should, of course, be allowed to speculate about the meaning of each myth, but they should also be asked how it complements Socrates' dialectic efforts in each dialogue. Perhaps they will discover that each dialogue is, as it seems to me, a distinct conversational universe. In any case, they might wonder why a dialogue is in one respect like a geometry text: There are words and there are pictures. What is it that the verbal vision can do that the dialectical passages can't? Why are the myths always about the cosmic vault above or the underworld below? Such questions

lead students at one and the same time to join Socrates' inquiry *and* to read Plato's dialogues.

To conclude, let me put succinctly my notions about the way a teacher should read Plato with young students: Don't lecture; don't retail doctrines; forget a time-efficient agenda. Give some discreet direction toward the subtleties of the text, but mostly ask questions inducing students to participate in the dialogue. And be in it with them.

NOTES

1   INTRODUCTION TO THE PHAEDO

1. Ariadne, the Minotaur's half-sister, fell in love with Theseus but was left stranded by him on the way home.

2. In addressing the difficulty raised by Cebes, Socrates suggests that they "come to close quarters in Homeric style." Throughout what follows we must recall that, although Socrates now fights ostensibly for the deathlessness of the soul (which has been threatened by the images of lyre and weaver), more importantly he fights for the renewed trust in the guiding power of philosophic arguments or *lógoi*. The interlude with "Phaedo himself," in other words, has in effect displaced the fear of the soul's death with the fear that *all* arguments "die" in the end.

The epic, Homeric stature of what Socrates undertakes in the dialogue is not only signalled in the intimation that the stay-at-home Socrates has something in common with the widely travelled Odysseus, who "knew the mind" of many men, fought to save his comrades and descended into Hades. It is also indicated in the Homeric allusion of the very first and the very last words of the *Phaedo*. When Echecrates opens with the words "You yourself, Phaedo—were you present on that day . . . or did you hear from somebody else?" he is virtually quoting the question Odysseus is asked before he tells of his wanderings: "Were you yourself present or did you hear it from somebody else?" (*Odyssey* VIII 491). And Phaedo's final summation of Socrates, that he was "the best and, yes, the most thoughtful and the most just" of all men they have met, echoes what is said of old Nestor, that "he knew justice and thought beyond all others" (*Odyssey* III 244).

3. We translate Phaedo's description of the last moment differently from others. The sense usually rendered is that when the attendant uncovered Soc-

rates, his eyes were fixed, and when Crito saw this he closed his mouth and eyes. The first word for eyes, *ómmata,* also means visage or countenance; the second one, *ophthalmoí,* means just the eyes. Moreover, the verb is active: It is Socrates who fixes, or better, composes his own features. Xenophon, in his *Defense of Socrates,* says that when Socrates had been condemned to death, "he went off blithe in countenance, demeanor and gait" (27). So not: "his eyes were fixed," but: "he'd composed his countenance."

There is a terrible case that seems almost the counterpart of Socrates' last moments: In Dostoevsky's *Demons,* a man called Kirillov believes that he can prove his ultimate freedom by willfully killing himself, but in the minutes before his self-annihilation he is seen to turn into a bellowing terrified beast, whose death disproves the claims of his life.

3   THE OFFENSE OF SOCRATES: **APOLOGY**

1. John Burnet, ed., *Plato's Euthyphro, Apology of Socrates and Crito* (Oxford: Clarendon Press, 1924). I would like here to draw attention to a very fine treatment by Thomas G. West, *Plato's Defense of Socrates* (Ithaca: Cornell University Press, 1979).

2. Herbert Spiegelberg, ed., *The Socratic Enigma, A Collection of Testimonies Through Twenty-Four Centuries.* (Indianapolis: Bobbs-Merrill, The Library of Liberal Arts, 1964), 99, 112, 243, 262, 203, 278.

3. Helmut James von Moltke, *Briefe* (Berlin: Henssel Verlag, 1971), 63.

4. *Socratic Enigma,* 43, 66, 187, 228, 285; Hegel, *Philosophy of Religion,* Part Three, C II 3.

5. William Roper and Nicholas Harpsfield, *Lives of Saint Thomas More* (London: Everyman Library, 1963), 175.

6. Burnet, 103.

7. E. Seymer Thompson, ed., *The Meno of Plato* (Cambridge, Eng.: W. Heffer and Sons, 1961), xxiv.

8. An immediate occasion for this essay was the textbook controversy of 1974 in Kanawha County, West Virginia. It arose from a clash between parents whose moral and religious sensibilities were offended by some of the books assigned to their children in the public schools, and educators in whose judgment such reading was necessary for the children's intellectual development.

9. Søren Kierkegaard, *The Concept of Irony, With Constant Reference to Socrates* (London: Collins, 1966), 221; cf. *Socratic Enigma,* 291.

6   THE MUSIC OF THE **REPUBLIC**

1. *Plato's Republic,* ed. B. Jowett and L. Campbell (Oxford: Clarendon Press, 1894), III, p. 4; *The Republic of Plato,* ed. J. Adams, 2nd edition (Cambridge 1963), I, p. 1. For prosography and dialogic dates see Debra Nails, *The People of Plato* (Indianapolis: Hackett Publishing, 2002).

2. Liddell and Scott, *Greek Lexicon,* see *Peiraieus.* It is, however, certainly permissible to omit the article, cf. 439 e 7.

3. Pauly-Wissowa, *Real-Encyclopaedie der klassischen Altertumswissenschaft* (Stuttgart 1937) XIX, I, p. 78.

4. Ibid., III, I; see "Bendis," 269. The torch race mentioned may be accounted for by the fact that Thracian Hecate had the epithet *Phosphorus,* Lightbearer.

5. Adams, *op. cit.,* I, p. 5.

6. Jowett, *op. cit.,* II, pp. 2, 7, and 79, on 368 a 3.

7. Also *Gorgias* 461a, 466c; *Phaedo* 98e; *Phaedrus* 228b. The scholiast to *Wasps* 83 says that Sosias is imitating Socrates' oath "By the Dog"; *Aristophanis Comoediae,* ed. Dindorf (Oxford 1837) III, 460; cf. *Plato: Gorgias,* ed. Dodds (Oxford: Clarendon Press, 1959), 262; also Lucian, *Philosophies for Sale* 16, who connects Socrates' dog with Anubis, Sirius, and Cerberus.

8. Pauly-Wissowa, *Suppl.* III, see "Heracles," pp. 1007 ff., 1018 ff., 1077 ff.; also Aristophanes, *Frogs* 108.

9. See *Phaedrus* 267 c 9, and Aristotle, *Rhetoric* 1400 b 19, on Thrasymachus's notorious violence.

10. Socrates, having completed the refutation of Thrasymachus, begins anew and in a new mode: "Socrates no longer comes forward with questions in the character of a man who is ignorant . . . , but as one who has already found what he seeks." *Schleiermacher's Introductions to the Dialogues of Plato,* trans. W. Dobson (Cambridge: J & J.J. Deighton, 1836), 356.

11. Aristophanes actually compares Socrates to Odysseus, another famous visitor to Hades. But in the *Republic* the comparison is, if suggested at all, made mildly to discredit Odysseus. For the Myth of Er is offered as an improvement over Odysseus's supposedly boring and false "tales of Alcinous," that is, as a new "Descent to the Underworld," a *Nekyia* (614 b 1, see scholia; cf. also Kierkegaard, *Concept of Irony* 130, note). Furthermore, his soul, disenchanted with ambition, chooses the perfectly private most un-Socratic life (620 c 6).

12. E.g., Plutarch, *Against Colotes,* 1126 c-d.

13. Compare Hippolytus's wish that human generation could be circumvented and children's seed could be temple treasure to be bought for "gold, silver, or a weight of brass" (Euripides, *Hippolytus* 621).

14. The old saying is used by Socrates in a similar way in the *Apology* (34 d 5). He too, he says, quoting Homer, has a family and is not sprung "from oak or rock," that is, he too has a private genesis. The original meaning of the phrase, which occurs in the *Odyssey* (XIX 163), was evidently no longer known to the scholiast on 544 d 8.

15. See Adams *op. cit.,* I, pp. 345 ff.

16. See F. M. Cornford, *Plato's Cosmology* (London: K.Paul, Trench, Trubner, 1937), 4–5. For a totally different point of view and concomitantly different years for the dramatic date of the *Republic,* see A. E. Taylor, *A Commentary on Plato's Timaeus* (Oxford: Clarendon Press, 1928), 15–16, 45.

17. A similar case is found in Xenophon's *Cyropaedia* and is expressed in the apparent lack of a match between the title, which seems to promise an account of Cyrus's upbringing by the Persians (I, ii, 2), and the content, which turns out to be instead the education Cyrus gave the Persians. This is because Cyrus, whose name means "Lord" in Greek, is at once the beneficiary and the source of Persian customs; *Cyropaedia* therefore means "The Lord's Education" both in the objective and the subjective sense of the genitive.

18. Cratinus, from a lost play, *The Thracian Women*. The cult of Bendis evidently was a good subject for comedy; it seems to have been the subject of Aristophanes' lost *Lemnian Women*.

19. See R. Hackforth, *Plato's Phaedrus* (New York: Library of Liberal Arts, 1952), 118. Plato founded a shrine to the Muses in the Academy (Diogenes Laertius, IV 1, cf. III, 25).

20. An otherwise silly ancient story to the effect that the whole *Republic* was stolen from the writings of Protagoras (Diels, *Fragmente der Vorsokratiker,* Berlin: Weidmannische Verlagsbuchhandlung, 1954, II, p. 265) seems at the least to indicate that on matters political there were points of apparent similarity, probably equally shocking to sober citizens, between Socrates and the sophist.

21. Glaucon's Gyges story is a witty transformation of Herodotus's version. In the latter, what is right and lawful is for every man to keep private things private or "to scan his own" (I, 8, 16); this barbarian counterpart of justice, a sense of shame, is tacitly transformed into the definition of what is just in Greek cities, namely "to do one's own," that is, to find and hold one's political place. Furthermore the main fact about Gyges' crime in Herodotus, that he is forced to do injustice precisely because he is *seen* in the act imposed on him by the king, is inverted in Glaucon's story, where by reason of the invisibility afforded by his ring Gyges becomes a criminal voluntarily and with impunity.

22. Note that in this context Socrates first acknowledges the natural world as the setting and source of human nature. The character of peoples is, as in Herodotean ethnology, dependent on the clime under which they live: Thracians, Scythians, and northerners in general are lovers of honor, Phoenicians and Egyptians are lovers of money, and the Hellenes *in the middle* are lovers of knowledge (435 e; cf. *Timaeus* 24 c; *Epinomis* 987 d). Thus even in the geographic place philosophy is at the center.

23. See Adams *op. cit.*, I, p. 144, note on 435 b.

24. See *Charmides* 164 d 5 for Critias's version of the Delphic background of this saying (p. 77).

25. See J. Klein, *A Commentary on Plato's Meno* (Chapel Hill: U.N.C. Press, 1965), 112–15.

26. See *Meno* 80 c, *The Meno of Plato,* ed. E. S. Thompson (Cambridge: Heffer and Sons, 1961), 112.

27. Throughout the dialogue Socrates' reiteration of themes, such as the "oft-told" tale of the One and the Many, as well as the recapitulations he often elicits from Glaucon, have the effect of making Glaucon "recollect" from time to time the springs and the course of the argument (e.g., 507 a 7, 522 b 1, 544 b 4). This is, obviously, not genuine Socratic recollection (see above, IV E 4 d) but an exercise of that power of memory which philosophers must possess as part of their natural endowment (535 c 1). Such memory-recollection (*anámnesis*) was especially cultivated by the Pythagoreans: "A Pythagorean man does not arise from his bed before he has recollected what happened yesterday. And he performs the recollections in this way. He tries to recover by means of *diánoia* what he first said or heard . . ." (Iamblichus, *Life of Pythagoras* 163, 20). The passage goes on to describe the discipline of completely recalling the *lógoi* and *érga* of the previous day, a discipline that was considered

part of the training needed for the acquisition of knowledge. It is a technique Socrates himself had mastered, for he remembers the whole dialogue.

28. The most important ancient reports of the "Unwritten Teachings" are conveniently collected in K. Gaiser, *Platons ungeschriebene Lehre* (Stuttgart: E. Klett, 1963), 445 ff. See also J. N. Findlay, *Plato, the Written and Unwritten Doctrines* (New York: Humanities Press, 1974).

29. Klein, *op. cit.*, 115–25, "The Dianoetic Extension of *Eikasía.*"

30. The Euclidean proof in (anachronistic) algebraic notation is:

Let the line be cut such that

$$\frac{a+b}{c+d} = \frac{a}{b} = \frac{c}{d}$$

Then $\dfrac{a+b}{c} = \dfrac{c+d}{d}$ (Euclid V 16, by alternation).

But also $\dfrac{a+b}{b} = \dfrac{c+d}{d}$ (Euclid V 11, by composition).

Therefore $b = c$.

31. Cf. Klein, *ibid.*, 191–99 on the "solidity" of the soul in the dialogues. For further sources on the "dimensional soul" see Gaiser, *op. cit. (supra,* N. 28), 545 ff.

32. See O. Toeplitz, "Mathematik und Ideenlehre bei Platon," *Zur Geschichte der griechischen Mathematik* (Darmstadt 1965), 59.

33. The objects on the Divided Line are only twice referred to in terms of *mímesis* (510 b 4 and 532 a 2, cf. 507 c 6).

34. In the *Philebus,* the Good as a human good comes to Socrates as a dreamlike reminiscence of a "third thing," other than and above both pleasure and human wisdom (20 b 8), that is, it is a "one" above the other "two." It has three characteristics: It is "perfect," "adequate," and "choiceworthy" (20 d); its power, again, cannot be "caught" in one idea but must be captured in three: beauty, symmetry, and truth (65 a 1); their relation is not unlike that of the three effects of the power of the Good, namely world, knowledge, and being, in the *Republic.* Eudemus (cited by Gaiser, *op. cit.* 480, note) says that Plato distinguished three ways the Good functions: as productive, as end, and as exemplary cause; these again correspond roughly to the Good as father, as end of learning, and as pattern of being. The whole complex is caught in a German word-play: the Good is the *Ursprung* (origin), that is, the *Ursache* (cause) of all *Sachen* and their *Sachheit* (M. Heidegger, *Platons Lehre von der Wahrheit* [Bern 1954], 40).

35. Gaiser, *op. cit.*, 531; see F. Cornford, *Plato and Parmenides* (New York: Liberal Arts Press, 1957), 3–11 for further references. For one playful allusion to the Indefinite Dyad in the Platonic dialogues themselves see J. Klein, "A Note on Plato's *Parmenides,*" in *Lectures and Essays,* ed. R. Williamson and E. Zuckerman (Annapolis: St. John's College Press, 1985), 285–88. Further terms used of the Dyad in *Metaphysics* 989 b 19 ff. are: material, the great and small, similar to the female, responsible for evil.

The identification of the *arché* Indeterminate Dyad, with the *eídos* Other does not, it must be said, work altogether for the *Sophist*. There the Other is enfolded in Being (ch. 11) rather than naming a principle beyond, or better below, Being. The reason seems to be that the *Sophist* is concerned with the analysis of duplicity and fakery in terms of *pure* ontology, while the Indeterminate Dyad is a *quasi-material* principle that distorts as it receives the forming One. Another way to put it is that the *Sophist* regards only the participation of the forms in each other and leaves their shaping of the material world—and hence its materiality—out of account.

For Being as the eidetic Two, see J. Klein, *Greek Mathematical Thought and the Origin of Algebra*, trans. E. Brann (Cambridge, Mass: M.I.T. Press, 1968), 93. (See also Note 11 of ch. 13 herein.) The dialectical name of this or of any other eidetic number is not given explicitly in any ancient source. On the Good as the "First" and "the source which is the whole" see Klein, *Meno,* p. 123 and n. 39.

36. The *hómoia* and associated terms like *parádeigma* and *analogía*, reduced however to mere principles of classification, figure largely in the work of Speusippus, Plato's successor in the Academy. Themistius (Gaiser, *op. cit.,* 535) says that Plato spoke of *méthexis* in the *Timaeus* but called participation *homoíosis* in the "Unwritten Teachings" (*Ágrapha Dógmata*).

37. Cf. Adams *op. cit.,* II, pp. 441, 470 ff.

38. There is also a curious story about an artificial Hades that Pythagoras is said to have built—a little chamber under the earth into which he disappeared for a long time and then ascended, announcing that he had dwelt in Hades (Diogenes Laertius, VIII 41).

39. Iamblichus, *Life of Pythagoras* 165, 12; see Note 27 herein.

40. See Jowett, *op. cit.,* III, p. 326.

41. Adams, *op. cit.,* II, pp. 163 ff.

42. Diogenes Laertius remarks on Plato's special use of the word *phaúlos,* pointing out that he uses it in the two senses of "simple, honest" and "bad" (III, 63). Actually, of course, Socrates often uses it ironically to mean "the great thing that everyone else overlooks."

43. The ancient texts are collected in Gaiser, *op. cit.,* 478–508. The difficulties in using these sources to reconstruct the *Ágrapha Dógmata* are (1) that they often mention Plato and the Pythagoreans indiscriminately; the longest account (Sextus Empiricus, *Against the Mathematicians* X, 248 ff.) even attributes the "dimensional" teaching to the Pythagoreans alone; (2) that they rarely tell by whom, to whom, or with what pedagogical purpose such a scheme was proposed. Aristotle, for instance, refers to the *Timaeus* in this context (*On the Soul* 404 b 16) which should give one pause—the account there is, after all, proposed as a myth (29 d 2). Nor can the frequent references in the ancient literature to *On the Good* help here, since no one knows whether that was one public lecture or a series of lectures or a kind of seminar. In other words, it is not possible to say what Plato himself thought of "dimensional generation," whether he approved it only for certain pedagogical purposes or became himself a thoroughgoing Pythagorean. In any case, since we know that the dialogues often play on certain differences between the author himself and Socrates, it would, even if Plato's opinion were well known, still be necessary to investigate Socrates' understanding of the Pythagorean order within the dialogue itself.

The *locus classicus* for such a cosmogenic order is the *Epinomis,* a dialogue said to have been tacked on to the *Laws* by Philip of Opus (Diogenes Laertius, III 37). Its purpose was to expound that astronomical theology which was to be the wisdom of the "midnight council," the rulers of the non-philosophical city of the *Laws.* Here the cosmos arises from a continual doubling of the unit, which produces a series of terms, 1:2:4:8, such that each term duplicates the ratio that the previous term has to the unit. These duplicating *lógoi* express the relations of the dimensions of the cosmos, from the dimensionless *one,* through that doubling of the point which gives rise to the line, up to the solid that is the cube of the "linear" number *two,* that is, *eight* (990 e ff.). The duplication is to be understood as the effect of the dyadic *arché.*

44. Plutarch, in the third *Platonic Query* (1001 c ff.), in which he discusses the (undecidable) question which segment of the Divided Line, the uppermost or the lowest, ought to be the longest, attempts to conflate the opinion that "the *diánoia* is as *nous* among the mathematicals, which are as *noetá* appearing in mirrors" with the genetic dimensional theory. The difficulties into which this leads him are instructive. He first makes Plato *induce* the mathematical cosmos from the noetic principles: "He leads the *nóesis* concerned with the *eíde* out of its abstraction and separation from body, going down in the order of mathematics . . ."; next we *reduce* that cosmos by abstracting its dimensions until "we will be among the noetic ideas themselves"; and finally, the sensible world is *deduced* from these by reading the realms of the Divided Line roughly downward, as stages of dimensional growth. In this account it is entirely unclear in what way the *noetá* are the principles of mathematics on the one hand, and of the sensible world on the other, and whether the mathematicals are the work of human *nóesis* or have the *noetá* as sources.

45. A centered sphere (as opposed to Parmenides' partless, centerless sphere) seems at least to convey more of the expressible characteristics of the Whole than the usual pyramid (cf. *Sophist* 244 e). The center, which in my diagram marks the end of the dialectic ascent, is, according to Aristotle (*Physics* 265 b 4), at once the *arché,* the *méson,* and the *télos* of a sphere, so that, in a manner of speaking, it encompasses the periphery. This corresponds to the fact that Glaucon's assumption, that the top of the dialectic ascent is "a rest . . . and an end" (532 e 3), is quite wrong—there still must follow a *syllogismós* that takes the argument back again to the periphery, where the power of the center as cause, *aitía,* is first fully apprehended (516 b 9; this noetic *syllogismós,* which is preceded by an ascent, as in *Statesman* 267 a 4, is not to be confused with the dianoetic deduction, as in *Republic* 510 b 5). It is, of course, convenient that all three of Aristotle's terms are also terms used of the Good. The radial lines may then represent the indefinite dyadic source, which is doubly delimited by the center and its periphery to produce the actual finite sphere of Being. But I must admit that extended attention to such diagrams makes the head reel and thought cease.

46. See Proclus, *Les Commentaires sur le premier livre des Éléments d'Euclide,* ed. Ver Eecke (Paris: Albert Blanchard, 1948), 58–62. On the motto over Plato's shrine to the Muses (*mouseíon*): "Let no one unversed in geometry enter here," see Elias, *Commentary on the Categories, Commentaria in Aristotelem Graeca* (Berlin 1900), Vol. XVIII, Pt. I, pp. 118, 13 ff.

Socrates' resistance to the advanced and technical study of mathematics is attested—indirectly—also in Xenophon's *Memorabilia* (IV, vii). Xenophon represents him as advocating a kind of mathematics, namely useful and applied mathematics such as earth measurement, exactly the opposite of that which he repeatedly insists on in the *Republic*. But when Plato and Xenophon differ in a deliberately diametrical way there is usually a vital point of agreement to be found. Here it is Socrates' deep objection to mathematics as a technical study independent of philosophy pursued by private experts and mired in fancy applications, a study that would fit into the doxastic rather than the noetic segments of the Divided Line. The very mental virtues required and acquired by such studies, keenness and sharpness (*Republic* 526 b, 535 b 5), are regarded by him with a certain suspicion because they tend to live in a little soul (519 a). His parodies of professional talk (527 a, 531 b) remind me of Swift's "large-thinking" Laputa.

47. See Klein, *Greek Mathematical Thought*, Pt. I, 6.

48. Of course, mathematical studies provide practice not only in what might be called cosmic oversight (*sýnopsis*) but also in that preliminary collection (*synagogé, Phaedrus* 266 b 4) which consists in "seeing together and bringing under one idea things scattered everywhere" (265 d 3), that is, in collecting particulars under one *eídos*.

The necessity of cosmic *sýnopsis* was emphasized by Speusippus, in whose opinion "it is impossible for anyone to define *any* of the things that are unless he knows *all* the things that are" (ed. P. Lang, *De Speusippi Academici Scriptis*, Fr. 31 b).

49. Sources in Gaiser, *op. cit.*, 461–67. Aristotle (*Nicomachean Ethics* 1095 a 32) furnishes the general background by noting that Plato was concerned with the direction that the road of inquiry ought to take, whether toward or away from principles.

50. See *The Thirteen Books of Euclid's Elements*, ed. Heath (New York: Dover Publications, 1956), I, pp. 136–41.

51. See Klein, *Meno*, 82–87.

52. For the Simplicius passage see Gaiser, *op. cit.*, 464; for the "paradigmatic cause," 480, note; for Theophrastus's comment on the absence of a deduction of the visible world, 493–94.

53. See Euclid's *Elements* III, 1 ff., p. 438.

54. Two mean proportionals in continued proportion: If $a:x::x:y$ and $x:y::y:b$, then a cube with side a is to a cube with side x as a is to b, for example, as a unit is to its double. The Greek mathematician Hippocrates had discovered this solution to the doubling problem during Socrates' lifetime. The actual construction is not elementary.

55. See T. L. Heath, *A Manual of Greek Mathematics* (New York: Dover Publications, 1963), 154–55.

56. Klein, *Greek Mathematical Thought*, Pt. I, 7 C.

57. The image of a man possessing *phrónesis* at work—it might be called "Socrates in the city"—is to be found in Xenophon's *Memorabilia*, which is intended to be the practical record, the *res gestae*, of Socrates. I doubt, however, that Xenophon's Socrates looks to dialectic for his wisdom. Certainly Aristotle does not. Cut off from its philosophical source, *phrónesis* becomes Aris-

totelian "prudence," the practical virtue of the politician (e.g., *Nicomachean Ethics*, 1141 a 30). The different derivations of prudence are a just measure of the distance between the Platonic *Politeía* and the Aristotelian *Politiká*.

58. Pauly-Wissowa, *Suppl.* III, p. 1007.

9   TIME IN THE TIMAEUS

1. See "Plato" (E. Brann) in *Encyclopedia of Time,* edited by Samuel L. Macey (New York: Garland Publishing, 1994), pp. 467–68.

2. Plato, to be sure, set the astronomers the task of rationalizing the anomalous appearances of planetary motions; see p. 228.

10   INTRODUCTION TO THE SOPHIST

1. Here are two examples of apparently jumbled, but actually revealing passages. The first concerns the making of a division, the second the collection or recapitulation of a line of divisions.

1. Sophist IV (see diagram, p. 286) is ranged under "marketing," which is divided into self-selling of self-produced products and peddling of other people's products (224E). But in the summary of this division the Stranger, with apparent carelessness, confuses levels and slips in a third case: the marketing and "trafficking" of things produced by oneself and by others. Since the Greek word for "self" is also the word for "same," the stranger seems to confuse the divisions between stay-at-home peddling of things made by others and travelling sales of things made by oneself (Sophist III and IV in diagram). But he is really exemplifying that "interweaving" of Same and Other which will be a theme of the dialogue.

2. The dialogue ends with an apparently disordered collection of the sophist's titles, as one engaged in "making" (*poiesis*). They are said to be rewound like a skein from the last to the first (268C. The sequence is visible on the right-hand line of the diagram.) Yet in the presentation of the final winding-up, the account is artfully deranged so as to place Imitation not merely in a middle but in a pivotal position. All the lower subdivisions that characterize the sophist as an opinionated, dissembling argufier are represented as an *ascent* to the imitative division, while above it the sophist is shown as sharing with the poet one and the same *descent,* just as he had before been identified with the angler under "getting" and with the philosopher under "separating." This crafty listing of the divisions not only shows once again how the kinds of Expertise are interwoven, but also that imitation, non-genuineness, marks the sophist in his very being.

11   NONBEING ENFOLDED IN BEING: THE SOPHIST

1. The Furies are gentled and invited to reside in Athens, and the maddening guilt of Orestes' matricide is extinguished by Athena in her city in

Aeschylus's *Eumenides*. Oedipus, guilty of parricide and incest, is conducted by Theseus to his Attic place of disappearance in Sophocles' *Oedipus at Colonus*.

2. In his *History of Philosophy,* Hegel says, as if it were obvious, that the sophists drew their denial of the possibility of error from Parmenides' view of truth (vol. 1, pt. 1, sec. 1, chap. 1, C 2).

3. One of the great changes that Parmenides and his followers must have observed in the world around them was the rise of expertise-proud specialists. The *Sophist* gives, among other things, an expertise tree, whose branchings allow Plato a chance for a lot of neologic spoofing. Socrates, when he asks in his conversations what something is, is not really interested in a specifying definition; he wants the steadfast gist of the notion. But the Stranger does define. He begins with a universe, that of human expertise, and by division into branches pursues the kinds from superior to subordinate, *general* to *specific*. In this dialogue, accordingly, the greatest of the forms, the *eide* (Latin *species*), are for the first time distinguished as *géne* (Latin *genera*) from the lower *eide*.

The appellation "sophist" seems to have been accepted voluntarily by at least one sophist, Protagoras (Plato, *Protagoras*, 317 b).

4. The Stranger's analysis is more complex than reported here; for example, he distinguishes, within the imitative art, between "likenesses" and "apparitions," that is, between exact copies and copies that deform the original for the sake of effect (236 a).

5. It should, however, be said that the Stranger is familiar with all the schools of thought concerning Being. And his refutation of Parmenides is more extensive than I report here; the Stranger attacks Parmenidean Being itself, namely, with respect to its partlessness, its being One (244 e ff.).

6. Whether the Platonic forms, which are objects *for* thought and thinkable (*noeta*), are to be considered as themselves thoughts is a deep perplexity (Plato, *Parmenides* 132 b). The Stranger, perhaps mindful of Parmenides' teaching that thinking and Being are the same, says that Being is a power, *dýnamis,* a power of doing and being affected (247 e). And he intimates that therefore Being has mind and life and soul (249 a). Heidegger (*Platon: Sophistes,* 1924, para. 79 b), in fact, goes so far as to say that the *genos* of "Motion" (*kínesis*), one of the major forms, is "the aprioristic title for *psyche* and *lógos.*" The difficultly with this identification is that the Stranger also includes Rest among the beings necessary to mind (249 c). In any case, it does not help to have just one *noetón* think. Each form has its proper nature for itself, but *all* forms share the characteristic of being thinkable. The perplexity is: How does the power of being *for* thought differ from the power of being *a* thought?

I would not raise this question here did not the introduction of Nonbeing among the forms which the Stranger is about to accomplish have the effect of tacitly making the realm of Being more mindlike: the Stranger hints at this when he speaks of Nonbeing as "all chopped up—just like knowledge" (257 c). Since every form is *also* a—relative—non-being, Nonbeing will act among the forms, the beings, much as human reason, *lógos,* does in speech. Both relate all beings to each other, and both determine each being by its negations. Only the human *lógos,* however, has the additional negative capability of being false.

7. At least it is not calculable without some algorithm for the combinations. It seems to me possible that the Other is in fact infinite, that is, if it turns out,

upon reflection, to be the form that brings the infinite appearances of the sense world under the realm of Being. It mixes with opinion and speech, at any rate (260 b). Otherness does play this role for Hegel—Nature is conceptualized as the Other of the Concept: "Nature has presented itself as the Idea in the form of *otherness*" (*Philosophy of Nature,* para. 247).

8. The subject of the negative in the Platonic dialogues is of course much wider than my focus on the Nonbeing of the *Sophist* might indicate. A most serious and honest book by Nicolai Hartmann, *Plato's Logik des Seins* (1909), is very regrettably unavailable in English. Hartmann wrestles hard with the connection of the Socratic-Platonic method of dialectic to the result it attains. He maintains that both the inquiry and its termini are shot through with Nonbeing. Dialectic is a *via negativa,* which yields as results the ideas (i.e., forms), and these are entirely delimited by what they are *not*; they are, for example, uncolored, unshaped, untouchable. These negations are eventually perceived as determinations: Nonbeing becomes positive, governing the very character of the ideas. Hartmann's understanding carries a price (which he welcomes): The ideas are "subjective" in two senses, (1) as "the products of the negating dialectic of a human mind," as the "innermost, most proper achievement of the self," and (2) insofar as they are in and of the mind, "self-acting," active, self-perspicuous self-visions of their own truth; Hartmann thinks that this is expressed by the Platonic formula for a form—*itself by itself (autó kath' autó,* 192 ff.). One need not believe this understanding to respect its force.

In tune with it, Socrates, that first philosophical dialectician (whose dialectical perplexities, I here interject, seem to me, unlike the sophistic dialectic, not to be a sort of self-stymieing, willful abiding within the clashing rocks of positive and negative), embraces *not* knowing. Hartmann observes that the emphasis in Socrates' notorious announcement to the Athenian judges at his trial that "I know within myself that I know nothing" (*Apology* 22 d) is not on his ignorance but on his knowledge (79)—and, one might add, on his knowledge of *nothing.* That "nothing" would be, in Hartmann's spirit, the negative power of dialectic, which chisels away at the thing sought, striking off what it is not, until some shape, its form, finally emerges.

It seems to me possible that Plato has the Stranger of the *Sophist* agree to use Socrates' dialogic way rather than the unilateral presentations he is accustomed to (217 c) not only from courtesy but also because he knows that the dialogic mode is itself already on the way to Nonbeing since it emphasizes affimation and *denial.*

13   PLATO'S "THEORY OF IDEAS"

1. Let me add here that the next most important source of the Theory of Ideas, very difficult to use, is Aristotle, who reports its technical elaborations and problems and looks at it, so to speak, askance.

2. The meaning of *theoria* in Greek is, however, that of a viewing, a sight seen—contemplation, and in that sense the Ideas are very much "theory."

3. I am thinking of the so-called problems of participation and separability, of self-predication, of the Third Man, and of eidetic structure. Incidentally, in the *Parmenides* young Socrates is portrayed as the supporter of that very ver-

sion of the theory—that the ideas are "separate" from things—which Aristotle explicitly denies he held. Aristotle makes this claim in a puzzling passage that is the prime source for all denials of Socrates' authorship of the "theory" (*Metaphysics* 987 b).

4. A Socratic hypothesis is unlike a post-Baconian hypothesis; it is not a conjecture to be verified by observational experience. It is a little closer to an astronomical hypothesis, such as Plato is said by Simplicius to have been the first to demand, namely an intellectual construction, a mathematical theory, devised to "save the phenomena"—that is, to display the anomalous appearances as grounded in regularities acceptable to reason. A Socratic hypothesis, however, is not a mathematical rationalization but an intellectual supposition.

5. Nor is the translation "form" quite good, because it is too reminiscent of the Aristotelian distinction between form and matter. The *eídos* may "produce" a form in a thing (*Phaedo* 104 d), but it *is* not its form in the sense of "shape."

6. I have given this presentation a perhaps questionable coherence by ranging through the dialogues as if Plato's works constituted a planned-out whole. But then I believe that in some sense they do, and that what scholars consider the "development" of Plato's thought from early to late dialogues is largely the advancing of one or the other of these different beginnings and aspects.

7. Accordingly, the *Phaedrus,* in which this beginning of philosophy is preeminently set out, was once, probably wrongly, thought to be Plato's earliest dialogue.

8. Of course, the visible things do not collectively constitute the *eídos,* nor is the *eídos* their concept, if by a concept is meant an abstract universal or a definition. I want to mention also that, although it is not his fixed usage, Plato does refer to the greatest *eíde* as *géne,* genera, kindred groups (*Sophist* 254 d), thereby indicating that in the highest reaches eidetic shapeliness yields to associative characteristics.

9. For Socrates *méthodos* usually means a *path* of inquiry to be followed (*Republic* 533 b), not a preset investigatory *procedure.*

10. (a) The word *ousía* did play a role *analogous* to modern "reality" in common language. As we speak of "real" estate, Greeks used *ousía* to mean one's property, substance. (b) Scholars attribute to Socrates the distinction between two uses of the verb "to be," the predicative and the existential. In its predicative use "is" acts as a copula, a coupling between the subject of discourse and what is said of it, as in "This face is beautiful." The existential "is" occurs in the chopped-off sentence "Justice *is,*" meaning it is to be found sometime, somewhere in the world: "Justice exists." But distinctions in verbal usage are not Socrates' aim. When we say that "the face is beautiful" it is for him the occasion for asking what beauty is, and when we assert that "justice exists" he wants to know in what world—and it will not be one that has time and place. That is to say, his "is" is not existential but ontic.

11. *Greek Mathematical Thought and the Origin of Algebra,* 7c, 79 ff. In brief, it goes like this: According to the stranger the *eídos* of Being is composed of two *eíde,* Change and Stillness (or Motion and Rest; *Sophist* 254 d), since first of all everything that is, is either in motion or at rest, though never both at once; these *eíde* never mingle. Being is not either of these alone, or their mix-

ture, but *both together.* That, however, is just how number assemblages behave; Socrates himself draws attention to this in that favorite formula: each one,
both two (*Greater Hippias* 301 a; *Phaedo* 97 a; *Republic* 476 a; *Theaetetus* 14
e). Each unit in a number remains what it was, *one,* but both together have a
new name and nature, *two;* they are *together* what neither is *by itself.* Being,
the highest *eídos,* would then be the eidetic *Two*—not anything above or beyond the two eidetic units, Change and Stillness, that constitute it, but simply
their being together, their communion: to participate in Being is to be dynam-
ically stable, alive (*Sophist* 247 d–e).

Aristotle reports the Academy's interest in the arithmetic organization of
the *eíde* (*Metaphysics* 987 b). He also points out that the eidetic units are not,
like pure arithmetic units, indifferent, and so capable of being added and
"thrown together" any which way (1081 a). They can only associate into eidetic numbers uniquely, according to their nature; such eidetic counting, which
drives speech to and then beyond its limits, is dialectic proper.

SOURCES AND ACKNOWLEDGMENTS

The chapters of this book originally appeared or were delivered in somewhat different form as follows:

Introduction to the *Phaedo:* in *Plato's Phaedo,* translation, introduction, and glossary by Eva Brann, Peter Kalkavage, and Eric Salem, published by Focus Publishing/R. Pullins Company, copyright 1998, and used by permission of the publisher.

Socrates' Legacy: Plato's *Phaedo:* written for a student journal of Yale University, 2002.

The Offense of Socrates: *Apology:* in *The Past-Present: Selected Writings of Eva Brann,* ed. by Pamela Kraus, published by St. John's College Press, copyright 1997, and used by permission of the publisher.

The Tyrant's Temperance: *Charmides:* delivered by Eva Brann as a lecture at Middlebury College in October 2002.

Introduction to Reading the *Republic:* revised from *Plato: The Republic,* trans. and ed. by Ray Larson, copyright 1979 by Harlan Davidson, Inc., and used by permission of the publisher.

The Music of the *Republic:* substantially revised from *Four Essays on Plato's Republic,* ed. by Elliot Zuckerman, published in the *St. John's Review* XXXIX 1 and 2, 1989–1990, and used by permission of the publisher.

Why Justice? The Answer of the *Republic:* delivered by Eva Brann as a lecture at Goucher College in September 2002.

Imitative Poetry: Book X of the *Republic:* delivered by Eva Brann as the Brother Sixtus Robert Lecture at St. Mary's College of California in March 2003 and dedicated to Brother Robert Smith.

Time in the *Timaeus:* in *What, Then, Is Time?,* by Eva Brann, published by Rowman and Littlefield Publishers, copyright 1999, and used by permission of the publisher.

Introduction to the *Sophist:* in *Plato's Sophist or The Professor of Wisdom,* translation, introduction and glossary by Eva Brann, Peter Kalkavage, and Eric Salem, published by Focus Publishing/R. Pullins Company, copyright 1996, and used by permission of the publisher.

Nonbeing Enfolded in Being: The *Sophist:* in *The Ways of Naysaying,* by Eva Brann, published by Rowman and Littlefield Publishers, copyright 2000, and used by permission of the publisher.

On Translating the *Sophist:* revised from *Retracing the Platonic Text,* ed. by John Russon and John Sallis, part of the SPEP Studies in Historical Philosophy series, David Kold and John McCumber general eds., published by Northwestern University Press, copyright 2000, and used by permission of the publisher.

Plato's "Theory of Ideas": in *The Past-Present: Selected Writings of Eva Brann,* ed. by Pamela Kraus, published by St. John's College Press, copyright 1997, and used by permission of the publisher.

"Teaching Plato" to Undergraduates: delivered by Eva Brann as a lecture at Thomas Aquinas College in November 2002.

Page 270: Vincent van Gogh, Dutch, 1853–1890, *The Bedroom,* 1889, oil on canvas, 73.6 × 92.3 cm, Helen Birch Bartlett Memorial Collection, 1926.417. Photograph by Greg Williams. Reproduction, The Art Institute of Chicago.

INDEX